D0848886

Liberty and Property

Political Ideology in Eighteenth-Century Britain

H. T. DICKINSON

Weidenfeld and Nicolson
London

ISBN 0 297 77412 3

Printed in Great Britain by
WILLMER BROTHERS LIMITED BIRKENHEAD MERSEYSIDE

For Mark, Anna and Elizabeth

Contents

Contents

Acknowledgements

This book is based on a wide range of printed primary sources which could not have been read without the generous assistance of a number of institutions. The staff of the British Library and the National Library of Scotland have been unfailingly helpful over a number of years. The University of Edinburgh has helped to meet some of my research costs and also granted me sabbatical leave for much of 1973. In that year a Fulbright travel scholarship and visiting fellowships from the Huntington Library, California and the Folger Shakespeare Library, Washington D.C., enabled me to spend months studying in these major libraries where their sytsem of chronological cataloguing enabled me to discover hundreds of anonymous and little-known pamphlets which I might never have found in British libraries with their author and subject cataloguing system.

Although this book is the product of original research and is based overwhelmingly on printed primary sources, I have profited from the work of other historians. My general approach has been influenced by Bernard Bailyn's celebrated *Ideological Origins of the American Revolution* and by the criticisms levelled at it. On particular topics I have benefited from the work of Geoffrey Holmes, J. P. Kenyon, John Brewer, J. G. A. Pocock, Duncan Forbes, Caroline Robbins, Isaac Kramnick, Peter Laslett and Quentin Skinner. I have also learned a great deal from conversations with Jeffrey M. Nelson of Harvard University and from attempts to explain my ideas on eighteenth-century politics to my students at Edinburgh University.

My greatest academic debt, however, is to my friend and colleague, Dr F. D. Dow, who has discussed the subject with me at some length and who has read every chapter with great care and has offered me much valuable criticism and advice. The faults which remain are naturally my own responsibility.

My much amended manuscript was, as always, typed with great speed and accuracy by Anna Campbell, Secretary to the Celtic Department in the University of Edinburgh.

The years of research, the considerable amount of travelling to distant libraries and the long hours spent in writing this book have placed a heavy burden on my wife and children. Without their support and forbearance this book could not have been written. It is dedicated to them with love and gratitude.

April 1977
University of Edinburgh
Harry Dickinson

The first line of argument involves rejecting the sceptical approach of the Namierites and stressing instead that men do sometimes mean what they say when they articulate political ideas and beliefs. According to this interpretation political principles and ideas are not simply cant, mere rationalizations of a desire for power, but are expressions of the genuine reasons and motives for political action. At least some political agents believe what they say and only by studying their ideas and arguments is it possible to understand why these men acted in the way in which they did. This view was most forcibly put by Herbert Butterfield in a direct attack on the Namierite interpretation when that interpretation was at the height of its influence in the late 1950s. Butterfield insisted that human beings are the carriers of ideas as well as the repositories of vested interests. He warned that the Namierites were in danger of draining the intellectual content out of the things politicians did and he criticized them for being over-contemptuous of the political literature produced by eighteenth-century politicians. 'Here is an interpretation of history, which through an understandable anxiety to avoid being hoaxed – through an understandable desire to avoid the mistakes of the doctrinaire – is in danger of refusing to realize the operative force of ideas.'[2] Butterfield failed to stem the Namierite tide when he wrote this, but in the last decade or so a number of historians have followed his advice and have put principles and ideas back into the political history of the eighteenth century.[3]

The second challenge to the Namierite interpretation of politics is prepared to concede that Namier's scepticism about politicians' being genuinely motivated by political principles may well be justified. This approach accepts that principles and ideas are not, *by themselves*, a sufficient explanation of political action. It recognizes that ideas and principles are rarely the determinants of human action and that therefore there may be no direct causal relationship between political thought and political action. Nevertheless, it is argued, it does not follow from this that political ideas should be ignored in seeking to explain political behaviour. By condemning *all* ideas as the mere *ex post facto* rationalization of political action the Namierites fail to explain why certain specific ideas are regarded as the best form of rationalization to be adopted. Since ambitious and skilful politicians believed that the expression of certain ideas could be regarded as more appropriate than others to the achievement of particular political objectives, then these ideas deserve the

3

careful attention of historians. A political agent may well feel the need to disguise his baser motives even from himself. His attempts to explain his behaviour are therefore designed to attain an appropriate self-image and so legitimate his political actions to himself. Certainly those politicians who do not believe what they say or write seek to legitimate their behaviour in the eyes of those who may doubt the morality of their actions. They need to be able to describe and evaluate their apparently selfish and untoward actions by using ideas and terms which are accepted and approved by others. While they may not always do this effectively or successfully, the way in which they seek to do it does cast light on how they and their contemporaries view certain political ideas and certain forms of political action. Their political behaviour can only be properly explained if historians endeavour to understand why such able men believed that it was rational to use particular arguments both in attacking their opponents and in defending themselves.

This challenge to the Namierite interpretation of political motivation also claims that political agents who regularly and repeatedly express certain political ideas, even if these are used to disguise their self-interested desire for power, can become themselves the victims rather than the masters of their arguments. A political agent may be obliged, for his own self-esteem and to retain his influence over others, to behave in such a way that his actions remain compatible with his frequent declarations of principle. The course of action which is open to any rational political agent is therefore limited and to some extent determined by the range of ideas and principles that he can profess with plausibility. It becomes very difficult to pursue a particular course of political action if it cannot be justified and therefore legitimated in the opinion of the agent and of those he seeks to influence. Anyone involved in political action, whether by word or deed, can only use ideas and principles which make sense to him and to the age in which he lives. Ideas and principles therefore act both as a constraint and as a directive to his actions. They can be used to defend and legitimate only a certain range of action. If this were once forgotten, the political agent would lose influence and would probably be subjected to a devastating counter-attack. The ideas men express therefore are important guides to any understanding of the political action which some men take and which others favour or reject.[4]

Although these two attempts to stress the importance of political

4

ideas as aids to understanding political behaviour have approached the problem from different directions it is not necessary to adopt one to the exclusion of the other. Certainly the first tends to rest upon a higher opinion of human nature, while the second accepts Namier's more realistic, or perhaps more cynical, assessment of human motivation. Nonetheless, the two approaches are not entirely incompatible. Those who accept that ideas and principles do motivate men do not claim that this applies to all men or even to a majority of them. Neither do they seek to divorce ideology from personal ambition or vested interests. Geoffrey Holmes, for example, in his *British Politics in the Age of Anne*, has done more than any other historian to understand the ideas and principles of the Whig and Tory parties of the early eighteenth century, but he has not attempted to prove that the party struggle was merely a conflict of principles waged by disinterested politicians. He has gone to great lengths to show that Whigs and Tories were interested in power and were anxious to defend the privileges of particular interest groups.

Other historians besides Professor Holmes have found it impossible to separate principles from self-interest. They recognize that if the reason for political action is always reduced to a base desire for power then it becomes impossible to distinguish different types of human motivation. They insist that self-interest can take many forms and therefore historians need to discriminate between the various types of self-interest. One type of self-interested action might benefit only the individual concerned and might cause suffering to many others. Another self-interested action might benefit the individual *and* either a few or many others. Yet another action might benefit the individual *and* the whole society in which he lives. The psychologist might insist that all these actions are motivated by self-interest, but historians have to examine how contemporaries judge the consequences of these actions. All societies are composed of self-interested individuals, but the needs and desires of each society will lead the members of that society to distinguish between actions which they admire, publicly and/or privately, and actions which they condemn. These values may change over time or differ from one society to another. The historian cannot quite escape judging a society by his own standards, but he must also endeavour to judge that society according to its own estimation of men's actions. He must recognize those actions which that society is prepared to regard as admirable or 'principled' and those actions which it will

5

condemn or deplore. If he does not understand the political values of a particular society, then he will not understand the political agents of that society. To understand these political values he must examine the political rhetoric, the arguments, prejudices and assumptions of the age.

Those historians who stress that political agents are primarily engaged in efforts to justify and legitimate their political actions thereby imply that these explanations have a chance of being believed and approved by others. Those political agents who seek to legitimate their actions may be endeavouring to disguise their self-interested desire for power, but they clearly hope that either their audience will be misled into believing their protestations that they are acting out of principle or that the audience will realize that it is in its own interest to support these actions and to label them as principled. In other words, either the audience genuinely believes in certain principles or it wishes to register approval of what these agents are trying to do and, for its own self-image, prefers to describe these agents as men of principle. In either case men are recognizing that there are actions which the age is prepared to admire or condemn. Legitimation is only possible if a society makes it clear which actions it will deplore as being self-interested and which it will admire as being 'principled'. Politicians who are apparently able and skilful would indeed be acting irrationally if they believed that certain arguments could be used to legitimate their political behaviour when all the time it was quite clear that no one ever accepted their protestations and explanations. If we assume that men invariably act irrationally or if we insist that what they say can never offer any evidence for understanding what they do, then, as historians, we can never explain any political action. The past becomes irrational and chaotic; a chapter of inexplicable accidents.

If, on the other hand, we wish to make sense of the political actions and the political agents of any past society, then we need to recognize the political values of that society and understand what that society or sections of it admired and condemned. We cannot afford to ignore either the nature and terms of the political debate or the structure of political argument. This does not mean that historians must take the rhetoric and protestations of political agents at their face value. These arguments certainly need to be subjected to searching analysis and careful scrutiny. Historians who study political ideology must be fully conscious of how often self-interest motivates men and they must be fully conversant with the political and social reality which affects the needs and desires of men, but they should not be contemptuous of the ideas expressed by men who were frequently highly intelligent and who were often remarkably well informed about their own political world. In other words, there is no need to abandon the realism of Namierite historians or their discoveries about the structure of politics. Rather their conclusions have to be tested by a careful examination of the structure of political argument and political ideology. Only by studying both political ideas and political and social reality can we hope to understand political actions. Namierite historians insist that action is more important than thought, while other historians are more interested in thought than action. To understand politics fully historians must remember that political agents both act *and* think.

If we accept that political ideas, principles and arguments can help to explain political behaviour, then we need to decide how best to relate political ideology to political action and how to assess the enormous amount of evidence available. Historians have attempted to relate political ideas to political action in a number of ways. One obvious and popular way has been to study the voluminous political writings of an important political thinker and political activist, such as Bolingbroke, Paine or Burke, and simply relate these to their political actions. The same can be done for a group of influential propagandists and activists such as the leading members of the Yorkshire Association, the Society for Constitutional Information or the London Corresponding Society. It is also possible to study a major issue such as the Act of Union of 1707, the Excise crisis of 1733, or the dispute with the American colonies and see what arguments these events produced. In all of these approaches however, because the focus of attention is on political agents or political events, the tendency is to allow political action to dominate political ideas. As a result the latter can indeed appear to be simply the *ex post facto* rationalization of self-interest. A more fruitful approach is to concentrate on the political debate, to focus attention on the structure of the argument, in order to see how ideas reflect and confront political reality. By examining political arguments as they develop over the years it may also be possible to understand how the political and social order has changed. I have previously adopted this approach in examining the eighteenth-century debate on the sovereignty of Parliament and the rights of man.[5]

7

This book attempts a much wider perspective. It does not concentrate on a limited number of political thinkers, it is not preoccupied with a particular crisis, and it is not concerned with the ideological debate over a single notion or concept. It seeks instead to understand the ideological debate about the nature of man, about civil society and about civil government from the 1680s to the 1790s. It shows how political agents endeavoured to defend and justify their concepts of what the political and social order ought to be. Sometimes groups of politicians and political propagandists sought to prove that what is, is what ought to be. At other times these groups or others tried to change the existing political and social order so that it would correspond more nearly with their vision of an ideal civil society and civil government. In order to show how this ideological debate both mirrors and interacts with political and social reality I have adopted a roughly chronological approach by dividing the book into three parts corresponding to the three different periods into which most political historians normally divide the eighteenth century. Historians concerned with political structure and action at national level have generally recognized a period of intense conflict between Whigs and Tories from the 1680s to the early years of George I's reign; a period of stability in the early Hanoverian period when a political contest of a decidedly limited nature was waged between Court and Country; and a period from the 1760s to the 1790s when political agents became increasingly polarized between those who wished to reform the political and social order, sometimes quite radically, and those who were determined to defend the *status quo*. By examining the ideological debate within this framework it is possible to show quite clearly how this debate both reflected and shaped political reality. It has to be admitted however that not all political agents and not all ideological debates fit neatly into the broad categories of Whig and Tory, Court and Country, radical and conservative. Some political agents defy any attempt to label them and others shift rather disconcertingly from one category to the other. It was also possible to be a Whig or a radical, for example, without subscribing to all the ideas and arguments associated with that political platform. Certain important ideological debates, such as that over the Act of Union of 1707, have been omitted because they are not directly relevant to the themes of this book. While this book therefore is not comprehensive in its coverage of political disputes of an ideological nature and its attempt to explain general positions and broad platforms cannot do justice to every individual political agent, it is organized so that it can show most effectively the importance of the relationship between political ideas and political action.

Any historian who attempts to examine the different ways in which men perceived the nature of man, and the nature of civil society and civil government from the 1680s to the 1790s is confronted with a vast wealth of evidence, most of which has been neglected by those historians preoccupied with the structure of politics and with the consequences of, rather than the motivation behind, political action. This evidence is not limited to the speeches and writings of politicians or to the political treatises of men like Locke, Hume, Paine and Burke. It includes tens of thousands of political pamphlets and sermons with a political message; a vast range of periodicals and newspapers which published political arguments and disputes; and a wealth of imaginative literature from the pens of such politically conscious writers as Addison, Steele, Swift, Defoe, Pope, Gay, Fielding, Dr Johnson, Coleridge, Southey and many others. A great deal, although of course not all, of this material was used in the preparation of this book. No historian could have read all the available material, but the conclusions reached in this book do rest upon the treatises of all the major political thinkers and propagandists, the reported parliamentary debates from 1688 to 1800, and a study of thousands of pamphlets (many of them anonymous), dozens of newspapers and periodicals, and many works of imaginative literature. Since it was not possible to make an exhaustive study of all the material available and since it is not possible to produce incontrovertible statistical evidence to prove how often an argument was put forward, how often it was read, or what influence it had, the conclusions reached are inevitably impressionistic. An effort has been made however to limit the subjective element in the assessment of the frequency and impact of particular arguments. In the first place, there is fairly reliable evidence about the sales of particular pamphlets, periodicals and newspapers.[6] Second, by reading a vast amount of political literature in its many forms it was possible to gain what is probably a fairly reliable estimate of how often or how rarely particular arguments were put forward. Finally, although this book is overwhelmingly concerned to present the evidence of the ideological debate of the eighteenth century, it rests upon a careful study of the political structure and political events of the period. It would not have been possible to show how political ideology interacted with political reality without an understanding of the changing political and social order of the eighteenth century. The chapters below concentrate on political ideas, but most of the conclusions could not have been reached if considerable attention had not been paid to political actions.

Perhaps because this study of political ideology deliberately seeks to establish the *connection* between political ideas and political behaviour and because it rests upon a study of the structure of politics as well as the structure of ideas, some of its most important conclusions support or at least only amend those reached by Namierite historians who have neglected this evidence. Those who have worked on the structure of politics will perhaps not be unduly surprised to find that much of the ideological debate of the eighteenth century revolved around attempts to establish the extent of the government's authority and the limits of the subject's rights and that the ideological position which men adopted was invariably influenced by whether their primary concern was to promote liberty or protect property. Other conclusions reinforce the arguments made by Namierite historians. It is argued below, for example, that the political stability which was established in the early Hanoverian period was as much the result of ideological consensus and the symbiotic relationship between Court and Country as the consequence of changes in the structure of politics. On the other hand, several of the conclusions reached in this book do challenge directly the interpretation of politics which is generally offered by historians who have concentrated on political action to the exclusion of political ideology. It shows, for example, that Tory ideology did not collapse after the Glorious Revolution, but continued to influence political behaviour well into the eighteenth century; it concludes that Whig ideology was more often based on conservative notions of the ancient constitution rather than the more liberal ideas of John Locke; and it proves that the defenders of the Whig establishment throughout the eighteenth century developed an ideological position which was as coherent and sophisticated as that of their Country and radical critics.

Part One

TORY
AND WHIG
(From the 1680s to c.1714)

I

The Tories and the Ideology of Order

From the Restoration of 1660 to the Revolution of 1688 a majority of the landed proprietors of England and an overwhelming proportion of the Anglican clergy hoped to maintain order in Church and State by upholding a political theory which conceded absolute power or at least very considerable authority to the Crown. Many propagandists in Church and State came to the defence of the doctrines of divine right, indefeasible hereditary succession, nonresistance and passive obedience. Until the disastrous reign of James II these doctrines served the interests of the Crown, the Church and a majority of the propertied classes and they won the support of a powerful element within Parliament. They became the ideological base of the Tory party of the 1680s. The Glorious Revolution of 1688 dealt these doctrines a serious blow from which they never entirely recovered. Nonetheless, this does not mean that Tory principles became irrelevant to those who tried to cope with the political problems of post-Revolution England or that the Tory ideology of order was rapidly abandoned as the ruling classes accommodated themselves to a Whig view of politics and society. On the contrary, some of the principles and attitudes of the Tories, founded as they were on expediency and on appeals to Scripture, history and the nature of man, were adapted quite successfully to the new political situation. Although some elements of Tory ideology failed to emerge unscathed from the crisis of the Revolution, others proved surprisingly durable and were eventually incorporated into that conservative ideology of Hanoverian Britain which has all too often been labelled, somewhat misleadingly, as 'Whig'.

1 Tory Ideology before the Glorious Revolution

After the Restoration in 1660 most men of property were prepared to support a political ideology which put the greatest stress on authority, order and hierarchy. The upheaval and disorder of the

13

Civil War and Interregnum convinced them that their estates and their privileges could only be secured by a political society in which there existed a single supreme authority from whose decisions there could be no appeal. For a time it came to be widely, indeed almost universally, accepted that to preserve order and to safeguard their privileges it was essential for men of property to accept the arbitrary and irresistible authority of a single magistrate. A sovereign authority must provide a single undivided final power which was higher in legal authority than any other, which was subject to no law and which, indeed, was a law unto itself. Derived in part from the political theory of classical antiquity, from Roman law and from medieval thought, this theory of absolutism came most directly to England from the work of Jean Bodin in the sixteenth century. After the Restoration of 1660 a host of political theorists and propagandists insisted that the ultimate or sovereign authority in England lay with the monarch. Many conceded to the Crown a more extensive authority than that granted by Bodin. By sovereign authority Bodin had meant the supreme power in the State, but he did not regard it as an arbitrary power or a power operating entirely without any controls or restrictions. The English supporters of royal absolutism after the Restoration insisted that the king possessed absolute and arbitrary power and that his authority could not be limited or controlled by the people or their representatives. Robert Filmer, for example, whose most famous work, *Patriarcha*, was published posthumously in 1680, maintained that the laws of England were simply the expression of the king's will for he could amend them or abrogate them at his discretion. The king could, if he so wished, set aside statute law, ancient customs and even the common law. Whatever he did was lawful and irresistible. To take up arms against the king was a damnable sin. A king could never be punished by his subjects even if he broke the law of God. The only possible sanction against the king was divine retribution which would be exacted in the next world if not in this.[1]

It was not enough however to argue that a king's authority was absolute and irresistible. Order could only be maintained if subjects were in no doubt about who had the *right* to be king and hence who had the right to exercise this absolute authority. If subjects would recognize the absolute authority of a ruler only after he was in undisputed possession of the throne and if therefore subjects could legitimately contest who had the right to rule, then order could never be guaranteed. There would be a grave danger of political instability whenever a ruler died or whenever subjects were divided over who had the legitimate right to the throne. It was therefore essential that a king should be able to establish a clear and unimpeachable claim to his throne. It was not only important to determine who actually possessed power, but to discover who had the right to exercise absolute sovereign authority. Order could only be preserved if the claim to sovereign authority were based on a clearly established right and not merely on the exercise of superior might. The Tory theory of order based the right to rule on two powerful foundations: direct divine ordination and indefeasible hereditary succession. The Tories insisted that kings ruled by the direct command of God and that God had established a clear and inviolable rule, namely indefeasible hereditary succession, to prevent a dangerous hiatus between the death of one ruler and his replacement by another whose claim would be universally recognized as unimpeachable and unchallengeable.

The absolute authority of the king and the doctrine of divine hereditary succession could not be sustained unless it was also accepted that subjects could not lawfully oppose the commands of their rulers and could not legitimately decide for themselves who should rule them. The maintenance of the theory of order required therefore that subjects should accept the doctrines of non-resistance and passive obedience. The former commanded that subjects could never actively resist the commands of their king or take up arms against him even to protect their lives, liberties and properties. Since it had to be acknowledged that rulers might conceivably command subjects to do something which was contrary to the laws of God, it was essential to have the principle of passive obedience to fall back upon. This doctrine maintained that when a ruler issued a command contrary to the laws of God then subjects need not obey, but neither could they actively resist. They must simply refuse to act and yet must be willing to submit passively to the punishment inflicted upon them for their disobedience. Subjects must accept the chastisement of their earthly ruler, confident that both he and they must come before the highest judge in the next world.

This theory of order – with its five component elements of absolute monarchy, divine ordination, indefeasible hereditary succession, non-resistance and passive obedience – explicitly rejected the notion that subjects possessed certain inalienable rights which they could legitimately defend against an arbitrary tyrant. The supporters of divine right monarchy insisted that all men were born subject to their parents and subject to their king. Filmer and others utterly rejected the notions that men were by nature free; that they had once shared the fruits of the world in common; that they had entered political society by means of an original contract; and that this contract guaranteed the rights of subjects and limited the authority of rulers. They insisted moreover that to make obedience a conditional obligation and to allow appeals to mythical natural rights or to a non-existent original contract would be to dissolve all order in the world. In popular or democratic states therefore there could be no stable systems of law because the opinions of the volatile masses were always subject to rapid change and were easily influenced by ill-designing men. Nor could property be protected in any society where men could claim an equal right to the fruits of the world. Even liberty could not be preserved when subjects elevated their rights above the authority of the king and when laws were enacted by their will. In such a society liberty became licentiousness and all order was reduced to anarchy. The tyranny of the multitude was undoubtedly the worst fate which could befall any political society. The only way to avoid such a nightmare situation was to accept that the authority of the king was absolute and divinely ordained. The natural consequence of this was that the obedience of subjects must be total and unconditional. Even a system of mixed government, which divided sovereignty between King, Lords and Commons, was little better than a democratic form of government for in such a system there was no means to secure absolute unanimity or universal consent. Either these three institutions would be involved in continual disputes or one of them would manage to possess absolute power without securing the right to it. It was therefore preferable to submit to the will of one man than to be at the mercy of warring factions.[2]

This willingness of men of substance to put their liberties and privileges at the mercy of an absolute king can only be explained by their horror of the 'mob' and their fear of social revolution. They had witnessed the collapse of political and social order in the 1640s and 1650s and they were determined that there should not be another such breakdown of established authority. Most of them would have agreed with Roger North when he declared: 'I would certainly, upon the competition, rather yield to one absolute potentate . . . who had power sufficient to govern and protect, than to live in perpetual fear and without proper guard against injury and oppression from the most cruel of all sorts, that is (not superiors so much as) equals, or rather inferiors.'[3] Men of property clearly feared that the common people might be encouraged to rebel against all established authority, but they were even more terrified that the rabble might initiate a social revolution which would destroy their privileges and their exclusive property rights. This alarm, though largely motivated by self-interest, could be and was defended by frequent references to the inability of the masses to take responsible political action. The poor were regularly categorized as ignorant, lazy and licentious. As such they were too easily led into ill-considered and irresponsible action. The commonalty:

> are too too often the unhappy instruments to beat down truth in all kinds, and set up error; for they are not more fickle in their religion, than they are unto their government, or rather governors, from whom they are apt to be seduced ... being too prone to suspect their governors, they are too easily wrought on by popular officers, or tribunes, who represent them; and being of a mutinous disposition, they brutally nourish factions in a state, for things they do not understand, till they pay the price of it, with their own blood and ruine.[4]

Thus, to most men of substance democracy was simply mob rule. Rather than lose all their privileges and property by a collapse of authority they preferred to submit to the absolute and arbitrary rule of the king. One tyrant could do less damage than a multitude of tyrants.

The theory of absolute and divinely ordained monarchy and the doctrine of non-resistance were regarded by many men of property as essential bulwarks of the political and social order, but their powerful hold on men's minds was reinforced by the influence of those who propagated them and the arguments which they used to justify them. If the ideology of order had rested solely on the argument of expediency then it would have been destroyed almost overnight by the Glorious Revolution of 1688 which removed James II from the throne and replaced him by William III who was not his immediate heir. To understand why this ideology of order was so powerful and so durable that it could withstand the shock of the Glorious Revolution we need to examine how the ideology was disseminated and on what firm intellectual and psychological foundations it rested. It is not claiming too much to insist that the support for divine right monarchy formed part of a coherent and consistent view of the world as many men in post-Restoration England knew it and understood it. The ideology of order was sustained by a deep-rooted desire to find a universal and immutable basis for the claims of established authority and the duties of obedience. It also fulfilled the need to find a political and social order which was above considerations of mere expediency, which was superior to time and circumstance, and which did not depend upon particular historical developments or national peculiarities. The Tories certainly wished to defend those who actually possessed power, but they also wanted to discover a political and social ideology which would win widespread acceptance and obedience because it was based on firm moral and intellectual foundations and not merely on the exercise of might. They wanted a political and social ideology which would support the existing hierarchical society and the prevailing distribution of authority, but which would also be easy to defend on intellectual grounds and which could not be readily undermined by its opponents. In their efforts to underpin their ideology of order the Tories looked to the influential institutions of society to preach their political doctrines and they ransacked all sources of knowledge in order to discover a firm intellectual base for their opinions.

The monarchy quite naturally welcomed the opportunity to propagate an ideology of order which conceded absolute authority to the king. Both Charles II and James II were deeply influenced by the disaster which had befallen their father, Charles I, at the hands of his rebellious subjects and they looked with admiration at the authority of Louis XIV of France. Not surprisingly they turned for advice to men who held a high regard for their kingly authority. Besides promoting such men at Court they encouraged both their lay supporters among the Tory party and the clergy of the Church of England to uphold the authority of the Crown. Parliament itself, at least in the heady days after the restoration of the monarchy, declared that the king possessed absolute authority and explicitly denied that subjects had the right to resist the exercise of this power. A statute of 1660 enacted: 'That by the undoubted and fundamental laws of this kingdom, neither the peers of this realm, nor the Commons, nor both together in Parliament or out of Parliament, nor any other person whatsoever, ever had, have, hath or ought to have any coercive power over the persons of the kings of this realm.' By the Corporation Act of 1661 all officers in local government, and by the Act of Uniformity of 1662 all ecclesiastical persons, had to swear: 'that it is not lawful upon any pretence whatsoever to take up arms against the king'. The Militia Act of 1662 recited: 'That both or either House of Parliament cannot ... nor lawfully may raise or levy war, offensive or defensive, against His Majesty, his heirs, or lawful successors.'[5] After the Restoration both Houses of Parliament instituted the practice of inviting two eminent divines to preach to them each 30 January on the anniversary of Charles I's execution and every 29 May in celebration of the restoration of Charles II. These annual sermons were always the occasion for exalting the authority of the king and for inculcating the duty of obedience. If they had a single common theme it was the doctrine of non-resistance.

Besides reviving the authority of the Crown the Restoration re-established the Church of England as the most important institution in the land and as the natural ally of the Crown. The Church of England had preached the doctrine of non-resistance since the sixteenth century, but after the Restoration it became even more apparent that the vast majority of the Anglican clergy accepted without hesitation their roles as servants of an absolute monarch and as advocates of an authoritarian view of society. As a class the clergy became committed to a highly religious theory of kingship and to the notion that resistance to the Lord's Anointed was a damnable sin. The clergy were convinced that the monarchy and the Established Church must stand together. While the clergy preached reverence for the king, they expected that the revived and strengthened royal prerogative would be used to assist the Church. The bishops were regarded by the Crown as great officers of state and even the ordinary clergy were expected to report on the political condition of the country and to promote the return of Members of Parliament favourable to the Crown. Even more important was the clergy's willingness to preach the duty of obedience and to encourage subjects to accept the powers that be. Preaching in 1666 Dr Robert South expressed the political faith of the Restoration Church when he declared: 'The Church of England glories in nothing more than that she is the truest friend to kings and kingly government, of any other church in the world; that they were the same hands that took the crown from the King's head and the mitre from the bishops.'[6] Even Gilbert Burnet and Edward Stillingfleet, who were later to be two

19

of the foremost divines writing in defence of the Revolution of 1688, preached the doctrines of divine right and non-resistance in Charles II's reign.[7]

The Church of England utterly denied that subjects could actively resist the king on any pretext whatsoever. The two ancient universities, where the clergy received their education, fully endorsed the theory of divine right monarchy and the doctrine of non-resistance. In 1681, at the height of the Exclusion crisis, the University of Cambridge presented an address to Charles II which stated unequivocally:

We will still believe and maintain that our kings derive not their title from the people but from God; that to Him only they are accountable; that it belongs not to subjects either to create or to censure, but to honour and obey their sovereign, who comes to be so by a fundamental hereditary right of succession, which no religion, no law, no fault or forfeiture can alter or diminish.[8]

Two years later, no doubt in partial response to the discovery of the Rye House Plot, the University of Oxford attacked those who denied the absolute authority of kings. The university urged all teachers to impress upon the young 'that most necessary doctrine which in a manner is the badge and character of the Church of England, of submitting to every ordinance for the Lord's sake ... teaching that this submission is to be clear, absolute, and without exception of any state or order of men'.[9]

The only concession which the Church of England was ready to grant to subjects was the right to refuse to obey a royal command which would involve breaking the law of God. Yet even under such extreme provocation subjects were not allowed to resist actively, but were bound by the doctrine of passive obedience. Although they might refuse to obey the king, they must passively accept whatever punishment was inflicted upon them for their disobedience. Redress could only be obtained from God and could never be sought by any positive human action. This political teaching of the Church was summed up in that most widely read manual of devotion, *The Whole Duty of Man*. Generations of children were taught their duty to their king:

An obedience we must pay either Active or Passive: the active in the case of all lawful commands ... But when he enjoins anything contrary to what God hath commanded, we are not to give him this active

20

obedience; we may, nay, we must refuse thus to act; ... We are in that case to obey God rather than Man. But even this is a season for the Passive Obedience; we must patiently suffer what the ruler inflicts on us for such a refusal, and not to secure ourselves, rise up against him. *For who can stretch forth his hand against the Lord's Anointed and be guiltless?*[10]

The Church of England buttressed the authority of the king and in return the Crown protected the privileged position of the Church by such measures as the Clarendon Code and the Test Act. The theory of order was also supported by the alliance between the Church and the landed gentry. Men of property had as much reason as the king to cherish the Church as a bulwark against civil strife and religious anarchy. Closely associated with the religious theory of kingship was a religious interpretation of human society and social obligation. With obedience to kings went reverence and submission to parsons and squires, to fathers and employers. Men of landed property dominated the villages and most of the towns of England. The landed estate was the sole centre of political authority that most men encountered and the manorial courts still exercised jurisdiction over most of the countryside. In such a world, men of substance regarded rank, degree and order as the essential means of preserving their privileges. They were determined that the poor, who were economically dependent upon them, should accept the harsh realities of life and learn to submit to those in authority. Most of the common people were confronted by a patriarchal society and spent their lives in subjection to the authority of a father, master, employer or lord. Patriarchs, whether fathers, employers or magistrates, were expected to show love and concern for their inferiors, but, in the last resort, they could exercise considerable authority. Obedience to patriarchal authority was regularly and officially taught by the Church of England. In teaching the catechism the clergy laid great stress on the Fifth Commandment to 'Honour thy Father and Mother'. The injunction to obey paternal authority was easily and generally expanded to encompass masters and employers, and ultimately the king himself. Thus, for example, Humphrey Brailsford could claim: 'These words, Father and Mother, include all superiours, as well as a Civil Parent (the King and His Magistrates, a Master, a Mistress, or an Husband) and an Ecclesiastical Parent (the Bishop and Ministers) as the natural

Parent that begat and bore thee: to all these I owe Revereance and Obediance, Service and Maintenance, Love and Honour.'[11]

The ideology of order benefited most men of property and was propagated by the major institutions of society. These practical considerations made it a formidable political doctrine, but its influence also depended on the strength of its intellectual foundations. The absolute authority of the king could be justified by appeals to Scripture, history and the natural order of creation. For most men of the later Stuart period the Bible remained the true, unique and complete revelation of God's will in all things. Since it was widely held that the Bible contained the whole truth about the nature of the world and the nature of human society, it was impossible for most men to develop an entirely secular view of politics. Few men attempted to discuss political authority or the obligation of obedience without reference to the Scriptures. All men would in fact have agreed with Sir Robert Filmer that government was divinely ordained and that political authority was originally exercised by Adam, who had been master of the whole world. Most Tories, at least, would have followed Filmer in arguing that Adam had exercised absolute authority over his descendants during his lifetime and that after his death this authority descended down the male line according to the law of primogeniture: 'For as Adam was lord of his children, so his children under him had a command over their own children, but still with subordination to the first parent, who is lord over his children's children to all generations, as being the grandfather of his children.'[12] The evidence of earliest creation therefore showed that men were not born as free and equal individuals, but were born subject to their fathers and all fathers were subject to the great patriarchs who in turn could claim direct descent from Adam. God had granted Adam absolute authority over all earthly things and this sovereign authority had passed to succeeding patriarchs by the process of indefeasible hereditary succession. Even when this process of direct divine ordination had been interrupted by the Flood it had started again with Noah who divided his authority among his sons so that each possessed absolute power over his own individual kingdom or patriarchy. Unfortunately, such evidence of direct divine ordination was not available for modern European monarchs. Some propagandists might be prepared to assert, but none could in fact prove, that Charles II could claim descent from Noah. Whatever the Bible said about direct divine ordination and indefeasible hereditary succession – and there were of course those who denied that there was any scriptural evidence for such notions – it certainly could not be used to provide unchallengeable evidence to support the right of Charles II to the throne of England. Sir Robert Filmer was prepared to admit this and to acknowledge that there had been too many revolutions and usurpations in English history to sustain the claim of direct biblical support for the Stuarts' right to rule. Nevertheless, this did not stop him arguing by analogy and claiming that since political authority always rested on God's will and since this authority was absolute and irresistible, then the Stuarts ruled by God's will and the kings of England possessed absolute power. This was not the same however as proving direct divine ordination or finding clear biblical evidence for indefeasible hereditary succession. Filmer had to fall back on the rather lame suggestion that, despite revolutions and usurpations, divine providence would ensure that in the long run the crown would be restored to the true heir.[13] By recognizing that usurpations had in fact disrupted the practice of indefeasible hereditary succession Filmer came close to suggesting that possession, especially long possession, was a sign of God's approval for a particular usurper and his heirs. Other propagandists who endeavoured to use biblical evidence to support divine hereditary right also practised a degree of intellectual sleight of hand. They insisted that since God had chosen the rulers of Israel then he had also chosen modern kings. They also claimed that since God was concerned about good government he must approve of well established royal families. The first claim however was not supported by any evidence to link biblical rulers with seventeenth-century kings. The second argument converted the doctrine of general providence, which claimed quite reasonably that God cared about the welfare of man, into a doctrine of particular providence, which suggested that God directly ordained certain rulers and commanded sovereign authority to pass from one king to another by means of indefeasible hereditary succession.

Thus, the evidence of the Bible could not entirely support the doctrine of divine hereditary right. The Bible did however provide clearer proof that God favoured monarchies and approved of authoritarian forms of government. The Scriptures provided abundant evidence to suggest that God conferred absolute authority on particular patriarchs and kings. The Bible was also ransacked to show how numerous were the injunctions commanding subjects to render un-

23

B

conditional obedience to their rulers. In the Old Testament, for example, the evidence of Samuel was particularly useful and this text was frequently cited to prove that subjects should never resist their king even when he behaved like a tyrant. The New Testament, especially St Paul in Romans xiii, provided even more explicit evidence that the doctrine of non-resistance was divinely ordained. When Anglican clergymen wished to preach a political sermon they frequently turned to Romans xiii for their texts. They expounded on such texts as 'the powers that be are ordained of God'; 'whosoever resisteth the power, resisteth the ordinances of God'; and 'they that resist shall receive to themselves damnation'.

This scriptural defence of the theory of divine right monarchy and the doctrine of non-resistance was supported by historical inquiries which endeavoured to show that the kings of England had been absolute monarchs since at least the Conquest of 1066. In his historical investigations, chiefly in *The Freeholder's Grand Inquest*, Sir Robert Filmer maintained that the laws of England originated in the sovereign power of the king alone. Parliament could only offer advice and, indeed, could only exist by the king's grace. This claim rested on the historical argument that the king's authority was exercised long before parliaments ever existed. Those who argued that parliaments were immemorial and part of the ancient constitution were mistaken. Filmer was not a good historian and so he was unable to strengthen his argument by showing that the House of Commons did not exist until the reign of Henry III. Dr Robert Brady was a gifted historian however and in the 1680s he was able to write a history of England which justified the absolute sovereignty of the king and explicitly denied the antiquity of Parliament. For Brady the essential evidence for establishing the absolute authority of the king was the Norman Conquest. William I conquered the whole country and was therefore an absolute king. Moreover, by introducing feudal tenures, he had established a new kind of law. There was no land anywhere in England which was not possessed by a lord who held his estates of the Crown. Before Henry III's reign there was no House of Commons and even the king's council existed only at the discretion of the monarch. Thus, Brady's historical research was able to support the Filmerian thesis that the laws and liberties of the people and the privileges of Parliament were not inalienable rights: 'there is a clear demonstration, that all *Liberties* and *Priviledges* the People can pretend to, were the *Grants*

24

and *Concessions* of the Kings of this Nation and derived from the Crown.'[14] Without royal permission Parliament could neither meet nor deliberate. Without the king's approval its decisions could not become law. Parliament was therefore entirely subordinate to the king and in no way could it restrict or limit his authority.

The political ideology of order, besides being sanctioned by Scripture and history, was also sustained by a coherent view of the pattern both of human society and of all creation. Many theorists agreed with Filmer in identifying the kingdom with the family and in equating royal power with paternal authority. While they claimed that the power of kings over their subjects and of fathers over their children both originated in the absolute authority which God had bestowed upon Adam, they did not base their whole case on the evidence provided by biblical texts. They preferred instead to argue that human experience had proved that the authority of both kings and fathers is natural and must therefore be ordained by God, the author of nature. This argument marked an important transition from the claim that government was directly established by divine command to the notion that, since God is the author of nature, then whatever is natural has his sanction. Obedience as well as authority was also natural and therefore also ordained by God. All subjects must obey their ruler just as all children must honour their father. This patriarchal theory made a great deal of sense to men who lived in a society where fathers, masters, magistrates and kings did indeed exercise considerable, almost unquestioned, authority.[15] It also fitted into men's perception of the whole of creation. It was widely held by educated men that creation was arranged in a hierarchical order which descended from God and the archangels down to simple plants and inanimate objects. Mankind occupied a position in the middle of this Great Chain of Being, but, within human society, a similar hierarchical order prevailed from kings down to the humblest subjects. Spiritual beings above men and animal creation below them both exhibited a similar pattern of rank, degree and order. This argument by correspondence or analogy could be used to justify absolute authority presiding over human societies as it presided over the whole of creation. Kings were thus God's viceregents and ruled by his will. Disaster would result from any attempt to overthrow the natural and divinely ordained order of creation. A high premium was put on the maintenance of the existing order, which could be defended as God-given. A metaphysical sanction was provided for

25

the injunction of the Anglican catechism that every man should labour 'to do his duty in that state of life to which it shall please God to call him'. To attempt to leave one's allotted place in society was to endeavour to invert the providential order. Any demand for equality, any resistance to authority was a direct challenge to nature and to God. The order and hierarchy which God had designed for the benefit of man could only be maintained if all civil societies were commanded by an absolute king who could count upon the unconditional allegiance of his subjects.[16]

It is clear therefore that the theory of divine right monarchy and the doctrine of non-resistance were not only beneficial and expedient for men of property, but were also capable of being defended with evidence provided by religion, history and nature. Unfortunately, this ideology of order also put the interests and privileges of the propertied classes at the mercy of an arbitrary and absolute king. Provided the king did not make a determined assault on their position however most men of property showed quite clearly that they were prepared to contemplate a very powerful monarch rather than risk the danger of anarchy. The Tories explicitly defended the theory of divine right monarchy, but few of them concluded that an absolute king need be a tyrant or despot. The king's authority, in the last resort, might be absolute, arbitrary and irresistible, but the Tories did not expect him to use this power to alter the whole fabric of civil society. A king might occasionally act in an oppressive fashion or might betray unjustified hostility to particular individuals, but it was regarded as highly unlikely that any king would pose a permanent threat to the privileges and property of the governing classes or that he would endeavour to ruin the whole country. It appeared axiomatic to men like Filmer that absolute kings would in practice act with a certain degree of restraint and that they would recognize that it was in their own interests to combine justice with order. Clearly no king could be strong or secure if he alienated all his most powerful subjects. His private interest would coincide with the public interest when he governed according to known laws and rendered justice to all his subjects. Moreover any sensible king would realize that while his authority could not be challenged by any earthly agent, his power was still subject to the revealed law of God and the law of nature. The risk attendant on defying God appeared to be so great that the supporters of absolute monarchy were convinced that no Christian king would set himself up as an arbitrary tyrant in the manner of the Ottoman Turk.[17]

26

Even the most committed supporters of the theory of absolute monarchy did not believe that in practice the king would act as a tyrant. They acknowledged that in the last resort he was above the law and that his authority could not be limited by Parliament and yet they expected him to operate within a framework of law and with the advice of his greatest subjects assembled in Parliament. This led the more moderate Tories to conclude that a good king would keep within the framework of established practice. In other words, he would voluntarily recognize that England was blessed with ancient constitutional practices and that his own authority and dignity were at their highest when he governed with the assistance of his loyal Lords and Commons. Tories of this persuasion were thus able to exalt the authority of the Crown while in fact limiting the exercise of that power by the traditional practices of the ancient constitution. The inconsistency of the more moderate Tory position was not exposed until the actions of the Catholic James II forced them to choose between complete loyalty to an absolute king and their desire to protect both their own interests and the ancient constitution. The royal attack on their privileges and their Church compelled them to acknowledge that an absolute monarch could not always be trusted to act within self-imposed limits. Until James II's rash and ill-considered behaviour alienated many of his natural supporters the division between moderate and extreme upholders of the theory of divine right monarchy was not apparent. Even when the king's actions threatened to undermine their privileged position few Tories could support the Revolution of 1688 with a clear conscience. The high Tories might not be prepared to concede that there were any limits on the king's authority whereas the more moderate Tories evidently expected him to govern within the framework of the ancient constitution, but they were all committed to the doctrine of non-resistance. The Revolution therefore disturbed the conscience of every true Tory. None found it easy to reconcile the events of 1688 with the ideology of order which they had believed to be essential, expedient, natural and divinely ordained.

2 *The Impact of the Revolution*

The Glorious Revolution of 1688 delivered a severe blow to the extreme Tory position on the doctrines of absolute monarchy, divine right, indefeasible hereditary succession, non-resistance and passive obedience. These various elements in the Tory ideology of order could not all survive the events of 1688-9 which saw James II

27

removed from his throne and his place taken not by his son but by his daughter and son-in-law jointly. Some Tories did endeavour to remain loyal to all the component elements in their ideology of order, but this attempt forced them to take grave risks or at least to suffer the loss of place and power. They had either to join James II in exile, be prepared to fight a civil war to restore him or later his son to the throne, or passively accept the Revolution and give up position and status in public life. Not surprisingly many Tories of wealth and status were not prepared to make such enormous sacrifices, especially once it became clear that the new political order was becoming firmly established and the prospect of social revolution was rapidly receding. Nonetheless, while these more moderate Tories were anxious to preserve their privileged position in society they were not prepared to abandon their whole ideology of order nor were they willing to embrace Whig or Revolution principles. They remained convinced that a hierarchical society and an authoritarian political structure were essential to the defence of their own privileged position and to the preservation of order throughout the kingdom. This encouraged them to salvage as much as possible of their political ideology, though they recognized that they would have to make some adjustments to their views in order to accommodate the awkward events of the Revolution. Those Tories who compromised their principles to the extent of abandoning their loyalty to James II and accepting the Revolution settlement had to renounce their support for an absolute monarchy. They also had to give up their unconditional support for divine right and indefeasible hereditary succession, though they did not reject these notions completely. They strove instead to adjust them to the new circumstances which prevailed after the Revolution. As we shall see, they transferred their unconditional loyalty and their notion of divine ordination to the whole legislature of King, Lords and Commons instead of to the king alone and they only deviated from the principle of hereditary succession to the extent of excluding Catholics from the throne. These adjustments enabled the Tories to claim that the post-Revolution political order was still sanctioned by divine approval and possessed absolute and irresistible authority. These changes also allowed them to retain those other vital elements of their ideology of order, namely the doctrines of non-resistance and passive obedience. These were the two most important ideological weapons needed to defend an existing political order which was both hierarchical and authoritarian. If subjects remained convinced that they must always submit to those in authority then the privileged position of the propertied élite could be preserved. These adjustments to the Tory ideology of order were not, however, made readily, easily or painlessly. They were made gradually and grudgingly over the two or three decades following the Revolution as the Tories came to terms with the fact that they could not entirely restore the political and social order of pre-1688. While therefore some Tories refused to come to terms with the Revolution settlement, the majority of them realized that they would be best employed not in seeking to reverse the decisions of 1688-9 but in trying to minimize the political and social consequences of those momentous events.

Hundreds of men of tender consciences – the non-jurors among the clergy and the loyal Jacobites among the laity – did refuse to compromise their principles by transferring their allegiance from James II to William and Mary. They stuck rigidly to the old doctrines and made little effort to accommodate their principles to the new circumstances created by the Revolution settlement. Many of these traditionalists retired from public life, but others felt compelled to oppose the new regime by word or deed. The existence of a non-juring church until well into the eighteenth century and the persistent threat from Jacobitism until the collapse of the 1745 rebellion clearly prove that the high Tory views were not readily abandoned. Traditionalists of this sort also waged a paper war in defence of the old Tory principles. The most famous and persistent controversialists were George Hickes, George Harbin, Luke Milbourne and Charles Leslie. These men condemned the contract theory and insisted that absolute monarchs derived their authority from the direct grant of God. Divine right, indefeasible hereditary succession and non-resistance were all based on the declared will of God.[18]

Although Charles Leslie and others were still campaigning with their pens after the defeat of the Jacobite rebellion of 1715, most men of substance and influence had by then abandoned the extreme Tory position. This does not mean however that they embraced the principles of their Whig opponents. On the contrary, most Tories sought to salvage as much as possible from the ideology which they had built up since the Restoration. They recognized that the Catholicism of James II had made it virtually impossible for them to maintain their support for the full-blown Filmerian theory of absolute monarchy, but they endeavoured to retain what they could of a political ideology which, until the accession of a Catholic king, had served their interests so well. They were prepared to concede that their privileges and those of the Church of England could never be secure if the king's authority were entirely unlimited, but they were determined to resist those claims which put ultimate sovereignty and the right of resistance into the hands of the people.

At the end of 1688 the Tories were in an acute dilemma. James II had fled to France and could only be restored by force. William of Orange was in London and was supported by a considerable armed force and by the committed Whigs. The latter were a minority of the political nation and had even less support in the nation at large, but there was little popular support for the restoration of the Catholic James II. Since William was determined to have the executive power placed in his hands, the Tories had to come to terms with him without abandoning all their most cherished political principles. The first and most important problem was to find a lawful ruler. An influential body of Tories, led by the Earl of Nottingham, favoured the declaration of a regency. This scheme would retain James II as titular sovereign while placing the exercise of kingly authority in the hands of a more dependable Protestant regent. This would in practice limit the king's actions without destroying the power of the Crown as an institution. It would also avoid any suggestion that subjects possessed the right to remove their ruler and choose a new sovereign. The constitution would be preserved largely intact and the government would still appear indisputably legal and hence certain to secure widespread obedience. Unfortunately for the Tories William rejected the regency plan and insisted on securing the Crown. Unless the Tories were prepared to risk a civil war they had perforce to abandon their loyalty to James II and to recognize William and his wife, Mary, as the new joint sovereigns.

After several tense debates and much painful heart-searching the Tories in the House of Commons reluctantly agreed to renounce their allegiance to James II. They were careful to insist however that this was due to the voluntary actions of James II rather than to any resistance offered by his subjects. The resolution of the Commons on 28 January 1689 declared that James II had abdicated by his flight to France: 'having withdrawn himself out of this kingdom, [James II] has abdicated the government and that the throne is thereby vacant.' The Tories refused to accept that Parliament could judge the king and strip him of his sovereignty. Still less would they concede that subjects had the right to depose their ruler. They repeatedly pointed out that no violence had been offered to James II by his subjects and that in his Second Declaration of 14 October 1688 William himself had denied that he wished to use force against James and had maintained that 'the forces we have brought along with us are utterly disproportionate to that wicked design of conquering the nation.' The Tories were also anxious to stress that the abdication of James II did not mean that the whole system of government was dissolved and that the people were free to erect a new one. Such a dangerous claim would reduce the whole country to a state of anarchy and threaten every landowner's title to his estates. Parliament therefore should only concern itself with solving the political problem created by James II's abdication.[19] The Tories in the House of Lords found it difficult even to swallow this scheme. They tried hard to institute a regency and, even when this proposal was defeated, they endeavoured to substitute the more neutral term 'deserted' for the word 'abdicated' in the resolution devised by the House of Commons. Not until 6 February did the Lords give way and accept the resolution of the Lower House.

Even after they had conceded that James II had abdicated the Tories faced the problem of how to fill the throne. They opposed any suggestion that the throne was vacant since this would be a denial of the doctrine of hereditary right and would imply that Parliament had the right to elect a successor to James II. In their view the Crown was hereditary and no act of James II could bar or destroy the right of his heirs to succeed to the throne. While the Tories were prepared to regard the baby prince, James Edward, as supposititious, they found it difficult to recognize William of Orange as the next in line to the throne. If James Edward were passed over then William's wife, Mary, was next in succession to her father's throne but, unfortunately, William was not content to be merely a regent or consort. He insisted on being king in name as well as in fact. Some Tories refused to agree to this and would not support the resolution to declare William and Mary as joint sovereigns. The Earl of Nottingham spoke for the Tory majority which reluctantly accepted the new rulers when he confessed that he had opposed 'the Prince his accession to the crown, not believing it legal, but that since he was there and that he must now owe and expect his protection from him as King *de facto*, he thought it just and lawful to swear allegiance to him.'[20] The Earl of Danby supported him, admitting 'they had resolved to make them King and Queen upon this crisis of affairs, yet no man would affirm that they were rightfully so by the constitution.'[21] Both Nottingham and Danby declared that many subjects would be unable to take in their existing form the prescribed oaths to the new rulers, since these oaths would imply that William and Mary were the rightful and lawful sovereigns. The Tories successfully pressed for a new oath of allegiance which did not require any explicit repudiation of James II and which contained no reference to William and Mary being 'rightful and lawful' sovereigns. The new oath simply required the swearer to state: 'I do sincerely promise and swear that I will be faithful and bear true allegiance to their majesties King William and Queen Mary, so help me God.'[22]

The new oath was a clear recognition of the fact that many Tories regarded the new regime as provisional, as a violation of the constitution caused by exceptional circumstances and to be tolerated until better times returned. This was certainly the attitude of Lord Ailesbury, who bowed to present necessity though he hoped to restore James II at the first opportunity. He excused his decision to accept the new rulers with the words: 'I took the oath which I termed before like to a garrison one, for it was my opinion that he being declared king (although I did in parliament do all that lay in my power to obstruct it) he was to protect the kingdom, and that those that desired protection ought to take some oath.'[23]

Most Tories appear to have agreed with Nottingham, Danby and Ailesbury. They accepted the new rulers with extreme reluctance, but they knew that the only alternatives were either to embrace Whig principles wholeheartedly or to risk civil war by fighting for their own beliefs. They did neither. Although they sacrificed their lawful king, they did so in order to preserve their Church and to uphold authority and order in the State. Their property, their social privileges and their political influence could only be preserved if the vacant throne were filled, at least temporarily, by William and Mary. Thus large numbers of Tories surrendered to the commands of sheer political necessity. Many Tory squires must have shared Sir John Bramston's reasons for reluctantly accepting the authority of William and Mary:

By his [James II's] absence it became necessary that Governement should be by somebody, to avoid confusion. There can be no Governement without submission to it, that can, whether by one or more, have no assurance of submission but by a religious tye and obligation; the constant practice in all states is by oath to obleige obedience. When the Governement is fixed, obedience becomes necessarie to it, and conscience obleiges privat persons to yield obedience, as well as prudence and safety to prevent anarchy, and the rabble from spoilinge and robbinge the noble and wealthy. These assertions and reasons seem to me to arise out of pure necessity.[24]

3 The Tory Acceptance of the Revolution

One of the most important tenets of the Tory ideology of order was the conviction that only a lawful and rightful government could be strong, stable and certain of obedience. Since they were not convinced that the new regime which was established in 1689 was in fact lawful and rightful it is not surprising that most Tories regarded the Revolution as a provisional settlement which was unlikely to survive for very long. Moreover, while the Whigs could regard the Glorious Revolution as confirming their ideological position, the Tories could only regard it as a severe blow to every important element in their ideology of order. They had seen the authority of an absolute monarch limited by acts of Parliament, they had witnessed a divinely ordained king replaced by one chosen by Parliament, they had accepted a deviation from the principle of indefeasible hereditary succession, and they had done nothing to stop active measures being taken to drive James II from his throne. Even when the Revolution settlement proved far more durable than they had ever imagined and their resistance to it steadily crumbled, few Tories were prepared to abandon their whole ideology of order and embrace Whig principles about contract, popular sovereignty and natural rights. Instead, they sought to redefine their political principles in such a way that they could accept the Revolution without abandoning their support for a hierarchical society and an authoritarian political order. If the Tories were to succeed in this, their first task was to justify the decision to accept William III as the rightful and lawful successor to James II. Eventually, after years of discussion about the right of conquest, the operation of divine providence and the legitimacy of accepting the authority of a *de facto* ruler, the Tories were able to salve their consciences about deserting James II and his son, the Old Pretender.[25] Once this adjustment was made they were in a position to salvage much of their ideology of order. The Tories could still support a powerful though not an

33

absolute monarchy, they could still appeal to the notion of a divinely ordained political order though not to a king directly ordained by God, and they could still accept the general principle of hereditary succession though not the doctrine of indefeasible hereditary succession. There was certainly no need for the Tories to abandon their conviction that the only legitimate governments were those sanctioned by God and, until the Hanoverian succession in 1714, they were in a position to stress that they had made only the smallest deviation in the right of succession to the throne. They were to be even more successful in their attempts to retain the doctrines of non-resistance and passive obedience.

The problem of recognizing William III as a rightful and lawful king could be solved for those who were prepared to assert that his claim to the throne rested on the right of conquest. This was a plausible argument which did not violate the cherished doctrine of non-resistance. William of Orange was not a subject of James II but a sovereign prince in his own right. For him to use force against James II in order to protect his own interests was 'agreeable to the laws and practices of all countries, to the laws of our own nation, to reason, and which is more, unto Scripture itself'.[26] As a prince in his own right it could be argued that William posed the general right to attack another prince in a just war, but it could also be argued that he had a particular right in this case because he was seeking to defend his wife's inheritance after James II had attempted to make a supposititious son, James Edward, his immediate heir. By appealing to the conquest theory there was no need to assert that James II had been deposed for betraying his trust and certainly no need to claim that the people possessed the right to establish their own government. William could be accepted as king *de jure* because he had driven James II out of the kingdom. The people could not be accused of actively resisting James II and could therefore, in good conscience, accept William III as their lawful and rightful sovereign.

There were however too many inherent dangers in the conquest theory to make it acceptable to many Tories. The forces of William of Orange had been joined by a number of James II's subjects in November 1688. If it were once allowed that William had conquered James II, then these subjects would be guilty of taking up arms against their lawful sovereign. Since some of these subjects were Tories, then the Tories themselves could be accused of a blatant breach of the doctrine of non-resistance. Moreover, William himself was aware that very few of his new subjects would relish being regarded as a conquered people. His own declarations of 1688 explicitly denied that he was using force to protect his own interests. Instead, his declarations claimed that he had landed to defend the religion and liberties of the English people. Furthermore, while the conquest theory could be used by others to justify the use of force against James II, it could not be used by William to support a claim to the throne for himself when he was at such pains to deny that he had come to England to serve his own ends. When therefore the conquest theory was revived in 1693 with the publication of *King William and Queen Mary Conquerors*, both the King and the Whigs joined the Tories in condemning this assertion. Parliament ordered the book to be burned by the common hangman, while the House of Lords resolved: 'That the assertion of King William's and Queen Mary's being King and Queen by conquest was highly injurious to their majesties, and inconsistent with the principles, on which their government is founded, and tending to the subversion of the rights of the people.'[27]

Far less dangerous than the conquest theory and much more in accordance with the traditional Tory doctrine that thrones were filled by God was the assertion that William became king as the result of a particular act of divine providence. An appeal to divine providence had the advantage of asking the Tories to accept what none was prepared to deny: that in the last resort human actions were dictated by the will of God and that no man could occupy a throne against the wishes of the Almighty. God undoubtedly ruled the world and kings merely governed as his viceregents. Hence, when one king's position was usurped by another, though sinful men might be immediately responsible, God was the final cause. Even Sir Robert Filmer had acknowledged that kings had often been deposed in the past and yet he endeavoured to square such usurpations with the doctrine of divine right. He did so by claiming that such acts of resistance, while justly incurring God's displeasure, were nevertheless only possible by God's grace.[28] This notion could easily be applied to the Revolution. The astonishing events of 1688 could be readily interpreted as evidence of God's particular providence. His special concern for the Protestant religion and for the liberties of Englishmen had wafted William across the Channel on a favourable wind, had landed him in England on the anniversary of the Gunpowder Plot, and had ensured that James II would flee without a blow's being struck. William had risked all in an apparently hope-less cause, but God had smiled upon his venture. Divine providence had placed William on the throne without recourse to the sin of resistance or the spilling of innocent blood. Thus Gilbert Burnet, an Anglican divine who had previously preached the doctrine of non-resistance, could preach shortly after the Revolution:

Consider the steps of providence ... the prodigies and miracles of Providence, that have attended our deliverance ... We have before us a work, that seems to our selves a dream, and that will appear to posterity a fiction: a work about which Providence has watched in so peculiar a manner, that a mind must be far gone into atheism, that can resist so full a conviction as this offers us in favour of that truth.[29]

At first this appeal to divine providence was made by Anglican divines who were prepared to abandon their earlier Toryism in favour of a moderate Whiggism. Within a few years however there is clear evidence that even those who would never accept Whig principles were prepared to appeal to divine providence in order to justify their acceptance of the Revolution. Francis Atterbury, a high Tory and one of the most determined defenders of the traditional Anglican position, eventually made full use of the appeal to divine providence. In 1701 he delivered a sermon before the House of Commons which was entitled 'The Wisdom of Providence mani-fested in the Revolutions of Government'. His thesis was direct and simple. Resistance by subjects was always a sin, but God was always free to overrule and throw down any government. 'No people can be reduced to such a wretched and forlorn condition, but that the good Providence of God may and will, if it sees fit, come to their rescue and deliver them; even without hope and against hope.'[30]

The claim that the Revolution had received divine sanction un-doubtedly persuaded some Tories to accept the events of 1688-9, but probably the most effective argument with the Tories was the appeal to necessity. We have already seen how Tories such as Nottingham, Danby, Ailesbury and Sir John Bramston were pre-pared to recognize the authority of an established regime, even one of doubtful legality, rather than risk everything to restore an abso-lute, Catholic king. This argument from expediency became even more influential when it was given intellectual and moral backing by eminent Tory propagandists, including high churchmen and former non-jurors, who advanced the claim that it was lawful to obey a *de facto* king if it were not possible to have a king *de jure*. The *de facto* theory or the prescriptive right of a king in possession was acknowledged by Filmer, the arch-apologist of divine right. He confessed: 'It skills not which way Kings come by their power, whether by election, donation, succession or by any other means, for it is still the manner of the government by supreme power that makes them properly Kings, and not the means of obtaining their crowns.'[31] This *de facto* theory was given an unintended boost by William Sancroft, the non-juring Archbishop of Canterbury, who decided in 1690 to publish Bishop John Overall's *Convocation Book of 1606* which contained numerous political arguments supported by the Church of England at that time. These political canons had clearly rejected the notion that governments were established by the people and had explicitly accepted the doctrine of non-resistance, but, because they did not sufficiently stress indefeasible hereditary succession, James I had refused to license their publication. Sancroft's decision to publish the Convocation book enabled those who wished to come to terms with the new regime to do so while claiming to be obeying the injunctions of the Church of England. Canon XXVIII of Book One claimed that, while God might use rebellions to punish rulers, this did not mitigate the offence of resistance. But it then went on to declare that when any new form of government, even one begun by rebellion, was thoroughly settled, this authority must be regarded as divinely ordained.[32] In other words, a well established *de facto* regime was clear proof that it existed by God's grace and hence it could be regarded as the *de jure* government. A prescriptive government eventually proved that it was divinely ordained. In that case subjects must render it the same obedience as any government which had always been *de jure*.

This canon provided the Tories with an excellent argument for coming to terms with the Revolution without endorsing Whig principles. William Sherlock was the first prominent Tory to make use of it. Sherlock, who had been a leading London clergyman, had refused to take the oaths to William and Mary and had been deprived of his living. In 1691 Sherlock recanted and published *The Case of Allegiance due to Soveraign Powers, stated and resolved*. In this treatise Sherlock argued that subjects owed obedience to divine authority rather than to any power which might claim a legal right to rule. It was evident that God could overthrow kings and set up new ones in their place. Whenever he did so, subjects must obey the new king because he ruled by divine authority. To ensure that subjects did not transfer their allegiance to any usurper as soon as he had secured the throne, God gave men a clear sign by which to judge whether the new regime had his approval or not. The test which subjects must apply was to ask themselves whether the new government was firmly established. Once they were sincerely convinced that this was the case then there could be no justification for refusing to render obedience.

When the whole administration of government, and the administrative power of the nation is in the hands of the Prince; when every thing is done in his name, and by his authority; when the estates of the realm, and the great body of the nation has submitted to him, and those who will not submit, can be crushed by him, when ever he pleases; if this be not a setled government, I despair of ever knowing what it is; for there is no government in the world so setled, but that by some unseen accident, or by greater force and power, it may be unsetled; and in this sense it is impossible ever to know, when a government is setled; for no government is, or can be thus setled against all events.[33]

On this basis Sherlock was convinced that subjects must obey the king in possession, William III, because he could protect them rather than James II, the king with the legal title, because he could not. There was a higher law than that of indefeasible hereditary succession. This was the law of self-preservation. The end of civil government was the preservation of human society and for that reason subjects must obey that government which could clearly protect them. An obstinate allegiance to a dispossessed king would endanger all order and would end in anarchy. It could never be in the interests of society to let all authority collapse.[34]

The *de facto* justification for the Revolution was bitterly attacked by non-jurors and by committed Whigs because both sides recognized that it had considerable appeal for those prepared to offer the new regime a conditional acceptance. The non-jurors rightly feared that their strength would be sapped if the theory of divine right could be undermined by a prescriptive right to the throne. They therefore charged Sherlock with selling his principles for the sake of preferment and ridiculed the notion that William could acquire a prescriptive right to the throne in a mere two years.[35] The Whigs feared that the *de facto* theory would allow the Tories to enjoy the benefits of the Revolution settlement without any commitment to

38

Whig principles and without conceding the legality of the Revolution. It could therefore act as a cloak for crypto-Jacobites.[36]

These fears were entirely justified. The prescriptive argument did persuade more and more Tories to accept William as king *de facto*, though many Tories remained reluctant to accept him as king *de jure* and hence to renounce all allegiance to James II. It is clear that an increasing number of Tories came to recognize that the preservation of order might be impossible if they did not accept a monarch whose title was held *de facto*, but they always regarded such a claim as inferior to a title which was clearly *de jure*. Possession only gives the best right when it is impossible to find or support a right *de jure*. When the Whigs attempted to pass an abjuration bill which would compel the Tories to abjure James II the Tories always opposed it. Tories like Humphrey Prideaux were prepared to take the new oath of allegiance to William III, but they were not ready to take an abjuration oath.[37] When, after an attempt to assassinate William III had been frustrated in 1696, the Whigs advocated an Association which required subscribers to accept William as their rightful king some ninety-two Tory Members of Parliament refused to sign. That in most cases this refusal indicated nothing more than a tender conscience rather than a positive loyalty to James II can be surmised from what occurred in the House of Lords. When the upper chamber decided to omit the term *rightful*, only about twenty Tory peers refused to sign the Association.[38]

By the beginning of Anne's reign the majority of Tories, though by no means all, had reconciled themselves to the demise of divine right monarchy. Before his death William III had managed to secure Tory support for the Act of Settlement of 1701 which designated the Protestant House of Hanover as the successors to Anne should she die childless. Once again Parliament abandoned the strict line of hereditary succession in order to ensure that a Protestant would sit on the throne. Although they did not entirely abandon the principle of hereditary succession the Tories were compelled to take a fresh and searching look at their attitude towards a divinely ordained monarchy and indefeasible hereditary succession. After a painful struggle with their consciences most of them were prepared to abandon their loyalty to these doctrines. The overwhelming majority of Tories voted for the Act of Settlement, though the bitter pill had to be sweetened by several clauses critical of William III and restricting the future actions of the Hanoverians. The death of James II in

1701 and of William III in 1702 undoubtedly made matters easier for the Tories. While Anne was on the throne the principle of indefeasible hereditary succession did not have to be abandoned. After all if the Pretender's claim were regarded as dubious, then Anne had the clearest right to the throne. Moreover, James II's failure to recover his throne could be regarded as a sign that God approved of the Revolution. It was therefore easier for most Tories to regard Anne as sovereign *de jure* as well as *de facto*.

The Tory party in general welcomed Anne's succession with undisguised relief, though this did not mean that all Tories had irrevocably turned their backs on the doctrines of divine right and indefeasible hereditary succession. Some of them still cherished the notion that Anne could be regarded as monarch by divine right even though she herself insisted that her right to the throne rested on the Revolution settlement. When, in 1710, she received a loyal address from the City of London, 'she immediately took exception to the expression that "her right was Divine," ... she could by no means like it, and thought it so unfit to be given to anybody that she wished it might be left out.'[39] The residual Tory support of indefeasible hereditary succession was also revealed in their attitude to the Pretender. Many Tories, who had reluctantly come to terms with the Revolution settlement and who had then welcomed the accession of Anne, still found it difficult to abjure the Pretender when this was required of them by an act passed in the last months of William's reign. The Earl of Nottingham was eventually to accept the Hanoverian succession, but, as a high churchman of scrupulous conscience, he found it extremely difficult to abjure the Pretender. He required the reassurance of John Sharp, the Tory Archbishop of York, before he could bring himself to take the oath.[40] Viscount Weymouth was only persuaded to take the oath because the accession of Anne presented an opportunity for the Tories to rally once more to the monarchy and the Church. He informed his brother in late March 1702: 'though I have not absolutely resolved to take this new oath, yet ... I am much nearer doing it than I ever thought I should bee, and may possibly submit to doe it, the case beeing so much altered by the death of King Wm, and the old as well as new lawes beeing on the Queens side. And if conscience will allow, I am sure prudence will prompt to strengthen her Government, and restore the Church to the ground it has lost.'[41] Even after the Tories in Parliament had taken the oath they still sympathized with those

Tories out-of-doors who wished to put off taking the abjuration oath. In 1703 the Tory majority in the House of Commons passed a bill, entitled 'An Act for enlarging the time for taking the Oath of Abjuration'. As late as 1714 perhaps as many as a hundred Tory Members of Parliament wished to see the Pretender succeed Queen Anne, though most of these were not prepared to fight in order to realize this hope. Even these committed Jacobites recognized the importance of a monarch sanctioned by act of Parliament. In the last months of Anne's reign they hoped in vain for the repeal of the Act of Settlement and for a parliamentary resolution in favour of the succession of James Edward Stuart.[42]

In the final analysis the overwhelming majority of the Tories accepted the Hanoverian succession without putting up a fight for the Pretender. Not surprisingly most Tories did not wish to fight a civil war for a claimant who was a Catholic and who had spent nearly all his life in France. It is unlikely however that their decision was taken entirely on pragmatic grounds. Throughout the reign of Anne the argument in favour of accepting a *de facto* monarch and the support for the prescriptive right of a well established government had made significant advances among Tory intellectuals and propagandists. William Sherlock had not convinced the majority of Tories when he asked them to accept the prescriptive title of William and Mary when the Revolution settlement was barely two years old. By Anne's reign however many more Tories were prepared to argue that an authority which had long demonstrated its power had acquired a divine sanction and had earned a prescriptive right to govern. It had long been an expedient principle in matters of property to equate the *fact* of ancient possession with the *right* of possession. To secure the stability of society it might be necessary to reduce the period of time required to establish a prescriptive right to govern.

After the death of James II and the accession of Anne the doctrine of prescription became increasingly attractive to the property-conscious Tories. In 1705 Henry Dodwell, who had been a non-juror since the Revolution, finally accepted the claims of the juring bishops to their sees. As the non-juring bishops died off Dodwell was in a position to argue that those bishops in possession had acquired a prescriptive title and even divine sanction.[43] In 1709 Offspring Blackall, the Tory Bishop of Exeter, was using prescription to defend the existing political establishment and was implying that it had now achieved a *de jure* right to govern: ' 'Tis most reasonable therefore now that in every place that should be taken to be the most rightful government which is establish'd; the powers that be are ordained of God; and the best title to government is that which has prevail'd by prescription, or is settled by the constitution.'[44] In the same year another eminent non-juror, William Higden, came to terms with the existing regime. Like William Sherlock he too argued that a monarch in firm possession of the throne had clearly gained God's approval and possessed a prescriptive right to rule: 'by the demise of a king, whether de facto or de jure, his authority is by law determined and at an end, and the laws thence-forward administer'd by the authority of the king in possession, and by his authority only.'[45] Higden went on to show that since the Conquest only six English monarchs had possessed a hereditary title to rule and yet all the others had been recognized as *de facto* sovereigns. Indefeasible hereditary succession had rarely been able to challenge the fact of possession and the actual exercise of power. Higden's argument certainly convinced George Berkeley, a staunch Tory divine and a future philosopher of distinction. Berkeley admitted: 'Mr. Higden has in my mind clearly shown that the swearing allegiance to the king de facto (whether right or wrong) is conformable as well to the law of the land as to the Scripture and reason, and the practice of nations. That it is agreeable to reason is so evident from the very nature and design of government, as one may justly wonder it was ever made a question.'[46] When Tories of Berkeley's intelligence and integrity clearly accepted the moral, intellectual and expedient arguments for recognizing a prescriptive right to govern it is not surprising to find that by 1714 most Tories had abandoned their traditional allegiance to divine right and indefeasible hereditary succession. Their willingness to abandon these cherished doctrines was undoubtedly made more palatable by their ability to retain at least the general notions of divine sanction and hereditary succession and by their success in preserving other elements of the Tory ideology of order.

4   The Survival of the Ideology of Order

Although the success of both the Revolution settlement and the Hanoverian succession compelled the Tories to abandon elements of their ideology of order, it is a mistake to argue from this that the political and social structure of eighteenth-century Britain rested entirely on Whig ideological foundations. In fact the triumph of Revolution principles was far from complete and the Tories were able to retain important elements of their ideology of order. After all, the political events of 1688-9 had not sparked off a social revolution and a hierarchical society which conferred rank and status on men of birth and fortune had survived the Revolution almost entirely unscathed. It is therefore not surprising to find that men of privilege and property were anxious to safeguard the political and social order which had survived the Revolution. Many of these men recognized that the Tory ideology of order still had much to offer those who wished to preserve privilege and protect private property. In other words, social and economic realities continued to justify certain Tory principles. While men of property realized that it was no longer possible to support an absolute monarchy, because an absolute king had recently threatened to undermine their political and social privileges, they still hoped to establish a sovereign authority in the State whose power would be absolute and irresistible. By changing their opinion about the source and location but not about the nature of this sovereign authority, they could continue to preach the crucial doctrines of non-resistance and passive obedience. If they located sovereignty in the whole legislature of King, Lords and Commons, they could retain the injunction that subjects should submit to the powers that be and so still protect their own position as the privileged élite. Thus the decision to abandon absolute and divinely ordained monarchy and the principle of indefeasible hereditary succession did not compel the Tories to give up their defence of a hierarchical society and an authoritarian political order. Indeed, it could be argued that by adjusting and moderating their political doctrines the Tories were in a better position to safeguard those interests which they had always been most concerned to protect. By changing the location of sovereignty they found an absolute and irresistible power, the legislature, which was more able than an absolute monarch to protect the interests of propertied men. By abandoning indefeasible hereditary right and by accepting the Protestant succession they were in a better position to defend the privileged position of the Church of England than they had been under a Catholic ruler. It could even be argued that by limiting the arbitrary power of the monarch the Tories made it easier to defend the remaining prerogatives of the Crown.

Before the Revolution the Tory emphasis on divine right monarchy naturally led them to revere the sovereign's authority. With William III on the throne the Tories were less willing to defend the prerogatives of the Crown. They acquiesced in the restrictions which were placed on the Crown by the Bill of Rights and they positively promoted further limitation on the royal prerogative in the Act of Settlement of 1701. Throughout William's reign Tories can be found sniping at the king's policies and actions and yet much of this criticism was levelled at the person who wore the crown rather than at the institution of monarchy. Several leading Tories opposed the Triennial bill of 1693, which William III also disliked, because it limited the royal prerogative to call and dissolve Parliament. Sir Edward Seymour, for example, insisted that Parliament must have as much concern for the prerogatives of the Crown as for the liberties of the subject.[47]

With the accession of Anne the Tories were able to revert to their traditional reverence for the sovereign and respect for the royal prerogative. In *The Divine Institution of Magistracy* (1709) Offspring Blackall, without quite resurrecting the divine right theory, emphasized the authority of the Crown and insisted that monarchs ruled by the will of God. During the Sacheverell crisis of 1710, when a celebrated Anglican divine was impeached by a Whig-dominated parliament for preaching the traditional Tory views on monarchy and non-resistance, there was a flood of loyal addresses in support of the Queen's prerogative. Typical of these was the address from Gloucester in which the Tory subscribers declared: 'We are now, and always shall be, ready to sacrifice our Lives and Fortunes, in Defence of Your Majesty's most Sacred Person, Prerogative, and Government.'[48] During the same crisis a Tory courtier, Thomas Coke, claimed: 'The rule I have laid down to myself is to support ye Prerogative of ye Crown in all points, as much as in me lies.'[49] Jonathan Swift could write of the Tories:

As they prefer a well-regulated monarchy before all other forms of government; so they think it next to impossible to alter that institution here, without involving our whole island in blood and desolation. They believe, that the prerogative of a sovereign ought, at least, to be held as sacred and inviolable as the rights of his people, if only for this reason, because without a due share of power, he will not be able to protect them.[50]

The Tory support for the royal prerogative was not of course devoid of self-interest. The Queen favoured the Tories, chiefly because of their defence of the Church of England, and so they had everything to gain from protecting the Queen's prerogative over such matters as the disposal of places of profit and power. It often, although not always, suited the Tories to resist what they took to be encroachments on those discretionary powers which the sovereign still possessed. During the peace negotiations with France the Tories upheld the Crown's unfettered right to conduct foreign policy and insisted that Parliament could only give advice when requested to do so. Not surprisingly they defended the Queen's right to create twelve new Tory peers in order to push the peace preliminaries through the House of Lords.

Nonetheless, the Tories did not support the royal prerogative simply because of the tactical political advantages which they could derive from it when it operated in their favour, as it did for much of Anne's reign. In their view an authoritarian political order could only be sustained in a hierarchical society led by a strong monarch. The Crown was both the symbol and agent of authority and stability. Only by securing its rightful prerogatives could law and order prevail in civil society. On the other hand, if too much power were conceded to subjects then anarchy and mob rule would be the inevitable consequence. The Tories retained their deep-seated fear of the licentious mob and were horrified whenever the Whigs spoke of the sovereign rights of the people. Francis Atterbury, one of the most outspoken Tory divines, protested that 'the voice of the people is the cry of hell, leading to idolatry, rebellion, murder, and all the wickedness the devil can suggest ... nothing but fire from heaven can stop the cry, nothing but sulphureous flames can quell the voice of the people.'[51] The whole notion that subjects possessed inalienable natural rights was anathema to the Tory concept of an authoritarian political order. Subjects could only lay claim to the protection of the law and to those rights which the law explicitly allowed them. Offspring Blackall insisted:

This I take to be an undoubted truth, that no man has a natural right to anything in this world, more than to the necessaries of life. Whatever right any man has to estate, or dignity, or dominion, except only over the fruit of his own body, is meerly humane; that is, 'tis a right that is given by the law of the land, or the constitution of the realm.[52]

The defence of the royal prerogative and the attack on the doctrine of natural rights provide clear evidence that the Tories still feared anarchy far more than absolutism: 'Compare tyranny with rebellion, and you'll find no such mischief by the first, as by the last. If the people rebel, thousands of tyrants start up instead of one; then is hell broke loose, and more are destroy'd in one day, than could otherwise be in many months.'[53] Support for an authoritarian political order however could no longer be associated with the advocacy of absolute and divine right monarchy. The awful warning of James II's reign and the realization that the Revolution settlement could be used to safeguard the privileged position of the propertied élite persuaded most Tories to abandon their loyalty to the principles of absolute monarchy and divinely ordained, indefeasible hereditary succession; but it did not force them to abandon their support for the doctrines of non-resistance and passive obedience. On the contrary, throughout the reigns of William and Anne, and especially during the Sacheverell crisis of 1709–10, the Tory laity and a majority of the Anglican clergy consistently proclaimed the political value of the doctrines of non-resistance and passive obedience.[54] In order to continue preaching obedience to the powers that be and yet avoid the taint of Jacobitism, the Tories were forced to reconsider their view of what constituted the supreme authority in the State. Some Tories, of course, were still convinced that the Crown remained the sovereign power in the State even though the monarch had graciously agreed only to legislate with the advice and consent of Parliament. The more moderate Tories – and there was an increasing number of such men – recognized that the success of the Revolution had made it impossible for them to remain loyal both to divine right monarchy and to the doctrine of non-resistance. Only non-jurors and Jacobites, that is those who could never accept the legitimacy of the Revolution, could remain committed to both concepts. Most Tories eventually came to terms with the Revolution settlement, but, in doing so, they needed to abandon both divine hereditary succession and the absolute authority of the monarch. Since they wished to remain free to preach the doctrine of non-resistance, however, they had to recognize another absolute, sovereign authority in the State in place of the Crown.

Since the decisions of the Convention Parliament in 1689 had fatally weakened the concepts of divine hereditary right and absolute monarchy the Tories were compelled to follow the Whig example of considering the combined legislature of King, Lords and Commons as the sovereign authority in the State. In seeking to continue their attempts to instruct subjects in their legal, moral and religious duty to obey the powers that be, the Tories had little alternative but to suggest that the supreme authority was the legislature unless they were to adopt the radical Whig notion of the sovereign people. As they reluctantly abandoned the divine right of absolute kings and yet struggled to maintain an ideology of order, the Tories were driven to substitute the concept of the divine right of the sovereign legislature. Even before the Revolution some Tories had supported the concept of an ancient constitution and had recognized that for centuries Parliament had been consulted by wise monarchs. They had not denied that the monarch possessed sovereign authority in the kingdom, but they had conceded that wise monarchs would seek the support of Parliament when taking important decisions. Even Filmer had not expected kings to ride roughshod over the interests of their most important subjects. It is therefore not surprising to find that the awful warning of James II's reign persuaded many Tories to put more trust in Parliament. This shift in emphasis was assisted by two political developments. In the first place, the Tories grew to appreciate the political value of regular sessions of Parliament. They came to recognize that the legislative power of Parliament could be used to protect the privileged position of both landed men and the Church of England. This process was assisted by changes in the composition of the Tory party. During the reigns of William III and Queen Anne a number of men who had some sympathy with the Revolution settlement but no confidence in the policies of the Whig leaders swelled the Tory ranks. Some of these men, including Robert Harley, Henry St John, Simon Harcourt and Jonathan Swift, became influential in the Tory party but saw no need to attack the power of Parliament. Indeed, by Anne's reign few prominent Tories were committed any longer to the principle that absolute sovereignty resided in the monarch alone. They had transferred their loyalty to the sovereign legislature. While this change may have been the product of necessity and expediency, the Tories believed that it was essential to justify this transformation so that they could both deny the doctrine of popular sovereignty and continue to preach the doctrines of non-resistance and passive obedience.

The first clear sign that the Tories were prepared to preach obedience to the legislature appears in the famous sermon which John Sharp, the Archbishop of York, preached to the House of Lords on 30 January 1700. In pleading for the right of the clergy to teach the traditional Anglican doctrines of non-resistance and passive obedience the Archbishop made it clear that the authority which must be obeyed was that of the law of the land and not merely the expressed will of the monarch: 'To speak this as plainly as I can. As the laws of the land are the measures of our active obedience; so are also the same laws the measure of our submission. And as we are not bound to obey but where the laws and constitution require our obedience; so neither are we bound to submit but as the laws and constitution do require our submission.'[55]

Two years later Sharp, though on excellent terms with the new Queen, was still ready to acknowledge that Anne held her crown by authority of the sovereign legislature. 'I am of opinion that [princes] hold their crowns by the same legall right that your Lordship holds your estate,' he informed the Earl of Nottingham, 'and that they may forfeite their rights as well as you may do yours. And that the Legislative is judge in one case as well as the other.'[56]

Sharp's first tentative steps to accommodate the doctrine of non-resistance to the apparently irreversible fact of the Revolution was soon reinforced by contributions from several other Anglican divines. In a sermon preached before the Queen herself, on 8 March 1704, Francis Atterbury came close to asserting the same doctrine as Sharp. 'The Law', Atterbury declared, 'is as much a Rule to her as to the least of those who obey her; the first Measure, not only of her governing Power, but even of her will to govern; and she makes no other use of that power, with which the Laws have invested her, than to give life and force to them.'[57] Offspring Blackall was more explicit in acknowledging that the legislature was the sovereign authority in the State. The whole thesis of his treatise *The Subject's Duty* (1705), is of crucial importance in understanding the way in which moderate Tories could accept the Revolution without denying the doctrine of non-resistance. Blackall insisted that all governments were ordained by God and that therefore resistance to them was a sin, but he rejected the Filmerian claim that God had decreed absolute monarchies as the only legitimate forms of civil government. In Blackall's view God had left different societies free to develop their own peculiar political institutions, but he had enjoined all subjects to obey the powers that be. An absolute ruler, who had voluntarily agreed to share his sovereignty with a representative assembly – as kings of England had repeatedly done – could not subsequently recover his unfettered authority without the express consent of that assembly. Conversely, if a government had originally been established by some form of contract, the people could not thereafter dissolve civil society in order to recover their authority. Even though the people themselves had created the legislature, that sovereign authority could not be resisted by those who had agreed to be subject to it. No matter how the legislature was created or constituted the authority which made the law was sovereign and hence absolute, unlimited and irresistible. Thus Blackall could reject the extreme claims of both the Jacobites and the radical Whigs. On the one hand he could limit the Crown by compelling the monarch to act with Parliament when making laws, while on the other he could reject the notion of the sovereign people. By making the combined legislature of King, Lords and Commons the sovereign authority in the realm, Blackall could put great stress on the doctrine of non-resistance without also demanding adherence to the concepts of divine right, indefeasible hereditary succession and absolute monarchy.[58]

Bishop Blackall's thesis was invaluable to those Tories who were anxious to accept the Revolution and ready to renounce their allegiance to an absolute monarch. Jonathan Swift, an Irish Protestant who accepted the Tory position on many issues, could never reconcile himself to a Catholic monarch on the throne. It is therefore not surprising to find him advocating non-resistance to the sovereign legislature. George Berkeley provided a brilliant philosophical defence of non-resistance which did not require the supreme authority to be in the hands of an absolute monarch. William Higden, for twenty years a non-juror, astonished both friend and foe when he not only recognized possession of the throne as a stronger title than hereditary right, but went on to claim that the supreme authority in the kingdom was the combined legislature of Crown, Lords and Commons. He thereby combined the prescriptive argument of Sherlock with Blackall's claim that the legislature was the sovereign authority in the state.[59]

It was not until the trial of Dr Sacheverell in 1710, however, that the Whigs discovered the political advantage which the Tories could reap from their accommodation to a conservative interpretation of the Revolution settlement. The Whig leaders believed that the impeachment of Dr Sacheverell would rally moderate opinion to their party because it would convict a prominent Tory divine of preaching against the Revolution and disturbing the peace of the State. The Tory managers for the defence could not deny that

49

Sacheverell had indeed preached the utter illegality of resistance, but they hoped to confound the Whigs by claiming that the doctor had meant the whole legislature and not merely James II when he referred to the supreme authority in the State. Samuel Dodd, one of Sacheverell's defence counsels, asserted:

The supreme power is the Queen and Parliament, and to this supreme power the Doctor has prest the utter unlawfulness of resistance; and I have not heard it said by any that it is lawful to resist the Queen in Parliament. Here is the strength of the nation, and here there ought to be a standing obedience, otherwise it is setting up the people to be judges, and not the collective body of the people assembled in Parliament.[60]

It is extremely doubtful whether Sacheverell had preached any such doctrine in his notorious sermon, but it is highly significant that more moderate and politic Tories were prepared to accept this argument in order to retain the doctrine of non-resistance while accepting the established fact of the Revolution settlement.

Clearly the Glorious Revolution did not end the Tory campaign to propagate an ideology of order. Most Tories remained convinced that a society of rank and status and a stable political order could only be sustained by a conservative ideology of this kind. At the same time, the actual survival of such a society after the Revolution enabled the Tories to find powerful supporters and influential propagators of their ideology of order. The continued political, social and economic supremacy of landed men and the survival of a powerful Church of England meant that there were plenty of men anxious to disseminate an ideology which would protect their vested interests. They realized that an ideology of order would protect their privileged position in society, while, in turn, their position of influence enabled them to propagate such an ideology. The political campaigns and the ideological debates of the reigns of William and Anne show how concerned landed men and Anglican clergy were to support an ideology of order and how useful this ideology was in preserving the vested interests of such men. The survival of the Tory ideology of order undoubtedly depended upon the strength of the landed interest and the Established Church. On the other hand, the privileged position of landed proprietors and the Anglican clergy could only be sustained and justified by the continued propagation of an ideology of order. Thus the landed interest and the Church of

England continued to be the chief propagators and the main bene-
ficiaries of the Tory ideology of order.

The concept of the patriarchal origin of political authority, so
much stressed by Filmer, had been delivered a hard blow by John
Locke and other Whig theorists, but the social and economic realities of the post-Revolution period still made it possible to regard
a system of rank, degree and order as natural, inevitable and beneficial. The real and pervasive power of fathers, employers and the
great landowners could not be gainsaid by any intellectual construct.
When it came to the exercise of political authority most Tories
remained convinced that the natural rulers of society were the men
of landed estates. In their view only men of substantial property
possessed the qualities necessary to sit in Parliament or to act as magistrates: namely, leisure, education, independence and a sense of duty
and responsibility. The overwhelming majority of subjects lacked
all of these qualities, while even merchants and financiers were too
preoccupied with the business of making money to have sufficient
leisure to devote to public responsibilities. Furthermore, whereas
landed men had a genuine stake in the country and must protect
their country in order to defend their own interests, the possessions
of merchants and financiers were movable. In a crisis men of estates
would have to stay and fight to preserve their interests, but merchants and financiers might be free to escape with their wealth.
Thus, in the opinion of many Tories, a sense of political responsibility was largely confined to landed men. Certainly the stability
of the State would be threatened if political authority were conferred
upon those who were unfit to exercise it.

These prejudices and assumptions led the Tories to regard themselves as the protectors of the landed interest and encouraged them
to take a hostile attitude to the political pretensions of those who
secured their wealth from commerce, financial transactions or positions of profit under the Crown. In the decades immediately following the Revolution the rates of profit to be made from land were in
general not as high as those to be earned from commerce, finance and
office-holding. At the same time the long and expensive wars during
the reigns of William III and Queen Anne placed a heavy burden on
the squirearchy through the land tax, which was levied at four shillings in the pound, while an equivalent tax burden was not placed on
other forms of wealth. Moreover, these wars required unprecedented
funds and supplies and an increasing number of administrators. New

opportunities of enrichment and advancement were therefore opening up for financiers, merchants and office-holders just when the landed interest was shouldering a particularly heavy burden. Numerous Tory spokesmen feared that these economic and social changes would be followed by a threat to the political authority of landed men. Many Tories echoed Sir John Pakington's desire 'to prevent the monied and military men becoming lords of us who have the lands'.[61] Henry St John was just as angry but more explicit when he complained:

A new interest has been created out of their fortunes, and a sort of property, which was not known twenty years ago, is now encreased to be almost equal to the terra firma of our island. The consequence of all this is, that the landed men are become poor and dispirited. They either abandon all thoughts of the publick, turn arrant farmers, and improve the estates they have left: or else they seek to repair their shattered fortunes by listing at court, or under the heads of partys. In the mean while those men are become their masters, who formerly would with joy have been their servants.[62]

This fear, that their social and political influence was being undermined, provoked the Tory spokesmen for the landed interest to lead both a political and an ideological campaign to defend and justify the privileged position of those whom they regarded as the natural leaders of society. In order to prevent moneyed men using their wealth to buy their way into Parliament the Tories pressed for a landed qualification for those who wished to be Members of Parliament. In 1711 they finally passed an act which insisted that candidates for election must possess real estate worth £600 p.a. if they wished to contest a county seat and £300 p.a. if they wished to stand for a borough. The Whig Bishop Burnet was no doubt correct when he suggested that 'the design of this was to exclude courtiers, military men, and merchants from sitting in the house of commons, in hopes that this being settled, the landed interest would be the prevailing consideration in all their consultations.'[63] The Tory Sir William Massingberd rejoiced when this bill became law and went on to express the hope that another bill would be passed to make it necessary for Justices of the Peace to possess landed estates: 'for when landed gentlemen represent us in Parliament, and do our business at home in the country, we may justly look for better times, and that our tottering constitution may be once more fixed to the confusion and amazement of all its adversaries.'[64] A bill to restrict the office of Justice of the Peace to those who owned real estate worth £300 p.a. actually passed the Commons, but foundered in the House of Lords.[65] On this issue, as on others, the Tories were not able to prevent the political authority of the landed men being weakened, but their actions prevented this authority being seriously undermined.

The Tory desire to uphold order, rank and hierarchy explains not only their support for the landed interest but also the strength of their attachment to the Church of England after the Revolution. No doubt many Tories genuinely approved of the structure, liturgy and doctrines of the Established Church, but they were also well aware that the Church was an essential buttress to their concept of order. Indeed, now that the influence and authority of the Crown could no longer be relied upon to the same extent as before the Revolution, the Church had become the principal institution defending the political doctrines so dear to the Tories. The Church of England was so intimately bound up with government, landownership and the social hierarchy that it was impossible to ignore its influence or entirely to escape its jurisdiction. To the Tories it appeared to be an essential instrument for the preservation of social order and political stability. The great majority of the Anglican clergy could certainly be trusted to preach the doctrines of non-resistance and passive obedience. Even the more moderate clergy were convinced that it was their duty to preach a doctrine of subordination:

the generality of men must not by any means be left wholly to the workings of their own minds, to the use of their natural faculties, and to the bare convictions of their own reason; but they must be particularly taught and instructed in their duty, must have the motives of it frequently and strongly pressed and inculcated upon them with great authority and must have many extraordinary assistances afforded them; to keep them effectually in the practice of the great and plainest duties of religion.[66]

Since the Tories believed that the Church of England provided political society with its essentially religious character and with a system of moral sanctions to enforce obedience, then it is hardly surprising to find them rushing to defend the special privileges of the Church whenever these were attacked after the Revolution. For their part a majority of the Anglican clergy rallied to the Tory party and urged upon their lay allies the importance of the link between Church and State. In return for preaching obedience to the secular authorities the clergy desired to see the State protect the privileged position of the Church. Both the Tories and the clergy feared that the Dissenters would overturn the established order in Church and State. Thus, in his famous sermon of 5 November 1709, Henry Sacheverell insisted:

> Our constitution both in Church and State, has been so admirably contriv'd, with that wisdom, weight and sagacity, and the temper, and genius of each, so exactly suited and modell'd to the mutual support and assistance of one another, that 'tis hard to say whether the doctrines of the Church of England contribute more to authorize and enforce our civil laws, or our laws to maintain and defend the doctrines of our church ... So that ... whosoever presumes to innovate, alter, or misrepresent any point in the articles of the faith of our Church ought to be arraign'd as a traitor to our state; heterodoxy in the doctrines of the one naturally producing and almost certainly inferring rebellion and high treason in the other, and consequently a crime that concerns the civil magistrate, as much to punish, and restrain, as the ecclesiastical.[67]

The alliance between the lay Tories and the bulk of the Anglican clergy failed to prevent some weakening of the authority of the Church of England after the Revolution, but it was sufficiently powerful to preserve the Established Church as one of the major institutions of the State. The Tories recognized the value of the resistance put up by the Protestant Dissenters to James II's blandishments and were prepared to offer some alleviation of the harsh legislation of Charles II's reign, but they were determined to preserve the privileged position of the Established Church. In 1689 the Earl of Nottingham and other Tories supported one bill which would comprehend the less radical Dissenters within the Church of England and another bill which would tolerate the public worship of those Dissenters who remained outside the establishment. When William III suggested that the political disabilities imposed by the Test and Corporation Acts should be removed however the Tories took alarm at this threat to the monopoly which Anglicans enjoyed of public office at national and local level. The clergy and Tory laity were also alarmed at the King's recognition of a Presbyterian state church in Scotland. Many politicians, including some moderate Whigs, joined the Anglican clergy in support of the privileged position of the Church of England. Any hope of repealing the Test and Corporation Acts was abandoned and even the Comprehension bill was dropped. The Dissenters had to rest content with a limited

Toleration Act which allowed them the liberty of public worship if their meeting places were licensed, but denied them the political privileges enjoyed by members of the Church of England. To impress on William III the strength of the support which the Church still enjoyed the Tories secured as an addition to the coronation oath a proviso binding present and future monarchs to uphold the Church of England as established by law.

Even this rebuff to the Dissenters and their political allies did not satisfy the Tories or the Anglican clergy. The great majority of the parochial clergy were angry and demoralized by the concessions granted to the Dissenters. The Church of England could no longer enforce attendance at church and the disciplinary power of the ecclesiastical courts waned sharply. The Toleration Act may have been a limited and grudging measure, but it did allow an increasing number of subjects to escape the jurisdiction of the Established Church in a way which had not been possible before the Revolution. The number and size of dissenting congregations certainly increased after the Revolution and the Anglican clergy were naturally fearful of where this process might end:

If ye Toleration Act be continued in force as it is, without any alteration it seems impossible to keep up any due discipline in ye Established Ch[urch] because if pastors admonish, suspend or excommunicate any proud, stubborn, or conceited persons, as just occasion may require according to ye nature of their offence, whether it be for profanely or idly absenting from all religious worship (wch is now commonly done) or for anything else; they will utterly contemn and despise it, since they can herd themselves (under a pretence of conscience) amongst some of the Tolerated Dissenters.[68]

This concern of the parochial clergy, that religious order would collapse if the authority of the Established Church were undermined, led them to look for political support for the Church of England. At the same time the Tories were convinced that the clergy were essential agents in the propagation and dissemination of an ideology of order as well as virtual electoral agents for their party. The result was a powerful alliance between the bulk of the Tory party, especially the squirearchy, and the large high church element among the parochial clergy. During the 1690s this alliance became convinced that William III and his Whig supporters were conspiring against the authority and privileges of the Established Church.[69] The parochial clergy in Convocation and the Tories in Parliament waged a long,

55

c

bitter and, in some respects, successful campaign to preserve the privileged status of the Church of England. When William III needed the Tories to pass the Act of Settlement in order to secure the Protestant succession, the Tories were in a position to wring an important concession out of him. One vital clause in the act insisted that the monarch must in future be not simply a Protestant but an Anglican. Throughout Anne's reign the Tories and the parochial clergy endeavoured with some success to safeguard the privileges of the Church and to limit the concessions granted to the Dissenters. The Tories deeply resented those less scrupulous dissenting laymen who qualified for office by the cynical practice of occasionally attending the Established Church and they were perturbed at the success of the dissenting academies which infringed the Anglican monopoly of higher education officially enjoyed by Oxford and Cambridge. After three failures the Tories eventually passed a bill in 1711 to penalize the practice of occasional conformity. They hoped thereby to emphasize the Anglican monopoly of public office and to weaken the grip which the Dissenters had gained on a number of corporations. The Tories also conducted a long campaign against dissenting academies, which educated future generations of dissenting ministers and so perpetuated religious schism. In 1714 they finally managed to pass the Schism Act which limited the activities of these academies. During these campaigns the Tories and the parochial clergy frequently pointed out that the established order in Church and State faced a common enemy. The most famous sermon of Dr Henry Sacheverell was entitled 'The Perils of False Brethren in Church and State'. When the Whigs decided to impeach Sacheverell for this sermon they confirmed the worst fears of the Tories and the clergy and provoked such a fierce reaction that the Whigs were swept from office for the rest of Anne's reign. During one debate on the dangers facing the Church the Tory Sir John Pakington spoke for his party and for the majority of the Anglican clergy when he declared that one of the gravest threats facing the country was:

the great increase of dissenting schools and seminaries all over the kingdom, in which great numbers of our youth are poisoned with principles which make them disaffected to the Church, and considering the strict Union between Church and State, I may say to the monarchy too. I take them to be nurseries for rebellion.[70]

2

The Whigs and Government by Consent

Just as it is too readily assumed that the Tory ideology of order collapsed after the Glorious Revolution so it is too often implied that a Whig theory of liberty, based on the social contract, the natural rights of man and the ultimate sovereignty of the people, rapidly replaced that of the Tories. The Whigs were certainly not as conservative as the Tories, but only a minority of them were committed to political principles which might be regarded as genuinely liberal. Most Whigs were certainly opposed to absolute monarchy and were ready to support the right of subjects to resist an arbitrary tyrant, but in many other respects they were deeply conservative. It is essential to remember that the Whigs shared many of the prejudices, assumptions and ultimate objectives of their Tory opponents. Most active Whigs were also men of substance who wanted political power to be exercised by responsible men of their own type and who wanted a stable, orderly, even hierarchical society which would protect the privileges and property of the wealthy and influential. They were in no sense democrats who wished to put political power into the hands of the labouring poor and very few of them were republicans who had any desire to sweep away the monarchy. Even the substantial number of Whigs who were ready to grant a measure of religious toleration to Protestant Dissenters had no wish to dismantle the Established Church or to sever all the links between Church and State. Very few Whigs were ready to see power pass out of the hands of men of wealth and property and they were sufficiently conservative to be horrified at the prospect of social revolution. Whig support for liberal opinions was further weakened by the success of their Tory opponents. During the reigns of William III and Queen Anne the Tories proved that many of their opinions had the support of a majority of the political nation. The Tory success must therefore not be measured simply by their ability to accommodate their political principles to the Revolution settlement. The strength of the support for Toryism drove the Whigs to abandon some of their more liberal views and to stress their commitment to conservative principles. Thus, while the tactical mistakes of the Tories drove them into the political wilderness on the accession of the Hanoverians in 1714, their strength during the previous two reigns had ensured that the Whigs who triumphed over them were men of a decidedly conservative stamp.

Nonetheless, it has to be recognized that the Whigs did reject the Tory ideology of order and their own political ideology did contain some important liberal strands which marked them off from their highly conservative opponents. There can be no doubt that all Whigs repudiated the Tory claim that England was governed by an absolute monarch. They insisted that the power of the Crown was not arbitrary and unlimited. In their view the authority of the king was clearly limited by the power of Parliament, especially in matters of legislation and revenue raising. The Whigs also claimed that all subjects possessed certain liberties, chiefly the rights to life, liberty and property, which no government could infringe without due process of law. In the last resort subjects could actively resist the worst excesses of an arbitrary tyrant. These principles undoubtedly distinguished the Whig position from that of the Tories. Nevertheless, while Whig principles were always more liberal than those of the Tories, they were less liberal after the Glorious Revolution than they had been before. In their opposition to Charles II and James II the Whigs developed a whole range of arguments designed to undermine the Tory ideology of order. Some of these were quite conservative and aimed to limit the power of the Crown by appeals to the rights of Parliament and the legitimate influence of men of property. Others were much more radical and were based on notions about the universal and inalienable rights of man and the sovereignty of the people. Once James II had been removed from the throne however and the threat of an absolute monarchy receded, then most Whigs were ready to accept the moderate Revolution settlement. None of them contemplated a social revolution and nearly all of them were ready to tone down the more radical arguments which had been used before the Revolution. If the Whigs had been free to make their own political settlement in 1689 they would probably have placed more limitations on the power of the Crown, but they would not have established either a democratic system of government or a genuinely liberal social order. When, during the years following the Revolution, they came to realize that they now had the chance to enjoy the benefits of office and place the Whigs became even more ready to accept the conservative political settlement made in 1689. Their principles never became as authoritarian as those of the Tories, but most of the liberal arguments which they had once employed were toned down if not entirely abandoned after the Glorious Revolution.

1 The Whig Theory of Liberty

During the Exclusion crisis of 1679–81 and during the reign of James II the Whigs became convinced that political stability could not be achieved under an absolute and arbitrary monarch. While the events of the 1640s and 1650s had convinced the Tories of the need to develop an ideology of order the actions of the Stuart kings in the 1680s persuaded the Whigs of the need to challenge the arbitrary and unlimited power of the Crown. In their view an absolute monarch posed an intolerable threat to the influence and interests of men of property. Only by resisting the power of the Crown could men of property protect their privileged position in society. If constitutional limitations were not placed on the Crown, then men of property would have to turn to armed resistance in order to preserve their rights. The 1640s, however, had shown that an armed struggle could lead to a far more radical revolution than the opponents of absolute monarchy desired. In order to steer a course between the dangers of absolute monarchy and social upheaval therefore it was essential that the king should govern with the consent of his most important subjects. The Whigs, like the Tories, wanted stability and order and a world in which men of property would be safe. In their view these objectives could only be achieved under a limited monarchy.

Nonetheless, they were reluctant to rest their political aims on an appeal to expediency or a secular ideology which would ignore religious and moral considerations. Like the Tories the Whigs were not just concerned with the question of who in fact wielded power. They wished to determine who had the *right* to govern: 'To settle therefore mens consciences under an obligation to obedience, 'tis necessary that they know not only that there is a power somewhere in the world, but the person who by right is vested with this power.'[1] The Whigs felt the need to be able to justify their political principles on moral grounds. They believed that men did not make themselves or own themselves, but were the workmanship of God and were sent into this world to do his business and serve his ends.[2] Although the Whigs did not rely as much as the Tories on the scriptural evidence of God's views on government, they did feel that their political principles needed the appearance of divine sanction if they were to carry conviction. While they occasionally appealed to the Bible, they relied more heavily on reason, the law of nature, and historical evidence to furnish proof that their political ideas were in accord with the will of God. For the Whigs reason and the laws of nature replaced the Bible as the chief means by which God transmitted his wishes to man and established general principles of human behaviour. By appealing to such evidence the Whigs showed that they were determined to prove that their political ideology was not only practical and expedient, but morally superior to that of their opponents.[3]

One of the first tasks of Whig theorists and propagandists was to demolish the Filmerian argument that absolute monarchy was ordained by God. This required them to counter Filmer's biblical evidence and to deny his assertion that the authority of the king was but the patriarchal authority of fathers writ large. To the assertion that absolute hereditary monarchy was ordained by God, the Whigs ransacked the Bible to prove that this was far from being the case. They claimed that if Adam had only one heir then there ought to be only one lawful king in the whole world yet Filmer was not even able to prove who Adam's original heir was let alone which kings could now claim descent from either Adam or Noah. The Bible also showed quite clearly that indefeasible hereditary succession was not a fixed rule approved by God. Neither Saul, David nor Jeroboam had any hereditary right to the thrones which they occupied, while neither Solomon nor Benjamin were the eldest sons of the kings whom they succeeded. Moreover, the Bible could be used to provide evidence to prove that subjects had rights and that tyrants could be resisted. St Paul, when on trial, insisted on his rights under Roman law, while David was actually aided by God in his successful effort to depose Saul for maladministration.

Filmer's critics frequently pointed out that his fusion of biblical evidence and patriarchalism made it impossible to reconcile the multiplicity of rulers in the world with the origins of absolute monarchy in the universal, patriarchal authority of Adam. John Locke went further. In his *Two Treatises,* especially the first, he painstakingly dissected Filmer's patriarchal theory. Locke explicitly and emphatically distinguished between the power of kings and the authority of fathers. He insisted that subjects were not in the inferior position of children who could be governed without their consent. Even if patriarchal authority were the model for the power of kings this could never justify absolute monarchy. Fathers did not in fact possess absolute authority over their children. Since God is the creator of all life, children could not be regarded as existing solely for the benefit of their fathers. All children have the right to be nourished, maintained, educated and protected by their parents. For a time children are helpless and at the mercy of their fathers. Eventually, however, they become adults and are in a position to revoke the authority of their father. If they do not do so, then their acceptance of patriarchal authority is a voluntary act and rests on consent not compulsion. Thus, if patriarchal authority is indeed the origin of political power, then the authority of kings must be modelled on that of fathers over their adult offspring. Kings must earn respect by their actions and subjects must consent to be governed.[4]

Besides countering the biblical evidence and patriarchal theory of the Tories, the Whigs put forward their own political theories which rested more heavily on appeals either to history or to reason. Of these two approaches there can be little doubt that the historical appeal to the ancient constitution of England was more influential than the appeal to the full-blown contract theory, even though the latter is much more famous because of its association with the name of John Locke. Although the two theories are inherently contradictory and most Whigs preferred to rest their case on the ancient constitution, this did not prevent the Whigs appealing to both theories when it suited them. Their preference for the historical argument was based on a realization that the concept of an ancient constitution placed limits on the power of the English Crown and recognized the privileges and authority of Parliament, but did not confer universal and inalienable natural rights on all men. While it denied the legitimacy of absolute monarchy, it did not advocate a democratic system of government. Instead, it sanctioned the long-established social and political order which was dominated by men of property. The contract theory, as put forward by Locke and Algernon Sidney, was inherently more revolutionary because it was based on more radical assumptions about the equality of man, the existence of certain universal and inalienable natural rights, and the ultimate sovereignty of the people. As we shall see, even Locke and Sidney drew back from the radical conclusion that the only legitimate political system was a democratic republic, but even a conservative interpretation of the contract theory was too much for many Whigs. They much preferred to argue their case against royal absolutism on the evidence of English history because they believed that this approach would achieve their political ends without risking social revolution.

According to the Whigs the evidence of history provided ample proof that subjects could resist tyrants, that hereditary right was not indefeasible, that kings of England did not possess absolute power and that they themselves recognized the limits of their authority. It could be proved that subjects had actively resisted the actions of their kings and had secured concessions which acknowledged their own liberties. On this point the most important example was the revolt against King John which resulted in Magna Carta. The liberties vouchsafed in this great charter were regarded as applying to *all* men, even though this was a misreading of the text, while the frequent reissue of the charter was seen as proof that subsequent English sovereigns were freely prepared to concede demands which had been forcibly wrung from King John. The right of subjects to resist tyrants appeared to be sanctioned by the opposition shown to several English monarchs. It even seemed to be approved of by several monarchs themselves for Elizabeth, James I and Charles I had all helped subject peoples in Europe to rebel against tyrants. The Filmerian claim that the succession to the throne was based on primogeniture and indefeasible hereditary succession was easily undermined by references to the way the crown of England had frequently passed to someone other than the eldest surviving son of the previous king. Finally, the coronation oath of English monarchs, by which they swore to uphold the law and to offer justice impartially to all subjects, was frequently cited as evidence of the conditional nature of royal authority. Even William I had not claimed to rule his new subjects as a conqueror, but had sworn to uphold the laws of Edward the Confessor.

All of these appeals to the evidence of English history were incorporated into a general thesis about the ancient constitution which was used by the opponents of the Crown throughout the seventeenth century. This thesis maintained that English law was customary and immemorial, and that the supreme authority in the kingdom was the legislature of King, Lords and Commons. Building upon this foundation many Whigs asserted that the liberties of Englishmen and the political institutions of England were of ancient vintage, whereas claims about the divine right and absolute authority of kings were recent innovations. The one law which was known to all Englishmen and by which their land was possessed and their crimes punished was the common law. This was customary law whose origin was lost in the mists of antiquity. The statute law enacted by Parliament was simply a means of clarifying or re-stating, but not generally of overriding, the common law. The implication was that immemorial usage had made the common law more perfect than any law which the intelligence of any particular parliament or king could devise. Written laws contained no more than the wisdom of one man or one generation whereas customary law in its infinite complexity had been tested over many centuries and contained the accumulated wisdom of many generations.

The fact that the English people were subject to a customary law was regarded as proof that they had developed their own law out of their own accumulated wisdom and experience and had not had it imposed upon them by the conscious will of a particular king or parliament. Yet paradoxically, while holding that the common law was based on ancient custom, the common lawyers of the earlier seventeenth century and the Whigs of the later seventeenth century came to believe that both the common law and the constitution had always been exactly the same. Both the common law and the constitution were regarded as being exactly the same in the seventeenth century as they had been in the immemorial past, about which no historical records could be found. A few Whigs did suggest that both the law and the constitution evolved over time and adapted continuously to changing circumstances,[5] but the majority was convinced that the common law and the constitution had survived unchanged over centuries. It was firmly believed that this ancient constitution, which could be traced back to the Anglo-Saxon era before the Norman Conquest and even further back until its origins were lost in the impenetrable mists of a Germanic or Gothic past, was a limited monarchy or mixed form of government. The king had never been absolute, but had always governed with the advice of Parliament. Both Lords and Commons could trace their origin beyond the Conquest to the Anglo-Saxon Witanagemot. William I was not a conqueror who could legitimately assume absolute power, but a claimant who had vindicated his right to the throne and had subsequently confirmed the laws of his predecessor. Although the Normans had endeavoured to subvert the nation's liberties, they had no right to do so. Their English subjects were therefore quite justified in their efforts to throw off 'the Norman yoke'. Magna Carta was proof both of their success and of their right.[6]

The concept of the ancient constitution was used and embellished throughout the seventeenth century by the opponents of Stuart absolutism. In the later seventeenth century it figured prominently in the works of such leading Whig theorists as Algernon Sidney, James Tyrrell, Henry Neville and William Petyt. They all laid less stress on immemorial law and placed more emphasis on the antiquity of Parliament. This enabled them to insist that England enjoyed a mixed government in which sovereignty was shared by King, Lords and Commons. Even Charles I was regarded as having fully conceded this point in his *Answer to the Nineteen Propositions* of June 1642. In this document the King had declared:

There being three kinds of government amongst men, Absolute Monarchy, Aristocracy and Democracy, and all these having their particular conveniences and inconveniences. The experience and wisdom of your ancestors hath so moulded this out of a mixture of these, as to give to this Kingdom (as far as human prudence can provide) the conveniences of all three, without the inconveniences of any, as long as the balance hangs even between the three Estates, and they run joyntly on in their proper channell ... The ill of absolute monarchy is tyranny, the ill of aristocracy is faction and division, the ills of democracy are tumults, violence and licentiousness. The good of monarchy is the uniting a nation under one head to resist invasion from abroad and insurrection at home: The good of aristocracy is the conjunction of counsell in the ablest persons of a state for the publick benefit: The good of democracy is liberty, and the courage and industry which liberty begetts.

In this kingdom the laws are jointly made by a King, by a House of Peers, and by a House of Commons chosen by the people, all having free votes and particular privileges ...[7]

The Whigs seized upon this statement as proof of their contention that the power of the monarchy was limited and the sovereign authority was shared by the combined legislature of King, Lords and Commons. William Petyt argued that Parliament could repeal former laws and enact new ones, could transfer the rights and possessions of private persons, could legitimize bastards, could make laws concerning the worship of God, and could even alter the succession to the Crown.[8] Algernon Sidney claimed that Parliament could legally restrain the authority of the Crown and could decide who should be king.[9] All Whigs insisted that subjects could resist a tyrant who aimed to subvert the ancient constitution. Whether sovereignty lay in an immediate sense with the combined institutions of King, Lords and Commons or ultimately with the fundamental laws of the ancient constitution, the unconditional obedience of subjects must be paid to the legislature and to the constitution rather than to the king. A king who threatened Parliament or the constitution could not depend upon the allegiance of his subjects.

In addition to the historical argument which supported the concept of an ancient constitution, with the authority of the king limited by the power of Parliament, a few Whigs developed an alternative rebuttal to the divine right theory. This argument was based on an appeal to reason and to the law of nature. It claimed that all men possessed certain natural and inalienable rights and that a legitimate government must rest upon the consent of the governed. Algernon Sidney's insistence that legitimate governments were created by the consent of free men and that subjects could resist an arbitrary tyranny won widespread support among the Whigs,[10] but only John Locke developed a coherent contract theory which fully accounted for the origins of civil government and which explained both the authority of the supreme magistrate and the rights of the subject. Unlike Sidney and all the other leading Whig theorists, Locke did not base his arguments on an historical appeal either to the ancient constitution or to some actual original contract. In order to justify limited monarchy, government by consent, and the right of resistance, Locke appealed instead to reason and to the law of nature (which he tended to regard as the same thing). Reason, he believed, was the best means of interpreting the law of nature which was the unwritten law of God. Reason instructed man in the law by which he was to govern himself and made known to him how far he was left to the freedom of his own will and how far he must obey the will of God. The law of nature was sovereign over all human actions and set the bounds to man's freedom. Locke insisted that liberty did not mean license, for the law of nature imposed duties and responsibilities as well as allowing men free will. Where there was no law there could be no real freedom.[11]

From his rational and yet essentially religious assumptions about the law of nature Locke was able to argue that God made all men free and equal. No human being was created for the sole benefit of another. All men were endowed with the natural rights to life, liberty and property and with the authority to protect those rights. Locke believed that no man has the right to put any other man under his power or will without that man's express or tacit consent. If any man attempts to exercise such an arbitrary and illegitimate authority, the injured party has the right to resist even to the extent of destroying the aggressor.[12] Since in the state of nature there can be no arbitrary power of one man over another, it follows that civil government can only be created by consent, by the voluntary agreement of those who are to be governed. To that extent civil government is an artificial construct. God approves of government as a means of restraining the violence of men, but the actual institutions of civil government are man-made.[13] Civil government originates in the realization by most men that they lack the power to preserve their natural rights against the designs of their corrupt and ambitious fellow-men. In the place of their own inadequate powers of self-preservation they set up an impartial judge and a known, settled body of laws. Men agree to surrender their individual claim to defend their life, liberty and property to a civil government which will establish known laws for the public good, will appoint impartial judges for the administration of justice, and will create a force sufficient to preserve law and order in the community. Once this has been done men must go to law rather than resort to force in order to protect their rights.[14]

The only legitimate governments according to Locke are those which have been established by consent. An absolute monarchy is illegitimate because the ruler is free to overrule the law of nature and to infringe the rights of man with impunity. This is against all reason and religion. In a civil society created by the consent of the community the sovereign authority is the legislature because it represents the united force of the whole community and because it alone can make positive law. A separate executive may be established to put the law into effect and to apply the necessary sanctions, but, while the executive might enjoy considerable prerogative powers, it is ultimately subordinate to the legislature. To ensure that the government fulfilled the expectations of those who created it, Locke suggested that it was advisable though not essential to have the legislature in the form of a representative assembly and to have its decisions reached by majority vote. The head of the executive might be part of the legislature, but his power should be separate from and inferior to it. The terms of the initial agreement of the people and the sovereign authority of the legislature placed limits on the executive's power. Both the executive and the legislature should be restricted by the ultimate ends of civil society, which are to protect the life, liberty and property of the subject rather than to serve the interests of the government. If these ends are neglected then the government has betrayed the trust reposed in it and the contractual relationship between government and governed has been broken. Thus Locke uses the notion of a contract to explain the origin of civil government, but, when a civil government is actually in existence and he wishes to refer to the relationship between subjects and their government, he substitutes the term *trust* for that of contract. This allows him to develop both a conservative and a radical dimension to his political theory. His appeal to the concept of an original contract allows him to stress the ultimate sovereignty of the people and to claim that power originates with the people and is deputed to their government. When he discusses the operation of a government which is already in existence however Locke concentrates on the trust which is needed between the governors and the governed. To provide both a stable political order and government by consent Locke urged that subjects must recognize the sovereign authority of the legislature unless that legislature clearly betrays its trust. Without obedience no government can survive, but obedience is only rendered on condition that the government performs its duties towards the community. In the last analysis Locke put a higher premium on consent than on stability. He acknowledged that ultimately it was for the people to decide whether their trustees have acted contrary to the trust placed in them. Once they are firmly convinced that a breach of trust has occurred the people are then free to resist in order to force the government to mend its ways or to establish a new government. In such an extreme situation, when there is a recourse to arms, only God can judge whether subjects are justified in resisting their government.[15]

Seen in the context of his age Locke's views were certainly liberal and the implications of some of his opinions were quite revolutionary. While the Tories were defending divine right monarchy, Locke was suggesting that the people established civil government and retained the right to resist those in authority who would abuse their trust by threatening to destroy life, liberty and property. The Tories were horrified at such notions and even many Whigs were perturbed at the radical conclusions which might be drawn from Locke's major premises. Nonetheless, a careful scrutiny of Locke's position and of the views expressed by most of his admirers, makes it clear that there was no intention of using the contract theory to justify in practice either popular sovereignty or a democratic form of government. Locke granted that all men possessed natural and inalienable rights to life, liberty and property, but there can be no doubt that he was most concerned to protect private property. The rights to life and liberty were essentially civil liberties and not positive rights to exercise political power. These civil liberties included freedom of conscience, the right to subsistence and to the fruits of one's labour, and the recognition that a man's personal freedom could only be infringed after due process of law. They put limits on the actions which governments could take to interfere with the lives of their subjects. The right which men possessed to protect their property however was so important that it was necessary to grant property-owners an active political role in society. We do not have to accept C. B. Macpherson's extreme claim that Locke was anxious to defend unrestrained capitalism in order to agree with him that Locke was concerned above all else to protect private property from the depredations of an absolute, arbitrary monarch.[16] It is true that Locke sometimes used the term property in a loose sense to incorporate 'life, liberty and estates' and he was certainly critical of unrestrained greed and the misuse of wealth, but he quite deliberately sought to justify the private ownership of property as a natural right. He stressed that property was divided unequally in a state of nature, long before the creation of a civil society. Indeed, he repeatedly and explicitly stated that the prime motive for creating civil government was so that men of property could enjoy their possessions in peace and safety.[17]

Locke and other Whig supporters of the contract theory claimed that legitimate government required the consent of the people, but they expected this consent to be implicit more often than explicit. Any man who owned property, or who lived in a state and enjoyed the protection of its laws, or who was simply travelling along the highway could be regarded as tacitly submitting to the authority of the government. A man could be interpreted as giving his consent

68

when he had not been coerced and when he derived benefits from the civil government under which he lived. Explicit or express consent was only necessary when a government sought to infringe a man's right to his property. Such consent could only be efficiently obtained by the majority vote of some form of representative assembly.[18] When it came to playing an active part in this decision-making process, it appears likely that the Whigs expected only men of property to be represented. Locke is not entirely clear on this point. Some commentators believe that Locke regarded those who owned no property to be subjects but not full members of society. They might give tacit consent, but, since they were not economically independent and did not enjoy the leisure necessary to develop their rational capacity, they could not be trusted with the important task of giving express consent through some form of representative assembly.[19] Other commentators reject this distinction between subjects and citizens as a mistaken interpretation of Locke, but they admit that Locke had no quarrel with a legislature dominated by men of property or elected on a propertied franchise.[20] There is certainly no evidence that Locke desired a more egalitarian political system than that which prevailed after the Glorious Revolution. He was in no sense a democrat or a social revolutionary and there is no reason to doubt that he accepted the dependence of the majority of the population on the aristocracy, gentry and clergy. Other Whig theorists were more explicit than Locke and they certainly restricted active political rights to men of property. Algernon Sidney claimed that 'they who place the power in a multitude, understand a multitude composed of freemen, who think it for their convenience to join together, and to establish such laws and rules as they oblige themselves to observe.'[21] By the term 'free man' the Whigs always meant a man of independent means. James Tyrrell, for example, explicitly excluded all labourers and servants who did not own land or property from the exercise of active political influence.[22]

Thus, whether the Whigs adopted the full-blown contract theory or merely accepted the notion of government by consent they were clearly concerned to make the world safe for men of property. Algernon Sidney denied that he had any wish to set up a democratic form of government. Although he was in favour of an elected legislative assembly, Sidney wanted the franchise restricted to freeholders in the counties and to merchants and master craftsmen in the boroughs.[23] John Locke maintained that once civil government had been established then only the legislative power could exercise sovereignty by making laws and levying taxes. The rule of law and not the sovereignty of the people was the normal operating principle of civil society. By subjecting themselves to civil government all men submitted their natural rights to be regulated by the laws of their civil society. The members of the community surrendered to the sovereign legislature their individual rights and they could not recover these rights unless the legislature or the executive betrayed its trust. Once consent was given the decision was irrevocable unless the government thoroughly abused its trust. Individuals could not simply withdraw their consent whenever they saw fit. To allow them to do so would inevitably lead to anarchy and would deprive every society of stability and order. The survival of the rule of law required that the sovereign legislature must be obeyed; provided it operated within the bounds of the law of nature and within the terms of the fundamental constitution of the civil society in which it existed.[24]

The one active political right which Locke conferred on all men was the right to resist a government which grossly abused its trust. He acknowledged that in the last resort all men had the right to preserve their life, liberty and property. Yet, even on the right of resistance, Locke was careful to insist that it should only be used in an emergency in order to oppose manifest acts of tyranny. He did not allow subjects to claim the right to resist isolated abuses and he certainly rejected the notion that subjects could overturn their government simply in order to set up a better one. The degree of moral responsibility incurred by those who rebelled was huge and alarming. Overturning the frame and constitution of any just government was the worst political crime a man could commit. In Locke's view it was highly unlikely that the lower orders would rebel without just cause. In fact he anticipated that resistance would be led by men of substance enraged by a concerted attack on their property. Nonetheless, though he tried to allay the fears of his conservative critics, Locke did not attempt to restrict the right of resistance to the property-owning élite. All men had the right to resist and only God could be the judge of an appeal to arms.[25]

2   The Whig Defence of the Glorious Revolution

Before 1688 the Whig theory of liberty contained some radical elements, but it also had some very conservative features. The

Glorious Revolution provided the Whigs with an opportunity to decide whether they wished to emphasize the radical or the conservative strands in their political ideology. This does not mean that the Whigs had complete freedom of manoeuvre after the Revolution, but they were certainly in a better position than their Tory opponents. The Tory ideology of order could not survive the Revolution unscathed and the Tories were compelled to make some painful and difficult decisions in order to adjust their ideology to the new circumstances of post-1688 politics. The Whigs on the other hand were never faced with such stark choices as the Tories and were never under such inexorable pressure to adjust their political principles. They did of course have to take into account the political strength of their Tory opponents and the wishes of William III, but they were in the fortunate position of being able to welcome the most important features of the Revolution settlement. The manner in which they defended the Glorious Revolution however reveals how the overwhelmingly conservative bias of their pre-1688 ideology was confirmed and consolidated. The Whigs could have protested at the conservative nature of the Revolution settlement and could have pressed for more radical action. Very few in fact were prepared to do so. Most Whigs were quite content to make only minimum alterations to their political ideology in order to justify and explain the Glorious Revolution. Contrary to the views of many historians the political views of John Locke were not adopted wholesale by the majority of Whigs. Most Whigs remained as conservative in their ideological opinions as they were limited in their political objectives. This can be seen most clearly in their attempts to conflate the contract theory with the more conservative notion of the ancient constitution and in their willingness to reject the radical implications of Locke's political theory while accepting the most conservative features of his work.

Locke's political theory was a brilliant refutation of the Tory theory of order, but he did not wish it to be a charter for political or social revolution. Locke was as anxious as the Tories to maintain social stability and he had no objection to a hierarchical society of rank and order. Nonetheless his version of the contract theory was clearly too radical to be swallowed whole even by all the Whigs. It is certainly an exaggeration to claim that Locke's political theory was triumphantly vindicated by the Glorious Revolution or that it came to be widely accepted, even in Whig circles, thereafter. Indeed,

71

it is doubtful whether Locke's whole case appealed to more than a small minority of the articulate members of the political nation.[26] Although the claim has often been made, it is in fact very difficult to prove that the Revolution was justified by repeated appeals to the contract theory. Locke's *Two Treatises of Government*, although largely composed before the Revolution, was published in 1690 and reprinted in 1694 and 1698. Yet it failed to secure general acceptance or popular esteem. Even Locke's friend James Tyrrell only made five references to the *Two Treatises* in his mammoth *Bibliotheca Politica* (1694) and none of his numerous dialogues between Mr Meanwell and Mr Freeman involved a serious discussion of the contract theory. In the tenth and eleventh dialogues there are references to the original contract, but this contract is based far more on the notion of the ancient constitution than on the contract theory of Locke. The concept of the ancient constitution rests on what men thought was actual historical evidence, whereas Locke's contract theory is based on the rational concept of natural and inalienable rights. Most Whigs when they spoke of the contract, meant the relationship between King and Parliament which they took to be an essential feature of the ancient constitution rather than the contract theory which Locke expounded. While Locke ignored the ancient constitution and wrote only of rights which were inherent in man *qua* man, the vast majority of Whigs preferred to appeal to the ancient constitution in order to justify their opposition to James II. They chose to appeal to historical evidence about the English constitution rather than base their case on a rational theory about the nature of civil society and the rights of man. Even Algernon Sidney wrote far more about the ancient constitution than about the contract theory.[27] Most Whigs when they referred to the original contract related it to some actual historical agreement between the king and the people of England and not to Locke's rational explanation of how men left the state of nature and entered civil society. Typical of this approach is the argument of Daniel Whitby. Having provided his readers with an historical view of the English constitution, which showed that the king's power had always been limited, Whitby used this evidence about the ancient constitution to prove that a contract existed between king and people:

the kings of England were kings by virtue of an original contract, made between them and the people; this is apparent by the contract made by the Conquerour with the barons, and the nobility and

72

commonalty of England; and the so frequent repetitions of that, or a like contract by the following princes of this realm, by the oaths they took at the coronation, to preserve to the people their ancient rights, and liberties, their original customs and laws, and by the continual claim the people made to the laws of their country, the laws of King Edward, and the Magna Charta as their right.[28]

This conflation of the theory of an original contract with the notion of an ancient constitution, which is a feature of Algernon Sidney's *Discourses*, appears again and again in the Whig literature after the Revolution. Even when the original contract was mentioned a greater emphasis was invariably put on the historical appeal to the traditional constitution of England.[29] Few Whig propagandists relied heavily upon Locke. When Benjamin Hoadly, for example, examined the notion of contractual obligations in some detail, chiefly in the second part of *The Original and Institution of Civil Government Discuss'd* (1710), he concentrated almost entirely on the older contractual theory of Richard Hooker and others rather than on the more radical contract theory of Locke. Hooker wrote of a contractual relationship or trust between ruler and ruled, a relationship which involved rights and duties on both sides. This contractual relationship could exist even if the form of government conferred sovereign authority on the Crown alone and even when it was ordained by God. Locke, on the other hand, was expounding a more radical thesis. He was asserting that civil society was an artificial creation, resting on an original contract, and he was claiming that the people were the ultimate source of power. In his view the people created civil government in order to preserve their natural rights. Benjamin Hoadly, throughout his extensive polemical writings, eschewed all mention of Locke. Though he is frequently cited as a devoted disciple of Locke, he put very little emphasis on the notion that the people were the source of power and he rarely mentioned that civil government was created by an original contract. A few Whig propagandists however did express explicit support for the kind of contract theory to be found in Locke's *Second Treatise*. The author of *Vox Populi, Vox Dei : Being True Maxims of Government* (1709) stated quite clearly that: 'All politick societies began from a voluntary union and mutual agreement of men, freely acting in the choice of their governors and forms of government.'[30] Yet even this work made no reference to Locke. While this work did go through numerous editions, it remains highly doubtful whether, even

73

twenty years after the Revolution, the full-blown contract theory had won widespread support among the political nation.

This reluctance to base the Revolution settlement on a radical interpretation of the contract theory can be detected in the speeches of Whig politicians during the critical debates of 1689. In the famous debate in the House of Commons on 28 January 1689 only a few Members of Parliament were prepared to appeal to the contract theory as understood by Locke. Sir Robert Howard did state boldly that: 'The constitution of the government is actually grounded upon pact and covenant with the people.' John Maynard agreed: 'our government is mixed, not monarchical and tyrannous, but has had its beginning with the people.'[31] These opinions however did not express the sense of even the Whig section of the House. Most members did not wish to discuss the most fundamental questions of government. George Treby, for example, insisted: 'We have found the throne vacant and are to supply that defect. We found it so, we have not made it so.' Sir William Williams wished to avoid any inquiry into the origins of government, while Sir Robert Sawyer feared that any discussion about the dissolution of government would put power into the hands of the people rather than confining it to Parliament.[32] The final resolution of the Commons did contain a reference to the original contract, but little emphasis was placed upon it. The whole stress was placed on the claim that James II had abdicated. The House finally resolved:

That King James the Second, having endeavoured to subvert the Constitution of the Kingdom, by breaking the Original Contract between King and People, and by the advice of Jesuits, and other wicked persons, having violated the fundamental laws, and having withdrawn himself out of this kingdom, has abdicated the Government, and that the throne is thereby become vacant.[33]

When this resolution came before the House of Lords the peers sought the advice of lawyers about the existence and nature of the original contract. Those who gave evidence, and these were principally Whig lawyers, asserted that civil government did rest upon a contract between king and people, but they were unable to provide any convincing proof of its existence or its terms. They were reduced to claiming that it was implicit in the nature of common law and in the nature of government, and they referred to remarks made upon the subject by James I, Richard Hooker and Sir Edward Coke.

These references however referred to the older medieval version of the contractual relationship between ruler and ruled rather than to the much more radical concept of the contract theory which saw civil government as an artificial creation of the people designed to preserve their natural and inalienable rights. William Petyt, when he gave evidence, preferred to appeal to the ancient constitution rather than to the original contract. He maintained that England's constitution originated with the Anglo-Saxon tribes in Germany and he asserted that an essential feature of this constitution was that the kings of England had always acted with the advice and support of Parliament.[34] In the event the Lords made little use of any of the evidence provided by these legal experts and they avoided any further discussion of the contract theory. The Declaration of Rights, submitted to William and Mary on 14 February 1689 and later embodied in the Bill of Rights, contained no mention at all of the original contract. It did condemn the actions of James II and it described them as contrary to the known laws and established liberties of the country. Yet even then it was never explicitly stated that James II had been deposed because of his actions. Parliament adhered to the claim that James II, by fleeing the country, had abdicated and had thereby left the throne vacant. When the Declaration of Rights was laid before William and Mary prior to their coronation this was not meant to imply that the offer of the crown was conditional on their accepting the Declaration. Nor did it mean that the Declaration was an explicit contract between ruler and ruled, though a few men tried to make it so. In the debates on the abjuration bill, in April 1690, Lord Digby claimed: 'The foundation of government is the Bill of Rights: wherein the king promises his part, etc. and we swear fealty. This is our original contract: if there be any, I am of opinion that is it.'[35]

The Scots did go further than the English in accepting that the Revolution was justified because of James II's breach of contract between king and people. The Scottish Convention roundly declared that it had the right to dispose of the crown and to reshape the constitution. On 4 April 1689 the Convention declared that James had 'forfaulted' the crown by his misgovernment and the Scots endeavoured to secure explicit promises from William III about future legislation to remedy the grievances of his subjects. Few Whig politicians in England were ever prepared to go so far. When, in 1710, the impeachment of Dr Sacheverell involved the Whigs once more in a major attempt to justify the Revolution, they still did not rely heavily on the Lockean version of the contract theory. The Whig managers of the impeachment made no reference to the works of John Locke and, indeed, they made very few references to the contract theory at all. Sir Joseph Jekyll implied its existence, but only Nicholas Lechmere defended it directly; though even he spoke primarily of the contractual relationship between the king and his subjects, as seen in the coronation oath, rather than of the artificial creation of civil government by the people.[36] Neither of them attempted to argue that the Convention Parliament had forcibly deposed James II because his actions had breached the terms of the original contract. The Whigs were ready enough to condemn the actions of James II, but most of them still preferred to accept the convenient myth that he had abdicated and left the throne vacant. Thus by 1710 the standard Whig justification of the Revolution was based on essentially conservative principles.

Nonetheless, while it is important to realize that the Whig justification of the Revolution did not rest four-square on the political theory of Locke, this does not mean that the Whigs were opposed to the notion of a contractual relationship between ruler and ruled or to the idea that governors held their power in trust for the people. On the contrary, the Whigs frequently appealed to such fundamental principles of government, but it is essential to distinguish between these relatively conservative principles and the more radical theory of Locke. The contract theory of Locke actually implied two contracts. The first and more radical of the two was the notion that civil society was an artificial creation by which men left the state of nature and voluntarily agreed to live under a system of laws which would protect their natural rights. This radical concept, which enshrined the notion of the sovereign people, was the *pactum unionis*. The second contract, which may in fact take place at the same time as the first, entrusted political power to a particular form of government. This was the *pactum subjectionis*. This second agreement was less radical than the first since it stressed that the people were subjects not sovereign. Many Whigs feared the radical implications of the *pactum unionis*, but they could readily accept the *pactum subjectionis*. After all the claim that rulers had duties as well as prerogatives and that their chief concern should be the welfare of their subjects was a venerable one. *Salus populi suprema lex esto* had long been regarded as a law of nature. It implied that the ruler held his power as a trust for the benefit of his subjects. The people did not establish their own ruler, but any ruler who so abused his trust as to threaten the safety of his own people was acting so unnaturally that he could be resisted. This was not the same as the radical claim that kings could only govern with the consent of the people. It could simply mean that rulers should not be arbitrary tyrants. The concept of a *pactum subjectionis* had the added advantage of fitting neatly into the traditional Whig notion of the ancient constitution. The Whigs could refer to the coronation oath, to Magna Carta and, most recently, to the Bill of Rights as firm historical evidence of this kind of contract between king and people. A conservative justification for the Revolution could be provided by an appeal to the kind of contractual relationship established by the ancient constitution, whereas appeals to the concept of an original contract or *pactum unionis* raised the more radical notion of the sovereignty of the people. As men of property who feared for their privileged position in society most Whigs preferred to rest their defence of the Revolution on a legalistic appeal to the traditional liberties of Englishmen under the ancient constitution rather than a rational appeal to the abstract principles of government.

A careful examination of the voluminous political literature spawned by the desire to justify the Revolution clearly shows that the Whigs did not rely heavily on the contract theory as defined by Locke. Instead, they concentrated on showing that James II had betrayed his trust and they emphasized that subjects had the right to preserve their essential interests by resisting an arbitrary tyrant. It was on the notion of trust and on the doctrine of resistance that the Whigs agreed most fully with the position expounded by Locke. The Whigs insisted that a king of England's power was limited by the terms of the ancient constitution and it was the king's duty to preserve the laws and liberties of the people as defined by that constitution. By his attack on the Church of England and by his absolutist tendencies James II had forfeited the trust placed in him. Thus, Richard Claridge asserted:

> Let then every true patriot and Englishman fix here: that the king is intrusted with the executive power of the law for the good of the people, and the people are to obey and assist him in the execution of this high trust; but if he abuses this power, as the deserter [James II] did, to the manifest oppression of his people, the people represented in parliament may take that trust from him, and give it to another, who will govern them in justice and clemency, and defend them in their religious and civil rights.[37]

The Whigs therefore only rarely claimed that James II had broken the original contract which established civil society. They sought instead to prove that he had subverted the ancient constitution. Samuel Masters, for example, accepted that it was impossible to prove the existence of an original contract; but the facts of English history, he maintained, showed that there was a contractual relationship between the king and his people: 'that compact being nothing else than a tacit agreement between king and subjects to observe such common usages and practices as by an immemorial prescription have become the common law of our government.'[38]

The central concern of nearly all Whigs, both during the original debate on the Revolution settlement and in subsequent decades, was to defend the Revolution by justifying the people's right to resist a king who threatened the traditional constitution in Church and State. The most radical doctrine universally accepted by the Whigs was not the contract theory, but the right of resistance. Yet, even on this issue, the Whigs were careful to interpret this doctrine in as conservative a manner as possible. They rejoiced that the Revolution had been bloodless and they emphasized that resistance was an extreme response to a dire emergency. The Whigs never attempted to justify revolution as a means of simply improving the constitution or radically extending the liberties of the subject. Many Whigs suggested that resistance should only be offered by the nobility and gentry and not by the people at large. John Locke himself implied this, while James Tyrrell was quite explicit: 'I do by no means allow the rabble or mob of any nation to take arms against a civil government, but only the whole community of the people of all degrees and orders, commanded by the nobility and gentry thereof.'[39] At the trial of Dr Sacheverell in 1710, when the Whigs were desperately trying to justify their interpretation of the Revolution, the Whig managers took great care to stress that the events of 1688–9 were an exceptional response to a unique situation. They made no attempt to offer a general and unconditional defence of the right of resistance. Robert Walpole assured Parliament and the nation that

Resistance is no where enacted to be legal, but subjected, by all the laws now in being, to the greatest penalties; 'tis what is not, cannot, nor ought ever to be describ'd, or affirm'd, in any positive law, to be excusable: when, and upon what never to be expected occasions, it may be exercised, no man can foresee; and ought never to be thought of, but when an utter subversion of the laws of the realm threaten the whole frame of a constitution, and no redress can otherwise be hoped for.[40]

3 Whig Ideology after the Revolution

An examination of the Whig defence of the Glorious Revolution shows that only a minority of Whigs endorsed Locke's contract theory or expressed a desire for radical changes in the constitution. In their response to the Revolution settlement and to the actual political situation of the 1690s and early 1700s most Whigs betrayed essentially moderate political aims and an overwhelmingly conservative political ideology. They insisted that their aim was to restore the ancient constitution and to safeguard the traditional liberties of the subject. Their oft-proclaimed desire – and it seems to have been a genuine one – was to restore the prescriptive constitution which recognized the prerogatives of the Crown, the privileges of Parliament and the civil liberties of the people. The majority of Whigs had no desire to erect a new constitution on the basis of such radical notions as the contract theory, the natural rights of man and the sovereignty of the people. This does not mean however that in the aftermath of the Revolution the Whigs entirely abandoned the libertarian strand in their ideology. Not only was there a very small, though very vocal, radical wing of the party, which kept alive more liberal ideas about the desirability of placing effective limits on those in power and about the need to safeguard the rights of the subject, but the Whigs as a whole always remained more liberal on some issues than their Tory opponents. The effect of the Revolution settlement and its political aftermath on Whig ideology was in fact paradoxical. On the one hand, the opportunity and desire for office, plus the continuing strength and tenacity of the Tories, confirmed and in places accentuated the conservative elements in Whig ideology. On the other hand, the need to defend the Revolution settlement and the Protestant succession throughout the reigns of William III and Queen Anne did allow the limited development of certain liberal strands in Whig ideology. The need to win supporters at home and to conduct an expensive war abroad persuaded the Whigs to make concessions to the Protestant dissenters and to the financial and commercial interests. It did not however encourage them to seek the political support of the labouring masses. In general therefore, in the period from 1689 to 1714, the overwhelming emphasis of

79

Whig ideology remained conservative, though the Whigs continued to uphold more liberal political principles than their Tory opponents.

The overwhelming majority of the Whigs were in agreement about what they regarded as the essential features of England's ancient constitution. They all agreed that the legislature was composed of King, Lords and Commons and that the power of the Crown was limited by the need to govern with the advice and support of Parliament. The sovereign was not absolute and he did not hold his office by the direct ordination of God. He held his power as a trust in order to serve the interests of civil society. His subjects enjoyed certain civil liberties and had the right to enjoy the benefits of the English constitution in Church and State. Should the sovereign abuse his trust so grossly that the liberties of the nation were in imminent danger, the people had the right to resist him in order to restore the constitution. The Whig position therefore was far more liberal than the Tory ideology of order. The Whigs were convinced that governments could only be legitimate if they obtained at least the tacit consent of the governed. When the rights of property were involved then governments had to secure the express consent of either those concerned or their elected representatives. Nonetheless, even these liberal notions have to be seen in the context of the general conservatism of Whig ideology. A few extreme Whigs might have wished to reduce the power of the king to that of a Dutch Stadtholder or a Doge of Venice, but the Whigs were never a republican party. Once they had a monarch who would accept the limits of royal power, who would regularly consult Parliament, and who was not averse to employing them in offices of profit and trust, then the Whigs were ready to abandon radical attempts to weaken the royal prerogative.

In the vital debates prior to the drawing up of the Declaration of Rights there was little discussion of far-reaching proposals for altering the form and substance of the constitution. Some suggestions were put forward for a significant reduction in the power of the Crown, but most Members of Parliament took fright at these proposals and the majority of them were dropped. The Commons concentrated on asserting old rights rather than on demanding major constitutional innovations.[41] The actual limitations finally imposed by the Bill of Rights were not extensive. The Crown's suspending power was abolished, its dispensing power 'as used of late' was condemned, and Parliament's sole right to levy taxes was confirmed.

Nonetheless, the Crown retained its freedom to appoint all officers of state; to summon, prorogue and dissolve Parliament; to make war and peace, and to conduct diplomacy; and even to veto legislation passed through both Houses of Parliament. William III was to make full use of all these rights.

The clearest infringement of the royal prerogative by the Bill of Rights was the attack on the right to maintain a standing army in time of peace. Yet even on this issue it should be remembered that William III maintained a standing army in peace-time from 1697 to 1702 without receiving the parliamentary sanction of annual Mutiny Acts. Further limitations were imposed on the Crown by both the Triennial Act and the Act of Settlement, but once again these were not permanent checks. The Triennial Act was repealed in 1716, while many of the clauses of the Act of Settlement were later either repealed or simply ignored. Attacks on the Crown's ability to influence the deliberations of the House of Commons by the distribution of offices, places and pensions achieved only limited success. Four bills designed to prevent any royal official sitting in Parliament all failed to pass into law between 1692 and 1700, though more limited measures to exclude selected placemen were passed in 1694, 1700 and 1701. None of these acts however can be regarded as a significant reduction in the Crown's ability to influence Parliament. In the event the most important limitation on the Crown's freedom of manoeuvre was achieved, almost indirectly, by Parliament's firm hold on the purse strings. Parliament put direct curbs on the financial independence of the Crown by granting the monarch a civil list which was not quite sufficient to meet his normal expenses, but it was the demands of war which really made it necessary for the Crown to have continual recourse to Parliament for additional revenue. Indeed, it is arguable that the enormous costs of two successive wars against France, which were fought in part to defend the Revolution settlement and the Protestant succession, did more to strengthen the power of Parliament than did all the constitutional measures from the Bill of Rights to the Act of Settlement.

The conservative strand in Whig ideology is clearly shown not only by the unwillingness to put effective constitutional curbs on the power of the Crown, but by the reluctance of the Whigs to locate sovereignty anywhere but in the ancient constitution. John Locke and the more radical Whigs claimed that the legislature was ultimately subordinate to the sovereign people who created civil society and first made the rules of civil government. Most Whigs however would not go so far. They certainly denied that sovereign authority resided in the monarch alone, but they refused to endorse the radical notion that the people were the ultimate source of sovereignty. Nonetheless, this substantial body of moderate Whig opinion was not in total agreement on the location of sovereignty. On the one hand there were those who believed that the fundamental laws of the constitution were unalterable and provided guidelines for any future legislation. On the other hand there were those who claimed that the sovereign authority lay with the legislature of King, Lords and Commons. Many Whigs contrived to support both views and to see them both as essential elements of the ancient constitution. They failed to see that the two concepts were inherently in conflict. These Whigs believed that the sovereign legislature would respect what they regarded as the fundamental laws of the constitution, but they failed to recognize that if the legislature were genuinely sovereign then it would of course possess the authority to pass or repeal any law it liked. No law could be beyond its sovereign authority, otherwise these fundamental laws and not the legislature would be supreme.

The notion that the legislature was sovereign was given a boost by the major constitutional decisions which Parliament took after the Revolution. The fact that Parliament settled the succession to the throne and initiated measures which placed limitations on the royal prerogative – which happened in both 1689 and 1701 – is evidence that a majority of the Members of Parliament believed that the legislature had the authority to amend the constitution. Certainly many Whigs had no qualms about this. Sir William Petyt, for example, maintained that statute law was superior to the common law and to the decisions of kings or judges.[42] Another eminent Whig lawyer, Sir Robert Atkyns, insisted that the legislature of King, Lords and Commons was absolute, unlimited and irresistible. It could give the law to all subjects and to all courts. Even when it erred the only remedy was another Act of Parliament.[43] A substantial body of Whigs, however, and some Country Tories too, could not bring themselves to accept the doctrine of parliamentary sovereignty. To them it appeared that the Revolution was replacing an absolute and tyrannical king with an arbitrary and unlimited legislature. They appealed therefore to the spirit of the ancient constitution, but, in the absence of a written constitution, this was not always a strong card to play. They were on firmer ground when they maintained that certain fundamental laws clearly did exist. The examples which they most frequently cited were Magna Carta, the Bill of Rights, the Triennial Act and the Act of Union with Scotland. Thus Bishop Burnet could claim: 'It was a maxim among our lawyers, that even an Act of Parliament against Magna Carta was null of itself.'[44] It is therefore not true to claim that the doctrine of parliamentary sovereignty was fully endorsed at the Revolution. On a number of occasions a body of Whigs insisted that the authority of the legislature was limited.[45] It was perhaps not until 1716 that the majority of Whigs explicitly accepted the sovereign authority of Parliament. In that year the Whig majority passed the Septennial Act which prolonged the life of a parliament which had originally been elected for a term of three years. Thus Parliament overrode the Triennial Act, which had been regarded as a fundamental part of the Revolution settlement. This determined action was clearly taken for conservative reasons. The Whigs wished to reject the notion that the electorate could determine the life of a parliament.[46]

In their views on the nature of the constitution, the extent of the royal prerogative and the location of sovereignty the Whigs showed themselves to be essentially conservative. Their aim was to restore the ancient constitution by curbing the excessive power of the Crown and by safeguarding the political influence of Parliament. They wanted a strong monarchy and a powerful political voice for men of substantial property. Nevertheless, the Whigs did show some signs of wishing to preserve and even to extend in some limited ways the liberties of the subject. In their efforts to reduce the authority of the Crown and to increase the power of Parliament the Whigs claimed to be protecting the liberty and property of the people. There can be no doubt however that they were more concerned to protect the privileged position of men of property than to extend the rights of the lower orders. The most significant extension of civil liberty which they were prepared to make was in the area of liberty of conscience; a right which on the whole benefited men of education more than the labouring masses, especially as Dissent was strongest among merchants and craftsmen. The Whig commitment to religious toleration was by no means complete or unrestrained, however, but it did mark a significant advance on the position adopted by the Tories. Although he was not the only campaigner John Locke provided the most detailed moral and philosophical justification for religious toleration. While he affirmed the role of reason in religion, he also stressed that in such matters there could be no certain knowledge. Neither reason nor revelation provided absolute proof that God favoured particular theological, ecclesiastical or liturgical systems. The one essential requirement was to accept Jesus as the Messiah. The authorities in the State therefore should only command conformity to a simple form of religious belief and insist on good conduct. They should certainly not go beyond this to enforce acceptance of any particular doctrinal system. Religious persecution was an illegitimate exercise of power and was usually embarked upon to satisfy the pride, ambition and interests of the clergy. It was also futile since, at best, it could only produce outward conformity not inner conviction. Persecution was therefore both an immoral and an ineffective means of propagating truth. Nonetheless, the extent of religious liberty that Locke was prepared to concede was limited. He was ready to tolerate all Protestants, but not Catholics or atheists. Catholics could not be trusted because they owed allegiance to a power outside the State, while atheists could not be trusted to keep any oaths or promises to which they might swear.[47]

Some Whigs were prepared to follow Locke's example and to plead for a simple religious faith, a reduction in the power of the clergy and full toleration for all Protestants. Few Whigs however wished to destroy the privileged position of the Established Church and only a tiny minority tried to undermine orthodox Christianity. The Toleration Act of 1689 was a decidedly limited measure, though this was largely due to the political strength of the Tories. The act declared that the penal laws should not be enforced against those Protestant Dissenters who took the oaths of allegiance and supremacy, who accepted the doctrinal provisions of the Thirty-Nine Articles, and who made a declaration against transubstantiation. Roman Catholics and anti-Trinitarians were expressly excluded from the benefits of the act. The penal laws were not repealed and even Protestant Dissenters remained second-class citizens because of the continued operation of the Test and Corporation Acts. Throughout the reigns of William and Anne the Whigs remained resolutely prepared to stand by the Toleration Act. Most of them had little sympathy with the repeated Tory efforts to prevent the practice of occasional conformity or to close the dissenting academies. Yet only a minority of Whigs were anxious to go so far as to repeal the Test and Corporation Acts or to destroy the privileged position of the Church of England. Most Whigs accepted an established church as an essential feature of the constitution, though they were prepared to tolerate those Protestant Dissenters who were no threat to Church or State.

While the Tories were convinced of the need for an authoritarian order in Church and State and were prepared to sacrifice individual liberties in order to attain it, the Whigs were coming to appreciate that the public good could not be achieved if those in authority were able to ride roughshod over private, separate and sectional interests which were not subversive. The Whigs maintained that no legitimate government could secure either the moral right or the physical means to act unless it could claim to be protecting the lives, liberty and property of its subjects. Although the Whigs too often overlooked the rights of those without property, they were more prepared than the Tories to acknowledge the value of various forms of property and to recognize that the State must hold the ring between competing interests. Like the Tories the Whigs feared radical social change and they readily condemned the unrestrained pursuit of wealth and power, but they realized that the landed interest had to accept that the financial and commercial revolutions had created new forms of property. In their opinion English society must adjust to the fact that financial stability and commercial prosperity were the sinews of war, the sources of England's growing wealth and power, and the country's main weapons in the fight to safeguard the Revolution settlement. Moreover, since wealth was an important source of power, no government could survive for long if it ignored the interests of financiers and merchants and no society could remain stable if it refused to confer status on those with wealth and power.[48]

Whig propagandists and politicians frequently condemned the worst practices of stockjobbers and others who made fortunes playing the stockmarket, but they often came to the defence of the financial interest and the whole system of public credit. Although they readily admitted that the world of credit was a mystery which few men understood, many Whigs insisted that the Government's ability to borrow huge sums of money at relatively low rates of interest was one of the best defences of the Revolution settlement and the Protestant succession. Without the support of the financial interest the country could never prosecute a successful war against France and could not prevent a Jacobite restoration. The Tory critics of the national debt were either unconcerned about the defence of the Revolution settlement or had not realized that wars were won by those who could find the money to pay for them:

For war is quite changed from what it was in the time of our fore-fathers; when in a hasty expedition, and a pitched field, the matter was decided by courage; but now the whole art of war is in a manner reduced to money; and now-a-days, that prince, who can best find money to feed, cloath, and pay his army, not he that has the most valiant troops, is surest of success and conquest.[49]

The Whigs were therefore ready to stand by the 'moneyed men' who provided successive ministries with the cash to fight France and hence the means to safeguard the Revolution settlement and the Protestant succession. Unlike the Tories they were not averse to allowing City men both the political influence and the social status commensurate with their contribution to the welfare of the state.[50]

The Whigs were even more convinced that trade was essential to England's wealth and security. They recognized that England was rapidly becoming a commercial power and that even the prosperity of the landed classes depended heavily on the progress of trade. Without a flourishing trade the whole nation would be impoverished:

Trade is the life of the nation, the soul of its felicity, the spring of its wealth, the support of its greatness, and the staff on which both king and people lean, and which (if it should sink) the whole fabrick must fall, the body politick would sicken and languish, its power decline, and the figure it makes in the world, grow by degrees, most contemptibly mean.[51]

The Whigs were not only conscious of the economic importance of trade, but were ready to grant merchants political representation. They saw no reason why they should be excluded from Parliament or even from office under the Crown. When the Landed Qualification bill was brought before Parliament in 1711, one Whig Member protested:

that Corporations and Boroughs were erected chiefly to send up representatives to take care of trade and manufactures, which were then but in their infancy; yet now that trade was extended, and bore such a mighty proportion to land as to be in competition with it, to exclude those from Parliament who seem'd before to be the proper trustees for trade, and to commit the protection thereof to the Landed Men only, or in the common phrase, to the 'Country Gentleman', seem'd a great alteration of our constitution, and what might very much turn to the detriment of trade and manufacture.[52]

Most Whigs clearly regarded property in its various forms as the only sure basis of political authority and the rights of active citizen-

86

ship. They believed that the political representation of men of property was the best means of persuading such men to defend the Revolution settlement. They were convinced that those qualities of independence, judgement and virtue, which were essential to the defence of the political order established by the Revolution, could only be found in men who possessed sufficient wealth to give them a firm stake in society. Daniel Defoe, who was a great defender of credit and trade, and who believed that merchants should be represented in Parliament and perhaps in the Government, recognized the primacy of landed property as a qualification for political authority.[53] John Locke did raise the radical notion of a labour theory of property, when he acknowledged the natural right of every man to the fruits of his own labour, but he never suggested or even implied that the labouring poor could take an active role in politics except to resist tyranny. Nearly all his property-owning contemporaries, Whig as well as Tory, ignored the contribution which the masses made to the welfare of the community. They were convinced that the lower orders deserved little more than a subsistence wage and indeed they insisted that low wages were a necessary incentive to persuade the masses to work at all. Poverty was regarded as the natural condition of the great majority of mankind and the poor must therefore accustom themselves to a life of unremitting toil. Of course some Whigs did express concern about the misuse of wealth and did condemn the unrestrained accumulation of capital or property, but even these men with a social conscience would have been horrified at any suggestion that political action should be taken to ensure a fairer distribution of the material goods of this world. Even the most radical Whigs did not wish to turn the world upside down by encouraging a social revolution.[54] The Whigs were as conscious as the Tories that an ordered, hierarchical society could only survive if the poor were taught to accept their unfortunate lot. The Whigs might be more prepared than the Tories to recognize new sources of wealth and to adjust the hierarchical order accordingly, but they were not opposed to either hierarchy or order as such. The majority of Whigs still believed that the social order could only be preserved so long as the individual was taught to

attend the duties of that particular situation or condition of life, whatsoever it be, wherein providence has at present placed him; with diligence, and contentment; without being either uneasy and discontented, that others are placed by providence in different and superior stations of the world; or so extremely and unreasonably solicitous to change his state for the future, as thereby to neglect his present duty.[55]

Thus, for virtually all Whigs, the lower orders were regarded as a potential threat to the stability of society and had therefore to be kept firmly in their place. While they might be offered compassion and Christian charity, they could not be trusted with political power.

Although the Revolution encouraged the Whigs to strengthen the power of Parliament and to press for frequent elections, they made no effort to extend the franchise, to redistribute seats or to alter the system of representation based on property qualifications. When the Whigs spoke of defending the liberties of the people this invariably meant protecting the privileges of men of substance. While they were fully prepared to acknowledge that the right to vote should be possessed by the lesser freeholders, the more substantial tenants and the independent masters of businesses, they were opposed to any attempt to confer this honour on labourers or servants. In his massive and influential *Bibliotheca Politica* (1694), James Tyrrell warned his readers from the outset: 'I desire always to be understood, that when I make use of the word people, I do not mean the vulgar or mixt multitude, but in the state of nature the whole body of free men and women, especially the fathers and masters of families.'[56] Another Whig, while actually defending the notion of the original contract as the foundation of civil society, stressed that all governments were erected by men of property:

It is owned, that all governments are made by man, and ought to be made by those men who are owners of the territory over which the government extends. It must likewise be confessed, that the FREE-HOLDERS of England are owners of the English territory, and therefore have a natural right to erect what government they please.[57]

Daniel Defoe went further still and insisted that the vast majority of the inhabitants of England only lived in the country at the discretion of those who owned the land. Far from being full citizens, the labouring poor were the servants of the property-owning minority. Although he was one of the most vociferous champions of the sovereign people, Defoe was careful to define 'the people' in a highly restricted sense. Political rights, he insisted, belonged only to a minority of the population:

I do not place this right upon the inhabitants, but upon the *Free-*

holders, the Freeholders are the proper owners of the Country: It is their own, and the other inhabitants are but sojourners, like lodgers in a house, and ought to be subject to such laws as the Freeholders impose upon them, or else they must remove, because the Freeholders having a right to the land, the other have no right to live there but upon sufferance.[58]

Even the most radical Whigs, the Commonwealthmen, had no desire to extend the franchise to the labouring poor. They too despised the lower orders as ignorant and disorderly and as entirely lacking in the ability to resist bribery or to exercise independent judgement. John Toland insisted: 'By *Freemen* I understand men of property, or persons that are able to live of themselves; and those who cannot subsist in this independence, I call *Servants*.'[59]

Nonetheless, while it is abundantly clear that the Whigs had no desire to carry through a radical political revolution, still less a social revolution, their ideological position undoubtedly marked a significant liberal advance on the Tory theory of order. Although they may have been concerned to protect the interests of men of property, the Whigs also succeeded in advancing the liberty of all men. Their successful challenge to absolute monarchy and the increased authority which they secured for Parliament helped to establish the rule of law which benefited all subjects. The Whigs insisted that the rule of law was the mark of a free state. In their view it was essential to have laws passed by a legislature which represented King, Lords and Commons and to have the rights of subjects safeguarded from all arbitrary action by those in authority. The law must be known, must be available to all, and must be seen to be observed. While the Whigs regarded the rule of law as the essential curb on arbitrary tyranny, they were also careful to distinguish between liberty under the law and the excess of freedom which resulted in anarchy and licentiousness. They particularly feared the anarchy of a lawless society. They claimed that a proper degree of liberty could only be preserved if the actions of both government and subjects were bound by the operation of known, equal and impartial laws. Only the rule of law could curb both the arbitrary behaviour of an absolute tyrant and the anarchic tendencies of the licentious mob. Locke himself declared that the

Freedom of men under government, is, to have a standing rule to live by, common to every one of that society, and made by the legislative power erected in it; A Liberty to follow my own will in all things, where the rule prescribes not; and not to be subject to the inconstant, uncertain, unknown, arbitrary will of another man.[60]

On this issue Locke had considerable Whig support. Richard Claridge, for example, claimed: 'The standard then of our civil government is the law of the land, it is superior to all orders and ranks of men, and looks with an equal aspect upon the prince and the people.'[61]

The rule of law does of course have both a conservative and a liberal dimension. The law can be an instrument by which men of property seek to define and defend their privileged position, but it can also be a weapon which even the most humble subjects might use to protect their rights. In order to combat an arbitrary and tyrannical monarchy the men of property needed to be able to appeal to an impartial and just rule of law. When they created such a system however they could not then deny all justice to the lower orders. The law sanctioned authority and property, but it could also bind the hands of men of wealth and power with clearly defined, universal and impartial legal rules. The actions of the Whigs therefore had wider and more liberal consequences than they originally envisaged. The same can be said of many of the arguments which the Whigs used to justify the Glorious Revolution. Very few of those Whigs who appealed to the contract theory, to popular sovereignty, to the rights of men or to the right of resistance wished to carry through a political or social revolution. Yet they could not prevent later generations from perceiving and developing the revolutionary potential in the principles of Locke and other Whig defenders of the conservative revolution of 1688. The radicals of the late eighteenth century were to appeal to those same principles in order to challenge the political and social order which the Whigs themselves built up after the Glorious Revolution.

3

Court and Country

All modern historians of the political structure of the reigns of William III and Queen Anne, however much they might stress the existence of organized Whig and Tory parties in both Parliament and the nation at large, would accept that there also existed a division between interests which can be labelled Court and Country. While these historians would stress that most political issues, including disputes over the Revolution settlement and the Protestant succession and disagreements over the conduct of war against France and the extent of religious toleration to be granted to Protestant Dissenters, were fought over by Whigs and Tories, they would also acknowledge that on some questions – the methods which ministers of the Crown used to manage and influence Parliament for example – the political division ran along Court-Country lines. Moreover even those historians who have been most concerned to stress the coherence and organization of the Whig and Tory parties have admitted that there were factors which prevented the development of a simple two-party structure in the reigns of William III and Queen Anne. They recognize that the parties of this period could not be as well disciplined and as highly organized as modern parties because most Members of Parliament were independent country gentlemen who managed their own electoral successes and therefore owed no electoral obligation to their party. Many of these members moreover were reluctant to follow their party leaders in labouring unremittingly in the House of Commons. Thus, both parties are often described as alliances of two elements: a 'Court' element of professional politicians who wanted power and were anxious for office, and a larger 'Country' element of natural backbenchers who cared little for office and who could not always be trusted to support the political ambitions of their party leaders. In both parties the pull of office and the desire for power could persuade some of the more ambitious politicians to put loyalty to the Court above loyalty to the party. At

91

the same time, hostility to what was regarded as the excessive power of the executive and the corrupt tactics of the Court could provoke the Country elements of both parties to form a temporary alliance in order to oppose some particular measure of the Government.

Just as historians of political structure recognize that the political conflict in the reigns of William III and Queen Anne cannot be understood solely in terms of the dichotomy between Whig and Tory, so the student of political ideology comes to realize that the debate between the Tory theory of order and the Whig notion of government by consent does not comprehend the whole ideological debate of the period. A close scrutiny of the political arguments of the period reveals an alternative, but not necessarily a contradictory, ideological division between Court and Country. As we shall see in chapters four and five, the ideological debate between Court and Country came to dominate political arguments in the early Hanoverian period. In the reigns of William III and Queen Anne however it did not predominate because its full emergence depended upon two factors. The ideological debate between Court and Country could only become important when some common ideological ground was established between the Whig and Tory parties or when new issues appeared which divided both parties into their component elements of Court and Country.

In the period between 1688 and 1714 the ideological division between Whigs and Tories remained clear and unresolved. The failure of the Tories to unite in opposition to the Pretender's claim to the throne destroyed them as an effective governing party after the Hanoverian succession. On the other hand, the deep commitment of the Whigs to the Revolution settlement and the Protestant succession enabled them to triumph over their opponents once George I had ascended the throne. Nonetheless, as the argument of the last two chapters has endeavoured to show, the majority of both parties gradually found some common ideological ground after the Revolution. The Whigs did not stand four-square on the contract theory of Locke and most of them were reluctant to draw radical conclusions from the doctrine of resistance, the theory of natural rights and the notion of popular sovereignty. For their part most Tories abandoned the Filmerian case for absolute monarchy and indefeasible hereditary right. Thus when they were faced with the problem of coming to terms with the events of 1688-9 the Whigs became less radical and the Tories less conservative than their earlier ideological position might lead one to expect. Both parties were anxious to avoid civil war and social revolution and both were determined to preserve a hierarchical society in which private property was secured from the depredations of an arbitrary monarch or a licentious mob. Indeed, on a number of fundamental issues Whigs and Tories were in greater agreement than most of them were usually prepared to admit or most later historians have seen fit to recognize.

By the early eighteenth century a substantial body of Tories had abandoned divine right monarchy and indefeasible hereditary succession, while most Whigs preferred to defend the ancient constitution rather than the sovereignty of the people. Both parties were coming to support those appeals to history and prescription that justified a limited monarchy and a mixed form of government which combined the benefits of monarchy, aristocracy and democracy in the legislature of King, Lords and Commons.[1] By the end of Anne's reign a majority of the political nation was coming to accept that the legislative power in the State was divided between the institutions of Crown, Lords and Commons and that the country should be governed by the rule of law. The support either for absolute monarchy or for the sovereignty of the people was eventually reduced to negligible proportions. Even those who wished to see the Pretender succeed Queen Anne were rarely supporters of absolute monarchy, while none of those who can be termed a radical Whig was in fact a genuine democrat.

Once the bulk of the political nation came to accept both the Revolution settlement and the Protestant succession and came to recognize that the constitution divided the legislative power between Crown, Lords and Commons, then some common ideological ground was bound to be established between Whigs and Tories. As the conflict between Whig and Tory weakened, so the division between Court and Country came to dominate political and ideological debates. This process, however, was not completed until George I was seated securely on the throne. Nonetheless, even before this process was complete, an ideological division between Court and Country was intermittently apparent. While Whigs and Tories were gradually establishing some common ground between their conflicting interpretation of the *nature* of the constitution, some of the developments which followed the Glorious Revolution were beginning to create Court and Country divisions over the *working* of that constitution. The political revolution of 1688–9 clearly revealed the ideological

93

differences between Whigs and Tories. The financial and administrative revolutions which followed upon William III's accession to
the throne and his decision to declare war on France created an
ideological division between Court and Country and determined the
issues on which it would focus.

Although the Revolution settlement placed some limits on the
prerogative power of the Crown and established the political importance of Parliament, it did not show how Crown and Parliament
were to co-operate harmoniously and effectively. Indeed, it could be
argued that the consequences of the Revolution soon created new
sources of friction between the executive and the legislature. William
III wished to occupy James II's throne so that he could bring Britain
into the war against France. His efforts to bring Britain's full weight
to bear against France precipitated a financial and an administrative
revolution which transformed the size and power of the central
government. William III and his ministers soon discovered that they
could not finance the enormously expensive war against France out
of current taxation. They therefore turned to the leading financiers
and moneyed men for huge loans to finance the war. To secure these
loans and to ensure that the agreed rates of interest were regularly
paid on them the Government allowed its major creditors to set up
the Bank of England and also established the practice of earmarking
specific taxes to meet the interest rates on this ever-increasing
national debt. This financial revolution was carried through in order
to find the money to pay for the cost of the large army and navy
which were needed for the war against France. To raise the necessary
revenue and to administer these armed forces the Government had
also to initiate a bureaucratic revolution which increased the size of
the Admiralty, the War Office and the various revenue-raising de-
partments of the Treasury.

Both the financial and the administrative revolutions put considerable sums of money and a whole range of Crown appointments
at the disposal of the Government. Thus, while the political revolution of 1688–9 weakened the prerogative powers of the monarch, the
financial and administrative changes which rapidly followed upon
William III's accession to the throne greatly increased the patronage
at the disposal of the Crown. The political uses to which this patronage was put tended to divide men along Court and Country lines
rather than into Whig and Tory camps. While, therefore, the Revolution settlement and the Protestant succession produced an ideo-

94

logical debate which was waged between Whigs and Tories, the political consequences of the extension of Crown patronage sometimes provoked an ideological division which can be more properly labelled Court and Country. The ideological positions of Court and Country existed in a symbiotic relationship and one cannot be understood without reference to the other. It is essential for the sake of clarity however to treat each in turn.

1 The Court Interest

It is possible to recognize a Court interest in the reigns of William III and Queen Anne, but, because of the more powerful pull of party on many of the major issues of this period, this interest did not establish a coherent identity or develop a consistent ideology. It was composed in fact of various elements which had some attitudes in common, but which also came to support the Court for different reasons. Nearly all of those who served the Court in this period accepted the Revolution settlement and were loyal to the monarch who was actually in possession of the throne. Certainly they all recognized that the monarch still possessed considerable political influence and must be allowed to exercise this power. The prerogatives of the Crown might have been reduced and the power of Parliament might have been increased, but there were still many who believed that only the monarch could take a firm hold of the executive or give a political lead to the whole country. Governments were still led and administrations were still made by the monarch and not by Parliament or the major parties in the State. Nonetheless, while there was considerable agreement about the power of the Crown among those who supported the Court, men still supported the power of the monarch for different reasons. The leaders of the two parties sometimes supported the Court in order to satisfy their own ambitions and to pursue the interests of their parties. Those who did not belong to any party but who held offices, places or pensions at the disposal of the Crown were bound to the Court by ties of self-interest as well as feelings of personal loyalty to the sovereign. The leading courtiers and political managers also supported the Court out of self-interest, but they were convinced that political stability could only be achieved if a strong government achieved considerable influence over both Houses of Parliament.

Both the Whig and Tory parties were led by able and experienced politicians who realized that they could not achieve the aims of their parties unless they had influence at Court. The principles of the party had therefore to be tempered by the need to win favour at Court. Once in power moreover the temptations of office and place made the leaders of both parties ready on occasion to abandon their principles or more often to water down their policies in order to retain the support of the monarch. Thus, power and office moderated the policies of both parties. This is not meant to suggest that the leading Whigs and Tories readily and cynically abandoned their principles and declared policies once they were in power. There were clear differences between an administration dominated by Whigs and one dominated by Tories. Nonetheless, the fact that Whigs in power were not always so very different from Tories in power shows that the pull of the Court could moderate though never exceed the pull of party.

On occasions the leaders of both parties were prepared to defend the royal prerogative and Crown patronage when these were exercised in their favour. The Whig leaders, for example, maintained that it was the Crown's prerogative to control foreign policy when they came under attack for their support of the treaties to partition the Spanish empire in the last years of William's reign. In the last years of Anne's reign the Tories did the same when the Whigs bitterly attacked the Treaty of Utrecht. The Whigs were also quite ready to make use of the Queen's influence to defeat the Tory bills against the practice of occasional conformity which were introduced between 1702 and 1704, while the Tories defended the Queen's right to create twelve new peers in January 1712 so that they would have a majority in the House of Lords to defend the peace negotiations with France.

Nonetheless, although it is possible to point to the cynical use of royal power in order to serve personal ambition and party ends, there is plenty of evidence to prove that there still existed within both parties a natural respect for the royal prerogative and a firm belief that the Crown initiated government policy. These attitudes were not confined to those who were in power themselves or to those whose party was in office. In a debate on the Triennial bill in January 1693 the supporters of the Court argued that annual sessions and triennial parliaments would be an unjustified diminution of the royal prerogative and a threat to political stability. Sir Joseph Tredenham, a Tory, protested: 'I am for rejection of the bill. We ought to be tender of the king's prerogative, and the calling and dissolving parliaments, the chiefest flower of the crown.'[2] He was supported by Sir Edward Seymour, another Tory, who claimed: 'I am no prerogative-man; that is, to set up prerogative against law; but if you take away calling and dissolving parliaments, you take away the government itself ... The prerogative is as inherent in the crown, as the people's rights in them.'[3] In January 1694 the Crown's right to veto bills passed by Parliament was defended by Charles Montagu, a Whig. He told the Commons: 'I shall always be for the liberties of the people, and for the prerogative of the crown. If the crown hath a negative voice, then why not exercised on this bill as well as any other ... this is for altering your constitution, not to allow the king a negative voice.'[4] The Court interest not only defended the royal prerogative, but supported the king's right to maintain a professional standing army. When the Government's opponents criticized the standing army as a threat to the nation's liberty, the supporters of the Court insisted that a professional army was essential, that the sword must not be taken from the king's hand and that, in any case, Parliament could keep a tight grip on the activities of the army by the control which it could exercise over the voting of the necessary supplies.[5]

The Court could never depend upon the unquestioned support of the party leaders because these politicians were prepared in the last resort to put the interests and principles of their party above their desire for office. There did exist however a substantial minority of the Lords and a smaller minority of the Commons whose loyalty to the Court was stronger than the pull of party. This loyalty was partly the result of genuine attachment to the Court and partly the product of self-interest. Between a third and a half of those peers who were active in the House of Lords were obliged to the Court for offices, places and pensions and the voting records of these courtiers reflected these ties. Besides pensions and unpaid offices of trust which were bestowed upon peers the Crown also tended to give most of the places of profit and favour at Court to peers and it could further influence the House of Lords by appointing bishops and creating new peers. In the House of Commons over one hundred Members of Parliament held some office or place under the Crown, but many of these found loyalty to their party too strong to make them willing to support the Court on all occasions. Nevertheless, there was a small nucleus of non-party officials and placemen in the Commons whose first loyalty was to the administration of the day. This group, which included members such as James Brydges, William Blathwayt, William Lowndes and Josiah Burchett, formed a genuine Court party, but it was not strong enough to withstand the pressure exerted by the two parties. The Court could only secure a majority in the Commons if it allied itself with Whigs or Tories.

Neither William III nor Queen Anne was anxious however to allow their administrations to be dominated by the leaders of either of the two parties. Whenever possible they placed their confidence in political managers, such as the Marquis of Halifax, the second Earl of Sunderland, the Duke of Marlborough, the Earl of Godolphin and Robert Harley, all of whom could be trusted to put loyalty to the Court above loyalty to a particular party. These men recognized that the Revolution settlement had limited the power of the Crown and had made Parliament an indispensable part of the machinery of State, but had not furnished the means of establishing harmonious relations between the executive and the legislature. The managers employed by both William III and Queen Anne feared the political consequences of allowing the party leaders to dominate Parliament and to dictate to the Crown. They were convinced that this would polarize the political nation and would either paralyse the Government at best or reduce the country to anarchy at worst. In order to achieve political stability and to make the new regime in Church and State work effectively these managers urged all men of goodwill to support the Crown and the administration. In their opinion it did not matter who served the monarch so long as the monarch was served. Since most members of the political nation claimed to be loyal to the constitution established or restored by the Revolution settlement, then they should recognize its virtues and concentrate instead on solving the practical problem of how to make this constitution work. According to these royal managers the most pressing problem was not the nature of the constitution, which so exercised the Whig and Tory parties, but the working of a constitution to which all men in political life had sworn allegiance. In seeking to convince Members of Parliament of this the managers not only exploited Crown patronage, but endeavoured to convince men of the wisdom, indeed of the necessity, of supporting the Court. The creation of peers and bishops, the distribution of Court and government appointments, the granting of places and pensions, the promotion of serving officers and the awarding of government contracts, and the careful manipulation of certain constituencies, all helped to build up a Court interest in Parliament. As we have seen, however, the pull of party was too strong and the patronage at the disposal of the Crown was not sufficiently plentiful or attractive enough to produce a situation in which a majority of both Houses of Parliament could be counted upon to support the Court. The managers of the Court interest therefore could not depend upon Crown patronage alone, but had to conduct an ideological campaign which tried to convince the political nation of the wisdom of abandoning loyalty to party and supporting instead the ministers chosen by the Crown.

The Court interest was of course determined to defend the Crown's patronage which was rightly seen as a valuable weapon in managing Parliament. The Court contested every attempt by Parliament to pass Place and Pension bills which were designed to exclude many of the recipients of Crown patronage from sitting in the House of Commons. The supporters of these measures insisted that they were needed to ensure that Parliament would be independent of the executive. In their view the desired balance between executive and legislative could be achieved only by keeping the membership of each distinct and separate. The Court replied by claiming that harmonious relations between the executive and the legislature could be maintained only if there were close links between the two. This was best achieved by making sure that the executive had its spokesmen in Parliament and Parliament had some representation at Court. This was the general line of argument pursued by the Court, but embellishments were added at different times. During the opposition to a Place bill in 1692 the Court warned that such a measure would only force the Crown to turn to the House of Lords for its servants. If this were done, the Upper House would greatly increase its political influence and the House of Commons would find its authority reduced.[6] On other occasions the spokesmen for the Court condemned Place bills as unjustified attempts to stain the honour of those who served the Crown. They claimed that it was an odious reflection on the monarch and his servants to suggest that they were prepared to betray the interests of the nation.[7] Furthermore, the Court pointed out, the House of Commons itself could not serve the interests of the nation if it were denied access to government ministers and had no opportunity to question them openly and, if necessary, defeat their proposals. If the Chancellor of the Exchequer and the Secretary at War, for example, were not also Members of Parliament, the House

99

of Commons would be unable to hold informed debates on financial matters and foreign affairs.[8]

The supporters of the Court clearly recognized that the royal prerogative and Crown patronage were not enough to ensure harmonious relations between the executive and legislature while the political nation was divided along party lines. It was therefore to their advantage to condemn parties as unstable elements in the State. Natural trimmers, such as the Marquis of Halifax, frequently condemned the pernicious effects of parties which only served to increase divisions and to sow discord. Parties pursued narrow self-interest, whereas the country needed to be governed by moderate men of wise counsel who would seek to eliminate faction and bind up the wounds of the nation.[9] On this point the Court could count upon widespread support, though, paradoxically, this did not lead to the elimination of party influence. Many men who were attached to one party or the other acknowledged that parties posed a major threat to political stability. Joseph Addison, although a prominent Whig, regularly attacked the dangerous effects of party rancour: 'A furious party-spirit, when it rages in its full violence, exerts itself in civil war and bloodshed; and when it is under its greatest restraints naturally breaks out in falsehood, detraction, calumny, and a partial administration of justice. In a word, it fills a nation with spleen and rancour, and extinguishes all the seeds of good-nature, compassion and humanity.'[10]

A partisan Tory such as Jonathan Swift also argued that party strife would eventually destroy the nation if carried too far. He urged the moderates in both parties to recognize that they had far more in common than they generally realized: 'Do not the generality of Whigs and Tories among us, profess to agree in the same fundamentals; their loyalty to the Queen, their abjuration of the Pretender, the settlement of the crown in the Protestant line; and a Revolution principle? Their affection to the Church established, with toleration of Dissenters?'[11] Since parties could not in practice be easily eliminated the managers and spokesmen for the Court endeavoured to weaken their influence by persuading the most able, ambitious and moderate among the party men that they owed a higher allegiance to the nation than to their party. The Crown, they insisted, could not be expected to govern at the head of a party, though it might decide to seek the support of party men provided they did not control the Government's policy. With skilful management it might even be possible to wean the moderate majority from the ties of party. The message to the moderates of both parties must be that the national interest ran counter to the self-interest of either party and that wise men must learn which to choose:

'Tis time for us then to grow wiser, and for all such as sincerely desire the publick good and welfare of their country, to bury their imaginary differences, that they may no longer suffer themselves to be made use of as tools, and to be play'd against one another by crafty and designing men, who regard them no further than as they can make them subservient to their own purposes.[12]

The Court managers recognized that it was not only the existence of parties which made it difficult to attain political harmony. They were also conscious of the effect of political appeals from Members of Parliament to the people and of attempts to bring pressure upon Parliament from out-of-doors. In either case stability would be threatened because politics would be opened up to a wider body of opinion. When therefore the Court stressed the doctrine of legislative sovereignty and resisted any attempt to democratize the political process, it appealed to majority opinion within Parliament. It clearly suited most of the leaders of the political nation to insist that sovereignty resided with King, Lords and Commons, not with the people at large. If the people were sovereign then the mixed constitution would be transformed into a democracy and the threat of anarchy loomed large. The people must not set themselves up as a separate estate, but must rest content with their representation in the House of Commons. They must be taught to respect and obey the legislature. This was not possible if they were in the position either openly to criticize or, worse still, actually to control the actions of Parliament. Parliament must have the independence to act as it saw fit and not succumb to the demands of the giddy populace. Though the people might offer advice to their representatives it must be made clear that Members of Parliament represented the interests of the whole nation and they could not be regarded as the delegates of particular constituencies. Members of Parliament ought to remain free of outside interference from the electorate just as they ought to be free of party control within Parliament. The people were not fit to exercise power for themselves and so they chose representatives to act for them. That being the case, they could not then forbid their representatives to act as they saw fit. The people could not elect a

Member of Parliament and then seek to tie his hands by instructing him how to act on each or any occasion:

Parliaments are not to consult their electors in the great affairs of the publick, for their electors are incapable of giving their advice in such matters. In things relating to their particular boroughs, the electors may advise their representatives, for of these affairs they may be well apprised. But what could a freeholder know of the state of Europe, so as to advise a Parliament, when he had been following the plough-tail ever since the peace? That grand jury ought to be chronicl'd, that could see further into state affairs than the king, and both houses, and thought themselves injured because their advice was not taken.[13]

2 Country Ideology

The Country element in the House of Commons was of substantial proportions in the reigns of William III and Queen Anne, perhaps as much as half the House, though it rarely polled its full strength. It drew its support from men who, on other issues, were fiercely Whig or Tory. This is not surprising given the recent history of the two parties and the nature of the Country interest. The Whigs had developed originally as a party hostile to arbitrary government and in opposition to the Crown. Not all Whig backbenchers could reconcile themselves to the post-Revolution situation which saw their leaders competing for office and even ready to defend the royal prerogative. The Tory party, on the other hand, had begun political life as a Court party, but it often found itself in opposition to the Crown after the Revolution. Thus, there were strong backbench elements in both parties which could not readily bring themselves to give unequivocal support to any ministry in the post-Revolution period. Some Whig backbenchers could not escape their ingrained hostility to the executive, while many Tories could not stomach the actions taken by the administrations which were loyal to the Revolution settlement. On some occasions therefore both these groups of backbenchers were capable of acting together in opposition to the Court.

The Country interest not only incorporated men who were Whigs and Tories on other issues of the period, but also men of very different abilities. Its leading spokesmen in Parliament included some able politicians who were determined not to be corrupted or influenced by accepting places or pensions from the Court. They were supported by a larger number of backbenchers who also prided themselves on their political independence, but who were not so influential that ministers needed to offer them rewards in return for their votes in Parliament. Both types cherished their independence and resented the corrupting influence of the Court. In their view office tainted and power corrupted. Hence the health of the body politic required men of landed estates and independent opinion to act as honest critics of the administration. Their political aims, however, were usually limited to negative efforts to restrict the power of the executive. Another identifiable Country element, the radical Whigs (who were often described as Real Whigs or Commonwealthmen), developed a more positive ideology and offered a more coherent vision of the ideal civil society. Although small in numbers the Commonwealthmen were a more homogeneous group and developed a more constructive policy than most supporters of the Country interest.

The Country interest as a whole shared with an increasing majority of the political nation the conviction that the best constitution was a mixed government which combined the virtues of monarchy, aristocracy and democracy without their attendant vices. The correct mixture was attained by carefully balancing the institutions of King, Lords and Commons. In their view however it was particularly important to prevent the executive from corrupting the people's representatives in the House of Commons. This could be achieved by two means: by placing limitations on the power of the Crown and by encouraging the virtue and patriotism of the citizens. Excessive wealth and property gave the Crown and the aristocracy too much patronage which might be used to corrupt the people's representatives in Parliament. On the other hand, the liberties of the nation could not be entrusted to servants and labourers who were always dependent upon others. The rights and privileges of citizenship should therefore be conferred only upon independent proprietors who were in a position to withstand the corrupting embrace of the most substantial landowners.

The notion that civic virtue depended upon the possession of land and that political power was rooted in property was accepted by all the elements of the Country interest, but it was the Commonwealthmen who most fully developed the thesis that the constitution could only be safeguarded by men of property who cherished their independence and were prepared to put the public good before private gain. The Country interest wished to see in England a classical populus, a

103

community of virtue. It maintained that civic virtue could not be achieved unless citizens possessed freehold land. The Common-wealthmen went on to claim that the ancient constitution of England had always rested on the balance between King, Lords and Com-mons and that this equilibrium was maintained by civic virtue, independence and the ownership of land. The ancient free constitu-tion, which could be traced back to a Gothic and Anglo-Saxon past, had always depended for its survival on the virtue of the community of independent freeholders. This constitution had faced dangers throughout English history. In the past the most serious threat had come from the royal prerogative. The Glorious Revolution had successfully blunted that menace, but it had done nothing to meet the dangers posed by the existence of a professional army and by the corrupting effects of money and government patronage. Indeed, it could be argued that the combined effect of the employment of a professional standing army, the increasing influence of money and the growth of Crown patronage allowed the Court to undermine the independence of Parliament far more effectively than the blatant abuse of the royal prerogative. The balance and equilibrium of the constitution, having weathered a frontal assault by an absolute king, was now in greater danger of being subverted by the insidious forces of corruption.[14]

The function of Country ideology was to mobilize country gentle-men and their representatives in Parliament to resist changes which would corrupt this civic ideal of moral and constitutional virtue. The Country interest had a deep suspicion of courts and courtiers and of their ability to corrupt the people's representatives in Parlia-ment. It desired to secure cheap and honest government and to restrict the executive's influence over the lives and property of the people. These objectives became increasingly difficult to attain in the reigns of William III and Anne as a fairly limited and unsophisti-cated administrative machine was adapted to the needs of two wars of unprecedented scale. Within this bureaucratic system, which raised and disbursed large sums of money, corruption was endemic if not quite as rampant as the Country interest imagined. But it was not only the peculation and corruption of Crown officials which alarmed the Country interest. Their real fear was that war, money and patron-age would undermine the constitution, subvert the liberties of the subject and corrupt the nation at large.

The wars against France compelled the Government to raise a

professional standing army of unprecedented size, far in excess of the forces employed by James II. It was evident to the Country interest that such an army might become an instrument of tyranny at home. Arbitrary and absolute governments had been established during the Roman Empire, in most European countries in more recent times, and in England under Cromwell and James II, when the people had not been in a position to defend their liberties against professional standing armies. Even if a standing army were not employed in a direct attack on the people's liberties, its size and professional character could undermine the constitution by more insidious means. A large standing army necessitated the levying of heavy taxation, the appointment and promotion of numerous military officers and civilian administrators, and the awarding of lucrative contracts to merchants who would supply the multifarious needs of the troops. All this provided opportunities for ambitious, capable, even corrupt men to advance their careers and fortunes by the expense and miseries of war. It is therefore not surprising to find the spokesmen for the Country interest bitterly attacking those who made profits from commanding, administering and supplying the army: 'War, among other monsters it engenders in the womb of a state, begets and gives rise to a set of busy, undertaking, ambitious, light, and projecting persons, who are then brought upon the stage of business. These, whom peace would have left in their original obscurity in troublesome times shine forth.'[15] It was even suggested that the war-time profiteers prolonged the conflicts with France in order to increase their opportunities to make ill-gotten gains.

The Country campaign against a professional standing army, especially in time of peace, combined the fear that such an army would make the executive irresistible with a concern for the political independence of men of property. The most vociferous campaign on this issue was waged in the late 1690s when William III was accused of maintaining a large standing army even after the conclusion of peace in 1697. In Parliament the campaign united Country Tories and Country Whigs, while in the pamphlet war waged out-of-doors the leading critics of the Court were a small, closely knit group of Real Whigs or Commonwealthmen, including John Trenchard, Walter Moyle, John Toland and Andrew Fletcher. The Country Tories tended to resent the cost of maintaining the standing army, but the Country Whigs concentrated more on the political dangers. Although the Country Tories also recognized the political dangers of a standing army, it was the Country Whigs who were most concerned to prove that a standing army could be both a direct instrument of tyranny and an indirect means of increasing the Crown's influence over Parliament. They also emphasized that a nation which relied for its defence on a hired, professional army had taken a major step towards sacrificing its liberties. A professional army was made up of men who were paid to fight. No one could be surprised if the officers and men decided to follow the best paymaster. Thus, in an emergency, the nation might find itself defenceless if its hired mercenaries deemed it expedient or profitable to desert their posts. On the other hand, a citizen militia was under the control of the people rather than at the disposal of the executive. If the militia were properly organized on a nationwide basis it could be just as effective a defence force as any mercenary army. Moreover, a citizen militia encouraged the people to recognize that they must be prepared to bear arms and to fight if they were to preserve their property and secure their liberty. Civic virtue could only flourish in a society in which men were responsible for defending their own interests. A free government could only be established and maintained when the sword remained in the hands of the people. Of course by 'people' even the Commonwealthmen meant those who possessed an independent income. Men of landed property in particular were the best defenders of liberty. Such proprietors were most likely to be willing to defend both their estates and their political liberty. The right to bear arms therefore was as important as the right to vote or to sit in Parliament. The creation of a citizen militia would remove the need for an expensive standing army and would also arm the best defenders of the constitution.[16]

The Country interest regarded the financial and administrative revolutions, which also occurred in response to the unprecedented scale of the wars against France, as posing even more of a political threat than the standing army. There were frequent complaints that the financial revolution had created a separate interest, the moneyed men of the City of London, to which the whole nation was heavily in debt. The Country Tories in particular, since they had closer links than the Whigs with the rural squirearchy, feared that the landed interest would be reduced to a state of utter dependence on the moneyed men. They bitterly resented the way the moneyed interest could make profits out of war whereas the landed interest had to bear a heavy financial burden in the form of a land tax which was generally levied at the rate of four shillings in the pound. Thus, landed men paid the land tax so that the Government could secure enough revenue to pay the interest on the national debt. The Country Tories were not only concerned about their pockets however. They also feared the political consequences of the financial revolution. They believed that the ever-expanding national debt would mortgage future generations to the moneyed interest and would compel the landed gentry to join the scramble for money or see their political influence wither away. Those with money and those who profited out of war would gravitate towards the Court and would be prepared to support policies which were inimical to the interests of landed men and the welfare of the nation at large.[17] They would use their wealth to bribe the electorate and to secure their return to Parliament at the expense of the impoverished squirearchy. The people would then find that they were no longer represented by men of virtue and merit, but by men who were ready to corrupt the people and who, no doubt, would act in a corrupt fashion themselves once they were in Parliament. Thus, either moneyed men would control and corrupt the Government or the Court would use them to corrupt and influence Parliament. In either case money would triumph over virtue and among the first casualties would be the balanced constitution and the liberties of the subject.[18]

The Country interest realized that the political influence of the moneyed men could only be limited if the need for huge loans was reduced, but they also recognized that this was only possible if peace could be made. It is therefore not surprising to find most Country backbenchers, especially those who were Tories, pressing for peace sooner than the Court felt able to secure it. During the wars with France the Country interest could not reduce the level of taxation, but it did distinguish between different taxes. The land tax in particular was hated because it placed such a burden on the squirearchy and yet the Country spokesmen also recognized that at least this tax was levied by local landed men and not by royal officials. In many ways the excise caused more alarm. Not only could it be levied on an ever increasing range of goods, but it required an army of excise officers, who were all dependent on the Crown, to collect it. This growing body of officials strengthened the Court interest in a number of constituencies and thereby promoted the return of several Members of Parliament loyal to the Government of the day.[19] The Country interest had more success in its efforts to restrict the amount of revenue going directly to the Crown. A pronounced suspicion of the executive and a firm desire to keep the Crown dependent upon parliamentary supply convinced many back-benchers, both Country Whigs and Country Tories, that they must keep a careful watch on the size of the civil list. Some favoured limiting the grant of the civil list revenues to the Crown to a fixed term of years, while others advocated a permanent, but small, revenue. The example of James II made many reluctant to grant William III a substantial and permanent civil list which would at best increase his patronage and at worst might make him independent of Parliament altogether, at least in time of peace. In Bishop Burnet's opinion 'a jealousy was now infused into many, that he [William III] would grow arbitrary in his government, if he once had the revenue; and would strain for a high stretch of prerogative as soon as he was out of difficulties and necessities.'[20] In the event the Crown never again secured complete financial independence after the Glorious Revolution and even its civil list barely met the routine and unavoidable expenses of the monarch. In compelling the Crown to appeal regularly to Parliament for the revenue needed to meet both routine and extraordinary expenses the Country interest won one of its greatest victories over the Court.

The Country interest did not content itself with ensuring parliamentary control over the revenues of the Crown, but sought to investigate how the money was used. In January 1691, in the face of determined opposition from the Court, the House of Commons voted to elect Commissioners of Accounts to inquire into the management of public money. The commissioners, who have been aptly described as 'the front bench of the Country Party', regularly censured the way the executive spent the revenue granted by Parliament. They soon ceased to exercise a purely administrative function and took up a political role. They sought to exert parliamentary control over the executive and were particularly determined to root out corruption. Their reports fostered the belief in mismanagement and financial irregularities by the servants of the Crown and provided ample ammunition to attack the performance of the administration and to criticize requests for additional revenue. The very first report of the commissioners, for example, showed that money voted for secret service activities was being paid to Members of Parliament in order to influence their behaviour in the House. This revelation led Sir William Strickland to protest: 'If this was given for public service, let it be owned. This may be the reason we go on so slowly. Let every gentleman lay his hand upon his heart, and declare and vote, "That whoever has received money is an enemy to the king and kingdom, and the liberties of the people".'[21] At various times the commissioners brought forward serious charges of financial malpractice and the misappropriation of public money by servants of the Crown. Early in Anne's reign charges were levelled at the Earls of Halifax and Ranelagh, while later in the reign Robert Walpole, Adam Cardonnel and the Duke of Marlborough himself were condemned for financial malpractices.[22] Even these spectacular successes for the commissioners did not satisfy the Country interest's determination to root out extravagance and corruption wherever it could be detected. Bitter attacks were launched against William III's decision to grant to his courtiers and favourites some of the land confiscated after the defeat of the Jacobites in Ireland. A clause in the Act of Settlement forbade the Hanoverians to grant Crown property to foreigners. When Queen Anne came to the throne the Civil List Act prohibited her from alienating Crown lands in perpetuity, but it did not prevent the monarch rewarding its favourites in other ways. Various demonstrations against the Queen's grants to the Duke of Marlborough testify to the fact that even a popular sovereign and a successful general could not silence the Country demands for an honest and frugal administration.

The corrupting effects of a standing army and of the financial revolution were compounded by the impact of these developments on the machinery of government and hence on the amount of patronage at the disposal of the Crown. The money, places, offices and contracts which the Government could disburse enabled the Court to build up support both in the constituencies and in Parliament. The Country interest feared that Crown patronage would replace the royal prerogative as the greatest threat to the independence of Parliament and the liberties of the subject. It was believed that once a majority of Members of Parliament had been debauched by Court favours then arbitrary power would be firmly established and impossible to combat. The people's representatives would themselves have been corrupted and would no longer possess the public spirit and civic virtue needed to lead the resistance to arbitrary power. The electorate would also have been bribed and the people as a whole would be easily persuaded that the constitution was safe so long as elections were still called and Parliament continued to meet.

Corruption, like a flood, would have spread over the whole nation and civic virtue would be sacrificed to the pursuit of gold. Before it was too late the Country interest must preserve the constitution from the insidious embrace of the Court. Some spokesmen feared that it might already be too late:

It is to be feared that, of late years, by making the highest stations of the kingdom the rewards of treachery and base compliance, by bribing members of parliament with pensions and places, and by the immense gains which a negligent and corrupt ministry has suffered private men to make out of the kingdom's treasure, almost all ranks of men are come to be depraved in their principles; and, to own a sad truth, none are ashamed of having notoriously robbed the nation; ... The little publick spirit that remained among us, is in a manner quite extinguished. Every one is upon the scrape for himself, without any regard to his country; each cheating, raking, and plundering what he can, and in a more profligate degree than ever yet was known. In short, this self-interest runs through all our actions, and mixes in all our councils; and, if truly examined, is the very rise and spring of all our present mischiefs.[23]

The Country interest was convinced that the combined effect of a large standing army, a preoccupation with money and material gain, and the extension of Crown patronage would result in a dangerous corruption of both the manners of the people and the political institutions of the nation. To counter this double threat the Country spokesmen developed a two-pronged response. This was designed to protect both the manners and the institutions of the nation by improving the public spirit and the political strength of the propertied men who were represented in the House of Commons. In the first place the Country interest campaigned to improve the civic virtue of the men of landed estates so that they would possess the personal qualities needed to withstand the tide of corruption flowing from the Court and the moneyed interest. Liberty, it was argued, could only be preserved if public-spirited men were eternally vigilant and continually aware of the interests of the nation at large. It was not enough for men of property to be satisfied with their own integrity. They must also be prepared to take action in order to defend the liberty and interests of the nation at large. In the sphere of public manners civic virtue was the only sure defence against vice and corruption:

Where ever this public spirit reigns: and where this zeal for the common good governs in the minds of men; that state will flourish and

110

increase in riches and power and where ever it declines or is set at nought; weakness, disorder, and poverty must be expected. This love to their native soile where it has been deeply rooted and while it could be preservd has made little citties famous and invincible, as Sparta, Corinth, Thebes, and Athens, and from thence all the Roman greatnesse took its rise; but where they are wretchedly contriving their own ends, without any care of their countreys proffit, or trafficking its wealth and liberty for rewards, preferment and titles; where every one is snatching all he can from the public, and, where there is a general neglect of national interest; they grow luxurious, proud, false, and effeminate: and a people so deprav'd, is commonly the prey of some neighbour, season'd with more wise and better principles.[24]

A second Country response to the threat of vice and corruption was to campaign against the excessive power of the executive and in defence of the merits of mixed government and the balanced constitution. The Country spokesmen often argued that there was nothing factious or disloyal about combining to defend the constitution and the liberties of the subject. Freedom could not be secured unless the proper balance between the executive and the legislature and between the institutions of Crown, Lords and Commons was preserved. To achieve this objective the Country interest put forward various remedies to reduce the power of the Court and to safeguard the independence of Parliament. Country members were particularly concerned to place effective limits on the amount of patronage at the disposal of the Crown and to devise various schemes which would preserve the independence of the House of Commons.

As we have seen many Country backbenchers were anxious to ensure that the Crown was financially dependent upon supplies of money voted by Parliament. The more radical spokesmen for the Country interest, particularly those who were Country Whigs, were prepared to go to considerable lengths to limit the political power of the Crown. Henry Neville suggested that the monarch should be deprived of his prerogative to make war and peace, to control the armed forces, to appoint ministers and create peers, to manage the public revenue, and to call and dissolve Parliament. He proposed that these powers should only be exercised with the consent of a special council chosen by Parliament.[25] Another Commonwealthman suggested that all public officials and servants should be elected by those who would be most affected by their actions. Thus, privy councillors might be elected by the House of Lords, judges by lawyers, bishops by deans and chapters, and sheriffs by the local gentry. Most important of all, the great officers of state would be chosen by Parliament.[26] Walter Moyle advocated the rotation of office-holders so that men would not be corrupted by a long spell in positions of authority and more men would have the chance of serving their country.[27]

Most of the spokesmen for the Country interest were not prepared to go so far in limiting the prerogative of the Crown, but they did share with the radical Country Whigs a genuine fear that the growing influence of the Crown would undermine the independence of Parliament. They were convinced that if it were not curtailed then Crown patronage would eventually secure for the Court a host of subservient placemen and pensioners in the House of Commons. If this development went unchallenged, the Commons would become the obedient servant of the Crown and would eventually lose its ability to protect the liberties of the subject. The balanced constitution could not survive if the democratic element was seduced by the profusion of favours granted by the Crown. The undue influence of the Crown had therefore to be restricted and, in the opinion of most spokesmen for the Country interest, this could only be done by reducing the number of placemen and pensioners sitting in the House of Commons. Thus, throughout the reigns of William and Anne, backbenchers from both the Whig and Tory parties combined to make repeated efforts to pass Place bills or 'self-denying' clauses to restrict the number of royal supporters in the Commons. The first attempt, in 1692, aimed at a general exclusion of all placemen. Despite the hostility of the Court this sweeping measure actually passed the Commons and was only narrowly defeated in the Lords.[28] In 1693 a similar bill, though one which allowed excluded placemen to seek re-election, was vetoed by the Crown. This provoked a storm of protest from the Country members in the Commons[29] and sparked off a bitter pamphlet war. Placemen were accused of betraying the people and the electors were urged to reject all such candidates at the polls. John Toland, a Country Whig, claimed that placemen could not be trusted to preserve the balanced constitution, to protect the liberties of the subject or to investigate the abuses of the Court. The corrupt influence of the Crown was threatening to dash the hopes of those who had expected that the Revolution would establish an honest government which enjoyed the trust and support of the nation at large.

The only remedy therefore that remains is, to chuse such a parliament who lie under no temptations, and are activated by no other motives but the real and true interest of his Majesty and his dominions; . . . it is high time for the electors to look about them and disappoint their [i.e. the placemen's] unreasonable and exorbitant hopes, and to spew them out as detestable members of the commonwealth; not only as unfit to be trusted with their liberties, but as unworthy to breath in the air of a free government.[30]

Measures to exclude certain specified groups of revenue officials, including the commissioners of the salt duty and commissioners of customs and excise, from the House of Commons were passed later in William III's reign. A more sweeping measure was added to the Act of Settlement of 1701, though this was not to come into force until the Hanoverian succession. If it had in fact ever come into effect it would have ensured that rigid separation of executive and legislative which the Country interest believed to be essential to the preservation of the constitution. This triumph however was more apparent than real. Most Country members recognized that the Court was unlikely to leave such a measure on the statute book. The clause was in fact repealed before it ever came into force. The Country members therefore continued to campaign for more limited yet more realistic place bills which would exclude certain categories of office-holders. The nearest that they came to success was in the fierce struggle to add a self-denying clause to the Regency Act of 1706. The Commons actually passed a bill which was designed to exclude all placemen from the House except important officials up to an absolute maximum number of forty. The bitter opposition of the Court and the prolonged resistance of the Lords eventually destroyed such an ambitious plan. The Country interest did succeed with a more limited measure. This excluded a number of existing office-holders, disqualified the holders of all newly created posts from sitting in the Commons, and insisted that those members who accepted office under the Crown hereafter would have to seek re-election. This self-denying clause in the Regency Act was the one great success which the Country interest achieved in Anne's reign, though its effectiveness never matched the high hopes of its sponsors. A brake was applied to the growing influence of the Crown but it was not seriously weakened. It was soon apparent that the Court's influence over the Commons had not been significantly reduced, but renewed efforts to pass further place bills proved unsuccessful. Place

113

bills did pass the Commons in 1712 and 1714, but they were both defeated in the House of Lords.[31]

In their campaign to preserve the balanced constitution the Country interest not only sought backbench support, but endeavoured to secure the backing of the electorate as a counterweight to the influence of the Crown. It was realized however that the voters could only be in a position to help preserve the independence of the House of Commons if they themselves were not unduly influenced by the Court. It was essential therefore to secure free and frequent elections to Parliament, in order to reduce or even eliminate the influence of Court patronage. Free and frequent elections would also help to make Members of Parliament more responsive to the interests of the people than to the wishes of the Court. The Country interest made three attempts to secure the constitutional right to frequent general elections before they finally secured a Triennial bill in 1694. Thereafter no subsequent parliament during the reigns of William and Anne lasted for more than three years and several did not last so long. Even this victory did not satisfy the more committed Country spokesmen and they continued to campaign for annual elections. Their argument was that fewer Members of Parliament would allow themselves to be corrupted by the Court when they knew that they had to seek re-election every year.[32] In order to secure free as well as frequent elections the Country interest campaigned against a whole variety of electoral abuses. The unfair behaviour of returning officers, the practice of creating fraudulent votes by splitting up freeholds prior to an election, and the fairly common tactic of influential candidates standing for two or more constituencies were all condemned,[33] but most Country complaints concentrated on eradicating the more blatant attempts to corrupt the electorate. Some reforms were actually carried, though they rarely answered the high hopes of their Country sponsors. In William's reign an act was passed to keep electoral expenses within reasonable limits so that the price of fighting an election would not be beyond the means of the squirearchy.[34] Another act sought to prevent the most notorious electoral abuses practised by returning officers.[35] In Anne's reign three bills were introduced to condemn electoral abuses, but only one, to prevent the splitting of freehold property in order to create additional, fictitious voters, was passed.[36] The most forward-looking Country suggestion for securing free elections was to favour a secret ballot so that no one would know how any elector had voted.[37] This proposal was never adopted, though the secret ballot was temporarily adopted for voting in the House of Commons.[38]

In addition to trying to prevent the electorate from being corrupted, the Country interest advised the voters to choose only honest and independent men to serve them in Parliament. They warned them against electing courtiers, placemen, moneyed men and stock-jobbers; all of whom would be only too ready to sacrifice the people's liberties in order to ingratiate themselves with the Court. The voters were reminded that men who were corrupt themselves would endeavour to bribe the electorate so that they could sit in Parliament and extend their villainy under the protection of the law.[39] The independence of Parliament and the balance of the constitution, the voters must remember, could only be maintained by honest electors who used their votes wisely: 'to attempt to fill the House with mechanicks, tradesmen, stock-jobbers, and men neither of sense nor honesty, is tricking at the root, and undermining the nation's felicity at once; and 'tis a wonder the impudence of this attempt has not made them stink in the nostrils of the whole nation.'[40] Only men of substantial landed property should be allowed to represent the people in Parliament: 'He who has a large estate will not consent to have the laws subverted, which are his firmest security ... They who are well born will desire to preserve that constitution of which they and their ancestors have always been a part.'[41] If merchants and bankers wished to sit in Parliament they should purchase an estate as a pledge to the electors that they would not flee the country with their wealth in the event of a serious emergency, but would be prepared to brave the same dangers as the other landed proprietors of England.[42] This conviction, that independence and integrity were only to be found in men of landed estates, led the Country interest to wage a long campaign to establish that the ownership of landed property was an essential qualification for all candidates for Parliament. Bills to establish such qualifications were defeated in 1696 and 1697 and it was not until 1711 that the Country interest finally triumphed. In that year it was decided that candidates in county elections should possess real estate worth £600 p.a. and candidates in borough elections should own real estate to the value of £300 p.a.

The more radical elements of the Country interest were not content to advise the electorate to return honest men of landed estates to represent them in Parliament. They insisted that the voters must never fully trust their liberties to those who represented them in

115

Parliament. After all it was not unknown for even honest men to betray their trust when tempted by the Court and it was certainly not beyond the bounds of possibility that Members of Parliament would seek to increase their own authority at the expense of the people's liberty. A free people must therefore not only scrutinize the actions of the executive, but must keep a careful eye on the actions of those who represented them in the legislature:

'Tis possible for even a House of Commons to be in the wrong. 'Tis possible for a House of Commons to be misled by factions and parties. 'Tis possible for them to be brib'd by pensions and places, and by either of these extreams to betray their trust, and abuse the people who entrust them: and if the people should have no redress in such a case, then were the nation in the hazard of being ruined by their own representatives . . . if they [the Commons] employ those privileges and powers against the people, the reason of those powers is destroy'd, the end is inverted, and the power cease of course.[43]

Defoe and like-minded Country spokesmen did not propose that power should in fact be taken from Parliament and put into the hands of the electorate. Rather they wished to stress that Members of Parliament must be conscious of and responsive to the interests of those who returned them to Parliament. Members of Parliament were not free to regard themselves as independent agents who could act as they saw fit. They must regard themselves as the delegates of the people rather than as independent representatives who were not directly accountable to the electorate for their actions. It was therefore reasonable and legitimate for constituencies to instruct their Members of Parliament how to vote on certain issues brought before the House of Commons.[44]

A few Commonwealthmen or radical Country Whigs went further still in their efforts to weaken the Crown's influence over Parliament by strengthening the authority of the electorate. This led them to consider a measure of parliamentary reform. There was however no desire even among the most radical Country Whigs to give the vote to the labouring poor. Even Commonwealthmen despised the masses as an ignorant and disorderly mob and as entirely lacking in the necessary ability to resist bribery or to exercise independent political judgement. Indeed, when suggestions were made to tamper with the right to vote the intention was to restrict the franchise even further; perhaps in the counties to owners of freehold land worth forty pounds not forty shillings per annum.[45] One radical Whig did suggest increasing the number of voters in certain boroughs, but not to the extent of enfranchising those without property.[46] There were however several proposals for a radical alteration in the system of representation. It was pointed out for example that London, Westminster and Middlesex, areas of considerable commercial wealth, were particularly under-represented compared with the counties of the South-West.[47] Others were critical of the large number of small, decayed boroughs such as Old Sarum, Dunwich and Bramber which still sent Members to Parliament. It was claimed that their survival as parliamentary constituencies simply encouraged candidates to corrupt their tiny electorates. It would therefore increase the independence of the House of Commons if these seats were transferred to growing commercial centres, such as Leeds, Manchester and Halifax, which at present were entirely unrepresented in Parliament.[48] The most detailed examination of the inadequate system of representation is to be found in *The Freeholder's Plea against Stock-jobbing Elections of Parliament Men* (1701), a pamphlet which is usually attributed to Defoe. The author incorporated a number of radical Country proposals in his demands for a reform of the representation. On behalf of the freeholders and gentry of the counties he complained about the excessive number of borough representatives compared with knights of the shire:

We think 'tis no small misfortune to the English constitution, that so great a number of members are chosen by the corporations of England, and according to our weak opinions, it seems not equal, that all the freeholders of a county shou'd be represented only by two men, and the towns in the same county be represented by above forty, as it is in Cornwall, and near the like in other counties.[49]

The author went on to criticize those boroughs which so restricted the right to vote that even men of property might be denied the franchise. This only served to make them an easy prey for those who wished to buy their way into Parliament. Far worse were the decayed, rotten boroughs which were virtually devoid of inhabitants let alone men of property and yet still sent two representatives to Parliament. They stood in stark contrast to those large and opulent towns which elected the same number of representatives or perhaps had no representation at all. It was hardly surprising that such a system encouraged corruption:

117

This inequality, we humbly conceive, opens the door to the fraudulent practices, which have all along been made use of in elections, buying of voices, giving freedoms in corporations, to people living out of corporations, on purpose to make votes, debauching the electors, making whole towns drunk, and feasting to excess for a month, sometimes two, or more, in order to engage their voices.[50]

Such corrupt tactics, it was maintained, beggared the country gentlemen and threatened to flood Parliament with wealthy moneyed men who had no concern for the constitution, for their constituency or for the nation at large. Candidates who were prepared to corrupt the electorate would have no scruples about selling their own vote at a profit once they were elected to Parliament.

Part Two

COURT AND COUNTRY
(From 1714 to the 1760s)

4

The Defence of the
Whig Establishment

Historians working on the politics of the early Hanoverian period have rightly stressed that the major accomplishment of this era was the achievement of political stability. This stability is in such marked contrast to the political strife of the reigns of William III and Queen Anne that historians have been at pains to explain how the fierce party conflict between Whigs and Tories was transformed into the more subdued and limited dispute between Court and Country. Very often however their explanations have concentrated too narrowly on changes in the structure of politics and have tended to ignore or minimize important developments in political ideology. Important changes in the structure of politics certainly did occur. Much has quite rightly been made of the divided and demoralized state of the Tory party at the end of Anne's reign and of its gradual disintegration during the reigns of the first two Hanoverian monarchs. Charged with disloyalty to the Hanoverian settlement the Tories were purged from public office by their Whig opponents. Unable to gain office by peaceful means and unwilling to embark upon a civil war the Tories retreated into a sullen and generally ineffective opposition to the Whig supremacy. By the early 1720s the Whigs were firmly entrenched in power, whereas the Tories had ceased to offer a viable, alternative government. Although they embarked on a long period of political supremacy the Whigs themselves were also affected by the changed political circumstances of the early Hanoverian period. Whereas the Tories had to face the insoluble problems created by their exclusion from office and favour, the Whigs had to adjust to a virtual monopoly of power. Without serious political rivals to keep a measure of party discipline and with too many able and ambitious men competing for power the leading Whigs fell prone to personal and factious struggles. Soon the political and parliamentary arenas ceased to provide a clash between Whig and Tory parties, but saw instead continuous disputes among groups of Whigs about who

121

should be in and who should be left out of power. While the 'ins' looked to their Whig allies and to the Court for support, the 'outs' usually sought a temporary alliance with the Tory or independent backbenchers in order to force their way into office. Agreements between 'outs' and independent backbenchers usually proved to be alliances of convenience rather than of principle, but they could only be effective if the 'outs' adopted, at least temporarily, such 'Country' policies as would win the support of a considerable number of the independent backbenchers. Thus, the major political disputes of the early Hanoverian period were no longer waged between organized Whig and Tory parties, which were in fundamental disagreement over a number of important questions, but between Whig 'ins' who looked to the Court for political assistance and Whiggish 'outs' who hoped to rally enough Country support to help them force their way into office. Those Whigs in office used Crown patronage to sustain them in power, while those out of office took up Country arguments in order to condemn this exploitation of royal influence. Yet, once in office, these former 'outs' were almost always prepared to abandon their earlier support for Country policies. Changes in the administration therefore rarely led to changes in the fundamental nature of the policies of the Court.[1]

While there is much to commend this explanation of how political stability was achieved in the early Hanoverian period it is only a partial answer to the question. The surprising degree of political stability that was achieved owes as much to ideological developments as to changes in the structure of politics. The development of political stability cannot be appreciated without reference to the achievement of a substantial measure of ideological consensus. This ideological development which underpins the transformation of the political debate from a Whig-Tory division to a Court-Country dichotomy, has too often been either ignored or misunderstood. Many historians, especially those greatly influenced by the work of Sir Lewis Namier, have been so preoccupied with the power struggle between 'ins' and 'outs' that they have interpreted the entire political life of the period as nothing but a selfish pursuit of office and place. The politicians of the period are deemed to have been interested solely in power and to have had no interest in how or to what ends that power should be wielded. Since many of those who were actively engaged in politics did in fact refer to political ideas, principles and assumptions, historians have had to accuse such men of using these arguments as a respectable cloak for naked self-interest. All politicians are therefore depicted as simply paying lip-service to political ideas and principles in order to win support from the naïve and simple-minded. Patronage and influence, according to this interpretation of eighteenth-century politics, are the only weapons of any importance in the political conflict of the period. The arguments which men used in public debate both in Parliament and the Press can therefore be safely ignored or at least should not be taken very seriously.

Even those historians who have attempted to provide an ideological dimension to their explanation of the achievement of political stability have too often misunderstood the nature of this ideological transformation. They have invariably stressed that an ideological consensus was achieved in the early Hanoverian period because the political ideology of John Locke triumphed over the Tory ideology of divine right and indefeasible hereditary succession. This explanation suffers from two failings: it simplifies the changes in the structure of politics and, in doing so, it simplifies the ideological developments of the period. As we have seen, *both* parties were transformed during the early Hanoverian period so that the structure of politics changed from a division along Whig-Tory lines to one along the lines of Court and Country. Although the Tory party experienced the most profound changes, the Whig party was also transformed, albeit in a more gradual and subtle way. The same is true of the ideological developments of the period. The Tory ideology suffered the greatest damage because of the party's ultimate failure to accommodate itself successfully to the Revolution settlement and the Hanoverian succession, but the ideology of the Whigs was also gradually transformed by their long experience of power.

The first two chapters of this book have shown how both the Whig and Tory parties shared certain social assumptions and political aims which caused them to moderate their ideology after the Glorious Revolution. In the decades after 1688 the Whigs became less radical and the Tories grew less authoritarian. The Whigs in general preferred not to endorse the more revolutionary theories of John Locke, while the Tories gradually abandoned their loyalty to direct divine ordination and indefeasible hereditary succession. Increasingly, both parties put their trust in the ancient constitution, recognized the legislative sovereignty of Crown, Lords and Commons, and urged subjects to submit to the post-Revolution establishment in which political power was still confined to the property-owning élite. This meant that both parties were gradually abandoning their extreme positions, each was adopting arguments from the other, and hence some common ideological ground was being established between them. Chapter three showed how, even during the reigns of William III and Queen Anne, the ideological debate was not always centred on the fundamental nature of the constitution, but sometimes focused on the actual working of an agreed constitution. Once Jacobitism had been defeated and the Hanoverians were firmly established on the throne this ideological tendency came to fruition and a large measure of ideological consensus was attained. This ideological development, combined with changes in the structure of politics, transformed a Whig-Tory dichotomy into a Court-Country configuration.

Throughout the early Hanoverian period ideological developments and changes in the structure of politics acted upon each other and together they increasingly promoted political stability. While the degree of political stability that was eventually attained was in sharp contrast to the instability which characterized the late Stuart period, this does not mean that the reigns of the first two Georges were utterly devoid of ideological conflict. The ideological differences between Court and Country were certainly not as serious and fundamental as those between Whigs and Tories because there was now so much agreement on the actual nature of the constitution. Nevertheless, there was still considerable tension between Court and Country over the actual working of the constitution. Ideological stability does not mean the absence of any ideological disputes. The stability was the product of the fruitful tension and the symbiotic relationship between Court and Country ideologies. As we shall see in the next chapter, the Country opposition was convinced that the policies of the Court, if unresisted, would ultimately destroy the virtues and benefits of the British constitution. This opposition achieved few spectacular successes, but it did prevent the Court developing its authoritarian tendencies so far as to undermine entirely the balance of the constitution and the liberties of the subject. For its part, Court ideology helped to defend and justify the methods used to make the delicately balanced constitution work in practice. The need to accommodate to power and therefore to combat those proposals of the Country opposition that would have made it impossible either to create an effective administration or to establish harmonious relations between the executive and Parliament forced the defenders of the Court to develop a distinctive ideology. This Court ideology, which is the subject of the present chapter, examined the purposes and foundations of civil government, discussed the structure of the existing constitution and debated the best means of preserving it. These inquiries were all designed to justify the Court's support for that balance between liberty and authority which, it was claimed, was the chief virtue of the existing government and constitution.

1 Authority and Obedience

The Court or establishment Whigs were anxious to sustain a social system in which a small minority possessed wealth and status and a political system which represented property rather than people. They were not content however simply to have wealth, status and power on their side. They also believed that they must endeavour to provide moral and intellectual justification for the political and social system which they were attempting to preserve and operate. Thus, they implicitly acknowledged that it was not enough to claim that might was right. In their view the *status quo* had to be legitimized and this required them to examine the origins of authority and the nature of obedience in order to prove that the aims and purposes of the existing government were those which the best civil governments ought to pursue.

The Hanoverian succession and the failure of the Jacobite rebellion in 1715 put the Whigs firmly into power and gave them an excellent opportunity to impose their political ideology on the nation. In seizing this opportunity the Whigs did not rush to throw off their earlier conservatism or to endorse the more radical implications of their political ideology. Having defeated their Tory opponents they did not then seek to adopt the full-blown contract theory of John Locke or to stress such radical Whig notions as the inalienable rights of man, the sovereignty of the people or the doctrine of resistance. On the contrary, long years of power during the early Hanoverian period led to a consolidation of those conservative tendencies which had been developing within Whig ideology since the Glorious Revolution. As the argument in chapter two made plain the majority of Whigs had never endorsed the more radical implications of John Locke's political theory. Most Whigs had preferred to appeal to the ancient constitution rather than to the social contract as the origin and source of both the right to authority and the duty of obedience.

Under the early Hanoverians it was the more moderate and ambitious Whigs, chiefly those who had betrayed some desire to serve the interests of the Court, who found favour and office. Long years in power made these Court or establishment Whigs increasingly willing to accommodate their political principles to the needs of the Government. The retreat from the more radical Revolution principles, which had been apparent among the moderate element in the Whig party during the reigns of William III and Queen Anne, became increasingly marked among those Whigs who enjoyed power under the first two Georges. Indeed, the establishment Whigs developed a conservative political ideology which laid as much or even more emphasis on authority and obedience as it did on liberty and the rights of subjects.

In seeking to justify the right of a property-owning élite to exercise political authority over the property-less masses the Court Whigs believed that it was necessary to examine the origins and purposes of civil government. They hoped that the results of such an inquiry would decide who had the right to exercise power and also to what extent subjects must obey those in authority. In their opinion Locke's political theory was too dangerous because it could be used to justify the sovereign authority of the people and an extensive right of resistance. Locke after all had been seeking to justify the right to oppose those in authority. Now that they were firmly established in power the establishment Whigs required a political ideology which would persuade subjects to accept as legitimate their own exercise of authority. In other words, the Court Whigs no longer required an ideology designed to oppose those in power, but an ideology which would defend and justify the *status quo*. They were therefore careful not to endorse all of Locke's political views, though they did recognize the conservative side of Locke's work and did realize that this could be exploited to support the Whig supremacy. They appreciated that Locke had gone to great lengths to justify private property and the unequal distribution of wealth. Indeed, he had insisted that civil government was established in order to protect the individual's right to his property and to preserve the unequal division of wealth which had arisen in the state of nature. The Court Whigs did not therefore have to abandon all support for Locke's political ideology. What they had to do was to appropriate and endorse the conservative elements in Locke's work while rejecting the more radical implications of some of his views.

126

The Court Whigs fully endorsed Locke's view that property had been divided unequally in the state of nature, that civil government was erected to protect this natural right to private property, and that no authority could infringe the rights of property without the consent of the owner.[2] Government was still regarded as an artificial creation which had only become necessary when men had acquired private property and needed to defend it. Locke had therefore been right to argue that an equal division of the fruits of the earth or a system of communal ownership were both inconsistent with human nature. To allow such claims would create far more problems than the existence of an unequal distribution of private property. Since, the Court Whigs insisted, Locke was therefore right to claim that civil government was deliberately set up to protect the rich from the envy and violence of the poor, no government could possess the authority to infringe the rights of private property without the consent of the owner.

While the establishment Whigs did not deny that all subjects possessed a natural right to their life and liberty, there can be little doubt that they were chiefly concerned to defend the rights of property. Even an occasional critic of the Court Whigs like William Blackstone was convinced that the law and the constitution were designed to protect private property:

So great moreover is the regard of the law for private property, that it will not authorize the least violation of it; no, not even for the general good of the whole community ... the legislature alone can, and indeed frequently does, interpose, and compel the individual to acquiesce. But how does it interpose and compel? Not by absolutely stripping the subject of his property in an arbitrary manner; but by giving him a full indemnification and equivalent for the injury he has sustained ... All that the legislature does is to oblige the owner to alienate his possessions for a reasonable price; and even this is an exertion of power, which the legislative indulges with caution, and which nothing but the legislature can perform.[3]

It was assumed by the establishment Whigs and indeed by the vast majority of property-owners that the rights of property could be securely protected only when men of substance exercised authority and governed the country. It became a common maxim to argue that power always followed property. The notion that the poor should have any voice in the governing of the country was regarded as both dangerous and absurd. The natural inequality of wealth rendered it impossible to establish a democratic form of government. A legislative assembly which was filled with the poorer members of society could never survive for very long: 'How can he who has confined his views to his own subsistence or preservation be intrusted with the conduct of nations? Such men, when admitted to deliberate on matters of state, bring to its councils confusion and tumult, or servility and corruption; and seldom suffer it to repose from ruinous factions, or the effect of resolutions ill formed or ill conducted.'[4] A democracy was widely regarded as the most unstable form of government. Far from securing liberty democracies quickly degenerated into the worst forms of licentiousness. The reservations about allowing the poor to sit in Parliament also applied to extending the franchise to those without property. Those without sufficient property to render them economically independent were regarded as having no will of their own and thus easily influenced by others. Without a material stake in society they might be readily persuaded to upset the social order and to attack the property of their superiors. The rights of citizenship were therefore restricted to men of property since they alone were able to cultivate the civic virtues needed to exercise them. The constitution conferred political influence only on men of property because to give the poor a vote would be to risk rebellion and social revolution. Thus, 'when we talk of people with regard to elections, we ought to think only of those of the better sort, without comprehending the mob or mere dregs of the people.'[5] This same restricted view of citizenship excluded the poor from positions of authority in the maintenance of law and order. In the debates on the Militia bill of 1757 Lord Hardwicke opposed a suggestion that the poor should be allowed to serve: 'Our men of property are our only freemen, according to the meaning of the word among the old Grecians and Romans: their servants were all slaves; and they never put arms into the hands of their slaves.'[6]

Given such prejudices and assumptions about who should govern it is not surprising to find the conservative establishment Whigs cautious about accepting Locke's more revolutionary notions about the natural rights of man, about the social contract as the basis of civil society, and about the right of resistance.[7] Since they knew that they owed their political supremacy to the Glorious Revolution and the Hanoverian succession, it was impossible for the Court Whigs to deny that in the last resort the people could resist an arbitrary tyrant or that the right to govern was a trust which imposed limits on those in power. To this extent therefore they did endorse the theories of Locke, Sidney and Tyrrell and they did acknowledge that civil government rested on a contractual relationship between ruler and ruled. They accepted that no government could claim to be legitimate nor could it expect to survive for very long if it did not secure at least the tacit consent of the governed. To some extent therefore the Court Whigs remained loyal to their Revolution principles. On the other hand they certainly rejected the radical Whig claim that the people were in practice the sovereign authority in the State and hence possessed the right to resist any government which did not serve their interests.

Most establishment Whigs believed that God had ordained government for the benefit of man, but they insisted that he had allowed the various races and nations to devise different constitutions to suit their particular circumstances. Thus, while the authority of government in general came from God, the precise form of any government came from man.[8] No particular form of government could claim to be divinely ordained and hence unalterable by man. Each government must be tested by experience before it could be regarded as appropriate to the needs of a particular society. Over many centuries the English had recognized the merits of a limited monarchy in which the legislative sovereignty was shared by Crown, Lords and Commons. England's ancient constitution enshrined the principle of government by consent, but this was not the same as the radical claim that all legitimate civil governments were based on an original contract or on the sovereignty of the people. The Court Whigs readily accepted that governments might have originated in conquest or through a gradual extension of the patriarchal family, but, nonetheless, their authority was limited by the subsequent need to secure at least the tacit consent of their subjects. Originally certain leaders may have imposed their authority on other men, but no exercise of authority could be legitimate unless it was for the benefit of the whole community, and hence all power had to be held in trust. The need to safeguard the welfare of society placed limits on the authority of every government and also defined the subject's duty to obey. Civil society was undoubtedly created to protect life, liberty and property. Any government which sacrificed these ends betrayed the trust placed in it. When that happened the people had the right to resist.[9]

It is therefore clear that the establishment Whigs remained loyal to the concept of government as a trust and to the notion that the exercise of power required the consent of men of property. They did not however endorse the full-blown contract theory or the sovereignty of the people. Their support for a contractual relationship between ruler and ruled did not necessarily imply that civil government was established by an express contract. Furthermore, although the tacit consent of the people might be needed to confer legitimacy on a government, this did not mean that the Court Whigs believed that the people could dictate to the government which they had established: 'Tho' all right comes from the people, it does not follow that when a government is settled even by the consent of the people, that the people have a right (while the constitution is preserv'd) to exercise authority over the government.'[10] The Court Whigs emphasized that, while it was possible that in the distant past a particular civil government had been established by contract or by express consent, all men were subsequently born subject to the government so created. Certainly all men now alive had been born in a state of subjection and were obliged to submit to the established and duly constituted government. Even if a particular civil government had been established by a contract made by the sovereign people, the people surrendered their authority to this government, and it then became the sovereign power in the State. In no circumstances except the complete dissolution of civil society could the people reclaim their sovereign authority. To deny this would be to encourage the breakdown of all order. The claim must therefore be regarded as both unnatural and impractical: 'should we so far ascribe the power of the government to the people, as to give them a right to resume it, when they please, as this would undoubtedly make government precarious, and tend to civil discord and confusion, this notion must necessarily be false, and such an action of the people unlawful.'[11]

For the establishment Whigs one of the most alarming features of Locke's political theory was his defence of the right of resistance. While the Whigs of the late seventeenth century needed to appeal to such a right in order to oppose the development of an absolute monarchy, the Court Whigs of the Hanoverian period were fearful that this doctrine could now be turned against them. They were therefore anxious to preach obedience to the new Whig establishment. In the past the political sermons preached on the anniversary of Charles I's martyrdom had been used principally by the Tories to preach their doctrine of non-resistance. Under the Hanoverians the Whigs used these occasions to preach a similar message. Typical of these sermons was that preached before the House of Lords by the Bishop of Hereford in 1752. The Whig bishop declared: 'it appears absurd to suppose a society, and at the same time to suppose no subordination of the members of that society, or no obligation to the rules and governors of it. An opposition therefore to public authority, or in other words, *rebellion,* has a necessary tendency to the dissolution of society; and deprives men of all those benefits and blessings, for the security of which societies were framed and governments established.'[12] Many supporters of the Hanoverian establishment in Church and State therefore sought to justify the unique example of the Glorious Revolution, while playing down the abstract right of resistance. Blackstone, for example, feared that the doctrine of resistance might not be used simply to justify the opposition to James II, but might be used to justify opposition to any government and therefore might lead men to seek to undermine even the present constitution. He therefore explicitly took Locke to task on this point:

It must be owned that Mr Locke, and other theoretical writers, have held, that 'there remains still inherent in the people a supreme power to remove or alter the legislative, when they find the legislative act contrary to the trust reposed in them: for, when such trust is abused, it is thereby forfeited, and devolves to those who gave it.' But however just this conclusion may be in theory, we cannot adopt it, nor argue from it, under any dispensation of government at present actually existing ... No human laws will therefore suppose a case, which at once must destroy all law, and compel men to build afresh upon a new foundation; nor will they make provision for so desperate an event, as must render all legal provisions ineffectual.[13]

Blackstone was even reluctant to justify the resistance used at the Revolution. He preferred to argue that the Revolution settlement should be accepted more on the basis of its prescriptive authority than of right. He maintained the convenient fiction that James II had voluntarily abdicated and had therefore left the throne vacant. While he conceded that the opponents of James II had been motivated by a desire to preserve the constitution, he warned against using this example in order to justify the doctrine of resistance. This might lead men to think that they could resist the present regime: 'Whereas, our ancestors having most indisputably a competent jurisdiction to decide this great and important question, and having in

131

fact decided it, it is now become our duty at this distance of time to acquiesce in their determination; being born under that establishment which was built upon this foundation, and obliged by every tie, religious as well as civil to maintain it.'[14]

Other supporters of the existing establishment did not go so far as to deny the right of resistance, but they did insist that resistance could only be used in an absolute emergency in order to preserve the constitution from an arbitrary tyrant. Resistance for lesser reasons would make all governments far too precarious. The inevitable result of inveterate opposition to authority was anarchy and bloody civil war. The Court Whigs rejected the claim that resistance was a duty which kept governments from betraying their trust. In their opinion this would imply that governments and subjects were always natural enemies. They protested that resistance was not justified as a means of redressing private grievances or as a means of establishing a new constitution on a better basis than the existing one. To encourage men to resist for insufficient reason would undermine the best constitution in the world and would only serve the interests of the enemies of the State. 'When the people are injured and oppressed, let them resist ... What I condemn is the general doctrine of resistance now so industriously preached and inculcated ... it must tend to mutual enmity between prince and people and *at this time* it is opening a gate to the ruin of both by making way for the Pretender.'[15] The people must put their trust in Parliament for only Parliament could safeguard the constitution without needing to resort to armed resistance. Parliament had saved the people in 1688 and could be trusted to do so again.[16]

Most of the establishment Whigs perceived the dangers inherent in the contract theory and the doctrine of resistance, but very few were able to develop a more conservative political philosophy which did not rest on the speculative abstractions of Locke. They were content to draw out the most conservative features of Locke's work, especially the defence of property, and to play down the more radical implications of his political theory. A few establishment Whigs did however endeavour to develop an empirical political philosophy which would explain the origins of government and the nature of obedience in such a way that their arguments would fully support rather than to some extent conflict with a conservative political system in which power was held by a narrow oligarchy of propertied men. David Hume, although sometimes labelled a Tory and never fully accepted by the more partisan Court Whigs, was in fact particularly anxious to refurbish the ideology of the establishment so that all moderate men would accept the *status quo*. If his work had been fully understood he could have provided the Court Whigs with a conservative ideology which limited the authority of arbitrary governments without endorsing the sovereignty of the people. An arch-empiricist, Hume sought to explain the origins and nature of government in terms of human experience rather than by appeals to the Bible or to the unverifiable laws of nature. To a much greater extent than Locke he attempted to establish a purely secular political ideology which did not need to depend upon essentially religious assumptions about the law of nature or about the natural equality of man in the sight of God. In his political writings as in his philosophy Hume was primarily concerned with *what is* rather than with *what ought to be*. In order to counter the reactionary threat posed by the theory of divine right and the radical implications of the full-blown contract theory Hume set out to base his view of authority and obedience not on the law of nature or man's God-given reason, but on the evidence of human experience.[17]

Hume set about demolishing both the divine right theory associated with the Tories and the contract theory of the radical Whigs. The former he regarded as self-evident nonsense. In his opinion God clearly desired that government should be for the benefit of man, but this did not imply that he had chosen particular men to act as his viceregents or that all governments acted by his commission. Such a view, Hume claimed, would in fact enable every authority, whether usurper, pirate or bandit, to claim its power from God. As for the contract theory Hume was prepared to concede that government must initially have depended on consent if only because men are so nearly equal in strength and mental capacity that one man could never subject a whole people to his sole authority unless they agreed to be his subjects. Consent of this kind – a mere tacit acquiescence – was not the same as a compact expressly formed for general submission and it could not have been sufficient to establish civil society. When contract theorists argue that every individual is not bound to obey a government unless he has given his consent, either expressly or implicitly, they are, claimed Hume, guilty of ignoring the evidence of human experience. Any original contract is now literally so ancient and so obliterated by a thousand changes of government that it cannot be supposed to retain any authority. Almost all modern governments were founded on usurpation or conquest. Most men do not inquire into the origins of government before they decide to obey. Obedience to authority has become a habitual response in most men. Locke was therefore wrong to claim that absolute monarchy is inconsistent with civil society. On the contrary, it is the contract theory which appears to run counter to the experience of most men in all past history. Indeed, rather than support a theory which constantly threatened the dissolution of government, most men, in Hume's opinion, would prefer to be ruled by a military dictator. Common sense would inform most men that 'were you to preach, in most parts of the world, that political connections are founded altogether on voluntary consent or a mutual promise, the magistrate would soon imprison you as seditious for loosening the ties of obedience; if your friends did not before shut you up as delirious, for advancing such absurdities.'[18]

Hume's empirical and almost wholly secular political philosophy led him to claim that civil society and civil government were established not on the will of God nor on the intellectual creation of man, but on the overwhelming force of human necessity. He insisted that it was not possible for man to exist comfortably or to supply all his wants and defects except by living in society, for only in society could the individual acquire greater strength, greater security and, by the division of labour, greater abilities. Man was so self-interested that society arose not from a desire for liberty or justice, but from man's most powerful and well observed desire: to protect and augment his possessions. Only this selfish, materialistic desire is insatiable, perpetual and universal. In the last resort the preservation of liberty must give way to the protection of property: 'There are three different species of good which we are possessed of: the internal satisfaction of our minds; the external advantages of our body; and the enjoyment of such possessions as we have acquired by our industry and good fortune . . . The last only are exposed to the violence of others, and may be transferred without loss or alteration.'[19] Society is therefore founded on the self-interested desire to stabilize the possession of worldly goods and, secondarily, to facilitate their exchange. In effect men come to a mutual agreement not to appropriate each other's goods. This convention is not in the nature of an explicit promise, but is the common-sense recognition of the mutual benefit to be derived from abstaining from seizing each other's property by force. Once the advantages of this agreement have been recognized however men seek to establish rules of justice and to define the duties and obligations which all men ought to perform. Justice and laws do not emerge from man's natural morality, but from his needs and his experience. They are the artificial creation of man's intelligent appreciation of what is in his best interests. Men become so used to the restraints of such rules that they are eventually able to recognize and condemn acts of injustice which do not directly affect them. Thus, duties and obligations arise out of necessity and self-interest, but gradually acquire the stamp of moral approval and the support of rules of justice. At first all such conventions are artificial, but, through education, habit and experience, they come to be accepted unconsciously and unquestioningly.[20]

Hume traces the origins of government to the same pressures of necessity and self-interest that persuaded men to live in societies. In order to regulate the conventions needed to secure private property men are forced to establish civil government because without it there could be no peace or security. Thus, it is truer to say that governments are needed to uphold conventions than that governments are established by original contracts. A magistrate is needed to administer the rules of justice and to enforce promises. An effective promise is not possible until a government has first been established. While acknowledging that governments served a utilitarian function – to administer justice and to preserve peace and order – Hume did not accept that governments needed to be established by an originial contract. It was more likely that external dangers and the threats posed by other societies forced men to submit to authority. Over many generations men learned the habit of obedience and came to appreciate the advantage of an authority which upheld the conventions of society. Habit consolidated what necessity and self-interest had imperfectly founded. Once accustomed to obedience few men think of throwing off their rulers.[21] Thus, the legitimacy of any government depends not on its origins, but on *prescription*. The authority of a government is established, sanctioned and legitimized in the same way as an individual's right to his property – by present possession reinforced by long possession. 'Time alone gives solidity to their right; and operating gradually on the minds of men, reconciles them to any authority, and makes it seem just and reasonable ... Right to authority is nothing but the constant possession of authority, maintained by the laws of society and the interests of mankind.'[22]

Since the functions of government are utilitarian any form of

135

government which fulfils its duties can justifiably be deemed legitimate and may claim the allegiance of its subjects. The self-interested desire for order and security and the consequent fear of anarchy help to secure the survival of any reasonable government. Once subjects become accustomed to a particular form of government it requires considerable provocation to rouse them to resistance. Provided the government fulfils its primary functions then the people have neither a reason nor a right to withdraw their allegiance. The fact of possession combined with clear evidence that it is performing its duties are sufficient guarantees of any government's legitimate right to exercise authority and to command the subjects' obedience.

Although Hume's interpretation of what constituted a legitimate government is uncompromisingly and unequivocally in favour of a settled, established authority, and hence offered firm support for the Whig supremacy, he did recognize that subjects possessed the ultimate right of resistance when a government failed to perform its duties. The obligation to obey ceases when the government fails to serve the purposes for which it was instituted. Self-interest and necessity created government and the same forces could also dissolve its bonds. Hume was Whig enough to denounce the notion of enslaving men to the doctrine of non-resistance: 'It is certain, therefore, that in all our notions of morals we never entertain such an absurdity as that of passive obedience, but make allowances for resistance in the more flagrant instances of tyranny and oppression.'[23] While endorsing the right of resistance in theory, however, Hume sought to restrict it in practice. Resistance could be justified only in an extraordinary emergency and was the last refuge in desperate cases. In the ordinary course of affairs nothing could be more pernicious and criminal, tending as it did to the subversion of all governments. The duty of obedience ought to be inculcated far more than the right of resistance because the latter could so easily lead to anarchy or encourage rulers to use violent measures in order to enforce submission.[24] Hume therefore played down the right of resistance because he was convinced that any government, however bad, is preferable to no authority at all. Like all establishment Whigs he preferred tyranny to anarchy. In his view the excess of liberty was the bane of civilized society.

Because he believed that the maintenance of order and authority, chiefly to protect private property, was the main function of government, Hume was prepared to defend the legitimacy of absolute monarchy. Nevertheless, it is quite evident that he favoured a system of

136

limited monarchy which combined effective authority with the maximum degree of personal liberty. Hume wished to preserve freedom of expression as well as to protect private property. He regarded liberty as the perfection of civil society, though he believed that the protection of property was its first charge.[25] Britain, he argued, was fortunate in striking a delicate balance between authority and liberty, between absolute monarchy and mob rule. Ever since the early seventeenth century the country had experiencd a long conflict between authority and liberty, between Crown and Parliament, between Court and Country. Stability had been achieved by the Revolution settlement because authority had been maintained but reduced, while liberty had been secured but confined within reasonable bounds. The balance was precarious however. Although it was quite probably the most perfect system of government attainable, its survival could not be guaranteed. Should it collapse, Hume was in no doubt that he would prefer to see it become an absolute monarchy rather than a popular, republican government. Liberty might be preferable to slavery, but the collapse of the present government would almost certainly result in anarchy and civil war. Hume was convinced that most people would agree with him that absolute authority was better than no authority at all.[26]

Thus, while Hume desired to maintain the delicate balance between liberty and authority, he feared that speculative theories about the origins of government, undue emphasis on the right of resistance, and ill-considered innovations could undermine this precarious balance and destroy the best government in the world. It was therefore essential to inculcate respect for the present constitution:

As human society is in perpetual flux, one man every hour going out of the world, another coming into it, it is necessary, in order to preserve stability in government, that the new brood should conform themselves to the established constitution, and nearly follow the path which their fathers, treading in the footsteps of theirs, had marked out to them. Some innovations must necessarily have place in every human institution ... but violent innovations no individual is entitled to make: they are even dangerous to be attempted by the legislature: more ill than good is ever to be expected from them: and if history affords examples to the contrary, they are not to be drawn into precedent, and are only to be regarded as proofs, that the science of politics affords few rules, which will not admit of some exception, and which may not sometimes be controlled by fortune and accident.[27]

Although Hume constantly urged moderation and continually defended the existing constitution his political opinions did not entirely endear him to the Whig establishment. This was largely because Hume was not enough of a committed partisan to defend the whole range of government policies. He was worried for example about the size of the national debt and he preferred a citizen militia to a professional standing army. Moreover, although his political philosophy would have furnished the Whig establishment with a more secure intellectual base than any which the more partisan Court Whigs were able to devise for themselves, Hume provided too much evidence of seeing both sides of a political question to satisfy the blinkered activists. During the bitter disputes between Walpole and his opponents Hume remained the aloof, impartial spectator, observing both sides with almost complete detachment. His views of recent history certainly unsettled the committed. When he examined the Glorious Revolution he was prepared to condemn those who opposed James II, while admitting that the success of their venture eventually provided them with retrospective justification. Even though he opposed any attack on the present Whig establishment he confessed that he could appreciate why men had once supported the Pretender. Hume refused to take seriously the Whig claim that the Tories were potential traitors who wished to see the overthrow of the constitution. In his view the Tory party had so declined in numbers, authority and zeal that it was no longer a major threat to the established order. In the past the Tories had emphasized the need for authority and the Whigs had stood for liberty, but now the differences were only of degree rather than of kind. Moreover, while Hume was prepared to join the Court Whigs in condemning faction and fearing parties which might have fundamental objections to the existing constitution, he conceded that the division between Court and Country was a natural and inevitable feature of Britain's balanced constitution. Indeed, he believed that the very balance of the constitution, so much prized by most of his contemporaries, rested on the fruitful tension between authority and liberty which the Court and Country parties personified.[28]

Hume's attempt to undermine the contract theory and his efforts to base the authority of an established government on its prescriptive right to command obedience represented too clean a break with Locke and Revolution principles to win him much support from the establishment Whigs in the 1740s. Yet by the 1760s his views had begun to influence the major theorists of the Scottish school and, as we shall see in chapter eight, the attacks on the contract theory and the reliance on prescription both increased in the later eighteenth century. By the early 1760s Adam Smith was teaching his students that the contract theory was a recent speculative opinion which was not firmly based on a proper understanding of man and his history. Like Hume he stressed that government was either imposed on men by those with superior force or wealth, or it was accepted by men because of its evident utility. Whatever the first beginnings it was age and long possession which sanctioned the authority of any government. In words highly reminiscent of Hume, Adam Smith poured scorn on the notion that men need only obey a government erected on the basis of an original contract. Men obeyed their government because they feared punishment, because they saw others submit, because they believed that those in authority had some right to command them, or because they were convinced that God expected subjects to obey. Few if any would mention a contract as the foundation of their obedience. Even if an original contract had set up a particular government, later generations were no longer conscious of this agreement and did not feel themselves bound by it. The vast majority of men were not consulted by their government and did not expect to be. They had no expectation of power and no intention of withdrawing their allegiance from the government under which they had been born. Habit dictated their obedience and prescription confirmed the right of their government to command them. Nonetheless, despite this firm support for an established government, Smith, like Hume, accepted that subjects had the right to resist manifest tyranny. This principle justified the Revolution, though Adam Smith was careful to stress that this example should not be used to encourage opposition to the existing government. No government is ever perfect and men must be careful not to upset the established order except in a dire emergency. Fortunately, Smith declared, the present constitution of Britain secured both liberty and property to a greater degree than any other.[29]

Adam Ferguson was critical of certain aspects of Hume's political philosophy, but he joined with him in attacking the contract theory. He rejected the hypothesis of a pre-political state of nature and he denied that civil society was erected on the basis of any artificial scheme or plan of man. In Ferguson's opinion man was born into society and he had always lived in groups or companies. Civil gov-

139

ernment was the consequence of man's needs and desires and, as these became more refined and complex, so the nature and form of government evolved in response to these changes. 'No constitution is formed by concert, no government is copied from a plan ... The seeds of every form of government are lodged in human nature; they spring up and ripen with the season.'[30] The chief causes of political changes were the pressure of war and internal conflict, the desire of men to protect their private property, and the wish to secure greater wealth through commerce and the division of labour. Material wants, selfish desires and sheer necessity, not the yearning for liberty, led men to erect and change their government. Society could not survive and progress unless most men submitted to authority. Popular governments would, of all others, be most subject to errors in administration and to weakness in the execution of public measures.[31]

The more partisan Court Whigs did not immediately endorse this onslaught on the contract theory, though men of this type were prepared to do so by the later eighteenth century when the radicals made the contract theory more dangerous to the establishment than it had previously appeared. As early as the 1730s however some of the supporters of Walpole were attacking the other Whig myth, the ancient constitution. Instead of claiming that both the right to exercise authority and the liberties of the subject were based on an immemorial constitution which had been repeatedly renewed by the people's heroic struggles against tyranny, these Walpolean Whigs insisted that the balance between liberty and authority was of recent origin. Political liberty in any meaningful sense had only existed since the Glorious Revolution. For a time at least some of the leading ministerial propagandists abandoned the traditional Whig interpretation of English history which had justified the Revolution on the grounds that it had restored the ancient constitution. Now, in order to meet the criticisms of the Country opposition, some of the leading supporters of the ministry were prepared to accept the old claim put forward by the Tories that England had almost always been governed by arbitrary and absolute monarchs. The Walpolean Whigs argued that the English had in fact been slaves until the Glorious Revolution inaugurated an era of liberty. Efforts therefore to praise and restore the ancient constitution were misguided:

To bring the government of England back to its first principles, is to bring the people back to absolute slavery: the primitive purity of our constitution was, that the people had no share in the government, but were the villains, vassals, or bondsmen of the lords; a sort of cattle bought and sold with the land. The very parliaments of old were composed only of ecclesiastical and civil tyrants ... The business of this paper is to shew, that our Modern Constitution is infinitely better than the Ancient Constitution; and that New England, or England since the Revolution, is vastly preferable to old England, take it in any point of time, from the Saxons down to that glorious period.[32]

One ministerial newspaper stressed that there was no evidence to prove either that Parliament had existed continuously since the Anglo-Saxon period or that the Commons had long exercised considerable authority. In other words the establishment Whigs of the Walpolean period were prepared to accept the historical argument of Robert Brady, that arch-defender of late Stuart absolutism.[33] They claimed that even during the reign of Elizabeth, which was so idealized by the Country opposition, the people had been at the mercy of the Crown.[34] Fortunately, the old, tyrannical constitution had been remodelled after the Revolution and liberty now flourished because of the efforts of the Whigs. Lord Hervey, a Whig courtier and supporter of Walpole, proudly boasted: 'From King James the Second's banishment, abdication, deposition, or whatever people please to call it, I date the birth of real liberty in this kingdom, or at least the establishment, if not the commencement, of every valuable privilege we now enjoy.'[35]

The myth of the ancient constitution was too much part of the Whig ideological heritage to succumb easily to this attack. William Blackstone still endorsed it in the 1760s and it can be detected in Burke's writings. Blackstone claimed that both the constitution and the common law could be traced back to the Anglo-Saxon period. The Norman Conquest had undoubtedly made some violent alterations to the ancient constitution, but the people had never given up the struggle to safeguard their liberties and to restore the constitution. Even Blackstone acknowledged however that this struggle had not been entirely successful until the Glorious Revolution.[36] In the meantime many other establishment Whigs endorsed the view that the nation's liberties rested on the constitutional settlement of 1689. David Hume, for example, accepted the argument that the Revolution firmly established liberty in Britain for the first time.[37] Robert Wallace insisted that 'Before the Revolution the nation could place no confidence in its governors, for they were continually giving them

141

ground of jealousy and were secretly undermining, or openly invading, their constitution.'[38] Court politicians regularly claimed that the constitution was not ancient, but of recent origin. In opposing the repeal of the Septennial Act in 1734, Sir Thomas Robinson declared: 'For my part, I do not comprehend what is meant by our old constitution, and therefore when gentlemen make use of the expression, our old constitution, I must look upon it as an indefinite term, which can admit of no direct answer ... I know of no settled constitution till the Revolution; it is from that happy period I date our having any at all.'[39] Thirty years later Lord Chancellor Northington was even more emphatic: 'My Lords, I seek for the liberty and constitution of this kingdom no farther back than the Revolution: there I make my stand.'[40] Thus, by the 1760s the Court Whigs were abandoning both the contract theory and the notion of the ancient constitution. They insisted on resting the authority of the government and the obedience of the subject on the actual constitutional settlement made after the Glorious Revolution. On the basis of this settlement Whig governments could claim both a legal and a prescriptive right to rule.

2   The Balanced Constitution

By explaining the foundations and purpose of government far more in terms of the need to protect property than of the desire to preserve liberty the establishment Whigs hoped to justify a political system in which the few governed the many. Their chief concern was to enable men of property to protect their possessions. It was certainly not their desire to extend political rights to the labouring masses. In pursuing this aim they tried to show that the existing constitution was the best available means of establishing authority and preserving liberty. They sought to prove that the present constitutional structure was the best that could be attained because it possessed the inestimable virtues of being a mixed government and a balanced constitution. The existing constitution was regarded as being a mixture of monarchy, aristocracy and democracy because the legislature was composed of King, Lords and Commons. This mixed government, which was widely regarded as being superior to monarchy, aristocracy or democracy in their pure form, was preserved by the balanced constitution. The constitution was praised for its complicated system of checks and balances which established an equilibrium between the executive and the legislature and harmonious

142

relations between the three component parts of the legislature, namely Crown, Lords and Commons. Because the executive could not dominate the legislature or vice versa and because no one part of the legislature could control the other two the balance of the constitution was preserved. Because all three parts of the legislature had to act in concert and because King, Lords and Commons combined to form the sovereign authority in the State the balanced constitution was able to preserve liberty while establishing order.

The establishment Whigs were not alone in praising the virtues of the existing constitution. Most of their parliamentary opponents and many of the lower orders were convinced that the British constitution was the finest ever established in the history of the world. The Country opposition might protest that the constitution was in danger, but they recognized its theoretical merits. The Court Whigs were generally ecstatic in their praise for the beauty and virtues of the constitution:

there is one kingdom on earth where Liberty has taken up her dwelling; where the governors have every thing in their power, but to hurt the people; where the subjects enjoy the sweets of freedom, not the outward marks and pompous appearance, but the essence and substantial blessing of sacred liberty. *Britain* is the only kingdom, and *Britons* the only people who can truly say, we are free, we have a property in what we enjoy, and reap the advantages of government without the least alloy of arbitrary power.[41]

Almost all Britons in public life were convinced that a mixed form of government achieved the greatest number of advantages and the fewest evils of any political system. Following the teaching of the political theorists of ancient Greece and Rome, especially Aristotle, Cicero and Polybius, the political nation recognized three pure forms of government: namely, monarchy, aristocracy and democracy. Unfortunately, while each had its merits, it was also plagued by a serious threat to either liberty or authority. Monarchy avoided disputes over who could exercise authority and it allowed the sovereign to act promptly in an emergency; but it placed the liberty and property of the subject at the mercy of one man who might act as an arbitrary tyrant. Aristocracy provided an able élite capable of leading and of offering an inspiring example to the nation, but it too often degenerated into a narrow oligarchy of warring, self-interested factions. Democracy offered the greatest liberty to the ordinary subject, but it was too slow to act and was so

143

inherently unstable that it invariably soon collapsed into anarchy or mob rule. Almost all democracies either ended in bloodshed or were transformed into military dictatorships. Only a mixed form of government, which incorporated elements of monarchy, aristocracy and democracy, could secure the benefits of each while avoiding their disadvantages. Mixed governments maximized the constraints upon power and prevented its abuse, while also ensuring that the people enjoyed as much liberty as was consonant with political stability. Fortunately for Britain the constitution, at least since the Revolution, illustrated the merits of mixed government. As Robert Walpole himself boasted: 'It is certain, that ours is a mixt government, and the perfection of our constitution consists in this, that the monarchical, aristocratical and democratical forms of government are mixt and interwoven in ours, so as to give all the advantages of each, without subjecting us to the dangers and inconveniencies of either.'[42]

The benefits of mixed government were achieved in practice by the balanced constitution of King, Lords and Commons. Each of these institutions had its own peculiar privileges and distinct functions. As chief magistrate the king was above the law, was the fount of honour, was the unchallenged head of the executive and retained various prerogative rights, including the power to summon, prorogue and dissolve Parliament. The Lords enjoyed the highest honours of the State, sat in Parliament as of right and formed the highest court of justice in the land. The Commons were the representatives of the people and, as such, defended the liberties and put forward the grievances of the subject. They also enjoyed the privilege of initiating all votes of supply. Besides these individual functions all three, King, Lords and Commons, combined to form the sovereign legislature. No bill could become law unless it was approved by all three in the same session of Parliament. There was no strict separation of powers even though the king dominated the executive, the Lords were the supreme court of law and the Commons voted revenue. The executive and the judiciary interacted with the legislature and the sovereign legislature was a combination of King, Lords and Commons. The constitution was therefore a complicated system of checks and balances. It preserved the privileges of Crown, nobility and people while seeking to secure a harmonious relationship between all three. It was this delicate balance and equilibrium which ensured that those twin goals of mixed government were achieved: namely, liberty and authority. In the words of William Blackstone, the influential jurist and lawyer:

And herein indeed consists the true excellence of the English government, that all the parts of it form a mutual check upon each other. In the legislature, the people are a check upon the nobility, and the nobility a check upon the people; by the mutual privilege of rejecting what the other has resolved: while the king is a check upon both, which preserves the executive power from any encroachments. And this very executive power is again checked and kept within due bounds by the two houses, through the privileges they have of enquiring into, impeaching, and punishing the conduct (not indeed of the king, which would destroy his constitutional independence; but, which is more beneficial to the public) of his evil and pernicious counsellors. Thus every branch of our civil polity supports and is supported, regulates and is regulated by the rest: for the two houses naturally drawing in two directions of opposite interest, and the prerogative in another still different from them both, they mutually keep each other from exceeding their proper limits; while the whole is prevented from separation, and artificially connected together by the mixed nature of the crown, which is a part of the legislative, and the sole executive magistrate. Like three distinct powers in mechanics, they jointly impel the machine of government in a different direction from what either, acting by itself, would have done; but at the same time in a direction partaking of each, and formed out of all; a direction which constitutes the true line of the liberty and happiness of the community.[43]

The concept of the balanced constitution involved each part's having its independent privileges while all three were dependent on each other. Eventually the establishment Whigs explicitly denied that the balanced constitution required the complete independence of King, Lords and Commons and hence a rigid separation of powers too. During the debates on the Peerage bill of 1719 some of the Court Whigs did support the measure with the argument that the virtues of mixed government could only be achieved by a complete separation of powers. Joseph Addison, defending the Government's bill, claimed that:

it is necessary that these three branches should be entirely separate and distinct from each other, so that no one of them may lie too much under the influence and control of either of the collateral branches. For if one part of the legislature may any ways be invested with a power to force either of the other two to concur with it, the legislative power is in reality, whatever it may pretend to, divided into no more than two branches.[44]

145

Although he represented government opinion at the time Addison did not have the support of the majority of the Whigs. His long-time friend Richard Steele, and that typical establishment Whig Robert Walpole (who was temporarily in opposition), carried the day with the opposite argument. Steele complained that the Peerage bill would so unbalance the constitution by making the House of Lords a closed oligarchy that the aristocratic element would predominate. The Lords would be free of the Crown's prerogative to make as many new peers as it thought fit and commoners would not be able to secure a title as a reward for wealth, talent or service to the State.[45] Robert Walpole pursued the same line of reasoning. He too feared that the Peerage bill would render the Lords entirely independent of King and Commons when it ought to be influenced to some extent by both:

the strongest argument against the bill is, that it will not only be a discouragement to virtue and merit, but would endanger our excellent constitution; for as there is a due balance between the three branches of the legislature, it will destroy that balance, and consequently subvert the whole constitution, by causing one of the three powers, which are now dependent on each other, to preponderate in the scale. The Crown is dependent upon the Commons by the power of granting money; the Commons are dependent on the Crown by the power of dissolution: the Lords will now be made independent of both.[46]

The force of Walpole's argument produced one of the worst defeats any administration ever suffered in the Hanoverian period and it vindicated the view of the constitution normally upheld by the Court Whigs. Walpole's opinion increasingly became the orthodox view of the balanced constitution. After 1719 the Court Whigs regularly ridiculed the notion of 'government by powers absolutely distinct, and absolutely independent'. Opposition to the concept of the separation of powers led the Court Whigs, as we shall see below, to reject Place and Pension bills because these were designed to produce a House of Commons entirely independent of the Crown. It was stressed that an entirely independent House of Commons or an independent House of Lords would be as destructive of the balanced constitution as an independent king.[47]

By locating sovereign authority in the combined legislature of King, Lords and Commons the balanced constitution prevented one man or a narrow oligarchy from governing in an arbitrary or tyrannical fashion while it also prevented the masses from converting

146

their numerical might into the right to govern. The notion of legislative sovereignty therefore appealed to men of property because it protected them from the twin dangers of arbitrary tyranny and mob rule. The Whigs had defended the concept of legislative sovereignty even before the Glorious Revolution while the Tory party gradually endorsed it in the early eighteenth century. After the Hanoverian succession it rapidly became a constitutional maxim. It was given explicit endorsement by the parliamentary majority which passed the Septennial Act in 1716. Although the opposition insisted that the Triennial Act was a fundamental law of the constitution and therefore could not be repealed, the Whig majority asserted that nothing could limit the actions of the sovereign legislature. The Earl of Cholmondeley, speaking for the Court Whigs, claimed 'that he made no doubt, but that the legislature is vested with a supreme power to rectify any inconveniencies to which any former law may, by experience be found to be subject; and this being the case of the Triennial Act, they ought to remedy the same.'[48] The same case was made by the pro-Government Whigs when the opposition protested that Parliament could not amend the Act of Settlement, the act by which the Hanoverians had succeeded to the throne.[49] In fact it was repeatedly shown that the authority of the legislature knew no bounds. In his famous and influential *Commentaries upon the Laws of England*, published between 1765 and 1769, William Blackstone proclaimed the absolute sovereignty of Parliament in all matters concerning the State.[50] When the American colonies challenged the doctrine, the overwhelming majority of the political nation rushed to its defence. Even the Rockinghamites, who were disposed to conciliate American opinion, upheld the doctrine in the Declaratory Act of 1766. Governor Pownall, who had some sympathy with the American cause, warned the House of Commons:

And first, of the sovereignty and supremacy of parliaments. That is a line from which you ought never to deviate, which ought never to be out of sight. The parliament hath, and must have, from the nature and essence of the constitution, has had, and ever will have, a sovereign supreme power and jurisdiction over every part of the dominions of the state, to make laws in all cases whatsoever; this is a proposition which exists of absolute necessity — its truth is intuitive, and need not be demonstrated — and yet, there may be times and occasions when this ought to be declared and held forth to the eyes and notice of the subject.[51]

147

The legislative sovereignty of King-in-Parliament was not limited to temporal matters but was also exercised over spiritual affairs. The legislature decided the extent of religious toleration and defined the relationship between Church and State. Although politicians and clergymen frequently praised the alliance between Church and State, it was not an alliance between equals, each sovereign within its own spiritual or temporal sphere. The claims of the State were ultimately superior to those of the Church, at least in law. This view was stated quite bluntly by Benjamin Hoadly, a bishop of the Church of England. He asserted unequivocally that the State must possess the power to preserve itself, even against the Church should that prove necessary. 'It is absolutely necessary to the being of the civil power, that any ecclesiastical person should be deprived of his right to the exercise of his office, if that exercise of his office be inconsistent with the safety of the state.'[52] Not content with this extreme Erastian position, Hoadly went on in his famous sermon, 'The Nature of the Kingdom or Church of Christ' (1717), to argue that since the Church was an invisible society ruled by Christ it ought not to invoke the secular arm to support its establishment and authority. This sermon, with its threat to the whole notion of an established church, provoked an enormous controversy. Nonetheless, while the controversy proved that Hoadly's views were unacceptable to the overwhelming majority of the clergy, it also proved that Hoadly was right about the authority which the State could exercise over the Church. The controversy led to the prorogation of Convocation in May 1717. Apart from a short meeting in 1741 Convocation was not summoned again during the rest of the eighteenth century. The independence of the Church of England was clearly curtailed by the State. The survival of its privileged position depended on the willingness of the legislature to maintain the Test and Corporation Acts and its readiness to exert its authority and influence on the Church's behalf.

3 The Preservation of the Balanced Constitution

The political nation at large recognized the advantages of mixed government and the balanced constitution and usually endorsed the absolute and sovereign authority of the legislature. The Country opposition however frequently complained that the actions and policies of the Court were threatening to destroy this constitution. For their part, the Court or establishment Whigs claimed that the balance of the constitution was so delicate that it could not be preserved unless certain positive actions were taken. The arguments of the Country interest might be just in theory, but in practice the balanced constitution would not survive unless the Court took the necessary steps to sustain and support it. The Court must therefore combat and counter the arguments of those who, perhaps unwittingly, would destroy the delicate balance of the constitution. This required the supporters of the establishment to develop three basic arguments: they had to show that the existing constitution actually represented the most powerful interests in the nation; they had to counter the actions of those who, they believed, would undermine the balance of the constitution; and they had to preserve the influence of the Crown because it acted as an essential counterweight to the powerful democratic element in the legislature.

The Court Whigs were not only prepared to argue that the balanced constitution combined the virtues of monarchy, aristocracy and democracy and brought together King, Lords and Commons in one legislature. They also claimed that it established an equilibrium between authority and liberty because, in practice, it represented the most important interests in the nation. At first the supporters of the existing constitution claimed that the legislature represented all the estates of the realm because it was composed of monarch, lords spiritual and temporal, and knights and burgesses. The concept of a nation divided into estates however gradually ceased to have much relevance to the structure of eighteenth-century society and so the establishment Whigs sought other ways of explaining and justifying the representative nature of the existing constitution. Most of the political nation and especially the establishment Whigs opposed the radical claim that the legislature must directly represent every individual man in the kingdom. They developed instead the more conservative notion that the legislature represented the most powerful and influential interests in the nation. David Hume believed that the nobility and the people were two separate orders or estates, but he also recognized that Parliament might represent distinct socio-economic interests, chiefly those founded on trade and land. Hume accepted that factions based on such interests were to be expected, but he never entirely approved of the concept of the representation of interests.[53] It was not until 1770 that Edmund Burke first formulated the notion that Parliament ought to represent not every man individually but the major and legitimate interests in the State. As new interests arose, so they should be represented in Parliament: '... a great official, a great professional, a great military and naval interest, all necessarily comprehending many people of the first weight, ability, wealth, and spirit, had been gradually formed in the kingdom. These new interests must be let into the share of representation, else possibly they may be inclined to destroy those institutions of which they are not permitted to partake.'[54]

The notion that the equilibrium of the constitution depended upon the representation of the major interest in the kingdom was not given intellectual justification until the later eighteenth century. Nevertheless it is obvious that the political success of both Robert Walpole and Henry Pelham rested on their recognition of the need to conciliate these interests. In practice if not yet in theory the Whig establishment accepted that Parliament must represent the major interests in the kingdom. These Whig leaders preserved the balanced constitution by skilfully adjusting and adapting their policies to the political strength of the landed, commercial, moneyed, professional and religious interests in the State. In doing this the Whig ministers showed that they appreciated the realities of power. The overwhelming majority of the political nation recognized the same realities. Most of the Country opposition appreciated that Parliament must conciliate both the landed and the commercial interests and must recognize the privileges of the Established Church while conceding a measure of toleration to Protestant Dissenters. The Country ideology however rested upon a belief that land was the prime source of political influence and civic virtue and was based on the fear that excessive wealth would corrupt the people's morals and undermine the constitution. The Court Whigs on the other hand appreciated the political and social value of movable wealth whether it came from commerce or finance. A commercial or moneyed economy held relatively few fears for them. They were prepared to acknowledge the political importance of the financial and commercial interests and to recognize the important contributions which these made to the preservation of political stability and the balanced constitution.

Some of the establishment Whigs did fear that the size of the national debt might get out of hand and that men might be dehumanized by too great a love of money, but even these misgivings never made them denounce the financial interest in the manner of the Country opposition. They never accepted the Country argument that money and luxury would inevitably corrupt the constitution. David

Hume, Adam Ferguson and Adam Smith all accepted that the progress of society depended upon the growth of wealth and the advance of luxury. They acknowledged that there were inherent dangers in these developments, but they denied that corruption was the inevitable result. The ill effects of money and luxury could be avoided and economic progress might even encourage a people to strive for political liberty. David Hume claimed that the liberties of England increased rather than decayed with the advance of luxury and refinement:

where luxury nourishes commerce and industry, the peasants, by a proper cultivation of the land, become rich and independent; while the tradesmen and merchants acquire a share of the property, and draw authority and consideration to that middling rank of men; who are the best and firmest basis of public liberty ... How inconsistent, then, is it to blame so violently luxury, or a refinement in the arts, and to represent it as the bane of liberty and public spirit.[55]

Some Court propagandists went beyond this and lavishly praised the financial interest for providing much needed support for the balanced constitution. The very existence of the national debt was regarded as proof of the stability of the existing constitution. Men would not lend large sums to a government which they did not trust and no government could long survive unless it merited such trust:

The national debt was contracted in defence of our liberties and properties and for the preservation of our most excellent constitution from popery and slavery. This encouraged the best subjects at the Revolution to venture their lives and fortunes in maintaining a long and expensive war in a firm dependence on parliamentary faith and that public credit which arose from the force and unconfined liberty, so wisely given to every subject to dispose of his property and interest in the public funds ... This commerce, this freedom for every subject to attach his property in the Funds, as occasion or convenience required, may undoubtedly be affirmed to be the support of public credit. It is in a great measure to this liberty that we owe the happy effects of the revolution, the blessings of peace, and the succession of the present royal family.[56]

While the establishment Whigs were prepared to defend the small yet powerful financial interest, they showed no desire to give political representation to the numerically largest interest in the kingdom: the labouring masses. They insisted that the poor could not be

151

F

trusted with political power because their misuse of it would destroy the delicate balance of the constitution. The Court Whigs frequently referred to the common people as the 'mob', the 'giddy multitude' and the 'inferior herd of mankind'. The poor were condemned as turbulent, factious and unstable, and as forever coveting the property of those with greater possessions. Some commentators regarded them as barely human:

The lowest class of the English are very brutish and barbarous, much of the nature of their bull-dogs; they are insolent and abusive, and much addicted to ridicule and scandal; they are very treacherous to one another, insomuch that if one has entrusted his friend with a secret, the first quarrel discovers all; they are affronting to strangers; much addicted to drunkenness, it being common to see them, both men and women wallowing in the streets, and dying drunk; they laugh at the misfortunes of their neighbours, and triumph over misery; they are indeed very laborious, and in that capacity of great service to the commonwealth.[57]

The establishment Whigs were convinced that the constitution could function properly only if the most powerful interests in the State were represented in the legislature. Even when this was achieved however they acknowledged that the constitution would not be free from all danger because it was so delicately balanced that the actions of ill-designing men could easily undermine it. Extra precautions had therefore to be taken to frustrate those who would overthrow the balanced constitution in order to bring in the Pretender or who were prepared to create political unrest until they were brought into power themselves. The equilibrium of the constitution was maintained by the balance and fruitful tension between executive and legislature and between those three elements of the legislature, namely King, Lords and Commons. It could not be maintained in the face of an opposition which sought quite deliberately to destroy the constitution or an opposition which was so factious that it would sacrifice the constitution rather than abandon its ambitions for place and power.

The Court Whigs genuinely feared a Jacobite plot to overthrow the constitution, but they were also able to capitalize upon this fear in order to smear all their opponents with the charge that opposition to the ministry bordered on treason to the Hanoverian succession. To this end they were aided by the discovery of several Jacobite conspiracies and by the survival of a distinct, although politically impotent, Tory group in Parliament. When members of both Houses

152

of Parliament openly accepted the Tory label and indeed remained loyal to certain Tory principles, it did not take much ingenuity for the Court Whigs to accuse these men of being crypto-Jacobites. It was maintained that since an actual Tory rump survived then a potential Jacobite threat existed. Those men therefore who wished to preserve the constitution must forgo the luxury of opposition and rally to the king's ministers. Thus it suited the Court Whigs to insist that a Jacobite threat existed and that therefore men had a clear choice between supporting the existing government and threatening to undermine a much-cherished constitution. Those who attempted to deny the reality of a Whig-Tory division in politics were playing into the hands of the enemies of the constitution:

Nothing is more commonly said, than that all parties are now united, and that there are no *Jacobites* amongst us. If I were a *Jacobite* I should certainly promote this opinion and labour to have it believed by those who are no *Jacobites*; since there cannot be a more artful or more certain expedient to make *Jacobitism* triumph, than to extinguish the fears of *Jacobitism*; for where there is no fear, there will be no precaution.[58]

Since a Jacobite threat existed, then, the Court Whigs asserted, it was entirely legitimate for the Crown to place its confidence in those who had proved their loyalty to the balanced constitution. Only Whigs who had long defended the Revolution settlement and the Hanoverian succession could merit such trust. Even if those who consistently opposed an administration composed of such dependable Whigs were not Jacobites they were at least factious malcontents who were ready to destroy the constitution in their efforts to get into power. There might be good grounds for occasionally opposing a government measure, but to oppose every action of an administration was to allow self-interest to get the better of any concern for the constitution. There could be no justification for a regular, formed opposition when no Whig administration could fairly be accused of threatening either the constitution or the liberties of the subject. When oppositions claimed to be defending the liberty of the subject they were merely seeking to hide self-interest beneath a cloak of political respectability. Because the Court could not satisfy the ambitions of all those who desired office and place, the discontented raised an opposition to the king's ministers under the pretence of defending the rights of the people. For proof of this one merely had to look at the careers of such politicians as Pulteney,

Carteret and the Elder Pitt, who were seen to abandon the principles which they had upheld in opposition once they were admitted into office.[59]

The Court Whigs insisted that formed opposition, whether by Jacobites or factious malcontents, posed a serious threat to the constitution. Despite, perhaps because of, its intricate system of checks and balances the equilibrium of the constitution could not be guaranteed. The balance was not necessarily self-adjusting and could be easily disturbed. This being the case, the enemies of the constitution had to be countered by increasing the stability of the king's government. This could not be done by appealing to the ordinary people because the giddy multitude could not be trusted to exercise the required political judgement. Indeed, the mob was too easily led astray by ambitious and plausible politicians. The greater representation of the people therefore would undermine, not preserve the balance of the constitution. The only alternative was to increase the influence of the Crown. Since the democratical element was inherently volatile, political stability could only be achieved by strengthening the hand of the monarch. The establishment Whigs pointed out that the enemies of the constitution could most easily succeed if they won control of the House of Commons because the Commons represented so much property and controlled the purse strings. If it ever decided to abandon support for the balanced constitution and chose to exert its full authority, the House of Commons could give the law to both the House of Lords and the king. An unrestrained democracy would then replace a system of mixed government. In order therefore to curb the potentially exorbitant power of the Commons it was necessary to preserve and even strengthen the power of the Crown.[60]

There were several ways in which the Court Whigs endeavoured to preserve the power of the Crown. They insisted that the king must retain his freedom to choose his own servants and ministers. The majority in Parliament must not be allowed to circumscribe his choice so closely that the administration became the servant of Parliament and the executive became the prisoner of the House of Commons. The king must be granted a substantial civil list and secret service fund so that he retained his executive freedom and was not entirely at the mercy of Parliament. Finally, in order to be able to take prompt and effective action to defeat both external and internal enemies of the constitution, the king must be given control of a substantial standing army even in time of peace.[61]

These measures were not enough however to ensure that the power of the Crown could balance that of the House of Commons. Yet to increase the royal prerogative still further would be to risk creating an arbitrary, absolute monarchy once again. On the other hand, if the Crown were able to manage and influence a section of the House of Commons without being able to dictate to it, the balance of the constitution could be preserved. The Court Whigs therefore supported the exploitation of Crown patronage to give the king a body of supporters in Parliament capable of influencing the decisions reached therein. While the Opposition might protest that the existence of a Court party in Parliament undermined the latter's independence, the Court Whigs maintained that without such support the Crown would be at the mercy of the House of Commons. The king must be allowed to exercise his most important prerogative: the right to dispose of places of honour, profit and power to those who would support the executive and influence the decisions of Parliament. 'The king must have his real power, as well as the other parts of the legislature; and ... he can have no real power, (now the crown lands are gone, and he depends absolutely upon the people for money) but by those dependencies, which his power of disposing of all places, civil, military and ecclesiastical, creates.'[62]

The Court Whigs were careful of course to stress that the patronage of the Crown was not great enough to constitute a serious threat to the liberties of the subject or to the balance of the constitution. They claimed that the Crown's supporters in Parliament – who composed the Court and Treasury party – were never numerous enough to constitute a majority and hence were not strong enough to silence all opposition. The Crown's influence was barely sufficient to make it difficult for factious men to win control of Parliament and prevent them endangering the constitution.[63] The Court Whigs insisted that giving a man a place or a pension did not necessarily induce him to act against his better judgement. Most recipients of Crown patronage were men of substance in their own right and they were unlikely to forfeit their independence or besmirch their reputations simply to please the king. There was no evidence that placemen and pensioners voted against their convictions. To suggest that the Crown rewarded men who were willing to betray the liberties of the subject and to

155

corrupt the constitution was to imply that the king himself was an enemy of the people. A willingness both to serve the king and to protect the interests of the people could not be regarded as incompatible unless the king and his subjects were pursuing entirely different ends. The truth of the situation was in fact the exact opposite. There was abundant evidence to show that there was a natural harmony between the interests of the Crown and the people:

> The king's choosing a gentleman to serve him, whom the people have thought worthy to represent them; and the people's choosing a gentleman to represent them, whom the king has thought worthy of one of the highest trusts of government, is a means of preserving that union and harmony between king and people, which is necessary to the carrying on the great ends of government.[64]

Thus, the Crown's influence over Parliament was the best guarantee that the balanced constitution would be preserved. To exclude the recipients of Crown patronage from Parliament, and especially from the House of Commons, would prevent the administration from pursuing the legitimate course of seeking parliamentary support for its measures. It would also deprive the people's representatives of just the kind of accurate and detailed information from the king's ministers that they needed to inform their debates and determine their resolutions.[65]

To counter the activities of 'factious' critics the Court Whigs were prepared to defend the influence of the Crown even to the extent of defending what the Country opposition regarded as 'corruption'. The Court consistently opposed all measures, including Place and Pension bills, which would reduce the Crown's influence over Parliament. When it proved too dangerous to risk defeating these popular bills in the Commons the ministers quietly smothered them in the Lords. Robert Walpole once protested that a Place bill was the surest way to divide the interests of the king and his subjects and hence was the quickest way to undermine the constitution. He argued that if the Crown chose to honour men of substance and merit and these men were excluded from sitting in the House of Commons, then the chamber would be dominated by men of little interest and less talent. Conversely, if men of distinction had to make a choice and decided to represent the people in Parliament, then the king would have no alternative but to turn to men without fortunes or ability. Thus, either a capable ministry would be constantly faced by a House of Commons dominated by inferior men or a weak ministry would have to deal with a chamber full of more able men. In either event the equilibrium of the constitution would be disturbed. It would be impossible to have both a strong executive and an able House of Commons. Either the executive would be too strong for the House of Commons or the latter would make it impossible to procure an effective administration. The balanced constitution would be destroyed and the nation would be faced by the stark choice between an over-powerful monarchy or an unstable democracy.[66]

The Court Whigs feared that the House of Commons, the democratic element in the constitution, might increase its power and escape the control of the Crown and the aristocracy. This fear was reinforced whenever the opposition in Parliament endeavoured to enlist the support of the people 'out-of-doors'. The Court Whigs passed the Septennial Act in 1716 in part because they believed that frequent appeals to the electorate might make the House of Commons too responsive to the interests of the voters. This attitude was made explicit when the opposition sought to repeal the act in 1734. In his response to this proposal Robert Walpole argued that more frequent elections would encourage faction, sedition and insurrection, and would disturb the balance of the constitution by increasing the influence of the electorate over their representatives. Similar objections were raised to the opposition's practice of encouraging constituencies to send 'instructions' to their representatives as a means of influencing the way these Members of Parliament voted in the House. Even more inimical to the calm deliberation of the House of Commons were the attempts by the misguided multitude to surround the House when it was in session, as happened during the stormy debates on the Excise bill in 1733. Once elected, the Court Whigs maintained, a Member of Parliament must be free to speak and vote as his conscience dictated and not as the people urged:

When the Parliament is chosen, that part of the power of legislation which belongs to the people is no longer in them collectively, but is devolv'd upon, and remains solely in their representatives. If we don't like what they have done, we are at liberty, when the time is expired, to chuse others; this, and this only is our power. But to send threatning letters, and authoritative orders and commands, to those in whom we have lodg'd the supreme powers of legislation; and, after that, to come up by the thousands; to beset their House; to affront them as they pass

157

by, is an unexampled piece of licentiousness, tending to a total dissolution of government.[67]

It clearly suited the Court Whigs and indeed the vast majority of conservative-minded Members of Parliament to regard themselves as representatives but not delegates of the people. They insisted that they were elected because of their wealth, status and abilities, which were all superior to those of most voters. That being the case it was sheer nonsense for the electorate to seek to dictate to them. The electors could never be as well informed of public affairs as their representatives and these representatives could never fulfil their obligations to the whole nation if they were controlled by those who voted for them. Members of Parliament were free to listen to the views of those who returned them to Parliament, but in general they must consider the wider interests of the whole people and not the narrow interests of their constituents. As Sir William Yonge, a staunch Court Whig, put it: a Member of Parliament 'may receive, he may ask, he may even follow the advice of his particular constituents; but he is not obliged, nor ought he to follow their advice, if he thinks it is inconsistent with the general interest of his country.'[68]

Beneath the prolonged and impassioned campaign[69] to ensure that Members of Parliament could retain their independence and freedom of action lay the deep-rooted assumptions that only men of property were fit to rule and that the people could not be trusted with any share in the decision-making process. If power were to be restricted to a narrow élite of propertied men, then the people, even most of the electorate, must be excluded from an active role in parliamentary politics. The balanced constitution was in fact essentially aristocratic: it gave power to a narrow oligarchy largely composed of substantial landowners. If Members of Parliament were to be regarded as simply the delegates of the people, as men who could be instructed and even intimidated by the people at large, then the balance of the constitution would be tipped heavily in favour of a democracy. The people might then be sovereign in fact and not merely in theory. The alarming consequence might be a social revolution and an attack on property. Thus, conservative opinion agreed with Lord Hardwicke when he warned Parliament: 'if you allow the dregs of your people to prescribe to, or controul the legislative authority of the kingdom, in opposition to what is

158

approved of by all those of a superior rank, not only our present establishment, but government itself must be at an end: anarchy and confusion must ensue.'[70] Contempt for the people and for the notion that Parliament should follow the popular will is even more apparent in an essay by one of the propagandists for Walpole's administration. This commentator admitted that a majority of the people in the country might be against the administration, especially a Whig administration, but he insisted that this was only to be expected in view of the prejudices of the squires and rural parsons who taught the people to hate the Court. For this commentator at least it mattered little what the people thought. The Court should not be over-preoccupied with either its own popularity or public opinion out-of-doors:

To conclude: Supposing it true, that the majority of the people are against the ministry, what doth that prove? The people are sometimes right, and sometimes wrong: They have been in the right against kings and parliaments too; and they have been in the wrong against both.[71]

4   Liberty, Authority and the Rule of Law

Among all the defenders of the Whig establishment there prevailed the firm conviction that authority could be maintained and liberty preserved only by the rule of law. The balanced constitution was not only supported by the rule of law, but realized its ultimate political and social purpose by embodying the principle of the rule of law. The aims and purposes of civil government – to maintain public order, to protect private property and to preserve the liberty of the subject – could only be achieved when the rule of law operated. The delicate balance between the authority of the magistrate and the liberty of the subject could only be safeguarded by the rule of law. One of the most essential features of the balanced constitution – the sovereignty of the combined legislature of King, Lords and Commons – sustained and in turn was upheld by the rule of law. Finally, the social and economic aims of the conservative, property-owning élite could only be safeguarded by a political system in which the fundamental and guiding principle was the rule of law.

The establishment Whigs and indeed a majority of the political nation accepted the maxim that there must be a supreme, irresistible and absolute power in every orderly state and that this authority must be a legislature which could impose laws on each and every subject of that state. Without the rule of law civil society would rapidly degenerate into either arbitrary tyranny or licentious anarchy. Laws might perforce restrain individual liberty, but without them society would regress to a state of nature in which the powerful overawed the weak and no man's life, liberty or property was safe. Men might lay claim to the natural right to life, liberty and property, but none of these claims could be upheld without the rule of law. The law alone could free men from the dominion of arbitrary will, whether by one man or by a multitude, and only the law could determine when the magistrate had the authority to command and when subjects had the duty to obey. The Court Whigs clearly recognized that the rule of law would safeguard them from the threat of absolute monarchy and the danger of mob rule. Above all they believed that political stability could not be achieved unless liberty was defined and limited by the law so that it did not degenerate into licentiousness.[72] In their view the opponents of the Court were too prone to ignore the truth of this and hence they put all property in peril:

Who then are the greatest friends to Britain, those who are for the establishment of such laws, and the preservation of such polity, as afford the subject so much liberty only as will preserve him in the security of his property; or those who under pretence of love to their country, are for introducing such a deluge of liberty, as must sweep away all property?[73]

This strong emphasis on the rule of law was designed to provide civil society with both a stable political regime and a clearly defined legitimate authority without the necessity of submitting to an absolute king or meeting the expenses of a large police force. The establishment Whigs, indeed the whole political nation, wished to support a political system in which authority was exercised by men of property. It was clearly recognized that the most important liberty of the subject was the right to protect his property from any arbitrary exercise of power. In order to maintain such a political system, in which the property-owning minority governed the labouring masses without recourse to a grossly illiberal and excessively authoritarian regime, those in authority had to use the law itself as a means of social control. The principle and practice of the rule of law could combine to provide an ideological weapon which would limit the authority of the government while encouraging the subject to obey. As Douglas Hay has shown so convincingly, the actual administration of the law enabled the ruling classes to display majesty, justice and mercy, and so allowed them to overawe the people without the need for frequent appeals to naked force. Courts and trials were conducted with pomp, ceremony and elaborate ritual in an attempt to arouse in those who witnessed them a sense of the majesty of the law. Judges and magistrates frequently used the courts to preach secular sermons on the virtues of established authority and the necessity of obedience. They endeavoured to impress on the accused, the jury and the assembled onlookers the need for law and order and they sought to convince them that law and order could be preserved only when subjects submitted to the powers that be. The administration of the law was upheld as an example of impartial justice unparalleled anywhere else in the world. The public nature of trials and the observance of strict procedural rules, at least in the higher courts, could be offered as convincing proof that all men were equal before the law and that the law was the guardian of the liberty and property of every subject. The rule of law could be justified even when its operation was halted by displays of the prerogative of mercy. Judges and Justices of the Peace could exercise considerable discretion in imposing sentences. Pardons and commuted sentences were frequently secured either to please a man of consequence or to show that the law had a human face. The law itself would remain apparently impartial, but its operation could be halted or its sentences mitigated. Thus the ruling classes could use the law to protect as well as to chastise the erring subject. The quality of mercy could sometimes reinforce social deference more effectively than a rigorous enforcement of the letter of the law.[74]

The rule of law undoubtedly benefited all subjects. The law was made by a representative legislature or by the decisions of an independent and often highly qualified judiciary. The law applied equally to all subjects and could be enforced against all subjects. It was often, although not always, administered in an open and impartial manner. Most subjects were therefore conscious of the advantages which they reaped from the rule of law. Nonetheless, there can be little doubt that men of property had the greatest influence in the making and the administering of the law and that therefore the rule of law conferred more benefits on men of property than on the labouring masses. Not only were peers and Members of Parliament men of considerable wealth, but judges, Justices of the Peace, sheriffs and even jurymen were invariably men of property. These men of property could invoke the law in order to prevent the lower orders gaining power commensurate with their numerical strength. A propertied franchise was maintained and various acts were passed and enforced to prevent dangerous crowds assembling and to make illegal all combinations of workers for the purpose of improving pay and conditions.[75] Certainly both the legislature and the courts more often used the law to protect property rather than to extend the liberties of the subject. While it is true that no eighteenth-century administration saw its priorities in terms of a legislative programme, every session of Parliament passed numerous bills on such matters as turnpikes, enclosures and river navigation that were designed to benefit men of property and influence. Parliament also greatly increased the number of capital crimes involving offences against property and passed a mass of legislation about crimes involving grain, wood, trees, fruit, dogs, cattle, horses, hedges and game – crimes that affected the gentry in particular – which allowed these cases to be tried by summary conviction. Thus, men of property did not have to worry about the problems of drawing up formal legal indictments or about acquittals being granted by tender-minded juries. As Justices of the Peace they could deal summarily with those who dared to attack their property.[76] The rule of law therefore preserved the existing constitution, held the balance between authority and liberty, and preserved the particular interests of the propertied élite.

5

Country Ideology

During the early Hanoverian period some individual politicians, including Robert Walpole, Henry Pelham and the Duke of Newcastle, stayed in power for many years and very few administrations suffered major defeats in Parliament. Even when an administration ran into difficulties in Parliament it could generally recover its majority by beating a strategic retreat on a particular issue or by bringing into office its most vociferous critics. Occasionally a minister might have to be sacrificed to appease parliamentary opinion, but there is no case of an entire ministry falling together and being replaced by a completely different administration. It was rare for any administration to face, and rarer still for it to be defeated by, a united opposition. Moreover, when former critics of the Government were brought into office they invariably adopted the same policies and indeed were prepared to propagate the same Court ideology as those politicians whom they had replaced. It cannot therefore be denied that many opposition spokesmen conducted a factious campaign designed simply to push ministers out of and themselves into office. Malcontent Whigs or 'outs', such as Carteret and Pulteney, might claim to stand for certain principles, but their willingness to be bought off by an offer of a place and their readiness to abandon their oft-proclaimed ideals once they had secured office confirm that their opposition was motivated by political ambition rather than by constitutional principles. This kind of behaviour has led many historians to dismiss all opposition in this period as factious and to see all contests for power as revolving around 'ins' and 'outs' who shared very similar principles.

It is certainly true that in the early Hanoverian period it proved very difficult to organize an effective opposition with a distinctive ideology and coherent policy. There were two main reasons for this. In the first place, the Country opposition which most frequently criticized the Court had in fact much in common with those in

163

power. Both the ministers and their opponents were not only drawn from the propertied élite and shared the same basic social assumptions, they were also in agreement about the nature and merits of the British constitution. On the other hand, the Country opposition was divided within itself because the disparate elements which composed it traced their ideological origins to the Whig and Tory parties of the late seventeenth century. The elements in the Country opposition could not agree, for example, about matters of religion or about who should enjoy active political power. Thus, the different elements making up the Country opposition found it difficult both to establish a permanent and clear ideological distinction between them and their Court opponents and to develop a coherent ideology to which all opponents of the establishment Whigs could subscribe.

It undoubtedly proved difficult to develop a coherent opposition or Country platform because it was not always easy to discover clear ideological grounds for disagreement with the Court Whigs since both sides accepted many features of the 'Whig' constitution. The ideological consensus reached by the Whigs and Tories by 1714 meant that there was no unbridgeable ideological gulf between Court and Country in the early Hanoverian period. None of the various elements in opposition, except perhaps the tiny Jacobite group, wished to overturn the constitution. The radical Whigs in opposition are sometimes described as Commonwealthmen or classical republicans, but this does not mean that they were either democrats or opponents of the monarchy. They simply showed a greater readiness to impose limitations on the Crown and the aristocracy in order to safeguard the civil liberties of the subject. A monarchy limited by an effective representative assembly and a government which took every care not to restrain the freedom of the individual were essential features of their ideal commonwealth. The opposition or Country Tories, for their part, gradually severed all links with Jacobitism and all loyalty to divine ordination and indefeasible hereditary succession. These old loyalties did not promptly disappear after the disaster of the 1715 rebellion and indeed Bolingbroke spent many years seeking to wean the Tories from a firm attachment to many parts of their traditional ideology, but disappear they eventually did. By the time the Tories joined the Country opposition to Walpole in the later 1720s they had fully reconciled themselves to both the Revolution settlement and the Hanoverian succession. Indeed, Bolingbroke was able to persuade most Tories to accept the ancient constitution, which held that a monarchy limited by Parliament was an immemorial right of the English nation, and to reconcile themselves to the Revolution settlement which had restored that constitution.[1]

All the elements in the Country opposition joined the establishment Whigs in upholding the virtues of the rule of law and in praising the merits of mixed government and the balanced constitution. The radical Whigs feared tyranny more than anarchy, but they wished to be governed by laws and not by will, whether it was the arbitrary will of one man or many. The tyranny of the multitude usually ended in the tyranny of one man in any case and so in their opinion mob rule was little better than a dictatorship.[2] Most of the Country opposition would certainly have shared Bolingbroke's conviction that mixed government and the balanced constitution were capable of providing Britain with the finest system of government in the world.[3]

The overwhelming majority of the Country opposition which believed in the virtues of the balanced constitution was also convinced that political power must depend upon the possession of property. Whether in or out of office they all feared that the labouring masses might acquire ambitions beyond their humble station in life. Country Tories such as Bolingbroke were convinced that men of calm, deliberate reason – the aristocracy of talent, which happened to coincide with the owners of landed property – should govern. The vulgar masses were passionate, ill-informed and incapable of political judgement. It was their duty to obey. The only democratic element in the constitution was that which represented those men of landed estates who could be regarded as independent and equal citizens.[4] The Tory country gentlemen were not the only opposition group holding such opinions however for even the radical Whigs shared these prejudices about the common people. Commonwealthmen such as John Trenchard and Thomas Gordon were as convinced as any Tory that only men of property should govern.[5] Although the radical Whigs would have preferred a more equal distribution of property so that power should not be concentrated in the hands of a tiny élite group of great landowners, they firmly rejected any suggestion that there should be an attack on private property.[6] They condemned the notion that any government had the right to take action in order to redistribute property equally so that power would in consequence be shared more equally, because they believed that such action

165

would produce an unstable democracy.[7] It is quite clear that even the radical Whigs had little respect for the poor. They were convinced in fact that the masses should remain in their humble stations in life and should be so disciplined by the need to labour that they could have no opportunity to turn the world upside down. Thus, John Trenchard bitterly attacked the idea of establishing charity schools which, he claimed, would provide an unsuitable education for the poor and encourage them to desire to rise above their lowly station in society.[8]

The Country opposition's failure to defeat the Court Whigs was not due only to their inability to draw a clear line between their ideology and that of those who were in power. It also proved difficult to unite the disparate elements of the opposition into an effective force ready to mount a sustained campaign against the Court. The Whig malcontents, the ambitious 'outs' who were chiefly concerned with forcing their way into office, would adopt any platform or argument which would further their careers, but would also abandon these with equal facility whenever a tempting offer of place or pension came their way. The other elements normally found in opposition to the Court were no more united in their actions or in agreement about their ideology. The small body of radical Whigs or Commonwealthmen, who criticized the Court Whigs for abandoning Revolution principles by seeking to increase the power of the Crown, had nothing in common with the handful of Jacobites who still flirted with the idea of restoring the Pretender. The largest element in opposition to the Court was the body of Tory country gentlemen who were ready to accept the Hanoverian succession, but who found it difficult to unite behind a single leader or to discover any distinctive Tory issues on which to rally sufficient support to bring them back into office. The establishment Whigs accused the Tories of being crypto-Jacobites and so ruined their reputation at Court. Successive administrations also skilfully reduced the support for the Tories in Parliament and in the country by diffusing the two emotive issues which had aroused the squirearchy and the parochial clergy, the backbone of the Tory party, so often in the past. The ministers took care to reduce the financial burden on the landed interest by relying less on the land tax than they had done in the reigns of William and Anne, and they refused to countenance any serious or sustained attack on the privileged position of the Church of England. Thus, the remnant of the Tory party in Parliament never gained sufficient credit at Court nor enough powerful backing in the country at large to bring it back into office. Its membership in the Commons never fell below one hundred in the early Hanoverian period, but neither did it rise above one hundred and fifty. It was a permanent opposition whose leading members had either to desert to the Court Whigs or reconcile themselves to the fact that they would never hold office.

The Court Whigs were able to capitalize on the fact that the important elements which were opposed to them had different ideological origins and aims. Hence it frequently proved possible for the ministers to drive a wedge between the Tory and Whig elements in the Country opposition. Although the Court Whigs were able to conciliate the Anglican hierarchy through the judicious distribution of patronage and through the acceptance of the privileged position of the Established Church, the Tories retained their traditional connection with the ordinary parish clergy. The Tories still regarded themselves as the most dependable bulwark not only against Dissent, but against latitudinarianism and deism. Whenever they suspected an attack on the Church of England they mounted a campaign in its defence. Thus, in 1736 for example, when the critics of the Church supported the Quaker Tithe bill, the Mortmain bill and the repeal of the Test and Corporation Acts, the Tories raised the alarm. Sir John St Aubyn condemned all these measures as the first step towards the dismantling of the constitution. He insisted that the existing constitution in both Church and State must and would stand or fall together.[9] In 1753 the Tories again rallied in defence of the Church when they bitterly condemned the Jewish Naturalization Act and secured its repeal. Their spokesmen on this occasion protested that the Whigs were the enemies of both the Church and the Christian religion.[10]

The Whigs in opposition never shared these fears and indeed the radical Country Whigs were the most determined critics of the Established Church. The Country Whigs sympathized with the Dissenters and wished to extend religious toleration beyond the limited concessions made in 1689. They supported all the measures of 1736 which, had they all passed, would have seriously weakened the position of the Church. The most Erastian and anti-clerical literature of the age emanated from radical Country Whigs, most notably John Trenchard and Thomas Gordon. They wished to see the Church placed even more firmly under the control of the civil

167

power and they desired to eliminate all the special privileges of the Established Church. They hoped to see the day when there would be complete religious toleration for all Protestants and the temporal ambitions of the clergy would be destroyed.[11] Such views naturally horrified the Country Tories. Bolingbroke, who hoped to unite the disparate elements of the opposition into an effective Country party, tried to paper over this yawning gulf between the religious views of the Tories and those of the radical Country Whigs. He tried to steer clear of religious issues, but, in doing so, he aroused the suspicions of his Tory allies and abandoned the one weapon which might have united the squirearchy and parochial clergy against the Court.

The Tory and Whig elements in the Country opposition were also divided over the question of who ought to enjoy active political power. The Tories still believed that the natural order of society was hierarchical and authoritarian, and that only men of substantial landed property should take an active role in politics. They were always prepared to support any measure which would restrict political power to those who owned land. In 1732, 1733, 1734, 1740 and 1760 the Country Tories urged that the law concerning the landed qualifications required by parliamentary candidates should be strictly enforced. In 1732 they actually secured an act which ensured that Justices of the Peace should own land worth £100 p.a. and in 1747 they tried in vain to increase the land qualification to £300 p.a. In contrast the radical Country Whigs not only wished to safeguard the civil rights of all men to liberty of conscience, freedom of expression and equality before the law,[12] but were ready to allow all men the right to judge the government under which they lived. The radical Whigs did not wish to extend the franchise to the poor, but they acknowledged that in the last resort all men had the right to resist oppression.[13] While the Tories feared that such notions would lead to licentiousness and mob rule, the radical Whigs insisted that tyranny was a greater and more imminent threat than anarchy.[14] They feared a rigidly hierarchical society which would not accommodate new forms of wealth and property, and they believed that liberty was in danger whenever a huge gulf existed between the very rich landowners and the lesser landowners, merchants and tradesmen. Although they would not countenance any attack upon property they did believe that liberty flourished best where the possession of property was widely distributed among a substantial section of the population.[15]

While therefore it proved extremely difficult and at times impossible to unite into a coherent and cohesive party those disparate elements in opposition to the Court Whigs, this should not blind us to the ideological nature of the attacks launched on the policies and especially the methods of the Whig establishment. The fear of corruption, which involved hostility to placemen, standing armies and the political influence of money, united the disparate elements in the opposition to the Court and sharply distinguished the ideology of this Country opposition from that of the establishment Whigs. Although a political platform built upon a Country ideology was never likely to be adopted by any administration, it did provide the only means of creating an effective opposition to the Court Whigs. This Country opposition was rarely powerful enough to bring down a Whig administration, but it was strong enough to inhibit the Court's freedom of manoeuvre. The balanced constitution might never have survived so long if the Country opposition had not defended the cause of 'liberty' when the Court was so often emphasizing the needs of 'authority'. Because of its failure to secure power it is easy to deprecate the Country opposition as impotent and to ignore it as irrelevant. In fact, however, it is impossible to explain how the Whig constitution of the early Hanoverian period achieved its unique balance between authority and liberty unless we appreciate that Court and Country co-existed in a symbiotic relationship. We cannot understand the ideology of one without reference to that of the other.

1 The Fear of Corruption

The Country opposition may have agreed with the Court Whigs on the fundamental principles which underlay the constitution and it may have been divided into Whig and Tory camps over certain issues, but there can be no doubt that the fear of corruption divided the Country from the Court and often brought together disparate elements into an ideologically motivated opposition to the political methods adopted by successive administrations. The Country propagandists, both Whig and Tory, were prepared to accept the constitution established by the Revolution settlement, but they were alarmed at the way in which the seductive influence of power, place and money was threatening to undermine the balanced constitution. In seeking to preserve the constitution the Country opposition waged a campaign which was as much moral as it was political.

169

It was widely believed that in order to combat the social, economic and political developments which were upsetting the social order, disturbing the delicate balance of the constitution, and ultimately threatening the liberties of the subject, it was necessary to change both the manners of men and the institutions of the country. A rhetoric of virtue, which stressed the need for integrity, patriotism and self-sacrifice, was employed to stiffen men's resistance to corruption and to unite them in defence of liberty, while a campaign against large standing armies and the misuse of Crown patronage was mounted in an effort to impose constitutional limits on the executive.

Country ideology was founded on an ethic of civic virtue which maintained that society and civil government could only be preserved by the patriotic actions and public spirit of men of property. Those who possessed a real and substantial stake in the country were the only true citizens and the natural leaders of those who were merely inhabitants. Their property gave them both independence and a sense of responsibility, hence they alone were in a position to act in the best interests of the nation as a whole. This property had to have a real and stable value, not a fictitious and mobile one. Hence landed property and trade involving material goods were both capable of conferring civic status, though land was clearly the more substantial and important possession. Trade in money and shares, however, did not confer the rights of citizenship upon financiers because their wealth was based on fantasy and speculation. The value of paper money and stocks and shares fluctuated wildly and depended upon the state of public opinion. Moneyed men were not independent citizens, but the creatures of the Court. They enjoyed wealth and power, without possessing independence or a sense of responsibility. The whole system of credit was irredeemably unstable and posed a serious threat to the real world of land and trade.

The Country opposition, both Whig and Tory, mistrusted the new financial system of the national debt, the Bank of England and the great chartered corporations that had arisen in the 1690s. They resented the way in which the moneyed men, who were involved in this exclusive and powerful world of public credit, had prospered during the wars of William and Anne, while the landed men had been heavily taxed. This situation was not repeated until the later stages of both the War of the Austrian Succession and the Seven Years War, but even during years of peace the moneyed men frequently enjoyed a higher return on their investments than the smaller landowners and merchants. The jealousy and fears of the squire-archy, freeholders and merchants were reinforced by such spectacular cases of financial corruption as the bursting of the South Sea Bubble in 1720 and the collapse of the Charitable Corporation in 1732. It is therefore not surprising to find the Country interest protesting that the process begun in the 1690s must be halted before it ruined the nation and beggared all those who had a real stake in the country. The Country opposition shared Bolingbroke's conviction that the financial revolution was in danger of destroying the political and social gains secured by the Revolution settlement:

It is impossible to look forward, without horror, on the consequences that may still follow ... What will happen, when we have mortgaged and funded all we have to mortgage and to fund; ... when we have mortgaged all the product of our land, and even our land itself? ... Who can answer, that a scheme, which oppresses the farmer, ruins the manufacturer, breaks the merchant, discourages industry, and reduces fraud into [a] system; which beggars so often the fair adventurer and innocent proprietor; which draws continually a portion of our national wealth away to foreigners, and draws most perniciously the rest of that immense property that was diffused among thousands, into the pockets of a few; who can answer that such a scheme will be always endured?[16]

While such hostility to the moneyed men may have been an exaggerated reaction to the consequences of the financial revolution, it was an attitude widely and firmly held among the Country opposition. The landed interest undoubtedly resented the fact that taxes were levied on property, but not on the large profits made by successful financiers. 'Monied men, another vast body, contribute little or nothing to this [land] tax. Their stock in trade can never be known, and is always assessed but a trifle; money lent on mortgages is never taxed, and stock in the funds has the publick faith to exempt it, so that by having unequal advantages against the landed interest, the monied men devour the country gentlemen and work the most ancient families out of their inheritances.'[17] Many merchants, both the lesser traders of London and those of the outports, also resented the privileges, monopolies and power of the financiers associated with such great chartered trading companies as the East India Company and the South Sea Company. The radical Whigs were as critical as any Tory squire of the exorbitant wealth and undue influence of the moneyed men. They concentrated on showing how the money market attracted too much of the nation's wealth from the genuinely productive trade in material goods. In their view, while stockjobbing flourished, trade decayed. Yet it was trade which encouraged arts, science and industry, whereas the money market encouraged only greed and self-interest.[18]

The intensity of this hostility to moneyed men was not due simply to the higher profits made in finance compared with the returns on trade and land. The success of the financiers and stockjobbers was regarded as merely the most obvious manifestation of the desire for and the influence of money, both of which were corrupting the moral, social and political order. It was the constant theme of the Country opposition that the Court was encouraging the nation to worship luxury and to pursue inordinate wealth at the expense of the traditional civic virtues of industry, simplicity, honesty and patriotism. The Court was accused of favouring the financial interest and of fostering the vicious, debauched and corrupt offspring of the financial revolution. Under an honest administration a man could only advance his fortunes by small degrees, but under a corrupt system of government a small number of men could enrich themselves by cheating the public and by selling their support to the highest bidder.[19] To increase their political influence the moneyed men bought up seats in Parliament by using their wealth to corrupt the electorate. The moneyed men 'turn awkward statesmen, corrupt boroughs, where they have not, nor can have, any natural interests; bring themselves into the legislature with their pedling and jobbing talents about them, and so become brokers in politics as well as stock, wanting every qualification which ought to give them a place there.'[20] The moneyed men also provided the Court with the money needed to finance the growing bureaucracy and to provide the patronage and bribes needed to influence both voters and Members of Parliament. It was therefore widely feared that money, rather than merit, status or a permanent stake in the community, was the most important factor shaping the political decisions taken at Court, in Parliament and in numerous constituencies.

Enough damaging evidence about financial corruption became public knowledge to convince many men that the standards of public life were deplorably low. Alexander Pope lamented the way the system of public credit had become such an abuse that it corrupted all levels of political life:

> Blest paper-credit! last and best supply!
> That lends Corruption lighter wings to fly!
> Gold imp'd by thee, can compass hardest things,

Can pocket States, can fetch or carry Kings;
A single leaf shall waft an Army o'er,
Or ship off Senates to a distant Shore;
A leaf, like Sybil's, scatter to and fro
Our fates and fortunes, as the wind shall blow:
Pregnant with thousands flits the Scrap unseen,
And silent sells a King, or buys a Queen.[21]

Writers such as Pope, Gay, James Thomson and the young Samuel Johnson attacked the vices of the 'city'; vices which they believed were infecting not only London, but the Court and Parliament. The simple and honest virtues of rural life were contrasted with the corruption of city life where money ruled and vice threatened to destroy all moral values.[22]

While these fears were undoubtedly exaggerated there were clear indications that corruption existed at all levels of the political process. The cost of winning a parliamentary seat rose steadily throughout the first half of the eighteenth century although the size of the electorate remained fairly constant. Clearly more money was being spent per elector; not necessarily on outright bribes, though certainly on such electoral expenses as entertaining the voters. Corruption in public life reached much higher than the electorate. Several Court Whig Members of Parliament were convicted of fraudulent practices associated with the funds of the Charitable Corporation and the York Building Society and with the forfeited estates of both convicted Jacobites and former directors of the South Sea Company. In 1725 Lord Chancellor Macclesfield was impeached for selling masterships in chancery for exorbitant sums and then neglecting to supervise the way masters handled money lodged with them by litigants. Several leading politicians, including Robert Walpole and Henry Fox, made large fortunes out of public office. The greatest financial scandal of the age, the South Sea Bubble, involved several cabinet ministers and royal favourites and even touched the royal family itself.

The financial revolution was closely linked, both in fact and in men's minds, with the extension of the government bureaucracy, the enlarged civil list, the expanded armed forces, and the use of the secret service fund. All of these developments created a considerable amount of patronage and put it at the disposal of the Crown. Both George I and George II were prepared to allow their ministers to use this patronage for political ends. To their Country opponents it looked as if the influence of the Crown had replaced the royal pre-

173

rogative as the greatest threat to the constitution.[23]

Although the Country opposition exaggerated the extent to which the Crown could influence and corrupt Parliament, it is quite clear that the size and discipline of the Court and Treasury party had increased significantly since Anne's reign. The Court Whigs did not have an indestructible majority in the House of Commons, but they did have the support of a body of placemen and pensioners that was sufficiently large and dependable to meet the normal needs of the administration. Only in exceptional circumstances could the Country opposition find an issue which would allow them to rally their full support in the House and which would encourage desertions among the placemen and pensioners. Only then could the Country opposition feel confident of defeating the Court. In the House of Lords the situation was even more unfavourable to the Country opposition. The administration could invariably rely on the support of a majority of the Upper House because the Crown could create new peers and appoint bishops and because peers were given the highest posts both in the Government and at Court. Thus the Country opposition could claim, with some justice, that a number of unpopular acts were passed and many popular measures were defeated because Crown patronage had destroyed the independence of Parliament and did not allow a free vote by the elected representatives of the people.

The Country spokesmen maintained, vociferously and repeatedly, that the Court had so influenced the electorate and the members of both Houses of Parliament, that the balanced constitution was in serious danger. In the past, they claimed, the Crown had attempted to subvert Parliament by a direct assault upon its privileges and its authority. These attacks had been repeatedly repulsed, most recently by the Glorious Revolution. By the more surreptitious and insidious use of Crown patronage, however, the Court could pack Parliament and weaken both the aristocratic and the democratic elements of the constitution. The balanced constitution of King, Lords and Commons might survive in theory, but in practice the first was in the process of acquiring power over the other two. This threat to the constitution was probably not intended by the king, but, unfortunately, the Country opposition insisted, neither George I nor George II fully understood the constitution and they were misled by a corrupt faction at Court. Bolingbroke argued:

We all know that there are mercenary and abandoned wretches amongst us, who have dared to lead for a dependence of the parliament on the crown; not for that dependence of the several parts of the government on one another, which our constitution hath formed, and on the preservation of which the freedom of our government entirely rests; but for the most indirect, the most iniquitous, as well as dangerous dependence imaginable; for a dependence, to be created by corruption, which must always produce effects as infamous as its cause.[24]

If the nation did not heed the alarm bells rung by the Country spokesmen, then, the latter claimed, a corrupt administration would establish a tyranny by stealth and, in the process, would sap the patriotic spirit of the people. The flood of corruption would first weaken the moral fibre of the nation, then pack Parliament, and thereafter undermine the constitution and threaten the liberties of the subject. This dreadful train of events could only be halted if the patriotic spirit and civic virtue of the nation were aroused. It was the duty of the Country opposition and Country ideology to perform this task and to rescue the nation. Virtue and vigilance were to be the true antidotes to the poisonous effects of money, luxury and corruption.

2   The Legitimation of Opposition

Any attempt to preserve the constitution by organizing an effective opposition to the political methods of the Court had to overcome three major obstacles. In the first place, the majority of Members of Parliament, who were not committed to the administration, had to be persuaded to attend the Commons regularly and to vote consistently against the worst abuses of the Court. Second, the Tory and Whig elements in opposition to the Court Whigs had to be persuaded that the long-standing disputes between Tory and Whig were no longer important and that they ought to be abandoned because of the pressing need to rally a Country opposition to the Court. Finally, the widespread conviction, that formed opposition to the king's ministers was either factious or smacked of treason, had to be overcome.

While no administration could command a permanent majority of the House of Commons, the support of the Court and Treasury party was enough to ensure that the ministry could only be defeated in a well attended House. Unfortunately for those who wished to

175

create an effective Country opposition the most likely support for their policies came largely, although not entirely, from independent country gentlemen and natural backbenchers whose regular attendance in Parliament could hardly be guaranteed. Many Members of Parliament had no desire for office and did not regard themselves as professional politicians. They regarded their seat in Parliament as a recognition of their standing in the community and as a means of preserving their local and class interests. While such men enjoyed the social amenities of London and Westminster during the parliamentary session and paid the occasional visit to the House of Commons, many of them were reluctant to put in long hours carefully scrutinizing every action of the administration. In their opinion the government of the country at national level lay with the king and his chosen servants. The administration was expected to suggest ways and means of raising the necessary revenue for the public service and to initiate the relatively few legislative measures which applied to the country at large. Only when the ministers had proved that they were manifestly unfit for the trust reposed in them was Parliament free to defeat their measures and to urge the king to seek different servants and to pursue different policies. It was not for Parliament to impose ministers on the Crown or to dictate government policy. Formed opposition was legitimate only when there were clear indications that the policies and methods of the administration were leading to disaster. The spokesmen for the Country opposition repeatedly warned that the Court Whigs were embarked on policies which would subvert the constitution. Their whole press and parliamentary campaign was designed to encourage the belief that it was a patriot's duty to oppose the Court. The country gentlemen were warned year after year about the need to arrive in town for the beginning of the parliamentary session, about the importance of regular attendance at the House and about the wisdom of staying until the very end of the session. These were the only ways of frustrating the Court's attempts to slip measures through Parliament when the House was but poorly attended. It was not enough for the country gentlemen to claim that they approved of Country measures if they would not perform their duty by a regular attendance at Parliament. The corrupt methods of the Court could only be detected and frustrated by eternal vigilance. The defence of the constitution required men to love liberty and to perform their duty as patriots.[25]

176

The second obstacle to the development of an effective Country opposition was the persistence of a Whig-Tory dichotomy among those in opposition to the Court. The long-standing and bitter enmity of Whig and Tory made it difficult to persuade men to bury old quarrels in order to wage a campaign against the Court. This was made doubly difficult by the Court's deliberate policy of insisting that they were the only true Whigs and hence that their opponents were Tories who flirted dangerously with Jacobitism. Walpole and the Pelhams maintained that the differences between Whig and Tory were still valid. As long as the spectre of Jacobitism lingered to haunt the Hanoverian succession the Whig-Tory distinction could be exploited by the Court Whigs to stigmatize their opponents as a threat to the constitution. This allowed them not only to proscribe the Tories, but to denounce all opposition as verging on treason.[26]

The attempt to combat this kind of propaganda began with the work of those radical Whigs Trenchard and Gordon in the early 1720s. They warned their readers that the survival of Whig-Tory differences simply played into the hands of a corrupt Court. While the potential opposition to the Court remained hopelessly divided over issues which were no longer relevant, the ministers were surreptitiously subverting the constitution. The terms Whig and Tory were now mere labels and no longer explained the significant political divisions within the nation. As long as men were deluded by the mere appearance of Whig-Tory divisions the Court, having appropriated the Whig label for itself, would have a free hand in undermining the liberties of the subject. Those Whigs now in office were as arbitrary as any Tory, whereas the former Tories, who were now in opposition, were prepared to defend the ancient constitution. This being the case, it was better to ally with an honest Tory than to support a corrupt Whig. The true distinction to be made was between the party of power and the party of liberty. It was therefore the duty of the Country to restrict the power of the Court in order to safeguard the liberties of the subject.[27]

Bolingbroke developed much the same case during his long campaign against Walpole and his political methods. He confessed that there had once been considerable differences between Whigs and Tories, but, he claimed, these had been steadily eroded since the Revolution settlement which had been achieved by the united endeavours of both parties. It was now absurd for men to insist that a contest between Whig and Tory still prevailed:

177

the proper and real distinction of the two parties expired at this era [of the Revolution], and ... although their ghosts have continued to haunt and divide us so many years afterwards, yet there neither is, nor can be any divisions of parties at this time, reconcilable with common sense, and common honesty, among those who are come on the stage under the present constitution, except those of churchmen and dissenters, those of court and country.[28]

Former Whigs and Tories must now unite in defence of the constitution and in opposition to the handful of Jacobites on the one hand and the Court's mercenary detachments on the other. The only people anxious to retain the old, obsolescent party labels were the factious spirits around Walpole who were interested solely in promoting their own selfish ambitions at the expense of the whole nation. To allow the Court to divide its potential opponents along the old Whig-Tory lines was to risk the destruction of the constitution by the insidious means of corruption. The threat to liberty was so great that party distinctions and personal differences must be superseded by the patriotic desire to serve the national interest. A corrupt faction at Court must be opposed by a patriotic Country party representing the interests of the whole nation.

The central political question, in Bolingbroke's view, was not whether those in office called themselves Whigs or Tories. The nation had to ask itself whether a corrupt faction or the honest representatives of the Country interest should govern. Walpole and his hirelings were not upholding Whig principles, as they claimed, but were feathering their own nests by ignoble methods and dishonest means. In their selfish pursuit of wealth and power they were ready to sacrifice the constitution and the liberties of the subject. All men of goodwill must combine to save the nation from arbitrary power acting under the cloak of Revolution principles. To triumph over such a well entrenched Court faction the opposition had to rise above the narrow spirit of Whig and Tory. The defence of the constitution required all patriots to combine in a Country party. Liberty could only be preserved by union, industry and perseverance.[29]

Perhaps the greatest problem that confronted those who endeavoured to forge an effective Country party was the overwhelming conviction of many country gentlemen that formed opposition was at best factious and at worst treasonable. Such men prided themselves on their personal independence and integrity, and proclaimed their allegiance to the Crown. They might regard themselves as 'patriots' and as defenders of the national interest, but they were not prepared to combine into a permanent opposition against the king's ministers. They proclaimed their readiness to oppose 'measures not men'; to resist specific policies but not to conspire to bring down particular ministers. To them opposition was by definition partial. They could not see how it could claim to represent the interests of the whole nation or how it could preserve the harmony essential to mixed government and the balance needed to sustain the constitution. Opposition suggested the pursuit of private interest instead of the general good. A formed and regular opposition would have to abandon sober reason and independent judgement in favour of blind hostility. Base passions would triumph over individual conscience. A formed opposition only served to delude honest men into helping the ambitious and the factious into power or into aiding evil men to bring down the constitution. The actions of such opposition spokesmen as Pulteney and Bolingbroke convinced some country gentlemen that to support such men was to serve either unrestrained ambition or the cause of the Pretender. Furthermore, it could be argued that the much-vaunted constitution itself could not stand if opposition became a regular practice. To oppose the king's ministers in a sustained campaign was to constrain the legitimate powers of the Crown. The balance of the constitution could not survive if the House of Commons continually limited the Crown's prerogatives.

To combat these attitudes the Country spokesmen had to stress that the opposition which they sought to promote was neither factious nor treasonable. On the contrary, it was essential to the preservation of the constitution. This required them to emphasize that the Court was waging a conspiracy against the constitution and that the authority of the Government was being continually augmented by the extension of corrupt practices. Since the threat to the balanced constitution came from the exorbitant power of the Court, the Country opposition was justified in uniting to defend the cause of liberty. Individuals acting alone had little chance of successfully resisting the growth of arbitrary power. Liberty could not be preserved unless all honest men combined. A free government could be sustained only if there were free expression and free association. A government which could silence and divide its critics would find nothing to hinder its actions, however arbitrary or tyrannical. On the other hand, a Government which was faced by vigilant patriots, who would criticize and publicize every abuse of power, might be kept within the bounds assigned to it by the constitution. Freedom of expression was essential to the preservation of the constitution because by this means alone could the friends of liberty encourage a healthy distrust of power. Any attempts to silence these critics or to render reasonable opposition suspect suggested that the Court must have something to hide.[30]

The Country opposition was described by its spokesmen as being free of the taint of faction or treason. It was a loyal opposition which would preserve the constitution and protect the king from the dangerous advice of evil ministers. It was not attached to the personal interests of particular men, but was designed to make those in power operate within the principles of the constitution. The Country opposition would not condemn ordinary errors of judgement or seek to restrict the legitimate powers of the Crown. It would act only to preserve the constitution from being subverted by arbitrary power or corrupt practices. Far from being a threat to political stability, the Country opposition in fact preserved it by acting as the watchdog of the constitution:

> There ought to be especially in parliament, a spirit of enquiry; or, if you will, a spirit of jealousy ... I hope there always will be a party willing to inspect the actions, and ready to control the councils of every administration ... it encourages the people not to submit tamely to any grievances, it keeps up that life and freedom which ought to appear in parliamentary debates, and it serves to restrain men in power from the vain imagination that they may do what they will ... From all this it follows that men of the strictest honour, men of the greatest loyalty to their prince, men who have the utmost zeal for the constitution, may engage in such an opposition ... without any selfish views of profit, or personal prejudice against those whom they oppose.[31]

The Country spokesmen did not agree on the question of whether a formed opposition needed to be a permanent feature of political life. Bolingbroke did not appear to envisage and certainly did not advocate a permanent opposition. He appeared to believe that the Country opposition would eventually defeat the Court and put honest men into power. These new ministers would then remedy abuses and make a formed opposition to them quite unnecessary. A new Country opposition would be necessary only when corrupt or arbitrary ministers were once more in office.[32] Many 'Patriots' of the 1740s and 1750s proclaimed that they were against all corruption, but refused to join any formed opposition, even one which could be described as Country in its ideology. Some men did argue however that a formed opposition should be a permanent feature of parliamentary life. In their opinion the best security for a free state was the continuous scrutiny of government actions. Only by this means could the balanced constitution be sustained. The authority of the Court must be balanced by the liberty of the Country to oppose its abuse of power. Both David Hume and Bernard Mandeville perceived that the balanced constitution might require the existence of a permanent opposition party, but the case was put best by Edward Spelman. He stated quite explicitly that in all free states the contest of parties was the best support of liberty. The public reaped great benefits from a vigilant opposition which kept ministers on their guard and prevented the uncontrolled growth of Court power.[33]

Clearly, by the mid-eighteenth century, the case for a formed opposition had been explicitly stated. There was still no sophisticated analysis of what constituted a party or how the conflict of parties could be of benefit to the nation as a whole; but the recognition of the merits of a formed Country opposition which would act as the watchdog of the constitution had gained considerable ground.[34] A majority of the political nation was not completely convinced that such an opposition was entirely justified because, if it had been, the Court Whigs would have suffered many more defeats. Yet enough men were convinced to make the Country interest a force to be reckoned with and to make Country ideology an important curb on the ambitions of the Court.

3   The Country Platform

Perhaps only during the opposition to Robert Walpole in the reign of George II was there anything approaching an organized Country party. Nonetheless, throughout the early Hanoverian period there was an identifiable Country platform which appealed to a substantial minority in Parliament and to a growing body of opinion out-of-doors. It is possible to detect two major planks in this platform. In the first place there were repeated attacks on the exorbitant power of the Court and on the threat which this posed to the balanced constitution. These criticisms focused on the size of the standing army and on the money and patronage at the disposal of the Court. Second, the Country interest showed a readiness to question the sovereign authority of the legislature. Since it was feared that Parliament was becoming dependent upon the Court, the Country interest suggested that limits should be placed on the actions which this dependent legislature could take. This led to suggestions that either the constitution or the people could place limits on the actions of the legislature. With regard to the latter the Country opposition supported a number of measures, ranging from the right of electors to instruct their Member how to vote to tentative suggestions for parliamentary reform, aimed at making the House of Commons more responsive to the people and hence less dependent upon the Court.

The primary concern of the Country interest was the fear that the Court had acquired the means of corrupting the constitution. The most obvious political weapon at the disposal of the Crown was the vast patronage system created by the financial revolution, the large standing army and the administrative machinery needed to manage the national debt and supply the armed forces. Crown patronage not only built up a powerful Court and Treasury party in Parliament, but encouraged many more men to consider selling their political independence in return for places and profit. The Court was approaching the position where it might be able to count upon a subservient majority in Parliament to support its every action. To prevent this happening the Country spokesmen attacked what they regarded as the fraudulent practices of the moneyed men and what they condemned as the corrupt links between the financial interest and the Court. They pressed for parliamentary inquiries into a number of financial scandals; they criticized the privileges granted to the Bank of England and the great chartered corporations; they condemned the infamous practices of stockjobbers and the frauds in the customs service; and they insisted that the national debt should be reduced as quickly as possible before the whole nation was massively in debt to a handful of financiers.[35]

The ill-gotten gains of the stockjobbers and financiers excited considerable jealousy, but the real concern of the Country interest was that the Court's patronage was now so great that it could undermine the independence of the House of Commons. The bitter attack on Walpole's Excise bill of 1733 was motivated far more by the political than by the financial and commercial consequences of this measure. The Country spokesmen protested that the scheme would need a veritable army of excise officers to operate it. These excisemen would threaten the liberties of the subject because of their power to search shops and homes for goods on which the proper excise duty had not been levied. Worse still, in some constituencies the excise-men would be so numerous that they would be able to sway any election in favour of the Court candidates and hence increase the number of the Court's dependents in the House of Commons. Thus, William Pulteney elevated the debate on the Excise bill from a discussion on an administrative reform to an investigation of the nature of the danger facing the constitution:

It is certain, that the liberties of this country depend upon the freedom of our elections for members of parliament; our parliament, especially the representatives of the people in parliament assembled, are designed for, and generally have been a check upon those, who are employed in the executive part of our government, to have such an influence over most of the elections in the kingdom, as to get any person chosen they please to recommend, they will then always have a majority of their own creatures in every House of Commons, and from such representatives what can the people expect? Can it be expected, that such a House of Commons will ever be any check upon those in power, or that they will find fault with the conduct of the most rapacious, the most tyrannical ministers that may hereafter be employed by the crown?[36]

This reaction may have been due to a grossly exaggerated view of the consequences of the Excise bill, but it was typical of the Country response to the increased patronage at the disposal of the Crown. Bolingbroke, in attacking the Court's close links with the great chartered corporations, asked: 'Have not all Ministries an influence over those companies, and may they not by their means be able to influence the elections of every city and trading town in England? And what may we not justly apprehend from such a formidable, complicated power; which may, one time or other, destroy our happy constitution?'[37] When, in 1732, Walpole endeavoured to revive the salt duty Sir William Wyndham, a leading spokesman for the Country Tories, claimed that most country gentlemen would rather pay a higher land tax than suffer the political consequences of such a duty:

One of the great evils of a salt tax, I may say the greatest, because it strikes at our constitution, is the great number of officers which must be employed in collecting that small branch of the revenue. These officers are all named by the crown, and being spread all over the country, must have a great influence in elections: This, Sir, throws a greater power into the hands of the crown, than is in my opinion con-

o

sistent with the liberties of this nation. If it ever shall happen to be the misfortune of this nation, to have a set of wicked ministers in the administration, and a weak or an ambitious prince upon the throne, the great number of officers employed in collecting the revenue, must be the most dangerous consequence to the very being of our happy constitution; and therefore we ought not, upon any pretence whatsoever to increase the number of those slaves of an administration.[38]

In order to curb the Court's ability to influence elections and to create dependents in Parliament by the skilful distribution of places and pensions, the Country interest advocated measures which would reduce the political consequences of the Crown's patronage. Country spokesmen regularly introduced bills which would disfranchise revenue officers and which would exclude many categories of placemen and pensioners from sitting in the House of Commons. None of these bills was passed, but their defeat simply confirmed the fears of the Country opposition that the Court was successfully undermining the constitution. An independent Parliament, it was firmly believed, would have passed such popular and patriotic measures. Edwin Sandys, the most consistent promoter of Place bills, warned the Commons that placemen had lost their independence and their integrity. The constitution could not be safe in their hands:

I am convinced, there will always be a great number, by far, I fear, the greatest number, who will rather vote according to the directions of the prime minister for the time being, than run the risk of being turned out of the lucrative post or office he then holds at the pleasure of the crown: and if ever a majority of this House should happen to be composed of such men, I am sure it will become as contemptible as ever the senate of Rome was, after it became the political tool of their arbitrary and tyrannical emperors.[39]

While patronage and corruption were regarded as the main agencies of the Court's ability to undermine the independence of Parliament and hence encroach upon the liberty of the subject, the Country interest was almost as alarmed at the threat posed by the existence of a standing mercenary army which was at the disposal of the Court. Taking up many of the arguments voiced in the late 1690s, the Country opposition under the first two Georges stressed that a large standing army might subvert a free constitution by either direct or indirect means. The most direct way was for the executive to use armed force against the representative institutions of the people. This policy had been followed by Cromwell and James II, by the tyrants of the ancient world and by modern absolute rulers.

Although the Country opposition did not dare suggest that the Court had any such desire to destroy the nation's liberties by force, they could suggest that foreign mercenaries could not always be trusted, that even British troops were often recruited from the worst subjects and might easily be suborned, and that under other rulers and ministers such mercenary forces might not be kept in their place. No government which claimed to be ruling a free people and which remained loyal to the Whig principle of the subject's right of resistance could possibly justify the existence of a large standing army in time of peace.[40]

The attack on the standing army as a tool of absolute rulers and as inimical to Revolution principles was a particularly telling charge to level at Whig administrations which claimed to stand by the principle of government by consent. It was also a popular move with Country opinion inside and outside Parliament because the standing army was a focal point for many fears and grievances. A professional army, with large contingents of foreign mercenaries, was not only expensive to maintain in peace-time, but its existence was linked to the hatred of burdensome continental wars which required heavy taxes on land and trade to sustain them. Such land wars aroused popular xenophobia and led to widespread criticism of the way British money and blood was being spilled to defend 'the despicable electorate' of Hanover. The Country opposition and public opinion at large undoubtedly favoured naval wars which could lead to commercial and colonial gains rather than land wars which appeared to serve no British interest and which were an enormous drain on the nation's financial and human resources. Typical of such views were the comments of Velters Cornewall, a Country Tory, who advised the House of Commons:

As we are by nature disjoined from the continent, and surrounded with the sea; it ought always to be a maxim with us, to have as little to do as possible with the disputes among the princes of Europe . . . soon after the Revolution we . . . began to interfere in disputes upon the continent, more than we ought to have done: we then began to load our commerce and manufactures with taxes of various kinds; and we then began to supply the public expense by running in debt yearly, instead of raising the necessary sums within the year . . . we make ourselves the Don Quixote of Europe . . . if we leave the continent to take care of itself and confine ourselves to a naval war; we may carry it on with little expense and great success against France and Spain.[41]

This was precisely the Country attitude which William Pitt was able to rally to his support in his attacks on the foreign policy of the Duke of Newcastle in the 1740s and 1750s.

The expense associated with the raising and employing of a large standing army enabled the Court to extend its influence and patronage. The raising of loans for war, the officering of the army, and the awarding of contracts to feed and supply the troops all combined to give the Court political influence over important sections of the political nation. This in turn strengthened the Court and Treasury party in the House of Commons, weakened the independence of the Lower House, and therefore threatened to subvert the balanced constitution. Thus the standing army, like the national debt, was seen as one of the chief means of strengthening the power and influence of the Court and weakening the independence of the House of Commons. Furthermore, the Country opposition claimed, a nation which hired mercenaries to defend its liberties and its interests was corrupting its own public spirit. The spirit of patriotism, the *virtù* needed in a free state, could not survive when men forgot their primary duty of being prepared to fight and even to die for their liberty. A nation which lost the willingness to defend itself had already surrendered its right to remain free. A free people must bear arms and be able to use them in its own defence. A citizen who was not also a soldier had alienated a vital part of his freedom and had lost his independence. It was therefore a vital plank in the Country platform to urge the disbandment of a mercenary standing army and to place the nation's defence in the hands of a citizen militia. Such a militia would not only be cheaper, but would renew the public spirit of the citizens in its ranks. It would make it impossible for a tyrant to use force against liberty, it would reduce the patronage at the disposal of the Court, and it would make the people responsible for the defence of their own freedom. Once again these were the Country attitudes which William Pitt harnessed to carry through a reorganization of the militia in the later 1750s.[42]

The preoccupation of the Country opposition with the fear that Crown patronage was corrupting Parliament and hence destroying its independence led to various attempts to control what Parliament could do. One approach was to suggest that Parliament did not possess unlimited authority but was restricted by the fundamental laws of the constitution. Thus certain statutes were unconstitutional because they were contrary to the very nature of the ancient con-

186

stitution under which Englishmen had lived for centuries. During the great debate on the Septennial bill in 1716 the Country opposition insisted that the repeal of the Triennial Act was contrary to the constitutional settlement made after the Revolution and was thereby invalid. William Shippen protested that Parliament could not act in such a manner as to betray those who elected it. The people had not elected it to amend or abrogate parts of the constitution and hence the Septennial bill was a breach of the trust which the people had placed in their representatives.

Though it is a received maxim in civil science, that the supreme legislature cannot be bound; yet an implied exception must be understood, viz. that it is restrained from subverting the foundations on which it stands; and that it ought not, on any pretence whatsoever, to touch or alter those laws, which are so far admitted into the constitution, as to become essential parts of it.[43]

The same argument was repeated by the Country opposition to the Peerage bill of 1719, the size of the standing army, the Heritable Jurisdictions Act of 1747 and the Jewish Naturalization Act of 1753.[44] The doctrine of legislative sovereignty did not therefore go entirely unchallenged, but it always carried the day against its critics.

The sovereignty of Parliament was too attractive and serviceable a constitutional doctrine to be rejected. Even the Country opposition was aware of its usefulness in combating the twin dangers of absolute monarchy and popular sovereignty. It was only occasionally that the Country opposition endeavoured to limit the exercise of the legislature's sovereign authority. The Country opposition was clearly reluctant to challenge the power of Parliament by endorsing the notion of popular sovereignty because this would lead inexorably to a democratic constitution. Yet, in order to prevent the Court undermining the independence of Parliament, the Country spokesmen had perforce to appeal to the electorate to return representatives who would not become clients of the Court. Thus in resisting the corrupting effect of Crown patronage the Country opposition was driven to adopt policies which required the support of the nation outside the parliamentary classes. These policies were designed to purify the existing constitution, but they were imperceptibly extended by some commentators until they came near to advocating reforms of the constitution which would alter its nature. The Country opposition in Parliament stopped short of advocating fundamental constitutional changes, but their policies undoubtedly suggested the way to achieve such reforms.

Since the Country opposition was unable to secure Place and Pension bills which would reduce the Court's influence over the House of Commons, it tried to devise means of ensuring the return of more independent country gentlemen. It urged the electors to vote for independent gentlemen of large estates who could be trusted to preserve their integrity instead of becoming clients of a corrupt administration. In order to reduce the cost of elections and to make it easier for country gentlemen to challenge courtiers at the polls, the opposition regularly campaigned for the repeal of the Septennial Act. Triennial or even annual general elections would, the Country opposition claimed, enable independent gentlemen to bear the costs and would make it easier for the electorate to reject representatives who sold out to the Court as soon as they were elected. The Septennial Act made it worthwhile for mercenary wretches to spend small fortunes on corrupting the electors because the outlay could be recouped during seven years' service to the Court. More regular elections would reduce both the value and the cost of a seat and would therefore increase the likelihood of a contested election and also give the voters frequent opportunities to repent of their decision to elect the hirelings of the Court.[45]

These attempts were chiefly designed to increase the influence of country gentlemen in the Commons rather than to put more political power in the hands of the electorate. Nonetheless, they would have made those Members of Parliament who represented the larger constituencies more responsive to the electors who returned them to Parliament. The Country opposition may have been concerned only to protect the Commons against 'the corrupting influence of the Court, but frequent elections would almost certainly have increased the influence of the electorate over their representatives. Such an unintended and largely unforeseen consequence certainly did result from the repeated efforts of the Country opposition to persuade constituencies to instruct their Members of Parliament to vote against the Court. In 1733, 1738–9, 1741–2, 1753 and 1756 the Country opposition deliberately organized nationwide campaigns to encourage constituencies to draw up instructions to be sent to Members of Parliament in order to push their representatives into opposition to the Court. In 1733, for example, 'instructions' came in from fifty-four constituencies across the length and breadth of

England and Wales. This was a remarkably well organized extra-parliamentary campaign to persuade Members of Parliament to defeat the Excise bill and it helped persuade Walpole to drop this controversial measure. In 1742 'instructions' were sent up to Parliament from no less than forty-five constituencies urging their Members to press for a strict inquiry into Walpole's past conduct and to vote for a Triennial Act and Place and Pension bills. In 1756 some seventeen counties and nineteen boroughs sent 'instructions' condemning the loss of Minorca. This particular campaign undoubtedly helped to bring down Newcastle and it eventually brought William Pitt into office.[46]

It has been suggested that the 'instruction' campaigns did not indicate grass-roots support for Country measures, but merely the ability of the leaders of the opposition in Parliament to organize their own constituencies in support of those policies which they planned to put forward in any case.[47] It is certainly true that the Country leaders deliberately encouraged these campaigns and that their own constituencies were often ready to oblige them with 'instructions'. It is also clear that most Country spokesmen had no desire to encourage the radical doctrine of popular sovereignty. They cherished the independence of Members of Parliament and did not wish to escape the influence of the Court only to fall under the power of the people. They did not wish to subordinate the House of Commons to the electorate. One supporter of 'instructions' warned: 'I do not affirm this privilege of instructing our members should be so literally understood, as that nothing can be legally enacted in parliament, but what the people must first have instructed.'[48] Nonetheless, there is evidence to suggest that these campaigns were not fully orchestrated by the Country leaders within Parliament. Even though they might not have been initiated from within Parliament they began to encourage the electors to take their power seriously. The campaign of 1733 was not even initiated by the Country opposition in Parliament. The first suggestion of instructing Members of Parliament to oppose the Excise bill came from the commercial community of London. This independent initiative earned the approval of *The Craftsman* which went on to urge that it should be imitated: 'This is a laudable precedent for reviving the antient practice of the people in giving their representatives Instructions upon all great occasions, and we hope it will be followed by every county and borough in England.'[49] Not all the fifty-four

counties and towns which sent instructions in 1733 were in fact
represented by supporters of the Country opposition. Some were
represented by supporters of the Court and the instructions were
clearly the outcome of some spontaneous local hostility to the Excise
bill. Moreover, it is clear that the Country campaign was designed
to stir up widespread popular indignation and that, in seeking to do
so, some Country spokesmen went out of their way in their press
campaigns to advise the electors of their rights. Bolingbroke and
the Earl of Marchmont reminded the electorate that they only delegated their authority to their Members of Parliament, but did not
surrender it absolutely. Since Members held their power in trust
from the people, they were not free to sacrifice the liberties of the
people.[50] One contributor to *Common Sense* went much further. His
astonishing claim actually conceded that the people were ultimately
sovereign and could legitimately decide to exercise their power
directly: 'If the electors of England should declare to you (the
Parliament), you shall not make laws for us, we will do it for ourselves: will any man say, they may not do it.'[51] This claim was
probably designed to warn the Court of the alarming consequences
of its actions rather than to advocate that the people should take
power into their own hands. Nonetheless, the 'instruction' campaigns, especially when urged by the Press rather than by Country
Members directly, were a step in the direction of extra-parliamentary
organization. The electorate was beginning to learn to organize itself
and no longer relied entirely on the Country spokesmen in Parliament to provide a lead in organizing opposition to the Court.

In addition to their regular campaigns for frequent elections and
for the right of voters to instruct their representatives the Country
opposition occasionally suggested the need for some measure of
parliamentary reform. Yet once again the aim of such proposals was
to secure the return of more independent country gentlemen rather
than to give the electorate a greater influence over Parliament. Most
proposals suggested that rotten or pocket boroughs, with their handful of corruptible voters, should lose their representation in Parliament. On the other hand, the counties and the larger towns should
be given an increased representation. One Country Tory protested
at the way knights of the shire were 'outnumbered, 3 to 1, by a new
sett of representatives of little beggarly burroughs; which being
poor, are exposed to be venal, and having little or nothing of their
own, have yet by the majority of their attorneys, the sovereign

disposal of the property and liberty of the freeholders of England.'[52] *The Craftsman* twice condemned rotten boroughs and urged a redistribution of seats according to the contributions which counties and towns made to the land tax.[53] *Common Sense* asked why small rotten boroughs should return two Members of Parliament when each Member for Yorkshire represented ten thousand freeholders and when such towns as Birmingham and Leeds had no representation at all; and why Cornwall should return over forty Members when Middlesex, London and Westminster together, with twenty times the population and one hundred times the wealth, only elected eight representatives.[54] The *Westminster Journal* advocated a radical redistribution of seats according to population and wealth. It suggested that the decaying boroughs of the south-west should be grouped together to form larger constituencies, while Birmingham, Manchester and Halifax should be directly represented in Parliament.[55] Other Country spokesmen advocated the secret ballot as a means of eliminating corrupt tactics in elections.[56] It is highly significant, however, that nearly all the Country proposals concentrated on a redistribution of seats in order to improve the system of representation and hence to secure a more independent House of Commons. There was no campaign for an extension of the franchise which would have increased the power of the people and made Members of Parliament more responsive to the wider electorates that returned them to Parliament. The ownership of sufficient property to render a man independent was still seen as the ideal basis for the franchise. The Country opposition was as preoccupied as the Court Whigs with the need to resist any threat to the political, social and economic privileges of the parliamentary classes.

While Country ideology was not concerned with the political rights of the labouring masses it did have an important impact on public opinion beyond the restricted confines of Westminster and the narrow limits of the ruling oligarchy in the country. This was owing to the nature of the Country platform and its successful dissemination across the length and breadth of the kingdom. The constant criticism of the Court and the perpetual stream of propaganda about the need to defend the constitution from corruption undoubtedly helped to create a Country attitude among many of the middling and lesser property-owners. At certain critical junctures the Country ideology influenced and encouraged widespread hostility to the Court. This was certainly the case over the South Sea

191

Bubble of 1720, the Excise bill of 1733, the outbreak of war with Spain in 1739, the Jewish Naturalization Act of 1753 and the loss of Minorca in 1756. Country attitudes were widely disseminated in the provinces by such popular opposition journals as *The Craftsman* and *Common Sense* and by the many local newspapers which showed antipathy towards the Court. Several provincial newspapers not only attacked specific actions of the Government, but openly campaigned for such Country measures as more frequent elections and Place and Pension bills. With the successful distribution of opposition propaganda throughout the nation and with the continuous expansion of the provincial Press a steady diet of Country ideology was fed to the middling and lesser property-owners. While this large readership was not yet prepared to demand an extensive reform of Parliament which would alter the balance of power in the nation, it did show a willingness to defend the liberties of Englishmen. It was still firmly attached to Britain's much-vaunted balanced constitution, but it suspected that the Court's corrupt methods would destroy this constitution unless the nation was prepared to defend its freedom. In creating an attitude of mind and a climate of opinion, if not in securing power, the Country ideology achieved considerable success.[57]

Part Three

RADICAL AND CONSERVATIVE

(From the 1760s to the 1790s)

6

The Development of a Radical Ideology

From the 1760s the campaign of criticism levelled at the Whig establishment began to undergo significant changes. Under the first two Hanoverians the Country opposition had been directed from within Parliament or by spokesmen with very close ties with the parliamentary classes. Starting with the Wilkite petitioning movement of the late 1760s however the most important and vociferous opposition to the establishment was extra-parliamentary and was directed by men who were not among the parliamentary élite even when, like Wilkes himself, they sometimes sat in Parliament. This shift from an opposition campaign largely waged by men sitting in Parliament to one conducted by men outside the governing élite was accompanied by a significant change in the arguments and demands put forward by the critics of the establishment. Whereas the Country opposition had largely accepted the virtues of the constitutional settlement achieved by the Glorious Revolution and merely complained that a corrupt Court was not allowing the balanced constitution to operate as it should, the more radical extra-parliamentary opposition began to claim that the Revolution settlement was far from satisfactory and to assert that liberty could only be secured if there were a major reform of the whole system of representation. Instead, therefore, of concentrating on reducing the Court's influence over the House of Commons as the best means of preserving the balanced constitution, the radicals began to press for an extensive measure of parliamentary reform that would make the House of Commons more responsive to public opinion at large. The radicals showed far less interest in Place and Pension bills, although these were still desired. They eventually aimed instead to extend the franchise to all adult males.

This shift from a Country platform to a radical plan of parliamentary reform occurred gradually and there was never a clear dividing line between the two approaches. Indeed many of those who

195

eventually ended up campaigning for parliamentary reform had started out by suggesting ways of limiting the Court's influence over the House of Commons. Although the change from Country to radical is highly significant it does not necessarily imply a sharp division between the two forms of opposition to the Whig establishment. The radicals clearly accepted and endorsed the Country claim that the constitution was threatened more by Crown patronage than by the royal prerogative. Their hostility to the Court stemmed from their conviction that the ministers were able to dominate Parliament by the cunning distribution of Crown patronage. Like Trenchard and Gordon, Bolingbroke and Pulteney, the radicals protested that the balanced constitution had been undermined and that Parliament had become subservient to the Court. The constitution continued to exist in mere form only:

The people still continue to elect persons to represent them in Parliament; but as soon as such persons are elected, and sent there, they become the creatures of the Crown, and can no more be said to represent the people of England, than the people of Turkey. It will be said, that this is the people's own faults, and that they are themselves corrupt, and take money of the persons they elect for their votes, and in some degree it is so, but yet the great fault is in the Crown; for if the Crown did not bribe the Members when elected, they would not bribe the people to elect them.

Let ministerial persons say what they will, the source of all corruption is in the Crown; there the grand evil lies, and unless the people can find out some method of stopping that source of bribery, it matters very little whom they chuse to represent them. The power of the Crown hath been increased within this last century to such a degree, as is absolutely incompatible with the rights and liberties of the people.[1]

This could have been written in 1733 rather than in 1773. Where the radical campaign did mark an advance on the Country platform was in recognizing that Parliament was too corrupt to reform itself and in deciding that only the efforts of the people could secure a genuine reform of the constitution. Place and Pension bills – now usually referred to as 'economical reform' – were only a first step. An extension of the franchise and a redistribution of seats would be more effective in making the House of Commons the representative assembly of the whole people.

The methods by which the Country spokesmen appealed for support and justified their opposition to the Court were also adopted and imitated by the radicals. The exploitation of the power of the Press and the skilful dissemination of propaganda were copied from earlier campaigns against the Court. The radicals repeated Country arguments about the need to defend the freedom of the Press and they insisted that honest men had the right, indeed the duty, to unite together in order to curb the power of the Court. Opposition was clearly justified when the aim was not the pursuit of narrow self-interest, but the defence of freedom.[2] Where the radicals made a significant advance on the campaigns launched by the Country interest was in leading and organizing their opposition out-of-doors rather than from within the confines of Westminster. The Country opposition wanted the electorate merely to endorse its policies. The radicals wanted the people, even those at present without the vote, to exert a powerful influence over Parliament.

Before explaining in some detail the reform platform which the radicals developed between the 1760s and the 1780s two major causes of this important ideological change have to be examined. In the first place it is essential to understand the intellectual process by which the radicals came to abandon traditional Country remedies in favour of an extensive measure of parliamentary reform. It is also necessary to see how new divisive issues created political pressures which led to the development of extra-parliamentary organizations that adopted the reform of Parliament as the central plank in their political platform.

1 The Ideological Origins of Radicalism

The development of political ideology from a Country to a radical platform was the consequence of both further intellectual inquiry into the rights of man and the external pressures created by the appearance of new divisive issues. The second factor was probably the more significant cause of the development of a radical ideology, but it is also important to see how the ideas of the later eighteenth-century reformers were rooted in and were indeed an intellectual extension of Revolution principles, the rational optimism of the Enlightenment and the traditional belief in English liberties.

The radicals of the later eighteenth century were greatly influenced by the more liberal Whig principles which had been kept alive by some of the spokesmen of the Country opposition since the 1680s. They appealed to the contract theory and the right of resistance and they laid claims to both the natural rights of all men and the traditional liberties of Englishmen. In other words the radicals absorbed the political theories of John Locke, Algernon Sidney, James Tyrrell and other Whig propagandists of the late seventeenth century, but interpreted them in a straightforward, literal fashion. The radicals were convinced that God had created all men equal or so nearly equal in their physical attributes and mental capacities that there could be no justification for a gross disparity in their civil and political rights. They therefore claimed that no man had any legitimate right to govern any other without his consent. The natural equality of man was never entirely lost even after the creation of civil society, for men deliberately erected political institutions in order to protect their natural rights to life, liberty and property. These natural rights could only be preserved if they were converted into civil liberties. Unlike Locke, the radicals claimed that these liberties must include a positive role in the political life of the community. A man's liberty could not be guaranteed unless he had a say in the political decisions which would affect him and his family.[3]

In order to justify this claim the radicals insisted that all legitimate governments were erected by an explicit or implied contract to which all men assented. Since such governments were originally the creation of the people they must remain subordinate to the sovereign authority of the people. The power of any government was limited to the pursuit of the natural ends of society, namely the preservation of each individual's right to his life, liberty and property. The exercise of tyrannical or arbitrary power was illegitimate and could therefore be resisted by force if necessary. In civil society subjects gave up their individual right to act as judge in their own cause, but nevertheless civil government was an artificial creation designed to preserve certain rights and these natural rights could never be totally surrendered. All governments had the duty to translate man's natural rights to life, liberty and property into civil rights or civil liberties which would be protected by the law of the land. Sovereign authority remained with the people and hence all governments were limited in their power and their freedom of action. If those in authority betrayed the great trust which the people had reposed in them, then this abuse of power could be forcibly resisted. Joseph Priestley, stating this Lockean principle in unequivocal language, maintained that:

if the abuse of government should, at any time, be great and manifest; if the servants of the people, forgetting their masters, and their masters' interest, should pursue a separate one of their own; if instead of considering that they are made for the people, they should consider the people as made for them; if the oppressions and violations of right should be great, flagrant, and universally resented; if the tyrannical governors should have no friends but a few sycophants, who had long preyed upon the vitals of their fellow citizens, and who might be expected to desert a government, whenever their interests should be detached from it: if, in consequence of these circumstances, it should become manifest, that the risque, which would be run in attempting a revolution would be trifling, and the evils which might be apprehended from it were far less than these which were actually suffered, and which were daily increasing; in the name of God, I ask, what principles are those, which ought to restrain an injured and insulted people from asserting their natural rights, and from changing, or even punishing their governors, that is their servants, who had abused their trust; or from altering the whole form of their government, if it appeared to be a structure so liable to abuse?[4]

While Priestley and other radicals stressed that a revolution should not be lightly undertaken, their concept of the right of resistance went much further than that of Locke. The radicals insisted that the people retained their sovereign authority in civil society and could exercise it to bring down, reform or amend a government which did not serve their interests. Locke had made the people subject to a sovereign legislature until civil society was dissolved. The radicals allowed the people to sit in judgement on their governors, to dissolve a government which did not protect their political rights, and erect a new one in its place.[5]

The emphasis by the radicals on natural rights and on the sovereignty of the people derived from their firm belief in a pre-political state of nature which had existed before the creation of civil society. Locke's concept of the state of nature had been highly abstract and he had made no effort to prove that it had once existed at any particular time or place. The radicals of the later eighteenth century were convinced that the state of nature had been man's actual historical condition before the creation of artificial government. Locke, though to a lesser extent than Hobbes, had recognized the potential instability of the state of nature and had shown the advantages to be gained by the creation of civil society. Many radicals, however, had a utopian vision of an ideal state of nature. Preoccupied with the corruption of the present age and yet convinced of the natural benevolence and essential goodness of the vast majority of men, the radicals often contrasted the simple virtues of the primitive past with the refined vices of present-day society. The Country opposition had repeatedly warned the nation of the threat of corruption and the dangers of luxury. The radicals clearly absorbed this message. Even though many of them also managed, somewhat inconsistently, to proclaim their faith in a future of unlimited progress (provided of course the world followed their advice), the radicals often longed to return to a more natural state. In the golden age of the state of nature most men had been benevolent and well disposed and their reason had been clear and uncorrupted. The natural rights and liberties of man had been recognized by almost all men, but unfortunately the ambitious designs of a few evil and powerful men had forced mankind to establish institutions of civil government. These institutions in their turn often fell under the domination of cunning and ambitious men, who continually attempted to restrict the natural rights and liberty of all men. It was therefore suggested that if men were desirous of recovering their natural rights they ought to return to the state of nature. Richard Price, while advocating the need to live 'according to nature', advised men : 'Let us then value more the simplicity and innocence of a life agreeable to nature; and learn to consider nothing as savageness but malevolence, ignorance and wickedness. The order of nature is wise and kind. In a conformity to it consists health and long life; grace, honour, virtue and joy. But nature turned out of its way will always punish.' Thomas Paine carefully distinguished between society which he regarded as natural to man and therefore beneficial and government which he regarded as an artificial creation and therefore often a danger to liberty : 'Society in every state is a blessing, but government, even in its best state, is but a necessary evil; in its worst state an intolerable one.'[6]

This tendency to idealize the primitive past was not quite so marked among the radicals as the confidence which they expressed in future progress. Most radicals absorbed the Enlightenment's optimistic vision of man's future. Joseph Priestley in fact explicitly rejected the notion of an idyllic state of nature in the past, but he had every confidence in the future. He insisted that improvements would be made not by a return to nature, but by a conscious effort to take advantage of art and education. 'Idleness, treachery and cruelty are predominant in all uncivilized countries; notwithstanding the boasts which the poets make of the *golden age* of mankind, before the creation of empires.'[7] Priestley was convinced that there was no limit to the rational faculties of man and he insisted that as these were developed so society would progress towards perfection. Mankind was capable of unlimited improvement and, provided men pursued rational knowledge, there was every prospect of future happiness: 'Thus, whatever was the beginning of this world, the end will be glorious and paradisaical, beyond what our imagination can now conceive.'[8] Richard Price believed that man's cultivated reason would direct him towards the pursuit of virtue and the rejection of vice. Man would learn how to control his emotions and his reason would lead him to choose to do what he ought to do and to abstain from doing what he knew to be wrong. Although he acknowledged that man's intellectual powers were still in their infancy, Price was confident that ignorance and evil could be overcome and that there was no limit to the future moral, political and scientific progress of man.[9]

The rational optimism of many radicals convinced them that the political institutions of civil society were capable of continuous improvement if only men applied rational criteria. Since man could improve his lot and control his environment through the exercise of reason, he could re-shape his political institutions according to rational first principles. With reason as the guide and education as the means of enlightening all men it was but a matter of time before men abandoned the pernicious practices of the past and adopted a more rational system of government. Progress would not be limited to scientific knowledge, but would extend to man's ability to control his political institutions. William Enfield claimed: 'In the natural course of human affairs, which is evidently progressive, it must soon come to pass that enlarged views and a liberal spirit will obliterate the maxims of ignorance and bigotry, and that every institution which is manifestly contrary to sound policy and inconsistent with that share of natural or political liberty to which every member of a free state is entitled, will be abolished.'[10] The radicals in general were confident that the future belonged to them and that their political opponents appealed to the worst, most irrational passions in men. The full potential of human reason however could only be achieved if men were granted the fullest possible political liberty. Only a free man could exercise his reason properly and choose the right course of action. Further progress therefore depended upon men being granted greater liberty and so reason led men to demand political reforms in order to improve every aspect of human existence.

The influence of enlightened thought and the appeal to reason were most apparent in the campaign for religious toleration, but they also helped to extend the demand for freedom of conscience into pressure for radical political reforms. Those who campaigned most vigorously for religious toleration and especially for the repeal of the Test and Corporation Acts were often also at the forefront of the movement for political reform.[11] Moreover, a study of the literature disseminated in the campaign for religious toleration shows how the arguments used to defend the claim for liberty of conscience developed into demands for the inalienable rights of man. In their early attacks on the Test and Corporation Acts the Dissenters concentrated on defending their own practices and insisted that they posed no threat to the established order in Church and State. Since they did not demand power but only wished to be left in peace, the Dissenters could claim that there was no justification for the penal laws which persecuted them for their religious opinions. When they renewed their campaign against the Test and Corporation Acts in the later eighteenth century however the rational Dissenters laid greater stress on their right to intellectual liberty. Andrew Kippis argued that the Dissenters should concentrate on denying the right of either the Established Church or the State to exercise authority over the individual's right to judge for himself in matters of conscience.[12] David Williams, another radical dissenting minister, pressed his fellow Dissenters to change the basis of their demand for toleration:

Your very existence depends on your changing the reason of your dissent, which used to be an opinion of superior orthodoxy and superior purity of faith and worship, for another which is the only rational and justifiable reason of dissent—the inalienable and universal right of private judgment, and the necessity of an unrestrained enquiry and freedom of debate and discussion on all subjects of knowledge, morality, and religion. This may be called *Intellectual Liberty*. This should be the general reason of dissent.[13]

On this claim to religious liberty as a natural and inalienable right the Dissenters began to base their campaign for radical political reforms. They first argued that there was no reason why their religious opinions should incur civil penalties. Men should be judged by their actions and not by their thoughts. Moreover, since God had created all men equal and all men had an equal right to worship God according to the dictates of their own conscience, then the State had no right to impose civil disabilities on particular religious opinions. Liberty of conscience rested on both the rights of man and the law of God. Any government which created civil penalties for private opinions was therefore guilty of an act of injustice and was infringing the natural rights of the subject. This emphasis on religious liberty as a natural right which ought to be protected by every civil government led to demands for a complete secularization of civil and political rights. Churches should be free and voluntary institutions in a free state and no peculiar civil or political privileges should be attached to particular religious opinions. All men should enjoy the benefits of free citizens.

In shifting the demand for toleration on to a political rather than a theological plane the radical Dissenters were led to demand religious freedom as a natural right which ought to be enshrined as a civil right. This in turn encouraged demands for political liberty as the best means of securing and preserving religious freedom. Joseph Priestley, for example, regarded religious liberty as the most important natural and civil right of man, but he insisted that in order to safeguard this right all men must have a political voice.[14] Richard Price was even more determined to combine the demand for religious freedom with the campaign for political reform. In his view both religious and political liberty were derived from God and were therefore universal and inalienable rights. All men must be free both to judge and to legislate for themselves in matters of religion:

As no people can lawfully surrender their religious liberty by giving up their right of judging for themselves in religion or by allowing any human being to prescribe to them what faith they shall embrace or what code of worship they shall practice, so neither can any civil societies lawfully surrender their civil liberty by giving up to any extraneous jurisdiction their power of legislating for themselves and disposing of their property. Such a cession being inconsistent with the inalienable rights of human nature would either bind not at all, or bind only the individual who made it. This is a blessing which no generation of men can give up for another, and which, when lost, a people have always a right to resume.[15]

The radicals did not find inspiration only in the rationalist elements in Locke, the Enlightenment and the campaign for religious toleration. They also gave a radical twist to the traditional empirical arguments about the practical virtues of the ancient constitution and the actual dangers which threatened it. Their attitude to the ancient constitution reflected their more radical view of politics. In asserting that the English had enjoyed considerable political liberty before the Norman Conquest they did not merely claim that Parliament was an Anglo-Saxon institution, but maintained that in the distant past all men had possessed the vote and sovereignty had resided in the people.[16] In their interpretation of the history of the ancient constitution since the Conquest the radicals also went beyond the Country and even the neo-Harringtonian view of the earlier Commonwealthmen. Both the Country spokesmen and the Commonwealthmen had argued that the ancient constitution had been restored by the Revolution settlement, but, unfortunately, since then the corrupting effects of Crown patronage had started to undermine the restored constitution. The radicals of the later eighteenth century made much of the ancient constitution and of the Norman yoke thesis which argued that an arbitrary monarchy had set about destroying the immemorial liberties of the people ever since 1066, but they rejected the confident claim that the Glorious Revolution had fully restored the constitution. Catharine Macaulay, for example, insisted that the men who made the Revolution settlement had accepted half-measures because they were convinced that radical reforms were impossible or undesirable:

In all the great struggles for liberty, true reformation was never by the ruling party either effected or even intended; the flaws in the Revolution system left full opportunity for private interest to exclude public good, and for a faction, who by their struggles against former tyrannies had gained the confidence of the people, to create, against the liberties and the virtue of their trusting countrymen, the undermining and irresistible hydra, court influence, in the room of the more terrifying, yet less formidable monster, prerogative ... It would be invidious and even tedious to detail the moral and political evils which took place at the Revolution, and which had been regularly, and with little alteration systematically carried on from that period to the present times.[17]

Tobias Smollett, before he came to support the Court, made the same general point in his *History of England*. After acknowledging that the Revolution destroyed indefeasible hereditary right, he went

204

on to claim that not enough had been done in 1689 to limit the power of the Crown or to secure the liberties of the subject. This was largely because the Revolution settlement was made in haste by a defective parliament. It ought to have been made by the whole people or by the representatives of the whole people after they had been clearly instructed by their constituents.[18] A contributor to the *London Evening Post* was even more critical of the conservative nature of the Revolution settlement:

The Revolution ... was not so favourable to the liberties of the subject. It appears to me the most extraordinary, and I am afraid fatal event, that could possibly have happened to us. I consider it as the best opportunity we ever had of establishing our liberties upon a permanent foundation; and by neglecting, or at least not properly attending to it, the source of all the disorders which we have of late unhappily experienced.[19]

2 The Appearance of New Issues

The growth of radicalism from the 1760s owed a great deal to the intellectual development of political arguments which had long been part of the armoury of the Country opposition. Nonetheless, although it is possible to see radical ideas stemming naturally from this heritage of arguments in defence of liberty, it is difficult to imagine that the demand for parliamentary reform would have developed so rapidly and so strongly without the pressure created by changing political circumstances and the appearance of new divisive issues. A book on ideology and political argument is not the place for a detailed treatment of those social and economic changes which created an urban and commercial middle class that was increasingly interested in gaining political representation or for an examination of the practical means by which support for parliamentary reform was mobilized. Clearly the growth of London and other urban centres, the increased wealth of the middling ranks in society, the steady expansion of the Press, and the mobilization of public opinion through clubs and extra-parliamentary organizations, all helped to create pressure for a reform of the system of representation. These developments have been treated at length by those historians primarily interested in radical *activity*.[20] In a chapter devoted to radical *ideas* it is legitimate to concentrate on those new factors which caused a significant shift in the political arguments being used by the critics of the existing constitution. Social and economic changes may have created an audience more receptive to radical ideas, the development of the Press and extra-parliamentary organizations may have made it easier to transmit these ideas and to mobilize support for them, but it was the political crises associated with the policies of George III, the career of John Wilkes and the disputes with the American colonies that encouraged the critics of the Court Whigs to demand a radical reform of Parliament.

For the last fifty years, ever since the publication of the major works of Sir Lewis Namier in the late 1920s, many historians have attacked and destroyed the old myth that George III wished to increase the power of the Crown by unconstitutional means. Nonetheless, while it is true that the fear engendered by the actions of George III and his ministers was largely unfounded and certainly exaggerated, there can be no doubt that a considerable body of contemporary opinion did come to believe that the balanced constitution and the liberties of the subject were in serious danger. Alarm may have been deliberately spread both by politicians who resented their exclusion from office and by John Wilkes to further his own ends, but the policies of successive administrations over the Middlesex election case and over the handling of disputes with the American colonies convinced those with no particular axe to grind that there was indeed an insidious design against the liberties of the subject. It is possible, but inadvisable, to dismiss the arguments of the Rockingham Whigs and of John Wilkes as entirely self-serving. It is not possible however to dismiss the widespread support for these arguments. When a substantial body of opinion is genuinely convinced that there is a threat to the constitution, this belief may be unfounded but the myth still has the force of reality. Whether the threat to the constitution was myth or reality the manifesto issued by the Constitutional Society of Birmingham in October 1774 makes it abundantly clear that many beyond the narrow bounds of Parliament and Westminster did believe that liberty was in danger:

The sudden and unexpected dissolution of Parliament, while it plainly indicates the deep laid system of despotism of an arbitrary and unprincipled Administration, ought to rouse every friend to civil and religious liberty, to an active and vigorous defence of those sacred privileges which are the glorious inheritance of Freeborn Englishmen. — There is no time left for hesitation and delay; the designs of the Ministry are openly avowed in their late dangerous political manoeuvre. Every individual is called upon by the most sacred tie of liberty, to oppose, and endeavour to avert the diabolical machinations of a set of men, whose success must inevitably terminate in the utter subversion of freedom and independence; and in the entire extirpation of the best and noblest privileges of Englishmen.[21]

Such alarm about the policies of George III and his ministers was first expressed by the Newcastle-Rockingham Whigs in the 1760s. They resented the way the new king had pushed out of power and place many of the Old Corps of Whigs who had dominated politics under the first two Georges. Their exclusion from office and their hostility to the Earl of Bute, the 'King's Friends' and others who had usurped their position at Court, may explain why the Rocking-ham Whigs went into opposition; but it is still necessary to examine the political arguments which such sophisticated and experienced politicians used to justify their actions. During their long years in the wilderness the Rockingham Whigs developed a political plat-form designed to curb the power of the Crown and to justify an organized opposition party.[22]

The Rockingham Whigs believed that they had been excluded from power by malign influences at Court, but, as an essentially aristocratic group of large landowners, they wished to curb the power of the Crown without making Parliament more democratic by appealing to the people. They therefore adopted the Country pro-gramme of reducing the excessive influence of the Crown rather than endorsing any radical plan to reform Parliament. In supporting Place and Pension bills, or what was now called 'economical reform', the Rockingham Whigs were echoing the traditional Country claim that 'the power of the crown, almost dead and rotten as prerogative, has grown up anew, with much more strength, and far less odium, under the name of influence'.[23] In 1779 Edmund Burke, when intro-ducing a measure of economical reform, warned the House of Commons:

I cannot help observing, that the whole of our grievances are owing to the fatal and overgrown influence of the crown; and that influence itself to our enormous prodigality ... Formerly the operation of the influence of the crown only touched the higher orders of the state. It has now insinuated itself into every creek and crany in the kingdom ... What is worst of all, it soon surrounds a supine and inattentive minister with the designing, confident, rapacious, and unprincipled men of all descriptions.[24]

207

This particular motion was defeated, but, in April 1780, the Rockingham Whigs did secure considerable support for Dunning's motion that 'the power of the crown has increased, is increasing, and ought to be diminished'. In 1782 several economical reforms, including bills introduced by Burke, Clerke and Crewe, were passed, though they had less impact on the influence of the Crown than the Rockingham Whigs had anticipated.[25]

In their efforts to hold together during many years in the political wilderness the Rockingham Whigs were driven to justify the legitimacy of an organized party in opposition to the Court. They came to realize that only an organized party held together by clear principles relating to public policy could hope to defeat ministers who had the full backing of the Court. Edmund Burke, much the most sophisticated political thinker in the Rockinghamite ranks, argued that party ought to be a persistent and enduring feature of politics since it was the best means of safeguarding the constitution: 'this country will never be well governed, until those who are connected by unanimity of sentiment hold the reins of power.'[26] Burke utterly rejected the claim that parties were by their nature subversive, though he did carefully distinguish between a bigoted, self-interested faction and a party which pursued clearly defined principles in order to serve the public good. In his view a legitimate party was 'a body of men united for promoting by their joint endeavours the national interest upon some particular principle in which they are all agreed'.[27] Only such a political connection, based on principles held in common, could successfully oppose a Court cabal which was threatening to subvert the constitution. In the opinion of the Rockinghamites party unity was clearly needed in the present circumstances in order to resist the Court's abuse of power, but Burke went further than the previous supporters of a Country party when he insisted that parties of principle ought to be an inherent part of a stable political order. He looked back to the Whig party of Anne's reign for his model of how men of principle should and could act in concert. Burke acknowledged that free men would always disagree with each other, but he believed that groups of men could coalesce around leading general principles of government. Thus, for Burke, party was not merely an opposition group acting as the watchdog of the constitution, but a body of men who would be prepared to act together in office. It would not cease to exist, like Bolingbroke's Country party, once it had brought down the ministerial faction in power. Instead, it would take office in order to carry through measures which were in accord with its general principles of government. An administration should therefore be dominated by the members of a party so that it would possess the coherence and strength necessary to carry through its policies.

Burke saw the Rockinghamite party as dedicated to the principles of the constitution and as committed to the defence of liberty. In his view its existence was essential to the preservation of the balanced constitution and the best guarantee of responsible government. If the political nation wished to defeat the cabal at Court it must rally to the party which would best defend the liberty of the subject:

If the reader believes that there really exists such a faction as I have described; a faction ruling by the private inclinations of a court, against the general sense of the people; and that this faction, whilst it pursues a scheme for undermining all the foundations of our freedom, weakens (for the present at least) all the powers of executory government, rendering us abroad contemptible, and at home distracted; he will believe also, that nothing but a firm combination of public men against this body, and that, too, supported by the hearty concurrence of the people at large can possibly get the better of it.[28]

The Rockinghamites never succeeded in achieving either of their major aims. Their measures of economical reform had little effect in reducing the patronage of the Crown and, as a party, they never matched the coherence and effectiveness of the Whig party of Anne's reign. Moreover, it is obvious that the Rockingham party was never committed to radical policies. Edmund Burke was quite right to claim, in retrospect, that it was an essentially aristocratic party which was ready to oppose the Court but had no desire to endorse popular sovereignty: 'I understood it to be a party, in its composition and its principles, connected with the solid, permanent long possessed property of the country; a party, which by a temper derived from that species of property, and affording a security to it, was attached to the antient tried usages of the kingdom, a party therefore essentially constructed upon a ground plot of stability and independence; a party therefore equally removed from servile court compliances, and from popular levity, presumption, and precipitation.'[29] Nonetheless, the Rockingham party did help indirectly to further the development of a radical ideology. Their own policies may have been limited to economical reform, but, as members of the ruling classes, their hostility to the Court convinced public opinion out-of-doors that there must indeed be a conspiracy against the constitution and a threat to the liberties of the subject. The Rockinghamites may not themselves have wanted parliamentary reform, but they did establish links with and indirectly foster the activities of first Wilkes and the Petitioning movement and then Christopher Wyvill and the Association movement. The Rockinghamites hoped to control public opinion and to give a lead to opposition elements outside Parliament, but their propaganda campaign against the Court and their justification of organized opposition helped to create radical extra-parliamentary forces which escaped from their control and went far beyond their limited demands for reform. As an aristocratic party of substantial property-owners the Rockinghamites lent respectability to all those who were prepared to organize opposition in order to defeat the policies of the Court and to safeguard the liberties of the subject.

John Wilkes, even more than the Rockinghamites, has been accused of deliberately exploiting every opportunity in order to further his own career. Yet such charges should not obscure the fact that his contribution to the development of British radicalism was considerable. Wilkes showed great skill in bringing fundamental issues before a mass audience and in opening up political debate to the people at large. His ability to rally support not only in the metropolis but on a nationwide basis helped to create the first important extra-parliamentary organization and to establish the first radical society, the Supporters of the Bill of Rights. This achievement not only brought many more people into the arena of political debate, but also led to an elaboration and extension of more radical ideas. Wilkes himself was not a sophisticated political thinker and his own commitment to radical reform may have been suspect, but he did focus popular attention on the notion of liberty more successfully than many more committed radicals and the involvement of the people in politics did lead to more radical demands for reform. With unrivalled skill Wilkes managed to raise his disputes with the authorities into issues concerning fundamental constitutional principles. After his famous attack on George III in no. 45 of *The North Briton,* the ministry used a general warrant, which made no mention of Wilkes by name, in order to search for any incriminating evidence to use against him. Wilkes exploited this situation to condemn the authorities for abusing their power simply in order to silence an effective critic. In his speech in the Court of Common Pleas, on 6 May 1763, Wilkes managed to give his personal plight a more general application: 'The LIBERTY of all peers and gentlemen, and, what touches me more sensibly, of all the middling and inferior class of the people, which stands most in need of protection, is in my case this day to be finally decided upon: a question of such importance as to determine at once, whether ENGLISH LIBERTY be a reality or a shadow.'[30]

The issues raised by the Middlesex election case enabled Wilkes to condemn the Government for an even more alarming abuse of its power. After Wilkes was elected for Middlesex in 1768 the administration persuaded the House of Commons to expel him for seditious libel because he had published an accusation that the authorities were over-eager to employ troops to put down any popular disturbance by his supporters. Wilkes had never been convicted in a court of law of this particular charge and yet a majority of the House of Commons was still prepared to expel him even after he had been twice re-elected for Middlesex in February and March 1769. This decision gave Wilkes the opportunity of warning the public of the serious constitutional implications of his expulsion: 'If ministers can once usurp the power of declaring who *shall not* be your representative, the next step is very easy, and will follow speedily. It is that of telling you whom you *shall* send to Parliament, and then the boasted Constitution of England will be entirely torn up by the roots.'[31] This prediction was rapidly borne out by events. In a third by-election, in April 1769, the Court put up a candidate, Colonel Henry Luttrell, who was roundly defeated by Wilkes at the polls. Not content with expelling Wilkes yet again, the Commons voted that Luttrell, the defeated candidate, had in fact been duly elected as Member for Middlesex. The critics of the Court, both in and out of Parliament, could now claim that a major constitutional issue and not merely the personal career of Wilkes was involved. The repeated attempts to expel Wilkes could be regarded as an assault on the freedom of the electorate to choose its own representatives. The decision to accept Luttrell as the duly elected member for Middlesex was an even greater threat to the rights of the voters because Parliament not only decided who the electorate could not choose but did the choosing for it. It meant that, in principle, a ministerial majority could control who might be allowed to sit in Parliament and would be in a position to fill the House of Commons with those who would support the Government of the day. Electoral freedom would be a hollow mockery and the Court could simply co-opt members to fill any vacancy. Of course the ministry had no intention of pursuing such an extreme policy, but the principles upon which it acted in seeking to expel Wilkes and to seat Luttrell in his place would, if accepted, threaten the whole existing system of representation.

The Middlesex election case therefore raised a constitutional issue which far transcended the personal fate of Wilkes and which proved capable of focusing more sharply than before the ill-defined discontent of those who were dissatisfied with the oligarchical nature of eighteenth-century politics. The opposition to the Court was no longer based so heavily on hostility to Crown patronage, but was founded on the fear that representative government might be destroyed and the will of the electorate frustrated by the actions of an arbitrary administration. Economical reform might no longer be enough to safeguard the liberties of the subject. Something would have to be done to make Parliament more willing to accept the will of the electorate and perhaps of the people at large. Wilkes was able to exploit these issues in order to appeal to many of those who were unrepresented in Parliament and perhaps even more to those who had the vote but could not break the aristocratic stranglehold on the majority of the constituencies. The Middlesex election case posed the question of whether Parliament was meant to be the political forum for a narrow and propertied oligarchy which could control the electorate or whether Parliament was designed to represent the interests of a much wider public. Was Parliament erected so that the few could manipulate the many and mislead them into thinking that their interests were represented or was Parliament established by the people in order to serve the interests of the whole community? Such were the profound political questions raised by the Middlesex election case and brilliantly exploited by Wilkes and his radical allies.

Wilkes was a great propagandist who recognized the value of publicity, knew how to appeal to a wide public and exploited every available political medium.[32] Throughout his long campaign against the authorities he put himself forward as the personification of liberty and posed as an ordinary, honest citizen engaged in a struggle with arbitrary and potentially tyrannical ministers. He claimed that he represented the middling and inferior class of people and that, if they joined him in opposition to the Court, together they could break down the politics of oligarchy and privilege. Unlike his opponents he did not despise the lower orders of society, but encouraged them to see themselves as engaged in a great struggle against the abuses of constituted authority. Even humble citizens had a responsibility to participate in the battle with corruption and arbitrary power. He taught the people that success or failure could not depend on his efforts alone. He could do nothing without the active involvement of ordinary people. Wilkes told his supporters that they had the power to influence political events: 'In proving yourselves enemies to ministerial persecution, the eyes of the whole world are upon you, as the first and firmest defenders of public liberty.'[33] By appealing to the public at large however Wilkes did not simply disseminate his ideas to a wider audience, but brought public opinion into the political debate. The activity of the people began to influence parliamentary politics and the ideas which appealed to the people were more likely to be radical than Country.

Wilkes and such metropolitan allies as John Horne Tooke, John Sawbridge, William Beckford, James Townsend and Richard Oliver not only came to dominate London politics, but organized a nationwide extra-parliamentary campaign to reverse the decision in the Middlesex election case. Once the activity of the electorate began to have an impact on the political debate, the actual nature of political argument became more radical. The more radical Wilkites soon formed the Society for the Supporters of the Bill of Rights which was the first political club of the eighteenth century to combine the old Country platform with the demand for parliamentary reform. The Society was not content simply to campaign against general warrants or to insist that Wilkes must be allowed to take his seat in Parliament. It went beyond this to urge the electorate to instruct their Members of Parliament to vote not only for Place bills and shorter parliaments, but to press for more radical reforms such as the abolition of rotten boroughs, the redistribution of seats and the secret ballot.[34] Wilkes, at first, did not endorse such radical proposals and strove to restrict the Society to the causes which involved him personally. Yet, by June 1771, in order to compete with those former allies who had seceded from the Society, Wilkes was ready to encourage the Society to resolve:

that every person who shall from henceforth be a candidate to serve as a member in this or any future parliament shall be required to sign a declaration and confirm it upon oath, that in case he is elected he will vote for and use his utmost endeavours to procure a Bill to shorten the duration of parliaments and to reduce the number of placemen and pensioners in the House of Commons and also to endeavour to obtain a more fair and equal representation of the people, and that he will promote to the utmost of his power an enquiry into the causes of the troubles and discontents which have distracted this country during the present reign.[35]

When Wilkes was finally able to take his seat in Parliament, after the general election of 1774, he pursued several radical causes. He endorsed the American claim to independence and he resolutely opposed the war with America. He also spoke up several times for the extension of religious toleration. Moreover, he lent his name and his popularity to the first motion for a significant reform of Parliament. On 21 March 1776 he attacked the irregularities of the electoral system which allowed the over-representation of certain areas and the under-representation of others. Not content with a redistribution of seats, however, he proposed a radical extension of the franchise. This was the first time in the eighteenth century that Parliament heard a plea for a more democratic franchise.[36] Wilkes had already brought the people into active politics out-of-doors, but now he wished to give them a more important role in deciding the composition of the House of Commons itself.

The Wilkite movement is chiefly remembered as the first effective extra-parliamentary organization, but it also advanced radical ideology in two important ways: it established the first political society to campaign for a reform of Parliament and it immersed a mass audience in its own political ideas and in the political debate in general. The fundamental political issues raised by the quarrel with the American colonies played an even greater role in advancing the argument for parliamentary reform and in propagating these radical ideas to a wide audience. The policies of successive ministries in the 1760s and 1770s provoked the colonies into a successful resistance based on such radical notions as the sovereignty of the people and 'no taxation without representation'. At home the colonial dispute raised profound ideological questions about the very nature of the British constitution and it led to the demand for a radical reform of Parliament.[37] A number of politicians and propagandists on both sides of the Atlantic were convinced that there was an intimate connection between the Government's oppression of the colonies and its hostility towards Wilkes. The cause of liberty in both Britain and the colonies was seen as threatened by a corrupt and oppressive

Court. The opposition in Britain claimed that the Government's policy towards the colonies was clear evidence of a malign campaign against the liberty of the subject. The Court was manifestly engaged in a conspiracy against the constitution and was using the colonies as a testing ground for its policy of subverting liberty. If successful in the colonies it would redouble its attacks on liberty at home. At the same time, the colonial debate on sovereignty and representation greatly encouraged the opponents of the Court in Britain to abandon the traditional Country platform in favour of a more radical reform programme.

The first fundamental issue raised by the dispute with the American colonies was over the nature and location of sovereignty. Successive British administrations had the support of the overwhelming majority in Parliament for their assertion that the sovereign authority over the whole empire was the joint legislature of King, Lords and Commons. A minority within Parliament and an increasingly vocal section of public opinion out-of-doors feared that the doctrine of parliamentary sovereignty would lead to imperial disaster and could even be used to subvert the liberties of the subject within Britain. Edmund Burke and the Rockingham Whigs were ready to endorse the *theoretical* sovereignty of Parliament. Indeed, they passed the Declaratory Act of 1766 which enshrined the doctrine, but they urged that this sovereign authority should not be exercised in such a manner that it would unduly antagonize those subject to it. Prudential considerations ought to make the legislature cautious about how it exercised its sovereign authority. Burke pointed out that even within Britain it might not be advisable to exercise an authority which would only provoke fierce resistance: 'The completeness of the legislative authority of parliament *over this kingdom* is not questioned; and yet many things indubitably included in the abstract idea of that power, and which carry no absolute injustice in themselves, yet being contrary to the opinions and feelings of the people, can as little be exercised, as if parliament in that case had been possessed of no right at all.'[38] The Elder Pitt and his allies were prepared to accept that Parliament could legislate for the colonies, but could not tax them without their consent. They separated legislation from taxation and denied that Parliament could tax those, like the colonists, who were not represented in the House of Commons. The defence of property and the doctrine of 'no taxation without representation' were such fundamental tenets of Whig

215

ideology that they could not be abandoned even to safeguard the sovereignty of Parliament. William Pitt himself insisted that 'there is no such idea in this constitution, as a supreme power operating upon property.'[39] His ally Lord Camden was even more convinced that there were higher authorities than that of Parliament: 'The sovereign authority, the omnipotence of the legislature, my lords, is a favourite doctrine, but there are some things they cannot do. They cannot enact any thing against the divine law, and may forfeit their right. They cannot take away any man's private property without making him a compensation.'[40] Later he declared:

My position is this ... taxation and representation are inseparable; — this position is founded on the laws of nature; it is more, it is itself an eternal law of nature; for whatever is a man's own, is absolutely his own; no man hath a right to take it from him without his consent, either expressed by himself or [his] representative; whoever attempts to do it, attempts an injury; whoever does it, commits a robbery; he throws down and destroys the distinction between liberty and slavery. Taxation and representation are coeval with and essential to this constitution.[41]

Most Whigs had always been concerned with the need to defend property and they had regarded the doctrine of parliamentary sovereignty as a constitutional means of achieving this end. When this doctrine was used to subvert the rights of property some Whigs believed that they must demonstrate the limits of Parliament's authority. These Whigs were clearly reverting to Locke's position: in normal matters of government the legislature was sovereign, but it could not gravely infringe a man's right to his life, liberty and property. The fundamental principles of the constitution and the natural rights of man were ultimately superior to the authority of Parliament. Subjects had the right to resist tyranny even when it was parliamentary tyranny.[42] The Earl of Abingdon insisted that the authority of Parliament was bound by the principles of the constitution. Parliament had the power to act only when it was endeavouring to preserve the people's right to their life, liberty and property.[43] John Wilkes came even closer to the doctrine of the sovereignty of the people:

Government is only a trust from the people for their good, and in several instances, so far from possessing an absolute power, we [Parliament] ought to acknowledge, that we have no power at all. I will never admit arbitrary power to be lodged in any man, or body of men. Many

216

things are so closely woven in with the constitution, like the trial by jury, that they cannot be separated, unless the body of the people expressly declare otherwise, after free and full consideration. There are fundamental inalienable rights, land-marks of the constitution, which cannot be removed. The omnipotence of parliament therefore, which is contended for, seems to me a false and dangerous doctrine.[44]

As we shall see below, the radical Whigs outside Parliament, who consistently supported the American colonists in their opposition to successive British administrations, utterly condemned the doctrine of parliamentary sovereignty and, like the Americans, discussed the virtues of popular sovereignty, a written constitution and a system of judicial review.

The American stand on the principle of 'no taxation without representation' also had a profound effect on political argument within Britain. The Country opposition to the Court had long campaigned for Place and Pension bills and for shorter parliaments as the best means of securing a purer House of Commons. The political debate in the colonies however stimulated more radical demands for a reform of the system of representation. At first a redistribution of seats was the principal radical demand, but increasingly an extension of the franchise became the hallmark of a radical. Serious discussion of this type of franchise reform only appeared in Britain after it had first been raised in the American colonies.[45] The Americans themselves had adopted the Whig principle that a man's property could not be forfeited without his consent and turned it into the more radical notion that subjects could not be taxed unless their elected representatives had voted for such an impost. This led them to conclude that any man who could be expected to pay taxes should have the vote. This was clearly a radical extension of the Lockean principle that a man's property could not be alienated without his consent. Conservative opinion within Britain rejected such a democratic claim and yet insisted that, while few men possessed the right to vote, all men in Britain were virtually represented in Parliament. Members of Parliament represented the whole nation, not merely those who voted for them, and they were charged with the defence of the public good, not simply with the protection of the interests of their constituents.

This defence of the prevailing system of representation did not convince the American colonists. They denounced virtual representation as a specious defence of oligarchy. They pointed out that the

217

more the British defended the existing system of representation the more in fact they exposed its blatant absurdities and injustices. The British admission that millions of Britons were not directly represented was regarded as the clearest proof of the inadequate and inequitable nature of the electoral system. The argument that non-voters were virtually represented was condemned as an attempt to cloak an aristocratic system of government with the trappings of liberty. Moreover the sorry state of representation in Britain was no excuse for taxing the colonists without their consent. While conservative opinion in Britain positively relished pointing out the peculiarities of the electoral system the Americans concentrated on how this system undermined the principle of no taxation without representation. The American argument was so clear and rational that it could hardly fail to have an impact on liberal and radical opinion within Britain. Lord Camden ridiculed the notion of virtual representation and endorsed the principle that taxpayers should be directly represented.[46] By 1770 his ally William Pitt, now Earl of Chatham, was suggesting that rotten boroughs should lose their representation in Parliament and the seats should be transferred to the more populous counties.[47] Radical opinion outside Parliament moved both faster and farther. By linking taxation and representation the radicals were able to demand not only a redistribution of seats but a major extension of the franchise. The radicals protested that many small boroughs did not really deserve representation in Parliament, whereas several wealthy and populous constituencies merited increased representation and towns such as Manchester, Birmingham and Sheffield needed to be represented for the first time. Even more significant was the radical claim that the principle of no taxation without representation must mean that not only freeholders but all male householders and perhaps even all men should have the vote. After all labourers and servants paid indirect taxes on much that they consumed. By tying representation to taxation rather than to property the radicals were therefore able eventually to justify universal manhood suffrage.

The dispute with the American colonies not only sparked off a major debate on the fundamental issues of sovereignty and representation, but also encouraged the widespread dissemination of radical ideas and the creation of societies and extra-parliamentary organizations whose political platforms reflected the important shift from Country to radical demands. By 1779 the Government's disastrous

218

handling of the war with America had provoked expressions of dissatisfaction throughout the country. A group of Yorkshire free-holders, led by Christopher Wyvill, began to organize a nationwide movement to mobilize the electorate in order to challenge the domination of politics by an aristocratic oligarchy. Seeking support from associations of freeholders all over the country Wyvill and the Yorkshire Association campaigned on a platform which com-bined the traditional Country demands for economical reform and shorter parliaments with the more radical demand for a reform of the system of representation. Wyvill, the inspiration and driving force behind the Association movement, was concerned not only to eliminate the means of patronage and corruption available to the Court but to increase the influence which the freeholders could exert over the House of Commons.[48] By March 1780 deputies from twelve counties and four boroughs had adopted a three-point programme which incorporated economical reform, annual parliaments and a change in the system of representation by the creation of an addi-tional one hundred county seats.

A majority of associations, dominated as most of them were by substantial freeholders, refused to endorse even the proposal for a moderate measure of parliamentary reform. Their preoccupation with Country remedies did not prevent other associations however from adopting much more radical proposals for changes in the system of representation. The associations established in the metro-politan region soon went beyond the demands of Wyvill. Former Wilkite activists such as Brass Crosby, Thomas Brand Hollis, John Sawbridge and James Townsend were joined by such radical theorists as John Jebb and James Burgh in a campaign for a number of electoral reforms including annual parliaments, the secret ballot, a redistribution of seats and an extension of the franchise. The report of the subcommittee of the Westminster Association, drawn up on 27 May 1780, declared that: 'An equal representation of the people in the great council of the nation, annual elections, and the universal right of suffrage, appear so reasonable to the natural feelings of mankind, that no sophistry can elude the force of the arguments which are urged in their favour; and they are rights of so transcendent a nature, that, in opposition to the claim of the people to their enjoyment, the longest period of prescription is pleaded in vain.'[49] At about the same time several radical theorists, including John Jebb, John Cartwright, Granville Sharp and Capel

Lofft, formed the Society for Constitutional Information as a means of disseminating political propaganda in favour of a genuinely radical reform of Parliament. Although it co-operated with the Association movement the Society advanced much more radical proposals for reform. The leading metropolitan radicals were prepared to advance the most sweeping measures of parliamentary reform, including annual elections, equal electoral districts, secret ballot, abolition of property qualifications for Members of Parliament, payment of Members of Parliament, and universal manhood suffrage.[50] These same six points were to be endorsed by the Chartists sixty years later and were to remain the platform for parliamentary reformers throughout the nineteenth century. They clearly had no chance however of being accepted by the parliamentary classes of the late eighteenth century and yet as early as June 1780 these radical proposals were in fact put before the House of Lords by the Duke of Richmond.[51] The motion was defeated without a division, but clearly the most radical ideas on parliamentary reform had now become the subject of political debate. The nature of political argument had changed drastically between 1760 and 1780. The reform of Parliament had become the central issue dividing the supporters and the opponents of the existing political system. Although no reform bill was passed by Parliament until 1832, the younger William Pitt attempted to promote a modest redistribution of seats in 1783 and again in 1785, while Charles James Fox and his allies consistently campaigned for a moderate reform of Parliament throughout the 1790s. All these measures were easily defeated, but a significant minority within Parliament and a larger body of opinion out-of-doors were no longer convinced that liberty was safe under the existing constitution. The reform of Parliament was seen by these men as the only means of preserving the virtues of mixed government and of making the House of Commons more responsive to the nation at large.

3 The Radical Platform

By 1780 demands for political reform had reached a wider audience and had advanced well beyond the traditional remedies of the Country opposition. The metropolitan radicals and the rational Dissenters, though clearly in a minority, were advancing the six-point programme of parliamentary reform that was to be endorsed by the People's Charter of 1838. These radical proposals provoked a conservative reaction in defence of the existing constitution, but they also encouraged such moderate reformers as Christopher Wyvill and a minority even within Parliament to recognize that at least some measure of parliamentary reform was essential. The more liberal elements in Parliament, from the Chathamites and Rockingham Whigs through the Younger Pitt to Charles James Fox and his supporters, had steadily shifted their ground from traditional Patriot and Country remedies, which concentrated on economical reform, to more radical proposals which envisaged changes in both the distribution of seats and the franchise. The traditional Country ideology was gradually abandoned in favour of a reform of Parliament that would strengthen the democratic element in the constitution.

The traditional Country proposals did not disappear and indeed they remained an essential plank in the Association platform, but they were steadily superseded in importance by plans which would alter the composition of the House of Commons and make its members more responsive to the opinions of the nation at large. The constitution, according to the radicals, was so palpably corrupt that it could not be purified by measures of economical reform. An alteration in the system of representation was necessary in order to ensure that Members of Parliament accurately reflected the interests and wishes of the electorate and remained dependent on the people rather than on the Court. The Country ideal had been an independent House of Commons, free from the corruption of the Court and the instructions of the people. The radicals appealed to a different concept of a pure House of Commons. They still wished to see it independent of the Court, but they wanted it to be representative of the people at large and more responsive to public opinion.

Thus, while the Country opposition was ready to assert that the authority of Parliament was not absolute and irresistible, but subject to such superior authorities as the law of God, the law of nature and the fundamental laws of the constitution, the radicals chose to lay much greater stress on the subordination of Parliament to the will of the sovereign people. William Jones and other radicals did retain the traditional argument that the authority of Parliament was limited by the principles of the constitution, but they went on to insist that these principles included the freedom of election and the preservation of equal political rights. They regarded the right of the people to choose their own representatives as the pre-eminent feature of the British constitution. This led them to claim that the legislature could not infringe this right without exceeding the authority delegated to it by the sovereign people.[52] Obadiah Hulme protested that the doctrine of parliamentary sovereignty conferred power on a narrow aristocratic élite. Such a doctrine threatened rather than preserved the liberty of the subject:

There is not a more dangerous doctrine can be adopted, in our state, than to admit that the legislative authority hath any right to alter, the first principles of our constitution, by acts of parliament. Upon this foundation, they may mould it into what shape they please; and, in the end, may make us slaves, by law ... Upon this principle, our constitution may be one thing today, and another thing tomorrow. It is this, or that, or any thing that our legislative authority, for the time being, shall think proper to make it. If so, they might, sometime or other make a law, to continue themselves for life, and enact, that no man shall be an elector, for a member of the house of commons, that is not possessed of an estate, in land, equal to that required, for a qualification of one of their own members; by which means, they would elect one another, and then the aristocracy would completely throw off all disguise: this seems to be the point, to which our constitution is verging; and, without great care, in all probability it will die, of an Act of Parliament, at last.[53]

Richard Price based his doctrine of popular sovereignty on the claim that civil government was established by an original contract to which all men had subscribed. Parliament therefore only possessed a delegated trust for ultimate sovereignty was retained by the people. The legislature could never rightfully employ the power which it held in trust to infringe the rights of the people to choose their own representatives freely and to instruct them how to act. In the last resort the people were still sovereign and could reclaim the power which they had conferred upon Parliament. 'If omnipotence can, with any sense, be ascribed to a legislature, it must be lodged where all legislative authority originates; that is, in the PEOPLE. For their sakes government is instituted; and their's is the only real omnipotence.'[54]

The radical critics of the doctrine of parliamentary sovereignty insisted that the ultimate authority in the State resided in the collective will of the people, but while most of their plans for reform would have made Parliament more representative of the people, they would not have put effective limits on the power which the legislature could actually exercise. Annual elections would enable the electorate to reject quite quickly any Member of Parliament who had lost the confidence of his constituents, the secret ballot would free the voters from any undue pressure from their social superiors, while a reform of the representation and the franchise would produce a House of Commons more representative of the nation at large. While these reforms might change the composition of Parliament they would not curb the power of the legislature or ensure that sovereignty lay with the people. Other reforms would be needed to achieve these objectives, but, unlike the Americans, the radicals in Britain failed to devise means of actually locating sovereignty with the people. The radicals did explore the idea that the electorate should have the right and should be ready to exercise the power of instructing their representatives in Parliament. The traditional Country use of instructions was designed to secure support in the constituencies for the actions of opposition leaders in Parliament. The radicals changed the emphasis and suggested that Members of Parliament should be the delegates of the people and should be ready to take their instructions from those who elected them. Some radicals even suggested that the electorate could impose tests upon the candidates standing in their constituencies so that they could discover where the candidates stood on certain issues before they cast their votes for them. The aim here was to commit candidates to the support of parliamentary reform and other measures which secured popular support.[55]

Major John Cartwright did once suggest that limits on the power of the legislature might be applied by a system of judicial review, by which a supreme court could be set up to decide whether Acts of Parliament were unconstitutional or not.[56] He never explored the idea any further and the scheme found little favour with other reformers. Jeremy Bentham did explore the idea, but did not support such a system because he feared that it would give too much power to judges who could not claim to be representative of the nation at large.[57] By the 1790s, under the influence of both American and French examples, the radicals were to take up the notion of a written constitution as the best means of limiting the authority of the legislature and enshrining the rights of the people. Before reaching this stage however some radicals had considered setting up a national convention which would allow the people to resume their sovereign rights and enable them to decide the best means of securing their constitutional liberties. James Burgh was convinced that the reform of Parliament could never be achieved by legislative means because too many Members were already corrupted by the Court. In his view reforms could only be achieved if the people reclaimed their sovereign authority by establishing a Grand National Association for Restoring the Constitution. This would be a national organization with both a central committee and local committees in every county. Though Burgh recognized that these committees were likely to be dominated by men of property he hoped that they would establish links with taxpayers in every parish. By such means the whole nation might be able to express its support for important constitutional changes.[58]

The nearest to a national organization designed to pressurize Parliament into accepting constitutional reform was the Association movement of 1779–80, though Wyvill himself deliberately disavowed any intention of creating a representative body which might be regarded as constitutionally superior to Parliament. Some of the metropolitan radicals however had no such inhibitions. John Jebb enlarged upon James Burgh's idea of a national association which would organize popular support for constitutional reforms and which might have the authority to dictate to Parliament and perhaps even supersede it. Jebb proposed that a body of delegates should be elected, with representatives returned from all the counties and leading towns in proportion to their population. These delegates would then be in a position to claim to speak for the whole nation and could therefore legitimately regard themselves as superior to Parliament. Since Parliament had no authority but that delegated to it by the people, then Parliament must accept the constitutional reforms put forward by this democratically elected body of delegates. Should it refuse to do so, these delegates would have the power to dissolve Parliament and to erect a new representative legislature elected on the basis of an equal, annual and universal franchise.[59] Although the Middlesex freeholders, to whom Jebb put his proposal, could not be persuaded to adopt such a revolutionary scheme, they did endorse the idea of a national association and the doctrine of popular sovereignty.

The notion that the people might remodel the constitution as they saw fit and that they might do this by electing a national convention which would supersede the authority of Parliament was the most radical proposal to emerge before the 1790s. The most typical demand of this first stage of British radicalism however was for the reform of Parliament. It was certainly this demand which most

224

clearly distinguished the radical platform from that of the Country party. All the important elements in the extra-parliamentary movements, including the Wilkites, the county associations, the metropolitan radicals and the rational Dissenters, eventually took up the cause of parliamentary reform as the chief means of preserving the liberties of the subject and safeguarding the constitution from the corrupt influence of the Court and of the aristocratic factions in Parliament. In the end their arguments were to convince the liberal minority within Parliament that a measure of electoral reform was essential. There was however no agreement on the extent to which Parliament should be reformed. Liberal opinion within Parliament and the moderate supporters of the Association movement were chiefly concerned to increase the representation of the counties and hence the political influence of the middling and lesser landowners. These reformers came nearest to supporting the old Country ideal of a House of Commons representing those who owned sufficient property to make themselves economically independent. Wyvill wanted a House of Commons freed of royal and aristocratic influence. He showed little concern for the unrepresented condition of the new manufacturing towns and he had no desire to give the vote to the labouring masses. In his view only men who possessed at least sufficient property to render them fit to exercise their right to vote freely and for the public good should be granted the suffrage. Since the masses were far too dependent on their masters and employers for their livelihood, they could not be trusted with the political rights of an active citizen. Moderate reformers like Wyvill were certainly not democrats.[60]

The metropolitan radicals and the rational Dissenters eventually went far beyond the demands of the moderate reformers like Wyvill. In the end they came to accept the fundamental principle of the natural right of all men to political equality and, on this basis, they advocated a redistribution of parliamentary seats according to population and universal manhood suffrage. Initially however their demands were more modest. The metropolitan radicals of the 1760s originally confined their demands to annual parliaments, the secret ballot, and a redistribution of seats from the rotten boroughs to the wealthier and more populous urban centres. It was argued that the present system of representation was both inadequate and inequitable because it gave too much political influence to the great landowners and to landed property in general, while conferring very

225

little influence on the large towns and on the owners of other forms of wealth. The rich and populous metropolitan region, which contributed so heavily to the national exchequer, was grossly underrepresented in comparison with the poor counties of Devon and Cornwall. Such growing commercial centres as Manchester, Birmingham and Sheffield lacked direct representation altogether. The principal concern of the metropolitan radicals was still to secure the representation of property, though they interpreted property in such a way as to incorporate other forms of wealth than landed estates. There was no suggestion yet of abandoning a propertied franchise, though it was accepted that the suffrage ought to be granted to craftsmen, tradesmen, shopkeepers and the more substantial householders, 'whose property is sufficient to render them independent, and secure them, if they please, from undue influence'.[61]

Once it was recognized that Parliament should represent other forms of wealth than landed property it was not long before some radicals began to echo the American demand that all those who paid taxes should be represented. Obadiah Hulme claimed that, on the basis of the principle of the representation of all forms of property, the existing electoral system was hopelessly inadequate. Many towns which had once been important but which had fallen into decay still retained their representation in Parliament. Yet several large towns which had recently become wealthy had no representation at all. Not only should there be a redistribution of seats, but the suffrage ought to be extended to every male householder who paid rates and taxes.[62] An even more detailed exposition of the principle of granting representation to those who contributed significantly to the national exchequer was provided by James Burgh. In his influential *Political Disquisitions* Burgh provided detailed proof of the inadequate and inequitable features of the existing system of representation. He proved beyond dispute that the poorer and least populous rural areas were grossly over-represented whereas the richest and most populous counties and urban centres were either under-represented or, in some cases, entirely unrepresented. Burgh further argued that the great landowners had too much influence on the composition of the House of Commons, whereas the commercial, financial and manufacturing interests had insufficient representation in Parliament. Yet the contribution which these interests made to the prosperity of the country and to the nation's revenues was greatly in excess of that made by the landed interest. As a consequence the

226

Crown and the aristocracy dominated Parliament and were able to make it serve their own narrow and selfish ends often at the expense of other important economic interests. A major overhaul of the whole system of representation was necessary to preserve the constitution from corruption and to safeguard the true interests of the nation. Place bills, annual parliaments and the secret ballot were all required, but the most essential reforms were a redistribution of seats and a major extension of the franchise. Property was widely diffused among the population as a whole and the suffrage should be too. Every man owned property of some sort and even the poor contributed a portion of their possessions to the national exchequer through indirect taxes on items of popular consumption. From their wages the poor paid taxes on a whole range of goods, including malt, beer, leather, soap and candles. Since it was an established maxim that those who contributed to the expenses of government should be represented in Parliament, then, Burgh concluded, even the labouring poor could not be denied a voice in parliamentary elections. Burgh interpreted property in the widest possible sense: 'Every man has what may be called property, and inalienable property. Every man has a life, a personal liberty, a character, a right to his earnings, a right to religious profession and worship according to his conscience.'[63]

Burgh and other radicals probably interpreted universal manhood suffrage as meaning all householders and ratepayers, thus excluding paupers and domestic servants from the rights of active citizenship.[64] A few radicals however did wish to extend the suffrage to all men irrespective of their social and economic position. In Cartwright's view poverty was no justification for stripping a man of his natural rights. Indeed labour itself was an important species of property as Locke himself had recognized. Cartwright took the doctrine of 'no taxation without representation' quite literally. Since all men paid taxes of some kind then all men over the age of eighteen ought to have the vote:

The first and most natural idea which will occur to any unprejudiced man, is, that every individual of them, whether possessed of what is vulgarly called property, or not, ought to have a vote in sending to parliament those men who are to act as his representatives; and who in an especial manner, are to be the guardians of public freedom; in which, the poor, surely, as well as the rich have an interest.[65]

Because men ought to be represented as individuals and not as owners of property, then, in Cartwright's view, parliamentary seats ought to be redistributed according to population. For a time Cartwright clung to the notion that parliamentary candidates should still be men of substantial property, but, in 1780, he abandoned this qualification and accepted the complete political equality of all men.[66] A few other radicals followed Cartwright along the same route to universal manhood suffrage. David Williams, another rational Dissenter, maintained that:

All men, at the age of eighteen, who are not vagabonds or in the hands of justice, have a right to vote; because they contribute by their industry to the support of the state. I have had doubts concerning menial servants; on account [of] their dependence on their masters: but the injustice of excluding them, would bring greater inconveniences, than the trouble of preventing the ill effects of that dependence.[67]

By 1780 the more determined radicals of the Westminster Committee of the Association movement and of the Society for Constitutional Information were putting forward political demands which included universal manhood suffrage, equal electoral districts, annual elections, the secret ballot, the abolition of property qualifications for Members of Parliament, and the payment of Members of Parliament. While these demands were far in excess of anything likely to be conceded by Parliament, the radicals who endorsed them were not as democratic as might be suspected. Most of the committed radicals would have been satisfied with a reform which gave the vote to householders or ratepayers and none of them was prepared to argue that women should have the vote.[68] None of the radicals seriously expected the labouring masses to take an active role in national affairs beyond the exercise of the vote or the right to petition the Government. All the reform movements, even the Society for Constitutional Information, were dominated by members of the middling orders, by men of property and education. The radicals resented the excessive influence of the great landowners and were determined to increase the political power of the middling men of property, particularly the commercial interests in the larger towns. They were ready to speak up for the rights of all men, but they did not envisage a political society in which the poor would actually wield power. Even if the right to vote was conferred on all men the radicals anticipated that the poor would know their humble station in a hierarchical society and would willingly defer to those of superior fortune and a better education. While parliamentary reform would make the Government more responsive to the interests of the people as a whole, the decision-making process would still be dominated by men of property. The poor would certainly not govern. Once the masses had the franchise they could be expected to vote for their superiors. One radical claimed that: 'if we had really a Parliament chosen by unbought electors, it is reasonable to presume, that the people would choose able men, virtuous men, and men of property.'[69] Joseph Priestley was convinced that greater wealth should confer greater political influence and therefore only men of considerable fortunes should hold the highest offices in the Government.[70] Members of Parliament need not be rich men, but they should still be men of property so that they could represent the interests of the important middling orders in society.[71] Major Cartwright only reluctantly dropped the idea of retaining property qualifications for Members of Parliament and he may even have retreated from this position later. Clearly the radicals wished to change the composition of Parliament, but they did not wish to see poor men elected to the House of Commons. They merely wanted to reduce the number of wealthy landowners in the Commons and increase the representation of middling men from the commercial, financial, manufacturing and professional interests. They all made the tacit assumption that the common people would be content to follow their lead and would never endeavour to seize political power in order to serve their own ends.

The radicals wished to make the House of Commons more representative, but they did not desire to democratize the whole constitution. Their ideal constitution was still a mixed government of monarchy, aristocracy and democracy. While they wished to make the House of Commons more democratic, they were content to allow the King and the House of Lords to retain all their special privileges. James Burgh, Richard Price and Major Cartwright, for example, all explicitly denied that they wished to undermine monarchical government or planned to abolish aristocratic privileges.[72] They still expected that great wealth would continue to confer great political power on its possessors. There was no serious campaign by the radicals to alter the social and economic structure of Britain which distributed wealth in an extremely inequitable fashion. Several radicals did condemn the desperate circumstances in which the poor were expected to live and they wished to alleviate their distress, but this humanitarian sympathy very rarely led to demands for the Government to take positive action.[73] The reformers did give some support to measures which would alleviate the worst consequences of poverty and were ready to support schemes which would improve the system of poor relief. In general, however, nearly all the reformers, both moderate and radical, desired to see low taxes and cheap government. They wished to reduce the Government's power over the individual not increase the role of the State. Parliamentary reform was not seen as a prelude to government action to redress the blatant social and economic injustices in Britain. The notion of creating a more powerful State which would take strong action to redress social and economic abuses was anathema to the vast majority of reformers. Joseph Priestley, for example, admitted that wise statesmen would concern themselves with the conditions of the poor, but he warned that there would be grave danger in pursuing policies which were designed to eradicate the evils of poverty. If the State was over-concerned to provide the poor with the means of subsistence, then many of the lower orders would refuse to work. Rather than labour to provide for themselves, they would live improvidently, spending everything they were given by the State in an extravagant and profligate manner.[74] Priestley was so determined to reduce the power and expense of government that he would not allow it to promote even those reforms which he held most dear. Although he was personally convinced of the importance of education in improving society, Priestley was adamant that the State should not interfere in this sphere. Education had to be left to individual initiative.[75] There was even more opposition to any suggestion that the State could interfere with the rights of private property and almost total opposition to the idea of legislation to secure a redistribution of wealth. Christopher Wyvill rejected any suggestion that the rights of property should be infringed or that recourse should be had to the desperate expedient of an agrarian law which would restrict the amount of land any individual could hold.[76] Catharine Macaulay did favour an agrarian law, at least to the extent of wishing to see the great landed estates of the aristocracy reduced in size, but, apart from attacking the law of primogeniture, she offered no practical solution to the problem of how to redistribute wealth.[77] William Ogilvie, in a long rambling work published in 1781, favoured an agrarian law and went on to suggest that all males over twenty-one should be able to lay claim to a portion of land not exceeding forty acres. This land should be provided from waste land and from the great estates of the Crown and the aristocracy.[78] Thomas Spence, in a lecture on *The Real Rights of Man* delivered to the Literary and Philosophical Society of Newcastle-upon-Tyne in 1775, did advocate a complete redistribution of the property of Britain among the whole population, but his audacity led him to be expelled from the society. His lecture was not in fact published until the early 1790s. By then a new wave of radicalism had put forward a whole range of reforms far in advance of the plans for parliamentary reform put forward by the first generation of British radicals. Nonetheless, as early as 1780, radical opinion had endorsed the principle of the sovereignty of the people, had begun to demand an extensive reform of Parliament, and had started to bring the people into politics. These were major advances and they transformed the nature of political argument and involved more people in political debate.

7

Radical Ideology
in the 1790s

The more extreme demands for parliamentary reform were adopted by only a small body of metropolitan radicals and rational Dissenters, who were never able to exert much influence on Parliament and who showed little interest in enlisting the support of the labouring poor. The Duke of Richmond's motion for a radical reform of Parliament received no support from his fellow peers in 1780. The Younger Pitt's more modest proposals secured the support of fairly substantial minorities in the House of Commons in 1783 and 1785, but the defeat of these measures persuaded the Prime Minister to abandon hopes of reform in the immediate future. Christopher Wyvill remained loyal to the cause of moderate reform much longer, but his support among the rural squires and freeholders steadily waned in the later 1780s. The violence of the Gordon Riots of 1780 shocked the propertied classes and the ending of the war with America removed the most divisive issue from the political scene. The reduction of Crown patronage begun by the Rockinghams in 1782 was carried on indirectly but more successfully by Pitt's policy of retrenchment and so another emotive issue was diffused. Thus, for a variety of reasons, the pressure for parliamentary reform waned significantly after 1785. Yet, by the early 1790s, radicalism had not only revived but had made major advances on the position it had occupied in 1780. The reform movement became more radical in its ideology, more revolutionary in its aims and more influential in its impact on the masses.

1 The Radical Revival

A number of factors contributed to the revival of radicalism in the early 1790s. In the first place the centenary of the Glorious Revolution produced an outburst of political propaganda in defence of liberty. The more liberal Whigs in Parliament, who tended to gather round Charles James Fox, entered enthusiastically into schemes to commemorate the Revolution.[1] A new reform club, the Society for the Commemoration of the Glorious Revolution, most often referred to as the Revolution Society, was established. Its members resolved to support a demand both for the repeal of the Test and Corporation Acts and a radical reform of Parliament. They proclaimed: 'I. That all civil and political authority is derived from the people. II. That the abuse of power justifies resistance. III. That the right of private judgment, liberty of conscience, trial by jury, the freedom of the press, and the freedom of election ought to be held sacred and inviolable.'[2] The Revolution Society consciously encouraged an interest in the principles which underlay the Revolution settlement and provided a platform for those who claimed that the Revolution enshrined the doctrine of popular sovereignty. At one of its first meetings Andrew Kippis, a dissenting minister who had long been associated with the campaign for religious toleration and parliamentary reform, preached a sermon in commemoration of the Revolution. In it he rejected the conservative claim that the liberties of Englishmen were first established in 1688. He insisted that English liberties were ancient rights which had been enjoyed for centuries. The Revolution re-stated some of them, but much more might have been done to safeguard the rights of man.[3] A year later, on 4 November 1789, Richard Price, the veteran campaigner for the rights of man, was asked to address the Revolution Society. In his lecture he maintained that the Glorious Revolution had rested on an appeal to those rights inherent in the nature of free men: the right to liberty of conscience, the right to resist arbitrary tyranny, and, most radical of all, 'the right to chuse our own governors; to cashier them for misconduct; and to frame a government for ourselves'. Unfortunately, Price argued, the Glorious Revolution, although it was a major step in the right direction, had not fully secured those natural rights to which all men could lay claim. The Toleration Act was only a minor concession to the Protestant Dissenters and the Test and Corporation Acts remained on the statute book. Worse still the system of representation was left in its grossly imperfect state so that Parliament could not be said to represent the interests of the people. Fortunately, the recent success of revolutions in America and France would remind the people that their rights had not been sufficiently safeguarded in 1689 and would encourage them to renew their demands for reform. The time was ripe for all men to recover their inalienable rights.[4]

The members of the Revolution Society were not the only radicals to seize upon the centenary of the Glorious Revolution to justify renewed attempts at parliamentary reform. William Enfield insisted that the Revolution was proof of the sovereign authority of the people:

> The unequivocal language of this public act, was, that all civil power originates with the people; that whatever authority or prerogative resides in the crown, it is entirely in the nature of a trust, delegated by the people for the benefit of the whole; ... By this great Revolution two important points were gained: the *first*, that it established a precedent in support of the right of the people to resume any delegated trust which has been abused, and to secure, at any expence, the authority of the laws and the permanency of the constitution: the *second*, that it produced an express contract between the King and his subjects, in which their mutual duties are clearly settled, and in which the prerogatives of the crown are restricted within limits, which cannot be transgressed without hazarding the existence of the State.[5]

In contrast, other radicals condemned the Revolution settlement for not doing enough to safeguard the liberties of the subject. They pointed out that not enough had been done to limit the power of the Crown and nothing had been done to reform the inadequate system of representation. The politicians who had carried through the Revolution had missed a golden opportunity for genuine reform and the consequence was the survival of an imperfect constitution. This failure of the governing classes to reform Parliament had inevitably provoked the people into demanding improvements for themselves. Since reform would not come from within Parliament it would have to come from without. In the end the united will of the people would triumph over all the opponents of reform.[6] Thus, somewhat paradoxically, the Glorious Revolution was praised for enshrining the sovereignty of the people and condemned for not securing the natural rights of man.

The centenary of the Glorious Revolution might not have led to complaints about missed opportunities if recent revolutions in America and France had not convinced the radicals that so much more could have been achieved in 1689. The revolutionary nature of the political changes wrought in America and France made the Revolution settlement appear to be an inadequate and conservative attempt at reform. In the 1760s and 1770s radical opinion in Britain had sympathized with the American cause and had claimed that the

234

Americans were seeking to defend the rights of Englishmen. The radicals had then witnessed the efforts of the Americans to enshrine political rights which were far in advance of anything achieved in Britain. The principles enunciated in the Declaration of Independence were far more radical than those enshrined in the Bill of Rights, but it was not until the new state defeated Britain and set about establishing a new constitution that the radicals saw such principles put into practice. The American experiment proved that political claims which were based on rational and moral principles could be realized in practice. The United States provided a working model of a system of government created by popular action and designed to embody many of the ideas suggested by the radicals in both Britain and America.

The radicals rejoiced at the success of the new republic in demonstrating how the determination, the co-operation and the moral virtue of the people could erect a new form of government and stimulate almost every aspect of society. The Americans were credited with recognizing the vital importance of the contracts between man and man and between the government and the governed. They had set up a government for themselves and this government protected the interests of all the people. The United States appeared to be the ideal example of a free state in which there was no aristocratic élite enjoying undeserved honours and privileges. A nation of independent proprietors and merchants had shown how to establish institutions which would instil virtue while preserving liberty. With the American example to hand it was no longer possible to argue that authority and liberty could not be combined without the cement of Crown patronage and aristocratic privilege. The Federal Constitution of 1787 was hailed as the clearest example of a government being erected on the principle of the sovereignty of the people. A free people had managed to divide legislative sovereignty between three independent institutions and had effectively separated executive, legislative and judicial powers. The constitution was not only erected by the will of the people, but specifically guaranteed certain natural rights. The Dissenters in particular welcomed the absence of any established church and the extent to which the principle of religious toleration was written into the constitutions of several of the states. Above all the radicals rejoiced that the Americans had shown that a more equal representation of the people did not inevitably lead to social revolution. Political equality could in fact be reconciled with the defence of property and with the maintenance of a moderately differentiated social structure. The United States offered empirical evidence to prove that radical constitutional reform need not lead to anarchy or civil war. Thomas Paine, who had been very active in America during the revolution, later told a British audience: 'I see in America the generality of the people living in a style of plenty unknown in the monarchical countries; and I see that the principle of its government, which is that of the *equal rights of Man,* is making rapid progress in the world.'[7]

The American constitutional experiment undoubtedly enlivened the flagging spirits of the British radicals, but it did not have the dramatic impact and electrifying effect of the French revolution. The outbreak of revolution in a country long regarded as the prime example of absolute monarchy was hailed as convincing proof that a new age of liberty was clearly at hand. The revolution in France was altogether more sudden and surprising than the American revolution. Its influence on Britain proved to be both more profound and more diffused throughout the whole of society. Within a few short months the strongest monarch in Europe was humbled by his subjects, the entrenched privileges of the aristocracy were condemned, the inalienable rights of man were proclaimed, and a representative assembly was charged with the task of drawing up a new constitution. British reformers of all shades of opinion were galvanized into action. Samuel Romilly, rejoicing at the news from France, confessed: 'I think of nothing else, and please myself with endeavouring to guess at some of the important consequences which must follow throughout all Europe. I think myself happy that it has happened when I am of an age at which I may reasonably hope to live to see some of these consequences produced.'[8] Major Cartwright declared: 'Degenerate must be that heart which expands not with sentiments of delight at what is now transacting in the National Assembly of France. The French, Sir, are not only asserting their own rights, but they are also asserting and advancing the general liberties of mankind.'[9] Richard Price was convinced that the times were auspicious for a new campaign to enshrine at last the natural and inalienable rights of man:

What an eventful period is this! I am thankful that I have lived to see it ... I have lived to see a diffusion of knowledge, which has undermined superstition and error – I have lived to see the rights of men better understood than ever: and nations panting for liberty, which seemed to have lost the idea of it. I have lived to see THIRTY MILLIONS of people, indignant and resolute, spurning at slavery, and demanding liberty, with an irresistible voice; their king led in triumph, and an arbitrary monarch surrendering himself to his subjects ... And now, methinks, I see the ardour for liberty catching and spreading; a general amendment beginning in human affairs; the dominion of kings changed for the dominion of laws, and the dominion of priests giving way to the dominion of reason and conscience.[10]

2 The Moderate Reformers

In the long run the conservative reaction to the French Revolution was to cripple the whole movement for political reform, but initially both moderate and radical reformers drew new inspiration and new strength from the dramatic events in France. The moderate reformers were encouraged to argue that a modest measure of parliamentary reform, freely conceded, would avert the kind of violent revolution which had broken out in France. In March 1790 Henry Flood brought before the House of Commons a bill which would strip all rotten boroughs of one of their representatives, give an additional one hundred seats to the counties, and extend the franchise to resident householders. In an impressive speech Flood argued that developments in France had made reform more urgent than ever, though he claimed that the excesses of the revolution in France could be avoided by enfranchising tax-paying householders rather than the whole adult male population. In Flood's view the impoverished masses were a rabble that could not be trusted with the vote.[11] Even this concession to conservative opinion could not appease the majority of Members of Parliament and Flood withdrew his motion without putting it to the vote. Two years later the moderate reformers again urged Parliament to reform itself before the example of France encouraged the people to try more violent remedies. The liberal Whigs who formed the moderate Society of the Friends of the People in April 1792 used events in France not as a reason for resisting reform, but as a warning of what happened when legitimate demands for reform were opposed for too long. Moderate reform would prevent violent revolution:

The abuses in the Government of France were suffered to gather and accumulate, until nothing but an eruption could put an end to them. The discontent of the People was converted into despair. Preventative remedies were either not thought of in time, or were not proposed until it was too late to apply them with effect. The subversion of the ancient

237

government ensued. The inference from this comparison is at once so powerful and so obvious, that we know not by what argument to illustrate or enforce it. We mean to avert for ever from our Country the calamities inseparable from such convulsions.[12]

This argument, that a timely and temperate reform would remedy the abuses in the constitution while averting the danger of violent revolution, was reiterated by Charles Grey when, on 30 April 1792, he announced his intention of introducing a motion for parliamentary reform in the next session of parliament.[13]

Events in France and Britain made it increasingly difficult for the moderate reformers to stand between reaction and revolution. The execution of Louis XVI in January 1793 and the outbreak of war in February shocked the propertied classes, and their alarm was increased by the evidence that radicals in Britain continued to support the revolution in France. The moderate reformers had to work hard to win support for a measure of parliamentary reform which they believed would be the only means of averting revolution; especially as conservative opinion was beginning to argue that such a reform would in fact be but a prelude to violence and social upheaval. They therefore endeavoured to prove that the existing system of representation needed improving, while maintaining that their proposals would stabilize politics by improving the representation of property. Thomas Oldfield, one of the Friends of the People, produced the most detailed examination yet attempted of the inadequate and inequitable system of representation. He pointed out that the voting qualifications for the boroughs were neither regular nor rational and that the conduct of elections was marred by bribery, corruption and blatant partiality. Worse still was the inadequate system of representation which meant that the monarchical and aristocratic elements of Britain's mixed government were far too powerful while the democratic element was so weak that the balance of the constitution was subverted. It could be shown that a mere 11,075 voters elected 257 Members of Parliament, a majority of the House of Commons, and that these voters were controlled by less than two hundred great landowners. Armed with these figures Oldfield argued that there must be a major redistribution of seats so that the wealth of the great towns would be adequately represented, but he wished to retain a propertied franchise. He suggested that the vote should be given to copyholders in the counties and to rate-paying householders in the boroughs.[14] Using Oldfield's evidence George Tierney was able to produce a report on 'the State of the Representation of England and Wales' which was used to justify the proposals for parliamentary reform put forward by the Friends of the People in 1793 and 1797.[15]

Moderate reformers were convinced that nothing could be gained by making extreme demands. The principle of universal manhood suffrage raised the spectre of mob rule and frightened most men of property. The best that could be hoped for was the representation of the smaller property owners. This would make the House of Commons more democratic with granting the vote to the irresponsible masses. It was confidently maintained that the mob could not be trusted with the vote. In times of peace and stability the poor would succumb to the bribes offered by men of wealth. On the other hand whenever they were discontented the labouring masses would be easily inflamed by artful demagogues. Liberty could only be preserved by disinterested and independent citizens and these qualities could only be found among men of property. The moderate reformers refused therefore to abandon a propertied franchise.[16] Charles Grey's parliamentary motions of 1793 and 1797, both of which received only derisory support, would only have enfranchised copyholders and rate-paying householders.[17] In Christopher Wyvill's view the reformers should enlist the support 'not of that class at the lower end of society, many of whom wish for universal suffrage only to abuse it, but of those middle classes, who have had some education, who have some property and some character to preserve, and who probably would prefer some limitation of the right of suffrage, as more friendly to peace, to order, and even to rational liberty'.[18]

Events in France therefore undoubtedly encouraged moderate reformers to revive their demands for parliamentary reform, but the prospect of a violent revolution breaking out in Britain persuaded the reformers that they must retain a propertied franchise. As a result, a firm wedge was driven between those moderates who wished to reform the system of representation in order to prevent Britain following the French example and the new radicals who were inspired by the events in France to develop a more revolutionary ideology. Even a veteran campaigner like Major Cartwright moderated his demands for parliamentary reform because he feared that the new radicals would use universal manhood suffrage to introduce revolutionary changes. He explicitly repudiated any desire to secure social or economic equality and he was utterly opposed to republicanism.[19] Christopher Wyvill feared that the ideas of Thomas Paine would overturn the constitution and bring about a violent social revolution: 'If Mr Paine should be able to rouse up the lower classes, their interference will probably be marked by wild work, and all we now possess, whether in private property or public liberty, will be at the mercy of a lawless and furious rabble.'[20] To understand this reaction by such brave reformers as Wyvill and such long-standing radicals as Cartwright we need to examine the revolutionary elements in the new radicalism of the 1790s.

3 The New Radicalism: Aims and Assumptions

The French Revolution encouraged liberal opinion in Britain to demand parliamentary reform as a means of preventing revolution rather than as a prelude to more radical reforms. At the same time however the events in France stimulated the development of much more radical notions which challenged the very basis of the British constitution. The new radicals of the 1790s not only reiterated some of the old demands, but wished to carry out a more extensive reform of the political and social order. In extending their aims these radicals had to strengthen the intellectual basis of their demands. They still appealed to John Locke and his contract theory and right of resistance, to the ancient constitution which guaranteed the liberties of Englishmen, and to the Dissenters' arguments that all men were equal in the sight of God; but the most influential among them also developed two newer claims. The first, and in the 1790s the more important, claim was not to appeal to history and to the traditional liberties of Englishmen, but to stress the natural and inalienable rights of all men. The second, and in the long run the more effective, approach was to attempt to base demands for reform on utilitarian criteria.

Some of the radicals of the 1790s perceived the weakness of the traditional claim to the ancient rights of Englishmen. They recognized that the weight of historical evidence favoured the conservative claim that there had always been a propertied franchise and that most subjects only enjoyed limited civil liberties and certainly not the right to an active role in politics. This recognition compelled them to argue about the rights which all men *ought* to have because of their common humanity and natural equality. A rational and moral view of the rights of man would justify a more radical extension of political liberty than any claim to the actual rights which

240

Englishmen had once enjoyed in the past. James Mackintosh argued that the right to freedom did not depend on proving that particular liberties had been possessed in the past. 'It is not because we *have* been free, but because we have a right to be free, that we ought to demand freedom. Justice and liberty have neither birth nor race, youth nor age ... Let us hear no more of this ignoble and ignominious pedigree of freedom.'[21] By adopting this approach Mackintosh was able to support the principles which underlay the Revolution settlement while condemning the limited reforms which were actually achieved in 1689. The principles of the Glorious Revolution could be used to justify more radical reforms than those yet achieved.[22] Thomas Paine was even more explicit. He deliberately rejected the idea of appealing to the evidence of the past and insisted that each age had the right to establish any political system which would fit its own needs. Paine contemptuously dismissed the much-vaunted Glorious Revolution as insignificant compared to the recent revolutions in America and France. He utterly repudiated the notion that the Revolution settlement could establish the distribution of power and set the bounds of liberty for generations to come. The authority of this settlement could only last so long as its terms proved beneficial and acceptable to the British people. Each age must be free to reject the wisdom and the decisions of the past. It was the living not the dead who must exercise power and their decisions should be guided by universal principles of justice and not restricted by previous actions. The evidence of history could not be used to dictate how men should act in the present or in the future. It was time to escape from the dead hand of history and to reject the tyranny of the past:

There never did, there never will, and there never can exist a parliament, or any description of men, or any generation of men, in any country, possessed of the right or the power of binding and controlling posterity to the 'end of time', or of commanding for ever how the world shall be governed, or who shall govern it; and therefore, all such clauses, acts or declarations, by which the makers of them attempt to do what they have neither the right nor the power to do, nor the power to execute, are in themselves null and void. – Every age and generation must be free to act for itself, *in all cases*, as the ages and generations which preceded it. The vanity and presumption of governing beyond the grave, is the most ridiculous and insolent of all tyrannies ... The parliament or the people of 1688, or of any other

241

period, has no more right to dispose of the people of the present day, or to bind or control them in *any shape whatever*, than the parliament or the people of the present day have to dispose of, bind or control those who are to live a hundred or a thousand years hence.[23]

Other radicals followed Paine's example and sought to break from the fetters of the past. Those who contributed to *The Cabinet*, a radical periodical published in Norwich, launched an attack on the ancient constitution. For nearly two centuries men had appealed to the ancient constitution to justify their claim to political freedom, but the radicals were now prepared to admit that political liberty had been restricted in the Anglo-Saxon period to the owners of landed property. The bulk of the people had been the absolute slaves of their masters. Whenever improvements had subsequently been made to this unhappy state of affairs it was not through any return to the ancient constitution, but through a deliberate policy of innovation. Far from fearing the consequences of radical change men should welcome the opportunity to escape from the tyranny of the past. Partial reform was not enough. The friends of liberty must lay the axe to the roots of oppression and extirpate every political abuse.[24]

This rejection of the past stemmed from and further stimulated the belief in a future of unlimited progress. The radicals were convinced that they were living in an age of reason which would dispel ignorance and free men from ancient tyranny. The free and constant application of reason, so nobly begun in America and France, would usher in an age of unprecedented liberty. Thomas Paine was confident that: 'The opinions of men with respect to government, are changing fast. The revolutions of America and France have thrown a beam of light over the world, which reaches into man . . . Ignorance is of a peculiar nature: and once dispelled, and it is impossible to re-establish it.'[25] The Norwich radicals asserted that:

Liberality of opinion, and freedom of expression, are now spreading themselves more and more widely among mankind: the theories of ages, the accumulated errors of a thousand years, now totter at the touch of reason, and hoary prejudice hides its wrinkled countenance, while the scrutinizing genius of modern times, spurning its despotic influence, endeavours to attract the attention of an enlightened world.[26]

Mary Wollstonecraft claimed that reason had advanced so far that progress could not now be halted. Men were learning to master their environment and this would enable them to improve their conditions.[27] James Mackintosh was determined to prove that the advance of reason and the growth of knowledge must inevitably lead to political reform and greater liberty:

Who will be hardy enough to assert, that a better Constitution is not attainable than any which has hitherto appeared? Is the limit of human wisdom to be estimated in the science of politics alone, by the extent of its present attainments? Is the most sublime and difficult of all arts, the improvement of the social order, the alleviation of the miseries of the civil condition of man, to be alone stationary, amid the rapid progress of every other art, liberal and vulgar, to perfection?[28]

The rejection of history and the belief in progress were both the product of the rationalist approach of the radicals. The most important aspect of this stress on rationalism was the conviction that all men possessed natural and inalienable rights. The extent of man's claim to political liberty was not discovered by reference to history or to the laws of particular societies. It could only be appreciated by those who understood the moral nature of man and by those who appealed to the abstract principles of pure, unclouded reason. The appeal to natural rights was made by nearly all of the radicals, but the most detailed and explicit defence of the universal and inalienable rights of man was made by Thomas Paine. By abandoning empirical evidence and by relying on reason and morality Paine was able to add a radical dimension to Locke's notions of natural rights, contract and popular sovereignty. Paine was concerned to justify the natural equality of all men and to protect all their extensive natural rights. He insisted that all men were created equal and therefore each generation had as much right to be free as the first generations on the earth. No government, however long it had been established, could legitimately invade the natural rights of man. Civil government was only established in order to convert man's natural rights into civil rights. The natural rights which were transformed into civil liberties were very similar to those defended by Locke. They included the rights to life, liberty and property and the right to the pursuit of happiness. Like Locke, Paine also conceded that the one natural right which individuals had to sacrifice in civil society was the right to use force in one's own cause. If a man wished to protect his rights and his interests he must appeal to the combined force of civil society and not take the law into his own hands. Civil

243

governments were erected to protect men's rights not to invade them. To ensure that they fulfilled these functions and exercised their power for the benefit of the governed, it was essential to limit the authority of those in power and to enshrine the doctrine of popular sovereignty. Paine was able to lay much greater stress on the sovereignty of the people than Locke had done because he insisted that the more important contract was not that between the governors and the governed, but the prior agreement by which every individual had voluntarily agreed to establish civil society and to devise a form of civil government. This prior contract which was agreed to by every man, established the society's constitution and this constitution clearly marked out the limits of the power of both the executive and the legislature and explicitly protected every man's civil and political rights. Under any legitimate civil government every man had an equal right to express his political opinions. This was a natural right which had to be converted into a civil right. It could never be restricted by hereditary or property qualifications. Thus Paine gave every man an active voice in the decision-making process and went beyond Locke's notion that tacit consent was enough to legitimize a government's action. In Paine's vision of civil society the sovereign will of the people was actively and consistently expressed. It did not lie dormant, as in Locke's view, to be reactivated only when the bonds of civil society were dissolved. Sovereign authority always resided in the people and they therefore had the right to retain a perpetual and continuous supervision over the actions of those in positions of power.[29]

Most of the radical propagandists of the 1790s agreed with Paine that the case for reform should rest on a rationalist appeal to the natural rights of man. They believed that the law of reason, which they usually equated with the law of nature and the law of God, dictated that men had equal and inalienable natural rights. They were also convinced that men could be governed by reason rather than by passion and hence possessed the qualities which would enable them to discover the means of translating these natural rights into civil liberties. A few radicals however developed an alternative intellectual basis for reform. William Godwin accepted Paine's claim that men were more naturally equal than unequal and that they were governed more by their reason than by their passions. He maintained that all men enjoyed the same nature, sense and faculties and that they were all endowed with reason. Yet Godwin's rationalism did not lead him to place great emphasis on the natural and in-alienable rights of man. While he acknowledged that all men had cer-tain rights, he was more concerned to point out their duties because in his mind justice was ultimately more important than freedom. The right to participate in the deliberations of government was impor-tant, but it was not as significant as man's duty to obey the voice of reason and justice. No man had the right to do wrong. The voice of the people, Godwin made clear, was not the voice of God. Even universal agreement could not convert wrong into right. In the last resort Godwin was more interested in establishing a world based on reason and morality than a society in which all men possessed equal political rights. He was more anxious to stress that men should follow the path of true justice than to campaign for radical political reforms. In his view men should recognize that the performance of their duties in the pursuit of justice was more important than deter-mined efforts to secure their political rights.[30]

Nonetheless, when he examined different forms of government Godwin was convinced that a democratic government was most likely to pursue the path of justice because it gave men the freedom to follow the dictates of reason rather than submit to the commands of superior force. His support for a democratic government however did not rest on the doctrine of abstract natural rights. He urged instead that utility should be the criterion adopted to judge political actions and he insisted that the greatest general good should be the guiding principle of society. Jeremy Bentham was even more scath-ing in his denunciation of natural rights and even more committed to the utilitarian ethic of the greatest happiness of the greatest number. In his opinion political liberty was not a natural right, but a relative good: it was simply one possible way of achieving the greatest good. The objective must be to pass good laws. Like Godwin he recognized that justice might not necessarily be exercised by a democratic government. The aim of political institutions must be to enact good laws. Men might enjoy equal political rights and yet produce bad laws. Indeed, if men were allowed to claim equal natural rights this would certainly prevent the passing of any laws since subordination was based on differences in rights. If political equality were truly a universal and inalienable right of all men then all laws could be criticized as an infringement of someone's liberty. To live according to the doctrine of abstract natural rights would be to live without the benefit of civil society or civil government. According to Bentham, '*Natural rights* is simple nonsense: natural and imprescriptible rights, rhetorical nonsense, nonsense upon stilts.'[31] Bentham preferred the doctrine of utility, but he did not use it to oppose reforms as did most thinkers who adopted a utilitarian ethic in the later eighteenth century in order to defend expediency and resist change. By the early 1790s Bentham was discussing the value of radical political reforms, including universal manhood suffrage, the secret ballot and the unlimited freedom of the Press, but he preferred to base such changes on a utilitarian foundation rather than on the doctrine of natural rights.[32] Among the radicals of the 1790s Paine and the appeal to abstract rights undoubtedly had the greater influence, though future reforms were to rest far more on the utilitarian approach of Bentham. It was not Paine but Bentham, though relatively unknown in the late eighteenth century, who was to inspire the philosophical radicals of the nineteenth century.

The radicals of the 1790s did not only endeavour to base their reforms on a new intellectual framework. They also differed from the earlier radicals in their identification of the abuses that needed to be reformed. Their aims went far beyond those of earlier reformers. Reformers such as Richard Price and Major Cartwright believed that all would be well if they secured a democratically elected House of Commons. They had no quarrel with a mixed government and did not attack either monarchy or aristocratic privileges. They did not want a genuine democracy and still less a republican form of government. Even more significant was their failure to pay serious attention to the social and economic grievances of the poor. In contrast the new wave of radicalism in the 1790s was prepared to attack the whole basis of the British constitution and recognized that parliamentary reform would not be enough. It was now suggested that almost all aspects of civil society needed to be reformed. Some radicals realized that the plight of the masses stemmed from economic as well as political causes and they showed a greater readiness to alleviate the distress caused by poverty. Yet nearly all of these radicals believed that political reforms alone would inevitably improve the lot of the poor. Only one or two of them perceived that a social revolution might be necessary before the economic grievances of the poor could be remedied. Political reform was still widely regarded as the panacea of all ills.

Nonetheless the radical proposals of the 1790s went far beyond even those suggested by the Society for Constitutional Information in 1780. The radicals of the London Corresponding Society and other similar clubs in the provinces certainly continued to advocate universal manhood suffrage, annual elections, equal electoral districts, the secret ballot, the abolition of property qualifications for Members of Parliament and the payment of Members of Parliament. The leading radical theorists however were dissatisfied with plans which concentrated entirely on purifying the existing constitution by reforming the electoral system. They launched a forthright attack on aristocratic privileges and hereditary government. Titles, honours and special privileges, they insisted, could not be tolerated in a society based on reason and recognizing the natural equality of all men. Neither the monarchy nor the House of Lords could be justified by any rational principle and so they must be cast aside in the march of progress. Thomas Cooper, fearing a charge of treason, protested that he had no intention of overturning the present constitution and only wanted complete political equality: 'I would have the man, whose stake in the community consists of life, and liberty, and labour, with a penny in his pocket, to have an equal voice in the choice of legislators, by whose laws that stake is to be protected, with another man, who has life, and liberty, and labour, with a hundred thousand pounds in his pocket.'[33] Despite his protestation Cooper went on to argue that no rational man planning to set up a new system of government would adopt that of Britain as a model. There was no moral justification for hereditary legislators and no rational grounds for dividing the nation into the separate interests or corporations of King, Lords and Commons. It was a monstrous injustice to raise huge sums of money by taxing the poor to keep a few men in luxury. Far too much of the misery of the world was produced by the pride, arrogance and ambitions of kings. It was also contrary to the evidence of nature to claim that such qualities and virtues as strength, industry, intelligence, wisdom, honesty and goodness were inherited and moreover inherited only by the propertied and governing classes. Social, economic and political distinctions could be earned only by intrinsic merit not by birth, and such merit was diffused throughout the whole population.[34]

Other radicals were even more outspoken than Cooper. They showed no respect for the British constitution and were not afraid to speak out unequivocally in favour of a democratic republic. James Oswald bitterly attacked all hereditary distinctions and concluded that 'in a State really free, a privileged caste of men cannot possibly exist; for it could never enter into the minds of free people to establish so absurd a barrier between man and man. In a free state, there can be but one class of men, which is that of citizen; as there is but one will, which is that of the people.'[35] Several other radicals endorsed this view but the most determined and influential advocate of a democratic republic was Thomas Paine. He utterly condemned the British system of government. In his view it had been clearly established by force. It supported a host of titles, honours and privileges and rejoiced in creating artificial and unjust distinctions between men who were naturally equal. There could be no justice in a political system which tried to create hereditary legislators out of a tiny minority of the population. The only legitimate form of government was a democratic republic set up by the will of the people.[36] The people would never voluntarily set up a monarchy or approve of an aristocracy. A mixed government, such as the much-vaunted political system of Britain, was in fact corrupt, expensive and unjust. It ought to be abolished. In its place a republican government should be erected. The new government authority would be limited. Every man would be represented in the democratically elected assembly. In order to make sure that the people's rights would be guaranteed and the government's power kept within strict limits a written constitution would be necessary. The executive would be subordinate to the elected legislature and the latter would be under the authority of the sovereign people.[37]

Paine was determined that each man should enjoy the same active political rights. The right to vote should be attached to the person and not to the property of man. To deny any man the franchise was to cast a slur on his moral character and to assert that he was less than a man. The possession of wealth was no proof of moral worth and poverty was not evidence of the lack of it. Furthermore, Paine insisted, every man possessed a form of property in the fruits which he could earn from his labour. Locke had made the same point, but the notion of labour as a form of property assumed much greater significance in the work of Paine and some other radicals:

the faculty of performing any kind of work or service by which he acquires a livelihood, or maintains his family, is of the nature of property. It is property to him; he has acquired it; and it is as much the object of his protection as exterior property, possessed without that faculty, can be the object of protection of another person.

248

Hence each man had the right to a share in the decision-making process of his society so that he could protect both his person and the fruits of his labour.[38] In fact, every man over the age of twenty-one should be entitled to vote and should be qualified to sit in the legislature. Elections should be held regularly, and at periodic intervals or on any extraordinary occasion the entire constitution ought to be referred back to the sovereign people. They could then decide whether to retain it, reform it or replace it.[39]

Like Paine, William Godwin believed that civil government was at best a necessary evil. The comfort and progress of man owed more to society than to government, but unfortunately the rational faculties of man had not yet advanced far enough to allow them to live without government. Nevertheless it had to be acknowledged that every government relied too much on compulsion and therefore limited the absolute freedom which all men ought to enjoy. To make government at all palatable it should be so constructed that it was as agreeable as possible to the ideas and inclinations of the people. Only a democratic republic could possibly meet this standard. Even a government of this kind could not demand general and unlimited obedience. Subjects should never revere their government and should always be prepared to criticize those in power. Men must cherish their freedom. They must never willingly renounce their independence or voluntarily give up their rights. Those in power might be strong enough to compel obedience, but they could only earn it when their actions were just and when they were in accordance with the wishes of the people.[40] Godwin recognized that all men were fallible and that no one could therefore claim the right to dictate to others or to set up his judgement as a standard for other men. While complete equality was impossible, the treatment of men should be measured by their merits and virtues. There could be no equity or justice in a society which conferred special privileges or hereditary honours on some men or which refused to allow all men the free exercise of their private judgement. Governments should not rest solely on force and power should not be a matter of hereditary right. Since compulsion made men slaves the only legitimate form of government was one in which all men could influence the deliberations of the legislators and the choice of policies to be pursued.[41] 'The most insignificant individual ought to hold himself free to animadvert upon the decisions of the most august assembly; and other men are bound in justice to listen to him, in proportion to the soundness of his reasons, and the strength of his remarks, and not for any necessary advantage he may derive from rank or exterior importance.'[42]

While Godwin conceded that no government would grant subjects unlimited freedom he hoped that men would so improve and progress that civil government would become unnecessary. Until this rational and enlightened state of affairs could be achieved Godwin favoured a democratic republic as the best form of government. Only a government of this kind would treat all subjects with near-equal justice and would try to respond to the desires and inclinations of all men. Monarchical and aristocratic governments always allowed the few to dominate the many and tried to force the people into a blind submission to authority. In stark contrast:

Democracy restores to man a consciousness of his value, teaches him, by the removal of authority and oppression, to listen only to the suggestions of reason, gives him confidence to treat all other men with frankness and simplicity, and induces him to regard them no longer, as enemies against whom to be upon his guard, but as brethren whom it becomes him to assist. The citizen of a democratical state, when he looks upon the oppression and injustice that prevail in the countries around him, cannot but entertain an inexpressible esteem for the advantages he enjoys, and the most unalterable determination to preserve them.[43]

Despite this fulsome praise for a democratic system of government Godwin continued to maintain that all forms of government infringed the liberty which all men ought to enjoy. No representative system, no matter how democratic the franchise, could perfectly reflect the views of all the people. Even a decision taken by a substantial majority was imposing a judgement on the minority which opposed it. Since he recognized that governments would not rapidly disappear from the face of the earth however Godwin admitted that men had to choose between different forms of government. For all practical purposes and for the foreseeable future it was therefore best to strive for a democratic republic.[44]

The radicals' emphasis on the rights of man rather than the claims of authority led them to condemn all hereditary honours, titles and privileges. Nonetheless, despite their insistence that all men should enjoy equal political rights, it is not absolutely clear that all the radicals genuinely desired to live under a government *by* the people. Many of them were drawn from a middle-class background and few of them could entirely escape from the traditional asumptions not only that men of wealth, education and leisure should govern, but that such men should shape and influence the minds of the labouring masses. James Mackintosh, for example, entertained the highest opinion of the commercial and moneyed classes and regarded them as the most enlightened supporters of freedom and reform. On the other hand he spoke disparagingly of government by the mob or vulgar multitude.[45] John Thelwall, normally ranked as one of the most determined radicals of the 1790s, had reservations about instituting a genuinely democratic system of government. He certainly insisted that the legislature ought to consult the poor as much as the rich. He admitted that the mass of mankind appeared ignorant and un-fitted for a political voice, but he also maintained that this was because they had been degraded for too long. Restore men their rights, he claimed, and they would soon learn to exercise them properly. Yet Thelwall never expected the poor ever to become sufficiently qualified to govern or to hold any important political office. He insisted that government of any sort was only necessary because very few men were qualified to rule themselves or to choose good representatives. While therefore he supported a government of the people, Thelwall never envisaged a government by the people. He expected the lower orders to follow the lead of enlightened men from the middle and upper ranks of society.[46] Indeed, at times, he feared that democracy might obstruct progress. Like Godwin he argued that the voice of the majority was not necessarily the voice of truth and he insisted that the majority had no right to suppress the opinions of the minority.[47] Even Thomas Paine was not always committed to a policy of extending full political rights to all men. Although he was utterly opposed to a propertied franchise and was ready to give the vote to poor men, he did on one occasion suggest that he did not include domestic servants in the ranks of active citizens. Like children and wives domestic servants did not have their own homes and were entirely dependent on their masters. In taking up such employment servants had voluntarily forfeited their independent character, the true test of a free man. Should they cease to be domestic servants and resume their independence then, how-ever poor they might be, they would be entitled to the full political rights of men.[48] Paine had abandoned this reservation by the 1790s, but he and almost all other radicals still ignored the rights of women.

In the struggle for the rights of man most radicals were concerned quite literally with the liberty of adult males rather than the rights of all mankind. They regarded the position of women as analogous to that of children or domestic servants; that is, they were entirely dependent on their masters and hence incapable of exercising the rights of an independent creature. A few radicals however were prepared to campaign for the rights of women. This effort is generally associated with the work of Mary Wollstonecraft, the wife of William Godwin, though she was not alone in lamenting the underprivileged position of half the adult inhabitants of Britain. Mary Wollstonecraft concentrated on the social and economic position of women which rendered them subordinate to and dependent upon men. It was this inferiority which made them unfit to play a full role in the public life of the nation. The law made it difficult for all but a tiny minority of women to dispose of their own property or income. All important careers were closed to women and even opportunities for education, particularly higher education, were severely limited. The vast majority of women were expected, indeed compelled, to limit their activities to the home, to domestic or menial occupations, or, for the rich, to an empty life of leisure. It was almost impossible for a woman of ambition or talent to find an occupation commensurate with her abilities. Even those who became teachers, governesses or nurses were denied the rewards, status and opportunities for promotion which would come the way of men in the same or similar occupations. In Mary Wollstonecraft's opinion this situation was created by the evident desire of men to keep women subordinate and, as far as possible, tied to domestic chores and duties. It was not the result of genuine distinctions between the sexes and it could only be remedied when all human beings were treated as equals and were allowed the full enjoyment of their natural rights.[49] Although her case now appears unanswerable there were few prepared to accept it at the time. Mary Wollstonecraft herself appears to have had little confidence in the ability of women to improve their own situation. They were so oppressed that they could only be saved by the intervention of men: 'Would men but generously snap our chains, and be content with rational fellowship instead of slavish obedience, they would find us more observant daughters, more affectionate sisters, more faithful wives, more reasonable mothers – in a word, better citizens.'[50]

Aware of the enormous difficulties in the way of securing redress for women Mary Wollstonecraft did not even bother to campaign for equal political rights for women. She was fully conscious of the fact that very few radicals were prepared to extend the suffrage to women because they regarded women as incapable of exercising a free, rational and independent choice. Charles James Fox spoke for liberal Whig opinion in Parliament when he opposed giving women the vote on the same grounds as he rejected universal manhood suffrage:

In all the theories and projects of the most absurd speculation, it has never been suggested that it would be advisable to extend the elective suffrage to the female sex; and yet, justly respecting, as we must do, the mental powers, the acquirements, the discrimination, and the talents of the women of England, in the present improved state of society ... it must be the genuine feeling of every gentleman who hears me, that all the superior classes of the female sex of England must be more capable of exercising the elective suffrage with deliberation and propriety, than the uninformed individuals of the lowest class of men to whom the advocates of universal suffrage would extend it. And yet, why has it never been imagined that the right of election should be extended to women? Why! but because by the law of nations, and perhaps also by the law of nature, that sex is dependent on ours; and because, therefore, their voices would be governed by the relation in which they stand in society.[51]

Major Cartwright argued that women had no right to claim to be represented in Parliament: 'women being by nature unable to qualify for and to perform various labours of magistracy and office in civil government, and of serving as the military defenders of their country, which are equally duties appertaining to *dominion,* and necessary to the preservation of *political liberty,* their right to the latter falls to the ground.'[52] John Longley claimed that nature fitted only men for public activity and designed women for domestic occupations.[53]

These were the voices of the moderate reformers, but few of the more radical reformers had any interest in the political rights of women. One exception was an anonymous contributor to a radical journal emanating from Norwich. He argued unequivocally for adult female suffrage and even for the right of women to sit in Parliament and to hold important public offices. Yet even he recognized that most men would laugh his arguments out of court.[54] Another essay on the same topic and in the same journal acknowledged that few radicals were concerned to promote the rights of women: 'Notwithstanding this general diffusion of liberal sentiment, however, I am aware that a disquisition on the rights of woman will expose the author to ridicule; and although he may not now draw down the thunders of an attorney-general, Bigotry will frown, and Folly, thrice-happy Folly! will jingle her bells, and laugh, at the attempt.' Even the activities of such able and educated women as Mary Wollstonecraft had not managed to weaken the ingrained male prejudice against recognizing the equality of women: 'it is the temper of the times to look on a learned woman with a kind of abhorrent awe, to regard her as we do an animal of uncommon magnitude, with curiosity and dread; we consider the acquirement of knowledge in a female, as incompatible with that delicacy of sentiment, and that refinement of feeling, which gives zest to the conversation of the sex.'[55]

The social and economic grievances of the poor received more attention than the rights of women, but concern over the plight of the labouring masses very rarely led to suggestions that social reforms were as necessary as political changes. Although the radicals deliberately sought to enlist the support of the lower classes and there is clear evidence that working men did join some of the radical clubs, most radicals remained primarily interested in securing political reforms. It may have been that these radicals genuinely believed that political reform would inevitably lead to economic changes which would improve the lot of the poor. Certainly Paine and others blamed poverty on such political causes as expensive governments and oppressive taxation. They claimed that a just government would leave more money in the pockets of its subjects. It seems more likely however that most radical spokesmen were afraid of the consequences of attacking the existing distribution of wealth. Either they feared that the governing classes would react violently to any threat to their property and so oppose any political reform or the radicals themselves were so conditioned to a hierarchical and propertied society that they were unable to endorse a levelling programme. In an essay justifying an extensive reform of Parliament Jeremy Bentham denied that this implied any attack on property: 'Equality in property is destructive of the very principle of subsistence: it cuts up society by the roots. Nobody would labour if no one were secure of the fruits of his labour. Equality in respect of the rights of voting is attended with no such inconvenience.'[56] Several radical societies went out of their way to deny that they planned any attack on property. In a broadside printed in 1795 the London Corresponding

Society protested that: 'In their ideas of equality, they have never included (nor till the associations of alarmists broached the frantic notion, could they ever have conceived that so wild and detestable a sentiment could have entered the brain of man) as the equalization of property, or the invasion of personal rights of possession.'[57] The Manchester Reformation Society claimed that it wanted political equality but not an equal division of property. Other radicals in the Merseyside region were of the same opinion:

> The equality insisted on by the friends of reform is AN EQUALITY OF RIGHTS ... The *inequality* derived from labour and successful enterprise, the result of superior industry and good fortune, is an *inequality essential to the very existence of Society*, and it naturally follows, that the property so acquired, should pass *from a father to his children*. To render property insecure would destroy all motives to exertion, and tear up public happiness by the roots.[58]

The radicals of Sheffield were even more explicit: 'we demand equality of rights, in which is included equality of representation; ... We are not speaking of that visionary equality of property, the practical assertion of which would desolate the world, and replunge it into the darkest and wildest barbarism; but that equality we claim is, to make the slave a man, the man a citizen, and the citizen an integral part of the state; to make him a joint sovereign, and not a subject.'[59]

Although the primary aim of the majority of radicals was to secure political equality some of them were fully aware that the real grievances of the common people were economic rather than political. Yet, even these radicals tended to accept economic inequality as an inevitable development and an intractable problem. Even Thomas Paine, despite his genuine concern at the plight of the poor, was convinced that property would always be divided unequally and that there could be no assault on the rights of private property. The State should no more interfere with the property rights of the rich than it should interfere with the labour rights of the poor.[60] What was wrong and what should be redressed was that men of property were allowed to monopolize political power. It was their political strength which enabled them to protect their own economic interests while sacrificing those of the poor. Thus, an economic inequality which was natural and unavoidable was compounded by the existence of political inequalities which were unnatural and remediable.

255

The economic grievances of the poor were made worse by an unsatisfactory political system and they could only be reformed, though not removed, by political reform. Paine condemned the excessive expenditure of governments which needed to support an unnecessary monarchy and a profligate aristocracy and which spent huge sums on corrupting the representatives of the people and in waging foreign wars of conquest. This vast expenditure had to be met by heavy taxes which burdened even the poorest subject and pushed many below the level of subsistence. If the common people were given an equal voice in electing the nation's legislature then taxes would undoubtedly be reduced. A democratic government would be a frugal administration.[61] Paine did not blame the poor for their desperate situation. He recognized that 'the great mass of the poor in all countries are become an hereditary race, and it is next to impossible for them to get out of that state of themselves.' To rescue a major part of society from misery and wretchedness, it was essential to reform the system of government and reduce the enormous tax burden placed on the poor.[62]

George Dyer shared Paine's conviction that extreme poverty was the inevitable consequence of a defective system of government which spent huge sums to enrich a privileged minority. An improvement in the plight of the poor must await a reform of the political system that would confer equal political rights on all men.[63] William Wordsworth argued that the existing political system made the economic situation of the poor much worse by passing 'innumerable statutes, whose constant and professed object it is to lower the price of labour, to compel the workman to be content with arbitrary wages, evidently too small from the necessity of legal enforcement of the acceptance of them'.[64] Daniel Eaton was convinced that the reform of Parliament would produce a host of changes which would improve the economic position of the poor. A democratic government would lower taxes, abolish the game laws, reform the poor law and remove from the statute book all those laws which infringed the right of workers to improve their own conditions.[65] John Thelwall bitterly condemned the present system of government which doomed the mass of mankind to lives of incessant toil. He insisted that every subject should enjoy more than the bare necessaries of subsistence. Yet his solution to the problem of long hours of work for low wages was to press for political reforms. He believed that the unrepresentative nature of Parliament was responsible for the situation in which nine-tenths of the population were condemned to be beasts of burden in order to maintain the privileged position of the other tenth.[66] Because only the rich were represented in Parliament then their interests were protected and those of the poor were neglected. The law allowed employers to combine to fix wages, prices and the conditions of labour, yet the poor were charged with breaking the law if they tried to do the same. 'Why – Because only the opulent and powerful are represented in Parliament; and therefore it is the opulent and powerful alone whose interest the representatives find it necessary to consult. If once every year the poor man's vote were as important as his employer's the poor could not be forgotten.'[67] Thelwall's conviction that annual parliaments elected by universal manhood suffrage would solve the economic grievances of the poor was both politically naïve and unduly optimistic. He came closer to recognizing the best means of improving the lot of the poor when he, incidentally, offered a radical redefinition of property. Developing the argument of Locke he insisted that property always originated in human labour: 'Property is nothing but human labour. The most inestimable of all property is the sweat of the poor man's brow: – the property from which all other is derived, and without which grandeur must starve in the midst of supposed abundance.'[68] Unfortunately, Thelwall did not develop this insight into a coherent theory of labour which might have enabled him to argue more effectively for a fairer distribution of the material benefits of this world.

A few radicals did show a greater awareness of the need to redress the grievances of the poor by reforms which would directly improve the economic circumstances of the common people. They recognized that the plight of the poor was largely the consequence of the unequal distribution of wealth rather than the result of a propertied franchise. William Godwin, for example, lamented that the unequal distribution of property had reached such alarming proportions that vast numbers of British subjects were deprived of almost everything which could make life tolerable or secure. This was not simply the lot of the idle and irresponsible. The unremitting toil of honest working men was scarcely enough to support them and their families above the level of bare subsistence. Such poverty inevitably bred many evils. It corrupted men by creating servility and dependence; it kept the poor ignorant and the rich idle; it discouraged intellectual attainments and it drove many men to crime.[69] If such evils were allowed to continue, then the rich would expose themselves to the

threat of violent revolution: 'the poor man will be induced to regard
the state of society as a state of war, an unjust combination, not for
protecting every man in his rights and securing to him the means of
existence, but for engrossing all its advantages to a few favoured
individuals, and reserving for the portion of the rest want, dependence and misery.'[70]

Samuel Taylor Coleridge was another who argued that an equality
of political rights was not enough to redress the grievances of the
poor. What the poor needed was an equality of condition: 'It is a
mockery of our fellow-creatures' wrongs to call them equal in rights,
when by the bitter compulsion of their wants we make them inferior
to us in all that can soften the heart, or dignify the understanding.'[71]
Coleridge was highly critical of most of the radicals for missing this
point: 'All that can delight the poor man's sense or strengthen his
understanding, you preclude; yet with generous condescensions you
would bid him proclaim "Liberty and Equality!" because, forsooth,
he should possess the same *Right* to an Hovel which you claim to
a Palace. This the Laws have already given. And what more do *you*
promise?'[72] James Oswald was another who protested at a situation
in which a few enjoyed every luxury while the majority was degraded
by the most wretched poverty. The rich 'have divided the earth
among them, as if it were the patrimony of a few individuals, and
not the common inheritance of the human race. Defrauded, even
before their birth, of their share of the genial gifts of nature, entire
generations rise and sink again into the earth, without having proved
a single joy, or tasted, in their cheerless journey through life, other
beverage than the bitter potion of toil, and pain, and disappoint-
ment.'[73] Yet he did not follow this protest with any proposals for
economic reforms to redress the grievances of the poor. Perhaps only
Thomas Spence promised the poor a remedy for their economic
grievances. He castigated the rich minority for usurping the economic rights of the majority and for monopolizing for themselves
what was designed for the benefit of all men. The plight of the poor
could never be remedied while the few retained their pretended
rights to an unjust and inequitable share of the fruits of the earth.
Poverty could never be eradicated and equal political rights could
never be achieved until wealth and property was fairly distributed
among all men.[74]

4   The New Radicalism: The Means of Change

The radicals of the 1790s were clearly divided over what reforms were necessary in order to remove the political abuses in civil society and to remedy the grievances of the people. Although they were united in demanding extensive political reforms, the radicals were uncertain about what should be done to deal with the evident plight of the labouring masses. When it came to thinking about the means of securing their demands the radicals were even more divided. Most of them based their demands for reform on an appeal to reason and on the conviction that reason could be relied upon to prove that all men ought to enjoy equal political rights. Faced with considerable opposition from those who did not believe that the law of reason dictated that men should set up a democratic system of government, the radicals had to consider abandoning a propaganda campaign which endeavoured to convert men simply by the force of argument. They were forced to turn instead to methods which would put severe pressure on the governing classes. Since most radicals thought political reforms would remedy all abuses they could only think in terms of political methods of putting pressure on those in power. They believed that extra-parliamentary agitation which was nationwide and which had the support of the majority of the population would compel Parliament to concede extensive reforms. If driven to it by Parliament's opposition to reform the people could summon a national convention to draw up a new constitution. This written constitution could then be submitted to Parliament. Very few radicals wished to see such a convention replace Parliament and fewer still were prepared to consider violent or revolutionary action. This emphasis on political reforms and this desire to change society by moderate political means meant that very few radicals thought about the need to redistribute wealth by legislative means and not one of them seriously considered using the economic power of the working classes to bring pressure on those who opposed them. While the workers themselves were beginning to combine to improve their wages and conditions of work the radical theorists failed to perceive that strikes and the protests of organized labour might be the most effective means of bringing pressure to bear on the propertied classes who opposed reform.

Given the fact that they were hopelessly divided about how best to achieve their objectives the failure of the radicals is hardly surprising. Perhaps the only area of substantial agreement among the radicals was the conviction that they should appeal to reason and the belief that they must educate the masses about their political rights. Many optimistically believed that a propaganda campaign alone would be enough to bring about a radical reform. A meeting of delegates from the various Constitutional Societies, convened at Norwich on 24 March 1792, declared: 'We believe that instructing the people in political knowledge and in their natural and inherent rights as men is the only effectual way to obtain the grand object of reform, for men need only be made acquainted with the abuses of government and they will readily join in every lawful means to obtain redress.'[75] Yet even while agreeing on the need to instruct the people the radicals disagreed on how best to carry out this educational policy. William Godwin was convinced that political progress required that the masses should use their reason and learn their duties, but he himself published an expensive philosophical work which was both over the heads and beyond the means of the lower classes. Many of the other radicals appealed at best to the lower-middle-class audience. Only a few radicals made a conscious effort to reach the labouring poor. Thomas Paine's *Rights of Man* proved to be the most popular work among the new radical organizations of the 1790s. This was owing in part to the fact that Part Two related directly to the working man's daily experience of economic hardship, but it was also owing to Paine's determination to reach as wide an audience as possible. The *Rights of Man* was published in many cheap editions so that it could be distributed by the thousand to the working-class membership of the new radical societies. There were few areas of Britain that Paine's work failed to reach and even fewer radicals who were not impressed by the force of his arguments. The enormous success of Paine's work owed a great deal to his ability to communicate ideas to ordinary men. Paine was very conscious of his audience and of the effect that he wished to have on his readers. His style was bold and clear, his case was well-ordered and carefully marshalled, and he had a rare gift for combining rational argument with the capacity to touch the heart and stir the imagination.[76] In his ability to speak to the masses Paine stood head and shoulders above the other radicals, though some, such as Daniel Eaton with his *Politics for the People* and Thomas Spence with his *Pigs's Meat; or, Lessons for the Swinish Multitude*, were as anxious to reach a mass audience. Both Eaton and Spence ransacked radical literature of the past two centuries in order to instruct the masses in their political rights and they disseminated this information in a cheap and easily digested form.

Since most radicals believed that rational argument and accurate information were essential to political progress, they regarded education as a vital agency of reform and yet they disagreed on whether education should be provided by the State. Thomas Cooper advocated a national system of liberal education so that the ordinary people would learn how to improve their own environment. He claimed that those in power had long attempted to keep the people in ignorance and to prevent them from enquiring into abuses and discussing remedies for their grievances. The masses were forced to labour without intermission so that they would have no time for mental improvement. The only political creed which they learned was one that urged them to submit without question to the orders of their self-appointed rulers. In contrast, those who wished to reform society wanted to teach the people to think for themselves as a prelude to their acting for themselves. Until a system of public education was established the middling and lower classes ought to establish clubs and societies which would encourage discussion and the dissemination of ideas and information. By this means the people might become more fully informed of their rights and of the political privileges to which they were entitled by nature.[77] George Dyer not only wanted the government to provide a system of state education, but suggested that the rich and the poor should attend the same schools. While they might not need the same kind of education they would benefit from being taught in the same public institutions. 'Such policy would humanize the heart, and prevent that proneness to insolence, which too often accompanies the wealthy, and that proneness to servility, which attends the poor. The principle which equalizes men, dignifies and exalts him.'[78] Of all the radicals of the 1790s William Godwin was perhaps the most convinced that the advance of reason and knowledge would lead to a future of unlimited progress. Sound reasoning and evident truth, when effectively communicated, would always triumph over error. 'Truth is omnipotent: The vices and moral weakness of man are not invincible: Man is perfectible, or in other words susceptible of perpetual improvement.'[79] Nonetheless, Godwin was as much opposed to a system of national education as he was to the suppression of any opinions in

261

politics and religion. Like Joseph Priestley he feared that any system of state education would seek to impose certain opinions on the people and to suppress others. Men would only be taught what served the ends of government and would learn to close their minds to many opinions which might be regarded as a threat to the prevailing establishment.[80]

The explosion of political controversy in the early 1790s led not only to efforts to disseminate political information to the masses, but to attempts to organize the people behind the radical reform programme. The new clubs and societies were more radical in their ideology than the Friends of the People and more interested in attracting a working-class membership than the Society for Constitutional Information. One of the first of the new clubs, the Sheffield Constitutional Society, soon attracted more than two thousand members from among the tradesmen, craftsmen and workers of the area. In campaigning for parliamentary reform the Sheffield society committed itself to the doctrine of popular sovereignty. In April 1794 the society resolved: 'We demand equality of rights, in which is included equality of representation; without which terror is law, and the obligations of justice are weakened, because unsanctioned by the sacred voice of the people ... that equality we claim is, to make the slave a man, the man a citizen, and the citizen an integral part of the state; to make him a joint sovereign, and not a subject.'[81] Other radical societies with similar programmes sprang up in Manchester, Norwich, Glasgow, Nottingham, Cambridge and Derby. The most famous and influential of the new radical societies was the London Corresponding Society, founded by the shoemaker Thomas Hardy in January 1792. Though a few men of substance joined this society it continued to be dominated by artisans and craftsmen. Like the Sheffield society it committed itself to the radical reform of Parliament and to the doctrine of popular sovereignty.[82]

The new radical societies and the theorists who inspired them were committed to major political and constitutional reforms, but they were not united and indeed far from certain how best to press their demands. Most appear to have believed, optimistically but quite unjustifiably, that a massive propaganda campaign and a national petitioning movement would persuade the governing classes to abandon their vigorous defence of the existing constitution. Others realized that more determined action would be necessary. They recognized that Parliament would never agree to reform itself and therefore the people must seize the political initiative. The idea of calling a national convention, first suggested by James Burgh in 1774, was advocated by Thomas Paine, Joseph Gerrald and several radical societies. They argued that individual petitions from separate associations could not express the popular will nor exert enough pressure on the ruling classes. Only a national convention established to draw up a new constitution which would enshrine the rights of man could offer an effective challenge to Parliament.[83] The radicals had neither the popular support nor the organization to take such revolutionary action. Nonetheless a few societies did send representatives to the British Convention which met in Edinburgh in late October and early November 1793. This convention proposed an extensive reform of Parliament and a massive, nationwide petitioning campaign, but it did not advocate violence nor regard itself as a popular representative body able to dictate to Parliament. John Richter of the London Corresponding Society and Henry Redhead Yorke of Sheffield may have regarded a national convention as a means of superseding Parliament, but Thomas Hardy, John Thelwall and most other radicals never endorsed this view and usually flatly denied it. Nevertheless the calling of a convention so alarmed the authorities that they broke up the convention and arrested some of its leaders. The Government followed this up with a policy of repression which within a few years effectively destroyed the radical societies and silenced their leading spokesmen.[84]

Faced with a determined and ruthless response from a reactionary and thoroughly alarmed Government many radicals showed great courage and remained loyal to their beliefs. Yet their capacity to defeat the Government was negligible because so few of them were prepared to contemplate a revolution on the French model and, even had they done so, there is little evidence to suggest that they would have secured much popular support. The radical societies had always explicitly renounced any desire to achieve their aims by force and even the leaders accused of treason during the famous trials of 1794 were acquitted of any charge of advocating a violent revolution on the French model.[85] Even the radical theorists were cautious about suggesting the need for revolution. John Thelwall thought that revolution might be provoked by a tyrannical government, but he himself wished to see a gradual transformation of society and opposed any violent or precipitate action.[86] William

Godwin utterly rejected violence as a means of securing reform:

nothing can be more indefensible, than a project for introducing by violence that state of society, which our judgements may happen to approve ... The most dreadful tragedies will infallibly result from an attempt to goad mankind prematurely into a position, however abstractedly excellent, for which they are in no degree prepared ... To dragoon men into the adoption of what we think right, is an intolerable tyranny. It leads to unlimited disorder and injustice.[87]

Thomas Paine certainly proposed revolutionary action, but he did not advocate violent revolution. He desired drastic changes and supported the idea of the people electing a national convention to draw up a new constitution, but he never advised the people to take up arms. Nonetheless, Paine, Thomas Spence and James Mackintosh all recognized that the stubborn resistance to reform by the governing classes might eventually compel the people to use force to achieve their ends. None of them, however, believed that such a resort to violence was imminent or unavoidable.[88]

Only James Oswald appears to have been absolutely convinced that radical reforms could never be achieved by peaceful means. He claimed that only violent revolution could secure the rights of man: 'Let us not be deceived, for it is force alone that can vindicate the rights of the people. Force is the basis of right, or rather right and force are one ... whoever shall dare to oppose the reformation of abuse, him let the besom of destruction sweep from the face of the earth; cursed be the eye that taketh pity on the enemy of the people; and may the tongue wither that shall plead in his behalf.'[89] Words alone, however violent, will not achieve a revolution against a determined and entrenched establishment. There is little evidence to suggest that many radicals were prepared to put their revolutionary sentiments into action. E. P. Thompson has uncovered evidence of revolutionary talk and secret organizations in various parts of Britain, especially in the months of desperation and repression between 1797 and 1798, but this material does not support the contention that a violent revolution was really planned or even desired by more than a handful of madcap conspirators.[90] The evidence of planned insurrection discovered by ministers, who were ready to inflate almost any radical demand into a revolutionary act, was in fact derisory. They discovered one hare-brained scheme to capture Edinburgh Castle; an attempt by William Maxwell to order several thousand daggers stamped with 'Rights of Man'; and the occasional handbill suggesting that the British should follow the example of the French in executing their king.[91] The most revolutionary acts of the 1790s were the naval mutinies at Spithead and the Nore in April and May 1797. The sailors protested primarily at their appalling conditions, but there is some evidence of radical ideas and revolutionary sentiments circulating among them. Nonetheless, it is extremely doubtful whether these mutinies, dangerous though they were, can be interpreted as a genuinely revolutionary movement which might have brought about a radical reform of the constitution. When the authorities made concessions and acted promptly against the ringleaders the mutinies collapsed. Some historians appear to regret that the British did not emulate the French in the 1790s, but this hostility to the repressive measures of the Government in these years cannot obscure the fact that most radicals never contemplated violent revolution. They believed, however mistakenly, that they could persuade their opponents to accept the desirability of extensive political reform. They never squarely faced the issue of what they should do if the governing classes refused to be convinced by their appeal to reason.

Since the radicals failed to devise effective means of achieving their primary objective of political reform, it is hardly to be expected that they should have had better success in their attempts to improve the lot of the labouring masses. In view of their own concern for private property and the widespread fear of social revolution it is not surprising that solutions to the economic problems of the poor proved beyond the radicals. William Godwin did claim that the fruits of the earth formed a common stock upon which each man had a valid title to draw for what he needed and that all men had an equal right to the means of subsistence. This led him to condemn the inequitable distribution of property and to come close to advocating a theory of 'from each according to his ability, to each according to his needs'. Yet Godwin offered no practical solution to the economic problems of the poor. He explicitly rejected the notion that the State could own all the sources of wealth and could distribute this income more equitably among all its subjects. He also opposed the idea of passing any law which would forcibly deprive the wealthy of their property. The law could not be used to set the bounds to any man's accumulation of private property. No right, however just and necessary, could be enforced by violence. Godwin was therefore reduced to hoping that with the progress of reason all men would become convinced of the advantages of a more equitable distribution of property. The rich would then voluntarily surrender their excess wealth to those who most needed it.[92] Thomas Paine was more realistic and pragmatic. He insisted that a just government must seek practical remedies to ameliorate the economic plight of the labouring masses. Although he always advocated cheap government and he never favoured too much state interference in men's lives, Paine did believe that money could be found to improve the economic circumstances of the poor. In Part Two of *Rights of Man* he provided a constructive programme of social and economic reforms designed to alleviate the distress of the labouring masses. He argued that a democratic government in Britain could save huge sums of money previously spent on the monarchy, on corrupting both Houses of Parliament, and on an aggressive foreign policy. A cheaper, more frugal government could then afford to reduce the high level of taxation which overburdened the poor since most of this revenue was raised by indirect taxes. In addition revenue could be raised from the rich by levying a progressive tax on all property worth more than £50 p.a. after deducting the land tax. This money would be used to assist the poor. Paine proposed child allowances of £4 p.a. for every child of a poor family until the child reached the age of fourteen; old age pensions of £6 p.a. for those over the age of fifty and £10 p.a. for those over sixty; maternity allowances of £1 for each child born to a poor family and a marriage grant of the same sum to every newly married couple among the poor; a fund to pay the funeral expenses of those who died some distance away from home and friends; and finally a scheme to employ the casual workers of the metropolis.[93] Thus, in a few remarkable pages, Paine made the most original contribution to the whole reform movement and suggested the basic elements of a welfare state. Nonetheless, despite the revolutionary nature of these proposals, Paine never challenged the rights of private property and utterly rejected any notion of forcibly compelling a redistribution of property. In *Agrarian Justice* he again returned to his scheme of taxing property in order to raise enough money to improve the living standards of the poor. On this occasion he suggested that since it was impossible to alter significantly the existing distribution of property the tax raised from the wealthy should be used to give a lump sum of £15 to every poor person on reaching the age of twenty-one.[94]

Paine was convinced that the amelioration of poverty by means of cash grants raised by taxes levied on the rich would avoid the need for any violent attack on private property. Despite the worst fears of his critics Paine had no wish to see a social revolution and he never advocated policies of social levelling or economic egalitarianism. John Thelwall also stopped short of demanding an attack on private property. He insisted that the appalling conditions of the poor must be improved, but he failed to offer any economic solution to the problem. Any attempt to redistribute property by force or by legislation would produce more problems that it would solve: 'Equality of property is totally impossible in the present state of the human intellect and industry; and if one of you once could be reduced to attempt a system so wild and so extravagant, you could only give to rascals and cut-throats an opportunity, by general pillage and assassination, of transferring all property into their own hands and establishing a tyranny more intolerable than anything of which you now complain.' Thelwall simply hoped that political reform would end the abuse of wealth by the rich and remove the economic grievances of the poor.[95]

A few radicals did suggest economic ways of improving the lot of the poor. James Oswald and an anonymous contributor to *The Cabinet* proposed that waste and common land should be divided among the poor while Mary Wollstonecraft suggested that large estates might be divided into small farms.[96] Only Thomas Spence however advocated a truly revolutionary scheme for redividing all the available land of the country equally among the entire adult male population. He was the only radical whose concept of natural rights led him to advocate a return to the state of nature when all men had enjoyed an equal claim to the fruits of the earth.[97] Nonetheless, while Spence's ideas were revolutionary they were also hopelessly visionary. There was quite simply no possibility that the propertied classes would agree to such a demand and the chances that the poor would take action to carry out such a scheme were little better. Spence was typical of the most radical theorists of the 1790s. He was too ready to believe that the rich would concede reform without a fight and that the masses would willingly follow those who advocated radical change. Moreover Spence, like the other radicals, had little grasp of the economic realities of the late eighteenth century. He concentrated all his attention on the agricultural sector of the economy just at a time when Britain was undergoing rapid commercial and industrial development. He believed that landed property was the sole basis of wealth and utterly failed to recognize that industry could produce wealth far more rapidly than agriculture. Not only did he believe that the wealth of the country was static and was produced from the land, but he was convinced that the population of the country was unlikely to increase. Once the agricultural land of Britain had been divided up among the existing inhabitants Spence believed that there would be no need to contemplate another redistribution of property at some subsequent date. Britain would become a contented land of small peasant farmers. Mines, factories and cotton mills had no place in Spence's vision of Britain's green and pleasant land.

Spence's plan for the redistribution of property showed no appreciation of economic realities or of the economic means which might be at the disposal of the labouring masses. Indeed nearly all the radicals failed to realize that the best hope of major change was to organize the working classes into an effective economic weapon capable of wringing important concessions out of the propertied classes. A few radicals did complain that the law did not allow the labouring poor to combine in order to improve their economic conditions, but they failed to promote the organization of such trade unions themselves. A Norwich radical protested that 'the law forbids combinations, the only means the poor could have of raising the price of their labour.'[98] John Thelwall complained: 'Why is it that factors, merchants, wholesale-dealers and opulent manufacturers enter into combinations with impunity? monopolize as they please? and fix, in their conventions, the price of commodities at discretion? while labourers and mechanics who enter into associations to appreciate their own labour are sentenced, like felons, to a gaol?'[99] Thomas Paine recognized that their labour was the most prized possession of the poor and protested that the law should not strip them of it. 'Several laws are in existence for regulating and limiting workmen's wages. Why not leave them as free to make their own bargains as the law-makers are to let their farms and houses? Personal labour is all the property they have. Why is that little, and the little freedom they enjoy to be infringed?'[100]

Nonetheless, while groping towards a theory of value that measured wealth according to the labour which produced it and while recognizing that workers ought to have the right to combine to protect their economic interests, the radical theorists failed to perceive that organized labour might be the most effective means of both economic and political change. John Thelwall did dimly perceive that the working conditions of the industrial poor might provide them with a political education. He claimed that 'every large workshop and manufactory is a sort of political society which no Act of Parliament can silence and no magistrate disperse', but this insight did not lead him to suggest that the workers might be the means of their own salvation if only they put their numerical and economic strength to good use.[101] None of the radicals advocated economic action, through the strike for example, as a means of putting pressure on the propertied classes in order to wring substantial concessions from them. There is plenty of evidence to suggest that the workers in certain industrial disputes were influenced by radical propaganda. For example, during the bitter and prolonged strike on Tyneside in 1792-3 crowds of workmen shouted 'No King. Tom Paine for ever' and threatened to attack the property of the rich, but the strikers were overwhelmingly preoccupied with increasing their wages.[102] Working men might combine to improve their conditions of work, but they did not see industrial action as a means of achieving political reforms or a general redistribution of wealth. While the governing classes were terrified of organized trade unions, their radical opponents had not yet grasped that industrial strength might be a powerful weapon of political, social and economic change. The radical theorists were still limited by their middle-class conceptions of society and still convinced of the strength of reasoned argument. Few of them seriously contemplated a political revolution and none of them considered organizing the working classes into an economic weapon of change. The radicals tried to convert the working classes to their rational schemes of political reform, but they did not spring from the poor, they did not really identify with the masses, and they entirely failed to appreciate the potential strength of organized labour, at least in the industrial areas of the country.

8

The Conservative Defence of the Constitution

Although the reformers in Britain developed an increasingly radical programme between the 1760s and the 1790s they failed to carry through any important political changes. Detailed arguments in favour of an extensive reform of Parliament were developed as early as 1780 and yet the first modest reform bill was not passed until 1832. It is not difficult to suggest reasons for this failure of the radicals. While external events did much to stimulate the growth of the whole reform movement, they also encouraged many people to rush to the defence of the existing constitution. The Gordon riots of 1780 convinced men of property that the common people were a swinish multitude who would destroy all order if they were not firmly restrained by the forces of law and order. The War of American Independence produced a wave of patriotic fervour as well as a surge of radicalism. The French Revolution, once it had developed into violence, terror and war, alarmed the governing classes and provided them with a reason or at least an excuse for a vigorous policy of repression which crippled and almost completely destroyed the reform movement by 1800. Nonetheless, it is probably a mistake to believe that the radicals would have succeeded but for the conservative reaction to the French Revolution. Historians of early British radicalism have been too prone to believe that the intellectual case for an extensive reform of Parliament in the late eighteenth century was unanswerable and that radical changes would have been implemented but for the panic reaction produced by the excesses of the French Revolution. The 'Terror' in France and the outbreak of war in 1793 undoubtedly made it more difficult to persuade the propertied classes that political reforms were necessary, but it is difficult to believe that the radicals had any chance of implementing their proposals at any time in the late eighteenth century. The most that they might possibly have achieved was the moderate changes suggested by William Pitt in 1785; that is, the redistribution of a small

270

number of seats and a modest extension of the franchise.

Despite their considerable efforts the radicals had quite simply not succeeded in persuading enough people to support their arguments and had failed to devise effective means of ensuring their success. The reform movement was hopelessly divided on what changes ought to be made and none of the competing elements could rally adequate support in or out of Parliament. It is significant that Birmingham, Manchester and Leeds, the three biggest towns without representation in Parliament, never organized petitions for reform. The radicals in fact failed to secure the kind of massive popular support which would have undermined the confidence of the governing classes and they never succeeded in organizing the working classes in such a way that their labour could become an effective weapon in the fight against the privileges of property. In the rural areas, where most of the population still lived, the radicals had little support and even in many of the largest manufacturing towns they were outnumbered by their opponents. These opponents dominated central and local government, commanded the forces of law and order, and controlled most of the wealth and property of the country. The radicals were in no position to match their power and effectiveness until industrialization and urbanization had transformed British society and the British economy. This transformation was only in its early stages in the late eighteenth century and so the failure of the radicals is hardly surprising.

It is therefore evident that the radicals had neither massive popular support nor an effective political organization capable of seizing power; whereas their conservative opponents possessed considerable power and were ready to use it. Yet these factors alone do not provide an adequate explanation of the failure of radicalism and the triumph of conservatism in the late eighteenth century. By concentrating solely on practical politics it remains possible to assume that the radicals won the intellectual argument about reform but lost the struggle for power. Indeed, this has become the orthodox interpretation of events. By paying more attention to the political arguments expressed by both sides however it is possible to offer an alternative explanation. The evidence of the last two chapters shows how the radicals were divided among themselves, how most of them failed to take their ideas to their logical conclusion and how all of them failed to devise any effective means of implementing their policies. The present chapter will consider the strength of conservative ideas and opinion. It will show that the propertied classes did not need the French Revolution to teach them to fear radical reform or to cherish the existing constitution. Events in France may have heightened their perception of what was at stake and may have encouraged the propagation of a more articulate conservative ideology, but a steady belief in the virtues of the British constitution and a firm resistance to change were apparent long before the 1790s. It can be argued and argued quite strongly that the radicals were defeated by the force of their opponents' arguments and by the climate of conservative opinion among the politically conscious, not simply by recourse to repressive measures and the forces of order. The conservatism of the late eighteenth century may have had its roots in an almost unthinking acceptance of the existing constitution and an instinctive fear of change, but these attitudes were firmly grounded in the realities of the situation and in unshakeable assumptions about the nature of politics and society. Once these attitudes and assumptions came under challenge from the radicals the defenders of the prevailing order began to develop a conservative ideology of considerable appeal, endurance and intellectual power. The first constituent element in the conservative campaign was to persuade the public of the practical virtues of the existing political system and to point out the dangerous consequences of reform. The second was to mount an attack on the intellectual foundations of the radical case and to formulate an ideology which would provide a strong buttress to the existing order. These two approaches were then combined in order to argue that those in power under the existing constitution also happened to be those who *ought* to exercise authority in a well constituted State.

1 The Virtues of the British Constitution

In seeking to explain the practical virtues of the existing constitution the conservatives pointed to all the positive benefits which the nation had reaped since the Glorious Revolution of 1688. In order to make it quite clear that these benefits were the direct result of the constitution as it actually existed and did not simply spring from the fundamental principles which underlay the Revolution settlement, the conservatives went to great lengths to explain the nature of the existing constitution and to show how the end-results which it produced were precisely those which practical politicians and men of property most desired. They insisted that the British constitution embodied the virtues of mixed and balanced government and they stressed that the reforms suggested by the radicals would destroy the balance which was so essential to the proper working of this constitution. In response to the radical complaints about the irregularities and abuses in the existing constitution the conservatives pointed out that these very faults actually helped to produce good government. The exploitation of patronage and influence and the irregular system of representation in fact produced the best legislators and helped to establish the delicate balance that was needed between liberty and property. The constitution as it existed in practice produced those end-results which the majority of the nation most wanted. It ensured both the preservation of liberty and the protection of property by ensuring the rule of law and upholding the sovereignty of Parliament. Most of all the constitution reflected and reinforced those social and economic distinctions which actually existed in British society.

The conservatives of the later eighteenth century could and did argue that the political and social order in Britain was one of the most liberal and stable ever established. They could compare it favourably with virtually every other system in the world and they could show how much it was admired by the most enlightened thinkers in Europe. The constitutional settlement achieved after the Glorious Revolution was credited with saving the country from absolutism and with inaugurating a period of unparalleled political liberty, social stability and economic advance. Under the Whig constitution Britain had become a major world power and praise was heaped upon it in pamphlets and speeches and from subjects high and low. According to William Blackstone: 'The idea and practice of this political or civil liberty flourish in their highest vigour in these kingdoms, where it falls little short of perfection, and can only be lost or destroyed by the folly or demerits of its owners: the legislature, and of course the laws of England, being peculiarly adapted to the preservation of this inestimable blessing even in the meanest subject.'[1] In the opinion of the Younger Pitt: 'The merit of the British constitution is to be estimated, not by metaphysical ideas, not by vague theories, but by analyzing it in practice. Its benefits are confirmed by the sure and infallible test of experience.'[2] In 1792 the humble members of the Church and King Club of Manchester proclaimed their absolute loyalty to 'one of the most beautiful systems of government, that the combined efforts of human wisdom has ever yet been able to accomplish'.[3]

The constitution was defended on the usual grounds that it was a mixed government which combined the virtues of monarchy, aristocracy and democracy while avoiding the dangers attendant on each of these in their pure forms, namely tyranny, a factious oligarchy, or anarchy. The institutions of King, Lords and Commons formed a delicate balance which secured liberty and stability while averting arbitrary power and mob rule. The king, as head of the executive and the fount of honour, could provide unchallenged authority and a firm lead. The Lords could normally be expected to support and buttress monarchy, but could also take the lead in any opposition to an arbitrary tyrant. The House of Commons represented the people and preserved their liberty and property, but was not sufficiently powerful to institute an unstable democracy. It was never easy, the conservatives argued, to establish and maintain a political order which was both stable and liberal. Since the ambitions and passions of men were not always firmly under control peace and order were easily lost. A political system that endeavoured to grant subjects considerable personal freedom risked creating a situation which was inherently unstable. Mixed governments were the best system that human wisdom had ever discovered, but even they were susceptible to corruption and dissolution if the three component elements did not co-exist in reasonable harmony. Each element had a natural tendency to pull in its own separate direction and it was only by carefully balancing them that they could remain harnessed together.[4] The British constitution could only stand firm while the institutions of Crown, Lords and Commons were delicately balanced. It would soon be toppled if the strength of any one of these component parts were weakened: 'take away ever so little weight from one, and the whole will immediately fall into ruins.'[5]

Before the development of extreme forms of radicalism in the 1790s most reformers would have accepted these oft-repeated arguments about the virtues and advantages of a mixed government and a balanced constitution. The reformers' case was that this wonderful constitution was being undermined by the excessive influence of King and Lords over the House of Commons. A measure of parliamentary reform was necessary to strengthen the democratic element of the constitution so that it could withstand the pressure exerted by the Crown and the aristocracy. The conservatives replied by warning that parliamentary reform, far from restoring the balance of the constitution, would in fact destroy it. Neither monarchy nor aristocracy could long survive once a democratic House of Commons had become a political weapon controlled by a sovereign people. It was therefore better to tolerate the minor abuses of the existing constitution than to institute reforms which would establish a democratic form of government. After all democracies were both more unstable and more corrupt than any other form of government. At best they were only suitable for small states and yet history showed that even the small states of ancient Greece and Rome had been torn apart by faction and insurrection. In democracies all subordination was destroyed and the voice of reason was drowned by the clamour of violence and enthusiasm. Before any order could be established in such states the common people, who were usually the most insolent and vicious of subjects, had to be caressed, bribed or intoxicated by those who would rule them. In Josiah Tucker's opinion:

> if experience shall be allowed to decide this question, it will almost universally tell us, that when a multitude are invested with the power of governing, they prove the very worst of governors. They are rash and precipitate, giddy and inconstant, and ever the dupes of designing men who lead them to commit the most atrocious crimes, in order to make them subservient to their own purposes. Besides, a democratic government is despotic in its very nature; because it supposes itself to be the only fountain of power, from which there can be no appeal.[6]

The conservatives' case did not rest simply on an unthinking opposition to change or on an unwillingness to listen to their opponents' arguments. They sought to counter the radical claims by endeavouring to show that there were many positive and practical reasons for those features of the existing constitution that appeared to be at best irregular and at worst corrupt and arbitrary. They went to considerable lengths to demonstrate that it was possible to offer sensible and pragmatic justifications for every feature of the existing constitution. While these might appear at first glance to be abuses further inquiry would show that they were necessary to the preservation of a mixed government and essential to the effective operation of the balanced constitution. Moreover, it could be clearly shown that the political system was rooted in the social and economic realities of the age. Since society was hierarchical and property was unequally divided, the political order must reflect these realities. The liberty of the subject, the protection of property, and the preservation of law and order could only be secured by a government controlled by the responsible elements in society. The British constitution had the particular virtue of allowing the leaders of society and the men of property to govern according to the rule of law.

While the reformers attacked the influence which the Crown and the aristocracy could exert over the composition and resolutions of the House of Commons, the conservatives insisted that the Commons could not be allowed to become entirely independent without destroying the virtues of a balanced constitution. The King and the House of Lords no longer possessed an effective veto over much of the legislation emanating from the Lower House and it was clear that no government could long survive without the approbation and support of a majority of the House of Commons. In these circumstances it was essential that the Crown and the Lords should exercise some influence over the composition and therefore the deliberations of the House of Commons. If the Crown and the aristocracy were not allowed to exercise influence naturally through their patronage then more open bribery and corruption would be attempted. If all influence of this kind were abolished then all power would devolve upon the House of Commons and 'our government would degenerate into the worst of all governments, namely, a democracy, with all the expence and trouble of a monarchy.'[7] No evidence could be provided, the conservatives claimed, to prove that the king and the aristocracy were in fact aiming to subvert the liberty of the subject. On the other hand the experience of the 1640s and 1650s clearly demonstrated the danger of allowing the House of Commons too much power.[8] Soame Jenyns insisted that:

An independent House of Commons is no part of the English constitution, the excellence of which consists in being composed of three powers, mutually dependent on each other; and of these, if any was to become independent of the other two; it must engross the whole power to itself, and the form of our government would be immediately changed. This an independent House of Commons actually performed in the last century, murdered the king, annihilated the peers, and established the worst kind of democracy that ever existed; and the same confusion would infallibly be repeated, should we ever be so unfortunate as to see another.[9]

William Paley claimed that the American colonies were lost precisely because the Crown had not possessed the influence over the colonial assemblies that it exercised over the House of Commons. A rebellion might break out nearer home if ever the House of Commons became independent of both Crown and Lords. As a political institution the House of Lords was not as strong as the House of Commons and so good relations could not be maintained between the two unless the nobility could influence the composition of the lower chamber. If the peers could not influence the election of some Members of Parliament then they would seek to exert their natural strength, which was firmly based on the possession of considerable wealth and property, in some other way. The most obvious tactic would be to increase the direct political influence of their own chamber, but any strengthening of the formal constitutional powers of the House of Lords would almost certainly provoke frequent disputes with the House of Commons. Political stability could never be achieved if the two Houses of Parliament were constantly at odds with each other. The same reasoning dictated that the Crown should have its leading servants sitting in the House of Commons. This was the only means of smoothing the relations between the executive and the representatives of the people. Without a body of royal supporters in the Commons a factious opposition would always be able to obstruct the decisions needed to implement the policies of even the best governments. This Court party was not in fact so large that it could be considered a serious threat to the liberties of the subject and if it were reduced it would not be strong enough to preserve the constitution. A mixed and balanced government could not be preserved unless patronage provided a link between the three elements in the legislature. Influence was in fact the cement of the constitution: 'many wise and virtuous politicians deem a considerable portion of it to be as necessary a part of the British constitution, as any other ingredient in the composition; to be that, indeed, which gives cohesion and solidity to the whole.'[10]

Soame Jenyns endeavoured to show that this kind of royal and aristocratic influence was not only necessary to the preservation of the constitution but was a natural response of those engaged in active politics. The working of the existing constitution corresponded in his opinion to the natural instincts of men and reflected the social realities of the age. Jenyns acknowledged that a numerous assembly had to be influenced to some extent if it were ever to work effectively with the king's ministers, but he went on to assert that it was natural to expect Members of Parliament to desire some material reward for their services to the nation. Able and ambitious men were not so altruistic that they would bear the costs of sitting in Parliament simply so that they could enjoy the satisfaction of serving their country. It was only natural that they would endeavour to serve themselves by the pursuit of power, honours and preferment. If these were not forthcoming then ambitious politicians would soon obstruct all parliamentary business until their demands were gratified by the Government.[11] Other conservatives used similar cynical and pessimistic assessments of human nature in order to support even more fundamental arguments about the operation of politics. One such commentator claimed that all political societies were inevitably composed of competing interests and ambitious factions. Reasoned arguments alone would never persuade enough men to support authority. No government therefore could survive for long unless it used a variety of apparently immoral tactics to compel, deceive, corrupt, indulge and cajole the people. It was easy to criticize influence, but the wise could see that it was in fact more necessary in a free government than under a tyranny where compulsion would suffice. Unfortunately, few men possessed the political wisdom to grasp this truth:

> The most ignorant can perceive the mischiefs that must arise from corrupt ministers and venal parliaments; but it requires some sagacity to discern, that assemblies of men unconnected by self-interest will no more draw together in the business of the public, than horses without harness or bridles; but, like them, instead of being quietly guided in the right road of general utility, will immediately run to riot, stop the wheels of government, and tear all the political machine to pieces.

Thus influence, like the other imperfections and abuses of the constitution, was only necessary because of the selfish and corrupt nature of men. It should only be eliminated when there was clear evidence that the nature of man had been radically reformed.[12]

Josiah Tucker reached a similar conclusion. He maintained that no government could survive unless it possessed the power either to compel or to influence the actions of men. Since too much compulsion produced an arbitrary tyranny, governors must be allowed to influence their subjects. While it had to be admitted that this political influence might not always be applied to the right ends, it could not be sacrificed without giving up all hope of a stable government. Fortunately, the evidence clearly proved that in Britain the Crown applied its influence to the best ends of society more often than not.

Moreover, Tucker argued, many of those who were most critical of Crown patronage were ready to defend the political influence of all other men of property. British society was replete with evidence that men of property, from the greatest landowners to the smallest tradesmen, sought to influence the actions of those dependent upon them. Where property was unequally divided, power would be unequally shared. Those who possessed greater wealth and power must be expected to seek to influence those with less. It was idle to condemn a particular form of political influence without criticizing the whole structure of society: 'Either therefore all influence ought to be condemned alike; or that of the Crown ought not to be branded more than the rest, as being peculiarly criminal, and held up as the only object of public hatred, and national detestation.'[13] Others made the same point. They maintained that the entire political and social system, from the sovereign down to the humblest labourer, could not operate without the exercise of natural influence and the firm ties which interest and dependency created. The British political system was but a microcosm of British society as a whole.[14]

The conservatives were convinced that the reforms suggested by the radicals would destroy the existing constitution. They were particularly alarmed about those reforms which would give the ordinary people direct influence over the composition and decisions of the House of Commons. Although they still adhered to the Lockean principle that the legislature should include a representative assembly chosen by the people, they also followed tradition in making a clear distinction between 'the people' and 'the rabble'. The former deserved to be represented in Parliament because they contributed to the wealth and strength of the country and because they could be trusted to exercise the vote with a due regard both to their own interests and those of the nation at large. The stability of the constitution rested on the representation of property because only men of independent means could be certain to possess the qualities needed to exercise a free choice among the candidates standing for Parliament. The possession of property attached a man to his country and gave him an interest which he would always strive to protect. The franchise therefore should never extend beyond the smaller proprietors: 'He who has a house, and family, and goods; and in his trade, at least, or other ostensible means of subsistence, a kind of independence, will be alarmed at every movement that may hurt or touch him, in any of these vulnerable parts. He will watch with an

279

anxious eye even the remotest inroads of oppression.'[15] In contrast, those without property were regarded as being in so mean a situation that they must be esteemed to have no will of their own. Such men could not be trusted with the franchise:

If these persons had votes, they would be tempted to dispose of them under some undue influence or other. This would give a great, an artful, or a wealthy man, a larger share in elections than is consistent with general liberty. If it were probable that every man would give his vote freely, and without influence of any kind, then, upon the true theory and genuine principles of liberty, every member of the community, however poor, should have a vote in electing those delegates, to whose charge is committed the disposal of his property, his liberty, and his life. But, since that can hardly be expected in persons of indigent fortunes, or such as are under the immediate dominion of others, all popular states have been obliged to establish certain qualifications; whereby some, who are suspected of having no will of their own, are excluded from voting, in order to set other individuals, whose wills may be supposed independent, more thoroughly upon a level with each other.[16]

The conservatives regarded the protection of private property as the most important duty of any legislature and they therefore concluded that only property-owners could be trusted to perform such a duty. The protection of property could not be entrusted to those who did not possess any property of their own and who might easily be tempted to acquire some by arbitrary means. The system of representation that existed in Britain was therefore entirely justified whatever the reformers might say. Edmund Burke calculated that at most there were some four hundred thousand men with the property qualifications deemed essential in a voter.[17] These were the men who could be expected to possess the disinterested and responsible attitude needed in an elector. Political stability could be guaranteed if such men were represented. On the other hand the masses lacked such qualities and to allow them representation would be to endanger the constitution. The radicals claimed that all men possessed the same abilities, but they ignored the actual situation of the masses. If only they would look at the circumstances which existed they would see that the masses could not be trusted with any active political rights. It was therefore right to exclude them from any direct representation in Parliament.[18] The poor were uninformed, were too ready to defer to their immediate superiors, and were easily deluded and inflamed by ill-designing men. They were without the 'discern-ment to perceive, or leisure to learn, or steadiness to pursue, the best, or indeed any effectual means of guarding against the power and artifices of the few'.[19] If such men had the vote then they would be certain to choose unsuitable representatives and sober men of property would have no confidence in a parliament of such men. Property, even liberty, could not be secured by a House of Commons which was without power because it lacked the confidence and sup-port of independent men of wealth and judgement.[20]

While most conservatives were content to stress the political ad-vantages of the existing propertied franchise, some occasionally gave vent to their contempt, fear and hatred of the masses. The ordinary people were occasionally referred to as the rabble, the mob, the com-mon herd or the swinish multitude. To appeal to such people was to entrust government to the most passionate, irresponsible and violent of men. If the vote was extended to such men then at elections 'such a scene of confusion, of drunkenness and riot, of rapine, murder, and conflagration, will present itself, as must shock us with horror, even in imagination.'[21] Should such men actually be in a position to influence the decisions of the legislature then all order would be subverted and anarchy would prevail.[22] Even to listen to such people was a mistake. Parliament should always reject out of hand those petitions for reform 'signed by the scum of the earth, the refuse of the people'.[23]

Until the events of the 1790s produced a fierce reaction among the governing classes the majority of those who sought to defend the existing constitution remained content to stress the political advan-tages of the representation of property rather than to warn of the dangers of an extended franchise. They insisted that the existing system had proved eminently satisfactory and was not widely re-sented. They pointed out that the radicals exaggerated the support for reform and they made much of the fact that the radicals were unable to drum up petitions from such unrepresented towns as Birm-ingham, Manchester and Sheffield.[24] The conservatives maintained that the general satisfaction with the constitution stemmed from the fact that the people recognized that they were virtually represented in Parliament even if they did not vote in any election. Men of property in the large unrepresented towns might still have a vote in county elections. Even if they were not qualified to vote in the county elections their commercial and manufacturing interests were repre-

sented by Members of Parliament elected for other towns with similar economic interests. The fact that a large town was unrepresented
did not mean that it had no influence over the decisions taken by
Parliament. No one could believe, claimed Lord North, that the
interests and petitions of Birmingham, Manchester or Leeds carried
less weight with Members of Parliament than those of such small
constituencies as Old Sarum.[25] Furthermore, it was argued, Members
of Parliament represented the whole nation and not merely the
constituency which returned them to Parliament. 'Every member
of the House of Commons represents those who voted against him,
as well as them who voted for him. Yea, wherever a man is chosen,
he ceases to be a representative of that city or county only, by which
he was chosen: and becomes a representative of the British people
at large. And every individual among that people is represented, not
by any particular Member of Parliament only; but by the whole
house.'[26] It therefore was of little account whether certain towns
were represented or not or whether certain individuals had the vote
or not. Provided Members of Parliament represented all regions of
the country, a wide variety of constituencies, and a sufficiently
numerous and responsible body of electors, then the House of Commons was in a position to represent the interests of the whole nation
and the entire population. Members of Parliament might be chosen
by men of property, but once elected they also represented the
property-less poor. Only by recognizing this concept of representation could there be a community of interest, a sympathy of feeling,
and an attitude of trust between the people and Members of
Parliament.

The concept of virtual representation enabled the conservative
defenders of the existing constitution to justify the exclusion of the
vast majority of the population from the privilege of exercising the
vote. By extending this notion of representation it also allowed them
to claim that Members of Parliament were the representatives of the
whole nation and not simply the delegates of those who actually
elected them. This had the advantage of allowing Members to serve
the general good of all rather than the particular interests of their
constituents. It meant that the House of Commons could be described as a deliberative assembly in which all members were free
to act to the best of their ability and in accordance with their independent judgement. While constituencies could offer advice to their
representatives they had no right to seek to instruct them or to bind

them to pursue certain courses of action in Parliament. To attempt to do so would rob a Member of Parliament of his personal independence and destroy his character as a representative of the whole nation. It would in fact prevent him from serving the whole community.[27]

The principle of virtual representation was an important part of the conservative defence of the existing constitution. It enabled men to argue that the irregularities of the electoral system did not mean that only a part of the nation was represented in Parliament. When the radicals derided this assertion that Members of Parliament represented the whole nation and not merely the minority who possessed the suffrage, conservative opinion replied by demonstrating that all the important interests in the State were represented in Parliament. Unwilling to contemplate the notion that the House of Commons ought to represent directly every adult male in the country, Edmund Burke had been the first to suggest that its strength lay in the fact that it represented the great and legitimate interests in the State. Parliament gained strength by representing not individuals, but interests. It acquired power, weight and stability by representing the landed, financial and commercial interests and also the official and professional men who served the country.[28] James Mackintosh, after he had ben converted by Burke, took up the same position: 'The best security which human wisdom can devise, seems to be the distribution of political authority among different individuals and bodies, with separate interests and separate characters, corresponding to the variety of classes which civil society is composed, each interested to guard his own order from oppression by the rest.'[29]

The concept of the representation of interests enabled the conservatives to defend the irregularities of the electoral system on grounds of utility and expediency. While the radicals concentrated on finding the logical and rational basis for extending the suffrage to all men, the conservatives preferred to stress that the prevailing system of representation, whatever its apparent faults, did in fact produce a House of Commons of the highest calibre. It was possible to criticize the system of representation as apparently irrational, but experience proved that it worked. The defenders of the constitution insisted that what was of greater importance was not who voted, but who was elected. If the composition of the House of Commons was carefully examined, then it could be clearly demonstrated that the irregular electoral system worked in practice. By the apparently arbitrary and illogical method of annexing the right to vote to different qualifications in different places a House of Commons was elected to represent all the important interests in the country. Among Members of Parliament could be found landowners, moneyed men, merchants and manufacturers as well as courtiers, government officials and representatives of all the learned professions and the armed services. Clearly men of the greatest wealth, highest status and most eminent talents were chosen to represent the people. These men were the best qualified and the most likely to promote the public interest. If the nation was not safe in their hands then no parliament could be safe from corruption. Since the best men were chosen it mattered little how they were elected. The rotten boroughs might be condemned by the radicals because they allowed a handful of voters to be influenced by outside forces, but it was precisely these constituencies which were most under the control of men of wealth and talent. A close scrutiny of the careers of Members of Parliament would reveal that many of those representing counties and the more populous boroughs rarely distinguished themselves in Parliament, whereas the chief men of business and the greatest men of talent, including the two William Pitts, Burke, Fox, Barré and Dunning, were often chosen for the smallest boroughs.[30]

This defence of the electoral system on pragmatic grounds became increasingly popular in conservative circles. When Charles Jenkinson spoke for the Government in opposition to Charles Grey's Reform bill of 1793 he urged Members to ignore the abstract question of who ought to have the vote and to concentrate instead on the practical objective of how to secure the best House of Commons. If the essential test was not who voted but who was elected, then it was evident that the existing system was working effectively. An extended franchise might well result in the return of Members who lacked fortune and ability and who would be too easily influenced by opinion out-of-doors. On the other hand, experience proved that the present system produced Members who were sober men of judgement. This was because the landed interest had the strongest representation, though the commercial and manufacturing interests had their due weight and influence in the House. The Commons also secured the advice and assistance of professional men, chiefly those in the army, the navy and the law. Moreover, the House could only conduct its business efficiently if it obtained the services of men who wished to pursue a career in government service. These were the men who could be counted upon to be active in debate and dependable in business. Popular opinion was generally hostile to such men and they were rarely returned for large constituencies. Without rotten boroughs the House would be denuded of much of its talent and its power would decline accordingly. Since therefore it was manifest that the existing system secured the election of the various types of Members needed to serve the national interest it would be rash indeed to alter it in favour of an untried system which could only be guaranteed to return men who were capable of swaying and being swayed in turn by public opinion.[31]

Conservative propagandists praised the constitution, despite its apparent irregularities and anomalies, because it worked effectively and because in their view it harmonized with social and economic realities. They praised it most of all because it produced precisely those political results which conservative men of property desired. The British constitution was regarded as the best means devised by the wisdom of man for combining liberty and stability. While the radicals criticized some of its illiberal features, the conservatives were more concerned with the preservation of law and order and the protection of property than with the extension of active political rights to all men. They believed that liberty could only exist when the rule of law was firmly established and they were convinced that the existing constitution was the strongest buttress to the rule of law. Their attachment to liberty was genuine enough, but they adhered to a restricted concept of liberty. The conservatives consciously and deliberately distinguished between liberty under the law and within the framework of a stable political order and the right of every individual to act as he saw fit. In their view the latter would produce anarchy and licentiousness and would end up by annihilating all liberty:

It is an error of very dangerous consequence to imagine, that we can never have liberty enough; and to fancy that every diminution of the authority of government is gaining so much fresh accession to the privileges and independence of the subject ... the licentiousness of subjects is no less fatal to liberty, than the arbitrary dominion of the most despotic monarch; that liberty, extended beyond its just bounds, leads to absolute tyranny.[32]

Conservative opinion was convinced that the existing constitution ensured that all men were regarded as equal before the law. In their view: 'The greatest degree of liberty, which any people can enjoy, is, to be governed by equitable and impartial laws.'[33] These benefits were secured by the British constitution. It guaranteed that a man's rights to his life, liberty and property were defined by the law and could only be infringed by due process of law. Liberty could not exist without such a constitution and the law could not be equal and impartial unless order and stability were secured by just such a government as the British enjoyed. In order to enjoy liberty men needed to live under a good and steady government which would maintain order and rule according to known and impartial laws.

Permit me ... to tell you what the freedom is that I love and that to which I think all men are entitled. It is not solitary, unconnected, individual, selfish liberty, as if every man was to regulate the whole of his conduct by his own will. The liberty I mean is *social* freedom. It is that state of things in which liberty is secured by the equality of restraint; a constitution of things in which the liberty of no one man, and no body of men and no number of men can find means to trespass on the liberty of any person or description of persons in society. This kind of liberty is indeed but another name for justice, ascertained by wise laws, and secured by well-constructed institutions.[34]

It was not essential to the preservation of liberty that every individual should possess the same active political rights. Men could be free to enjoy their life, liberty and property under the existing constitution because they were not subject to excessive government interference. The protection of such civil liberties did not require that all men should possess a voice in the decision-making processes of the State. In other words, since liberty was impossible without law and order, men must be content with a limited government like that of Britain and not seek to dictate to those in power. Liberty was impossible without the rule of law for law was the means of preventing an arbitrary and tyrannical government. The British constitution preserved the rule of law more efficiently than any other known system of government. The defence of liberty therefore did not require the direct representation of every individual in Parliament. In opposing Alderman Sawbridge's motion for a reform of Parliament, in 1784, Lord North asked the Commons:

Did freedom depend upon every individual subject being represented in that House? Certainly not; for that House, constituted as it was, represented the whole kingdom. Freedom depended on a very different

286

circumstance. He was free, because he lived in a country governed by equal laws. Where the highest and lowest were governed by the same laws, where there was no distinction of persons, there freedom might be said to exist as purely and as perfectly as in the nature of things it could exist.[35]

Edmund Burke spoke for many conservatives when he utterly rejected the notion that liberty could be complete and unrestrained: 'The extreme of liberty (which is *its abstract perfection, but its real fault*) obtains nowhere, nor ought to obtain anywhere ... Liberty too must be limited in order to be possessed.'[36] He was particularly horrified by the idea that liberty could only be achieved by giving free rein to the sovereignty of the people. This would be to put the will of men above considerations of reason and justice.[37] This would make might right and would lead to another form of arbitrary tyranny, namely mob rule. In order to prevent this it was essential that laws should emanate from a known legislature whose sovereignty was absolute and irresistible. In other words, the rule of law in Britain was secured by the existing constitution because that constitution recognized the sovereignty of Parliament not the sovereignty of the people. The legislature could only uphold the rule of law because it had the authority to impose on every subject any law which it passed. Equal and impartial laws could not exist if particular subjects or groups of subjects were beyond the reach of justice or were free to deny the authority of the legislature. The sovereignty of Parliament must be so extensive that it applied to all subjects and all questions.[38] The only limitation on its authority was that recognized by the wisdom, prudence and judgement of the legislators themselves.[39] The legislators might decide that certain actions were imprudent or unjust, but whatever they did decide to enact had the force of law and was in consequence supreme and irresistible.

Conservative opinion therefore refused to accept any limitations on the legal authority of Parliament because it would place the rights of the individual above the rule of law. The legislature must not be regarded as subordinate to the sovereign will of the people as the radicals endeavoured to prove. Subjects might have the right to liberty of conscience, but this right could not prevent Parliament from establishing a national church and endowing it with certain privileges, including a monopoly of public office for its adherents.[40] Subjects might also claim equality before the law, but they had no right to claim the authority to cashier their governors or frame a new government to their satisfaction. Any alteration in the constitution or in the distribution of political power had to be sanctioned by Parliament.[41] There was certainly no need to seek the endorsement of the people for the laws of Parliament: 'no man in his senses will pretend to say, that the laws and edicts of parliament are not binding, ' 'till they have received the sanction of some patriotic club, or popular assembly convened for that purpose: – or that taxes ought not to be levied, 'till the people shall appear to be willing to pay them.'[42] The House of Commons must act for the people and, if necessary, act against them. Otherwise the people and not Parliament would be sovereign.[43]

The doctrine of legislative sovereignty was immensely popular with conservatives because it could be brought to bear against all radical schemes to set up a rival authority to that exercised by propertied men sitting in Parliament. Members of Parliament who rejected the claim that the electorate could send them instructions were hardly likely to countenance more radical schemes to exert popular pressure on the legislature. Conservative Members protested vigorously against any attempt to inflame the populace against the House of Commons. During the Wilkite disturbances of 1770 Jeremiah Dyson warned the House: 'I am an enemy to tyranny, Sir, and therefore I cannot without indignation hear this House threatened with the most preposterous and horrid of all tyranny, that of a mob. To insinuate that the measures of a legislative body should be influenced by echoes of sedition from the rabble, is to insinuate that all government should be at an end.'[44] Even more alarming to conservative opinion was the extreme radical claim that the people could elect a national convention to draw up a new constitution. This was vigorously condemned as 'an open attempt to supersede the House of Commons in its representative capacity, and to assume to itself all the functions and powers of a national legislature'.[45] To the conservative defenders of the constitution all schemes designed to confer sovereign authority on the people were a threat to the sovereignty of Parliament, the rule of law and the genuine civil liberties of the subject. All the various plans to reform the existing constitution were therefore condemned. Any extension of the franchise would only swamp the opinions of responsible men of property with the violent and uncontrolled passions of the ignorant masses. A redistribution of seats would either give the landed interest too much influence if the counties secured greater representation or would subvert the landed interest if the large towns were given increased representation. The secret ballot would encourage more men to sell their vote and would make it impossible to judge which men took their responsibilities seriously. Frequent general elections would only increase the opportunities for dissipation, tumult, and corruption and would force Members of Parliament to spend more time nursing their constituencies than serving the nation. Members would either strive to be popular with their constituents or would succumb to tempting offers from the administration which would help them with their electoral expenses. In either case they would pursue selfish ends or sectional interests to the exclusion of the public interest. The consequence would be either perpetual instability as Members of Parliament bowed to popular pressure and refused to take difficult decisions or a House of Commons entirely corrupted by the Court. Both liberty and stability would then be lost.[46]

By the 1790s conservative opinion was convinced that radical demands would not only endanger the existing constitution and the rule of law, but might destroy the whole fabric of society. An increasing majority of the propertied classes both in and out of Parliament was ready to sanction repressive measures which would prevent the radicals emulating the revolutionary principles and the violent measures of the French. Conservative opinion feared that the attacks on the existing constitution would not only produce instability and lawlessness, but would be the prelude to the violent levelling of all social and economic distinctions. Most radicals might claim that they only desired a reform of Parliament, but the support which many of them expressed for the French Revolution convinced conservative opinion that the monarchy, the aristocracy and the Established Church would all be swept away in a reign of terror. While the radicals expressed good intentions and claimed that the rational basis of their theoretical schemes would ensure that their reforms would produce a just and stable government, the example of France provided the conservatives with evidence that violence and anarchy were the inevitable consequences of putting power in the hands of the mob. The tyranny of the people was far worse than the most determined despotism of any European monarch. The sovereignty of the people, once unleashed, would not be content to eliminate corruption and protect the liberty of the subject. It would attack all privileges, including all social and economic distinctions, and it would make a determined effort to remedy what the poor regarded as the greatest grievance in society, namely the unequal distribution of property. The conservatives were therefore convinced that the benefits of the existing constitution could not be reaped if the sovereignty of Parliament was replaced by the sovereignty of the people and if the rule of law was replaced by the will of the licentious mob. If the existing constitution collapsed then social revolution would soon follow since men of property would have no political or legal protection against the envious claims of the indigent masses. In Burke's view: 'The sovereignty of the people was the most false, wicked, and mischievous doctrine that ever could be preached to them ... The moment that equality and the sovereignty of the people was adopted as the rule of government, property would be at an end, and religion, morality, and law, which grew out of property would fall with it.'[47] Like Burke, Arthur Young was convinced that the French Revolution had proved that political reforms which put power in the hands of the indigent masses would inevitably lead to social revolution. Give the vote to the poor and:

it follows, by direct consequence, that all the property of the society is at the mercy of those who possess nothing; and could theory have blundered so stupidly as to suppose for a moment, that attack and plunder would not follow power in such hands; let it recur to France for *fact*, to prove what reason ought to have foreseen ... The leading conclusion, deducible from the French experiment, and written in characters, which he that runs may read, is this, IF PERSONS ARE REPRESENTED, PROPERTY IS DESTROYED. We know then what to think of the proposals for reform hitherto made in this kingdom.[48]

2 The Development of a Conservative Ideology

Most of those who defended and justified the existing constitution did so on practical and pragmatic grounds. In their view the British constitution had stood the test of time and had clearly proved itself superior to any other. Even its apparent abuses and anomalies could be shown to be essential to the working of its delicately balanced mechanism. Most important of all, the constitution secured the important advantages of good government: the rule of law, the protection of property and the preservation of civil liberty. These political advantages chiefly benefited men of property, though it was also claimed that even the ordinary subject gained more under the British constitution than he could secure under the arbitrary tyranny of a despot or a mob. Not surprisingly most men of substance preferred to keep the political benefits which they already enjoyed to the dubious promise of future benefits if they took the advice of the radicals. The conflict between radical and conservative can therefore be seen as one between those who put forward speculative hypotheses about the future benefits which would accrue if the constitution were re-established on rational first principles and those who already enjoyed considerable advantages under the existing constitution and were unwilling to risk political changes which might not only undermine these but also lead to violent social revolution. Nonetheless, the dispute was not simply between theoretical and speculative radicalism on the one hand and hard-headed, pragmatic conservatism on the other. After all, the radicals firmly expected that their proposals would reap considerable political benefits for the middle and lower classes. For actual proof they could point to the American experience and, at least for a time, to the reforms carried through in France. Conversely, the more philosophical and ideological conservatives were convinced that it was essential to counter the radicals with political arguments which would both undermine their principles and provide philosophical justification for the *status quo*. The conservative ideology which was developed in the later eighteenth century was less rationalist and systematic than the natural rights philosophy of the radicals, but some elements in it were far more profound and soundly based than the rather facile claims of Paine and his allies.

The development of an effective and influential conservative ideology owes a great deal to the speeches and writings of Edmund Burke, but he was only one of many conservative theorists and propagandists who endeavoured to provide a philosophical justification for the existing constitution. Burke undoubtedly played a major role in providing positive and constructive reasons for defending the existing establishment and he certainly had the greatest influence on conservative opinion in the 1790s. Many others did of course reach similar conclusions independently, though they failed to develop them so thoroughly or to express them so brilliantly as Burke. A number of able theorists did however contribute more than Burke to a powerful attack on the Lockean principles which underpinned so many radical claims. Burke wrote very little on the contract theory, for example, and what he did write was somewhat ambiguous. Yet the contract theory was a crucial plank in the radical platform and it needed to be undermined if the radical case was to be seriously weakened. The conservative theorists were not content simply to attack the principles which underlay the demands of their radical opponents. In seeking to justify the existing constitution the conservatives developed a distinctive ideology of their own. Nonetheless the conservative ideology developed from a determination to undermine three arguments used by the radicals. Conservative ideology emerged as a response to the radical interpretations of the natural state of man, of the origins and foundations of civil government, and of the aims and purposes of political society.

The political claims of the radicals rested heavily on the argument that all men were naturally equal. The radicals admitted that men differed in their intelligence, strength and talents, but they insisted that these were only minor differences and were unimportant compared to the equality that all men possessed in the sight of God and in the state of nature. Conservative theorists however utterly rejected this concept of natural equality. While they admitted that all men shared a common nature they denied that this meant in practice that all men were equal or could lay claim to the right to be treated as equals. To counter the radicals they stressed the observed inequality of men. Conservatives insisted that men had merely to look around them to see that no society existed in which all men were equal. Arthur Young claimed that 'equality is a romantic phantom of the imagination, never realized.'[49] Soame Jenyns maintained that the evidence of society clearly proved the inequality of men: 'for we daily see, that some are born with beautiful and healthy bodies, and some with frames distorted, and filled with the most deplorable diseases; some with minds fraught with the seeds of wisdom and genius, others with those of idiotism and madness; some, by the laws and constitutions of their countries, are born to the inheritance of affluent fortunes and distinguished honours, others to a life of poverty, labour and obscurity.'[50] George Pitt condemned the radical claim as dangerous nonsense:

Their fundamental doctrine is that of *the perfect equality of mankind*, than which nothing can be more dangerous, more impossible to practise, or more immediately subversive of all government. A doctrine, the fallacy of which is proved by the experience of every day, by the concurrence of all history, from the earliest times, and, above all, by the contemplation of all the works of the Creator, whether animate, or inanimate; the very essence of which appears to be *gradation, or inequality*.[51]

292

The conservatives insisted that men were born unequal in both body and mind and these inequalities increased in later years as men improved or damaged their initial prospects. It was therefore impossible, without violating the principles of human nature, to prevent a permanent distinction of ranks in society.[52] Bishop Watson preached that God's providential design required that men should differ widely in their talents and abilities. These differences were not only designed to demonstrate the extent and range of God's power, but also enabled God to show men what virtues and qualities they ought to develop. Industry and frugality were rewarded, while laziness and extravagance were punished. The poor and unfortunate must learn to reconcile themselves to the inscrutable designs of God and to labour against adversity. For their part the rich and talented must learn humility and charity so that they would bless God for his goodness to them and be ready to assist those less fortunate than themselves.[53] Soame Jenyns pursued a similar line and claimed that the divine plan required the highly unequal distribution of riches, understanding and health, but the equal distribution of happiness. God compensated the poor with more hopes and fewer fears, with better health and a greater appreciation of small enjoyments. Their very ignorance helped the poor to endure the miseries of poverty and the fatigue of endless drudgery.[54] Inequality was therefore not only natural and providential, but positively beneficial to all ranks in society.

The radicals not only claimed that men were naturally equal, but also insisted that men were naturally benevolent. Although they acknowledged that the passions of men frequently led them from the path of justice the radicals still believed that human reason, if properly cultivated, could restrain men's passions and guide them in the pursuit of truth and justice. Since reason and benevolence could be made stronger than passion and self-interest then all men could eventually be trusted with political liberty. Civil governments should therefore rest upon the principle of equal liberty and should allow men to use their reason for the improvement of society. Conservatives however had a very different attitude to the nature of man. They were convinced of the fallibility and imperfectibility of man. They claimed that both the Christian religion and the test of experience proved the sinfulness and selfishness of all men. Human reason alone had never proved adequate to the task of restraining the unsocial needs and desires of men. Without the legal restraints and coercion applied by those in authority civil society would soon collapse into anarchy as passionate and ambitious men used force to pursue their own selfish ends. The need to coerce men and to protect the weak from the strong and the virtuous from the selfish stemmed from the fact that men were not naturally benevolent and rational.[55]

Civil society, the conservatives insisted, must recognize and accommodate itself to the natural distinctions among men. Attempts to level all such natural distinctions could only be accomplished by force, but even the most violent revolutions would not succeed in permanently eradicating these differences. Although violence might temporarily level society it could not make men equal and so either the natural hierarchy must reassert itself or the natural leaders must be subordinated by the exercise of unnatural force. In the latter event a natural order would be replaced by an unnatural one. Once having overthrown a system of natural order and subordination the radicals would have to maintain the new order by force. Inferior men could only govern superior men if they governed by might and will rather than through justice and equal laws.[56]

In seeking to explain the origins and foundation of civil government in Britain the reformers appealed to three sources of authority: the original contract, the ancient constitution and the principles of the Glorious Revolution. The radicals, particularly in the 1790s, laid greatest stress on the contract theory. Their concept of natural equality led them to insist that all men possessed certain natural and inalienable rights. Civil society and civil government were artificial constructs designed to preserve and protect these natural rights by converting them into civil rights. This could only be done by contracts which were agreed to by all men and which conferred on all men the right to retain an active role in the political affairs of their society. In seeking to reject the democratic claims of the radicals the conservative theorists were compelled to challenge this interpretation of the contract theory. This led them to deny that there had ever been a pre-political or pre-civil 'state of nature'; to reject the claim that civil government was created by a contract agreed to by all men; and consequently to refute the radical demand that all men must have an active role in politics.[57]

Those conservative theorists who tackled the problem of the creation of civil society either rejected the notion of an original contract or at least laid little stress on it. Edmund Burke was not much concerned to trace the origins of civil society, but he did reject the notion that men had lived in a pre-civil state of nature in which they had enjoyed complete independence and equality. Burke denied any sharp distinction between natural and civil or artificial society. He regarded 'natural man' and 'civil man' as complementary rather than as opposed aspects of human nature. Furthermore, he believed that civil or developed society was more natural to man than the savage and primitive forms of society normally classified as natural : 'The state of civil society . . . is a state of nature; and much more truly so than a savage and incoherent mode of life. For man is by nature reasonable; and is never perfectly in his natural state, but when he is placed where reason may be best cultivated and most predominates. Art is man's nature. We are as much, at least, in a state of nature in formed manhood, as in immature and helpless infancy.'[58] Burke did not directly repudiate the notion of an original contract or claim that it was historically false, but the concept is not important to his idea of civil society. Any contractual relationships in society were but part of the ongoing historical process and no contract could be regarded as either the foundation of civil society or civil government or the basis for extensive claims about the rights of man. When Burke stressed the importance of a contract he did not mean the original basis of civil society established at a particular time by deliberate choice. In his view the only important contract was not this logical and artificial construct of man, but the eternal, binding and unchangeable relationship between man and man which resulted from the grand design of God :

It is a partnership in all science; a partnership in all art; a partnership in every virtue, and in all perfection. As the ends of such a partnership cannot be obtained in many generations, it becomes a partnership not only between those who are living, but between those who are living, those who are dead, and those who are to be born. Each contract of each particular state is but a clause in the great primaeval contract of eternal society, linking the lower with the higher natures, connecting the visible and invisible world, according to a fixed compact sanctioned by the inviolable oath which holds all physical and all moral natures, each in their appointed place.[59]

Many conservative theorists unequivocally rejected the radical claim that civil government was created by a voluntary contract, whether that contract was agreed to by all men or only by the most important men of property.[60] In taking this stand they were prepared to repudiate the political philosophy of John Locke which the radicals regarded as the chief basis of Whig principles. Josiah Tucker ridiculed the whole notion of an original contract:

> The Lockians have not yet vouchsaved to tell us, where any one single copy of this famous original contract is to be found, – in what language it was written, – in whose hands deposited, – who were the witnesses, – nor in what archives we are to search for it. But nevertheless they have taken care to supply us very amply with inferences and deductions resulting from it; – as if it had been a thing, which had been already proved and admitted, and concerning whose existence no further questions ought to be asked.[61]

In place of a man-made contract as the origin of government and subordination some conservatives were prepared to return to the notion of the divine institution of magistracy. They rejected the purely secular political philosophy of the radicals and insisted that the right to govern and the duty to obey derived from the will of God. Although they did not return to the old Tory doctrine that particular rulers governed by divine right, they maintained that government itself was an institution designed by God for the benefit of man. The submission of the individual was a religious duty which every man owed to God. Men could not choose to be free and unconnected, but must follow the providential design of God and live united in society and subject to government.[62] Although not alone in his views Burke, more than any other conservative theorist, stressed the divine origin of government. He was convinced that God willed civil society in which each man had different duties and obligations and that He willed the state in which men could best carry out these responsibilities. Both civil society and civil government were divinely ordained. They were not artificial constructs, the mere expression of human will:

> the awful Author of our being is the Author of our place in the order of existence; and that having disposed and marshalled us by a divine tactic, not according to our will, but according to his, he has, in and by that disposition, virtually subjected us to act the part which belongs to the place assigned us. We have obligations to mankind at large, which are not in consequence of any special voluntary pact. They arise from the relation of man to man, and the relation of man to God, which relations are not a matter of choice.[63]

Those conservative theorists who attempted a more profound study of the actual origins of civil society and civil government were convinced that both were the natural product of the needs and fears of man. In reaching this conclusion they were heavily influenced by the work of David Hume and the earlier writings of Adam Smith and Adam Ferguson, which were discussed in chapter four. In place of the contract theory, which they regarded simply as a speculative hypothesis, they sought a sociological and historical explanation which accorded more nearly with the known evidence about the nature of man and the origins of society. In doing so they rejected the concept of a state of nature as an abstraction which bore no relation to any reality ever experienced by man. All the earliest traces of man revealed him living in civil society, however primitive. There was abundant evidence to suggest that civil society was natural to man and was the product of his wants and needs. It was clear that men could not survive long without associating together and assisting one another. If any man were deprived of the advantages of society he would soon seek to make his way back into it. Civil society could be traced back to primitive beginnings, but it had always existed and it developed naturally as the numbers and wealth of the members of society increased and their needs and wants became more complex. Civil society was therefore a natural development and not the artificial creation of some original contract or convention. Not only was there no surviving record of any such contract, but none could ever have existed. Laws and institutions concerning agreements, contracts and conventions could be traced in all societies, but they were the product of those societies and not the foundations on which they were first erected. Men must have already formed themselves into a society and must already be concerting together before any form of contract could be agreed and enforced. Contracts and agreements were needed to deal with the defects of existing societies and could not therefore be the origins of society. Laws and institutions, government and subordination were established before conventions and contracts were possible. Civil governments were initially established by force or necessity, not by contracts based on voluntary agreements. Men were either compelled to subordinate themselves to those with superior strength, wealth or wisdom or simply found it expedient to do so. To imagine a civil society in which every man was absolutely free and equal and in which each man voluntarily agreed to the setting up of a civil government was both visionary and absurd. It was beyond proof and beyond belief. In rejecting the contract theory however the conservatives did not wish to justify any government, no matter how tyrannical and

297

arbitrary. They were prepared to acknowledge that no civil government could survive for long without the tacit consent of the majority of its subjects, but they denied that this implied that governments were erected by the express consent of all men. Those who accepted the protection of government had tacitly agreed that in return they would give allegiance and obedience. Thus, even conservative theorists admitted that a legitimate civil government must rest on a contractual relationship between governors and governed. A trust existed between rulers and ruled. Should one party betray its trust the other could resort to force to restore the relationship. But this was far removed from the radical notion of an original contract, agreed to by all men, which allowed the sovereign people to cashier their governors when they saw fit and to alter their government whenever it suited them.[64]

Besides rejecting the radicals' interpretation of the original contract the conservatives repudiated their view of the ancient constitution. Although Paine and other extreme radicals abandoned any appeal to history, many radicals still claimed that Britain's constitution was ancient and immemorial, though they also insisted that this constitution had been originally erected on rational fundamental principles. This claim enabled them to argue that the constitution of the late eighteenth century had been corrupted by the monarchy and the aristocracy and must be restored to its original principles. Since the conservatives denied that any existing government could trace its origins to rational first principles, they needed to undermine the radical concept of the ancient constitution. They did so by arguing that since the ancient constitution was immemorial it was quite literally impossible to trace its original features and principles. Nothing could now be inferred about its origins and so no attempt could be made to restore the constitution to its first principles. Despite their repeated assertions the radicals could not in fact provide any historical evidence for their views about the ancient constitution or for the changes which they claimed were needed to restore it. Edmund Burke protested:

On what grounds do we go to restore our constitution to what it has been at one definite period, or to reform and reconstruct it upon principles more conformable to a sound theory of government? A prescriptive government, such as ours, never was the work of any legislator, never was made upon any foregone theory. It seems to me a preposterous way of reasoning, and a perfect confusion of ideas to

298

take the theories which learned and speculative men have made from that government, and then supposing it made on those theories, which were made from it, to accuse the government as not corresponding with them.[65]

Far from suggesting that radical changes should be made to restore the ancient constitution to its original principles the conservatives insisted that such violent alterations would destroy the constitution. The example of France proved what anarchy and confusion resulted from a wilful violation of history and tradition. The experience of Britain proved that the essential features of the constitution could only be preserved by the most judicious and temperate action. By breaking with tradition and by seeking to establish a new constitution on rational first principles the French had produced the awful tyranny of mob rule. The Glorious Revolution of 1688 showed how to restore the fundamental features of the ancient constitution while avoiding the perils of violent and unnecessary change. In Burke's view 1688 had witnessed 'a revolution, not made, but prevented'. The natural leaders of society had made only a small deviation in the strict order of hereditary succession. The legal prerogatives of the Crown and the legislative supremacy of King, Lords and Commons were confirmed and the traditional liberties of the subject were restored. No attempt was made to establish an entirely new constitution or to endorse such revolutionary doctrines as the inalienable rights of man or the sovereignty of the people. The Glorious Revolution did not give the people the right to choose their own governors, to cashier them for misconduct or to frame a government for themselves. In seeking to restore the ancient constitution the politicians of 1688 had avoided making such revolutionary claims. The principles of 1688 could not therefore be used to justify the reforms demanded by the radicals.[66]

Conservative views on the origins of government in general and on the nature of Britain's ancient constitution in particular led them to conclude that constitutions developed gradually without conscious human contrivance or systematic design. They were the product of history and experience, not the deliberate result of reason or will. The British constitution was *prescriptive*. Its authority rested not on any original contract or known first principles, but on the evidence that it had existed time out of mind and had made thousands of adjustments to the needs created by altered circumstances and the changing habits of the people. The constitution was the fruit of experience and the result of trial and error over centuries. Its strength lay in the fact that it had been tested by time and found to correspond with the actual needs and wants of society. The wisdom and experience of many generations of men must be regarded as superior to the intelligence of any particular individual. It mattered little that the constitution was not founded on the free consent of the people. The fact that the constitution was fashioned out of a people's experience over centuries must weigh more heavily in the balance than either the nature of its creation or any rational plan for its improvement. Human experience must rank higher than human reason:

> It is a presumption in favour of any settled government against any untried project, that a nation has long existed and flourished under it. It is a far better presumption even of the *choice* of a nation, far better than any sudden and temporary arrangement by actual election ... [the British constitution] is a constitution made by what is ten thousand times better than choice; it is made by the peculiar circumstances, occasions, tempers, dispositions, and moral, civil and social habitudes of the people, which disclose themselves only in a long space of time. It is a vestment, which accommodates itself to the body.[67]

If the people are reasonably happy and content then, the conservatives insisted, it is dangerously conceited for even the wisest and shrewdest men to presume to elevate their reason above the judgement of centuries. 'Those who pull down important ancient establishments, who wantonly destroy modes of administration, and public institutions, under which a country has prospered, are the most mischievous, and therefore the wickedest of men.'[68]

For many conservatives prescription served the purpose which the doctrine of natural rights served for the radicals: it legitimized a particular political and social order. A constitution and a society which had existed for a long time could claim to have passed the test of experience and to have acquired the sanction of prescription. A prescriptive constitution, like that of Britain, was more soundly based than any form of government recently established by contract or choice. Prescription even sanctioned governments which had originally been established by force or conquest; prescription 'through long usage, mellows into legality governments that were violent in their commencement'.[69] By emphasizing the importance of long possession the conservatives could defend as legitimate the British political system which conferred political power on a narrow élite and denied political rights to the masses. Reverence for the past could be used to oppose any radical or violent change in the present or the future. The conservatives insisted that those who respected the experience of centuries would not seek to make changes in accordance with abstract general principles. They would only countenance minor adjustments which were in harmony with the wisdom of the past and the principles of an ancient, prescriptive constitution. Change was inevitable, but it must conserve what already existed rather than destroy and rebuild anew:

We must all obey the great law of change. It is the most powerful law of nature, and the means perhaps of its conservation. All we can do, and that wisdom can do, is to provide that the change shall proceed by insensible degrees. This has all the benefits which may be in change, without any of the inconveniences of mutation. Everything is provided for as it arrives. This mode will, on the one hand prevent the unfixing of old interests at once: a thing which is apt to breed a black and sullen discontent in those who are at once dispossessed of all their influence and consideration. This gradual course, on the other side, will prevent men, long under depression, from being intoxicated with a large draught of new power, which they always abuse with a licentious insolence.[70]

The doctrine of prescription was particularly appealing to men of property because it not only sanctioned the existing constitution in Britain but also buttressed the prevailing distribution of property. The preservation of the constitution could be combined with the defence of property. The two objectives could be mutually reinforcing. Both were the product of immemorial custom: 'Prescription is the most solid of all titles, not only to property, but, which is to secure that property, to government. They harmonize with each other, and give mutual aid to one another.'[71] By appealing to prescription the conservative theorists could provide the ruling classes with a weapon that was to prove more effective in the defence of order and property than the radical effort to base innovations on the natural rights of man. Burke could reinforce the self-interest of the propertied classes when he advised them: 'If prescription be once shaken, no species of property is secure, when it once becomes an object large enough to tempt the cupidity of indigent power.'[72] Many titles to property like the beginnings of many constitutions began in violence, but ancient violence, although wrong in the beginning, is consecrated by time and becomes lawful.[73] William Paley tried to teach the propertied classes the same lesson by deliberately using

301

prescription to sanction both established political authority and the ownership of private property. In his view the authority of Parliament and the willingness of subjects to obey both rested heavily on tradition and prejudice and these were the product of prescription:

They who obey from prejudice are determined by an opinion of right in their governors; which opinion is founded upon *prescription* ... Nor is it to be wondered at, that mankind should reverence authority founded in prescription, when they observe that it is prescription which confers the title to almost every thing else. The whole course, and all the habits of civil life, favour this prejudice. Upon what other foundation stands any man's right to his estate? ... It is natural to transfer the same principles to the affairs of government, and to regard those exertions of power, which have been long exercised and acquiesced in, as so many *rights*.[74]

Since the conservative theorists repudiated the notion that all men were naturally equal and they denied that legitimate civil governments were created by an original contract or that they developed according to any conscious design, this inevitably influenced their opinion about the aims and objectives of government. The radicals claimed that civil governments were established to protect the natural rights of man more effectively than they could be preserved in a state of nature. These inalienable rights were no longer the limited civil liberties defended by John Locke, but included the right to an active role in politics. All men had the right to vote for a representative legislature and the sovereign people retained the right to strip their governors of power whenever they saw fit and to establish a new government more to their taste. Conservative opinion claimed that the actions of governments should be guided by the laws of God and the laws of nature. The exercise of power without responsibility and without any concern either for the rights of the subject or for the higher duties of man must be avoided. Arbitrary tyranny which put all subjects completely at the mercy of their governors and an unrestrained democracy which converted might into right were both contrary to the wishes of God because they put the will of man before justice and morality. No government, whether it was an absolute monarchy or a popular democracy, was free to act entirely as it pleased. Governors had to be aware of those moral laws which are the foundation of order and of civilization itself. Their power had to be exercised on behalf of society as a whole and in accordance with the eternal principles of equity and justice. No government could claim that it possessed the right to exercise arbitrary power over the lives, liberty and property of its subjects. All authority was a trust and those who exercised it must remember that their own self-interest was subordinate to the welfare of society and the commands of God. 'All persons possessing any portion of power ought to be strongly and awfully impressed with the idea that they act in trust; and that they are to account for their conduct in that trust to the one great Master, Author, and Founder of society.'[75]

Since they emphasized that governments developed over many generations and since they insisted that political action must be guided by an insight into the underlying moral principles of human society, it is not surprising to find the conservatives concluding that political authority could be exercised only by a minority of able men. They maintained that the art of governing required men of solid judgement, ample intelligence and considerable experience. These qualities could not be found among tradesmen, artisans, servants and labourers, but only among men of birth and fortune who enjoyed the independence, leisure and education needed to prepare a man for the duties of governing. The British constitution with its propertied franchise and its property qualifications for Members of Parliament fully recognized that political power should be restricted to a narrow élite. Soame Jenyns insisted that the nation must be 'advised and directed by the most respectable members of it; who are possessed of rank, property, wisdom, and experience'.[76] Such qualities and virtues could not be found in the masses and so it was legitimate to deny them direct political influence. Burke acknowledged that the common people could judge when they were oppressed, but he stressed that this did not mean that they were equipped to exercise power:

the most poor, illiterate, and uninformed creatures upon earth are judges of a *practical* oppression. It is a matter of feeling; and as such persons generally have felt most of it, and are not of an overlively sensibility, they are the best judges of it. But for the *real cause*, or the *appropriate remedy*, they ought never to be called into council about the one or the other. They ought to be totally shut out; because their reason is weak; because, when once aroused, their passions are ungoverned; because they want information; because the smallness of the property, which individually they possess, renders them less attentive to the measures they adopt in affairs of moment.[77]

Burke, who, more than any other conservative theorist, stressed the complexity of political and social questions and the importance of being guided by moral principles, was not content that those who ruled should simply be well educated men or skilful pragmatists. He believed that the exercise of authority could only be sanctioned if those in power possessed exceptional qualities. Politicians were not required merely to weigh up conflicting evidence and to assess competing interests in order to make the most reasonable and expedient decision. What was needed was a profound understanding of the complexity of the historical process and of the political and moral principles which were the foundation of the constitution and the social order. Those in power had to possess that combination of common sense, circumspection, insight and imagination which Burke described as 'prudence'. This prudence was more ethical than intellectual. The prudence required of men of affairs was a practical wisdom which weighed changing circumstances, had the vision to see what was required and possessed the courage to carry it through. It was far more than common sense and sound judgement. Intelligence had to be informed by an understanding of the complex nature of man and an insight into the moral principles which guided human society. Political affairs were in continual flux and yet the underlying principles of government could be detected by long study and close observation. Reason offered some guidance and so did the evidence of the past. But present judgements required more than just the exercise of reason or the understanding of experience. It was essential to recognize a higher law than expediency and a more profound ethic than utility. Prudence was based on morality as well as on reason and empirical data; and it was informed by instinct, prejudice and feeling as well as by a knowledge of present circumstances.[78]

Burke argued repeatedly that politicians needed to develop a moral perception of the individual's place in his society and of that particular society's place in the providential order of God. This could only be achieved through a profound awareness of the common and the collective experience of men, through an appreciation of community instinct and sentiment, and through a respect for the traditions and inveterate prejudices of society. Those in power must be conscious of the bewildering complexity of society, aware that the consequences of their actions must always be uncertain, and ready to bow before necessity. The State was a complex organism which could not be easily remodelled and ought not to be lightly tampered

304

with. Politicians must not expect to make new discoveries in morality, in the underlying principles of government, or in the ideas of liberty. The best that they could achieve was an imperfect good, a form of justice which struck a happy mean between order and liberty. After all they must remember that 'an imperfect good is still a good. The defect may be tolerable and may be removed at some future time. In that case, prudence (in all things a virtue, in politicks the first of virtues) will lead us rather to acquiesce in some qualified plan that does not come up to the full perfection of the abstract idea, than to push for the more perfect, which cannot be attain'd without tearing to pieces the whole contexture of the Commonwealth.'[79] Abstract, rational principles were an inadequate guide to political action because they would not necessarily apply in all circumstances. It was therefore a primary dictate of prudence not to prefer pure reason above the rooted opinions and established order of society. Political actions had to be adjusted to suit human nature and particular circumstances and not founded on abstract, universal principles:

Circumstances are infinite, are infinitely combined; are variable and transient; he who does not take them into consideration is not erroneous, but stark mad; ... A statesman, never losing sight of principles, is to be guided by circumstances; ... You can hardly state to me a case, to which legislature is the most confessedly competent, in which, if the rules of benignity and prudence are not observed, the most mischievous and oppressive things may not be done. So that after all it is a moral and virtuous discretion, and not any abstract theory of right, which keeps governments faithful to their ends.[80]

The conservatives were not only concerned with the actions of those in power. They were also anxious to stress that the duties and obligations of subjects were defined by God and were subject to his will. In their view God was not primarily interested in the liberty of men, but in their reverence for his authority and their obedience to his laws. The radicals taught men what they *could* do, while the conservatives endeavoured to teach them what they *should* do. The latter insisted that men ought to perform what was just, not simply what was in their power to achieve: 'what is liberty without wisdom, and without virtue? It is the greatest of all possible evils; for it is folly, vice, and madness, without tuition or restraint.'[81] To elevate the individual will above man's duty to God was the gravest of sins. To submit to the laws of God as well as to the laws of man was the foundation of order and the support of civilization. The subordination of subjects was part of the eternal law and it must be inculcated in all men:

The body of the people must not find the principles of natural subordination by art rooted out of their minds. They must respect that property of which they cannot partake. They must labour to obtain what by labour can be obtained; and when they find, as they commonly do, the success disproportioned to the endeavour, they must be taught their consolation in the final proportion of eternal justice. Of this consolation whoever deprives them, deadens their industry, and strikes at the root of all conservation.[82]

Conservatives were convinced that the radical claim, that civil government should secure the liberty of men above all else, would threaten all established order. The recognition of universal, inalienable rights would mean that subjects would never submit to any authority. Edmund Burke condemned the notion of abstract rights as inimical to all government:

Abstract principles of natural right ... were the most idle, because the most useless and the most dangerous to resort to. They superseded society, and broke asunder all those bonds which had formed the happiness of mankind for ages. He would venture to say, that if they were to go back abstractedly to original rights, there would be an end to all society.[83]

The radicals claimed that their doctrine of natural rights was but a logical extension and a clear statement of the Whig principles of John Locke and the Glorious Revolution. The conservatives, most of whom still preferred to call themselves Whigs, were therefore compelled to challenge the view that Whig or Revolution principles proved that governments were erected to preserve the natural rights of man. They were prepared to condemn not only Locke's contract theory, but his claims that subjects possessed certain inalienable rights which governments must recognize. Locke did not in fact make the same extensive claims as the radicals of the later eighteenth century, but since these radicals claimed him as a major source for their ideas and insisted that their own notions were but a logical development of those of Locke then it is not surprising that conservatives such as Josiah Tucker felt compelled to repudiate the authority of Locke:

In the 2nd part of his Treatise of Government, he [Locke] supplies them with such materials, as put it in their power (were his scheme to take effect) to call for thousands and thousands of alterations in the forms and modes, management and administration of every government upon earth, and to unsettle every thing. In short, his principles or positions (whatever were his intentions) give them a perpetual right to shift and change, to vary and alter without end; that is, without coming to any solid establishment, permanence, or duration. Add to all this, that as the rising generation are not bound, (according to Mr Locke's system) to acknowledge the validity of the acts of their fathers, grandfathers, &c. they must of course have a new set of unalienable rights of their own; for they are perfectly their own masters, absolutely free, and independent of that very government, under which they were born. In consequence of this, they also have a right to demand as many new arrangements and alterations, as they please, agreeable to their own taste and humour: and if they are not gratified therein, have a right to stir up new commotions, and to bring about another and another revolution, &c. What could the most enthusiastic republican wish for more?[84]

Some conservatives were so alarmed at the use made of Locke and Revolution principles in the late eighteenth century that they were increasingly willing to play down the right of resistance. Although they were not prepared to assert that the people could never resist an arbitrary tyrant, they stressed that a general claim to the inalienable right of resistance would subvert all authority. The doctrine could only be appealed to in the gravest emergency and then only by the natural leaders of society. Henry Dundas pointed out how easily it could be misused: 'The expediency of resistance was not a point which the generality of mankind could safely consider ... Every ignorant man would conceive he had a right to resist everything which did not accord with his own opinions, and the result might be shocking to humanity. Such language tended to bring all government into disgrace, or at least, to render it precarious.'[85]

This hostility to the concept of inalienable natural rights led some conservatives to insist that the only rights a man possessed in civil society were those given to him by the law of the land. Since there had never been a state of nature and civil government had not been created by a contract agreed to by all men, then there was no justification for the concept of universal and inalienable rights. Civil government could not therefore be regarded as a means of preserving these rights. On the contrary, government was designed to maintain justice and to preserve law and order. The only rights to which men could lay claim were those which it was expedient and practical for a particular government to grant. In defending the Test and Corporation Acts, which denied Dissenters the same civil rights as Anglicans, it was frequently asserted that any civil government could decide that certain rights and privileges could be confined to particular categories of men.[86] Burke extended this kind of argument into a general principle. He insisted that men must rest their political claims not on abstract natural rights, but on those legal and historic rights which they could make good in a court of law. Men enjoyed different rights under different forms of government or even under the same form of government at different times.[87] A few conservatives were prepared to take this line of argument much further and to allow every government complete freedom in deciding which rights their subjects could enjoy. They came close in fact to conferring absolute and unrestrained power on the State:

Men may amuse themselves with ideas of natural, inherent, inalienable natural rights, as much as they please; but in a civil or political state, individuals possess no such rights any further than they are compatible with the laws of the state. They cannot oppose their separate wills and private judgments to the will and judgment of the state, but in all things must submit thereto; even supposing its judgment and will should be founded in error.[88]

This was a betrayal of Revolution principles with a vengeance. Such a doctrine elevated the rights of the State above the liberty of the subject. The authority of the government would be unlimited and the rights of subjects would be non-existent. Fortunately, even in the near panic reaction of the 1790s, most conservatives were unable to renege on Whig principles to this extent. They did not renounce the principle that no government had the right to act in an arbitrary or tyrannical fashion and they recognized that legitimate governments possessed only limited authority over the lives and possessions of their subjects. Civil government, they admitted, was designed both by the blessing of God and the wisdom of man to serve the interests of all mankind. All governments existed to secure the needs and wants of their subjects and so no government was free to act in such a way that it would betray the safety and welfare of its subjects. The authority of civil government was limited because men did possess certain rights which no legitimate government could grossly abuse. Although conservative theorists were reluctant to describe these rights as universal and inalienable, they were in fact those rights to life, liberty and property which Locke had assigned to all men in the state of nature. They were those limited civil liberties which the Whigs of 1688 had claimed no government could rightfully destroy. They included a number of auxiliary rights, including the right to live under the rule of law, the right to equal justice before the law, the right to the fruits of one's industry and the right to inherit from one's parents. It was reasonable, convenient, expedient and just that subjects should enjoy these rights because they benefited all men without undermining the essential authority of government. Yet even Burke accepted that these rights were not simply at the discretion of civil government, but were rights possessed by man *qua* man. In the final analysis therefore a tyrannical government might be regarded as intolerable and might be resisted by force.[89]

This recognition that all men had the right to enjoy certain civil liberties did not of course lead the conservative theorists to argue from this that all men had the right to claim the vote or to demand a fairer distribution of wealth. They were only prepared to claim that these civil liberties limited the right of the government to interfere with the private affairs of the subject and compelled the government to render justice to all subjects. These liberties did not include the right to interfere in the affairs of government or to change the system of government. A just government protected the limited civil liberties of its subjects, but was under no obligation to extend them unnaturally. The power to play an active role in political affairs was not a natural right, but one of those legal rights which any civil government was free to confer or deny as it saw fit. Burke was convinced that all men had the right to justice, but 'as to the share of power, authority, and direction which each individual ought to have in the management of the state, that I must deny to be amongst the direct original rights of man in civil society ... It is a thing to be settled by convention.'[90] A positive voice in public affairs was not a natural right because it could not be defended either as a necessary means of preserving civil government or as essential to the protection of the subject. Liberty itself could not be secured if all men had an equal share of power. No government could survive and hence no civil liberties could be protected unless an authority was set up with the power to restrain the passions and self-interest of individuals. If men could do as they pleased, then confusion and lawlessness would ensue and justice would collapse. If men were to be governed, then most of them must be taught submission rather than encouraged to interfere in the affairs of government. The functions of government inevitably involved imposing limitations on the freedom of men. These restrictions varied according to time and circumstance. Political liberty was a legal not a natural right and in all societies was enjoyed by a minority of subjects. No one could claim a divine or inalienable right to govern others. The matter was entirely one of expedience and prudence. It was a question of deciding who could safely be trusted with such power. Active political power was a privilege enjoyed by a few not a right to be claimed by all.[91]

The conservatives' determination to repudiate the radical claim that all men had an equal right to political power was undoubtedly dictated by their conviction that the most important right of man was the liberty to enjoy his possessions in peace and security. In their opinion the rights of private property could never be safeguarded in a civil society where all men enjoyed political power. Those with power but without property would not long be content to remain in this state: 'If the formation of government was committed to the no-property people, the first thing they would do, obviously would be, to plunder those who had property, and the next thing would be, to plunder and massacre each other.'[92] On the importance of protecting private property all the conservative theorists were in agreement with John Locke. They all agreed that the prime function of civil government was not so much to secure liberty as to preserve private property. The possession of property was treasured by those who enjoyed it and resented by those who did not. Institutions and laws were therefore needed to protect those who owned property from the attacks of those who desired it:

It is only under the shelter of the civil magistrate that the owner of that valuable property, which is acquired by the labour of many years, or perhaps many successive generations, can sleep a single night in security. The acquisition of valuable and extensive property, therefore, necessarily requires the establishment of civil government ... Civil government so far as it is instituted for the security of property, is in reality instituted for the defence of the rich against the poor, of those who have some property against those who have none at all.[93]

So great was the right of property that no civil government could violate it even for the general good of the whole community. Even those, like Burke and Blackstone, who readily endorsed the sovereignty of Parliament, still insisted that 'we have never dreamt that parliaments had any right whatever to violate property.'[94] This being the case, then the extreme radical demands for the redistribution of wealth, even for government action to alleviate poverty, must be utterly rejected. Property would always be divided unequally and poverty could never be eradicated. Attempts to remedy these harsh but unchangeable facts of life would damage the few without benefiting the many and would destroy all order and government:

> The characteristic essence of property, formed out of the combined principles of its acquisition and conservation, is to be *unequal*. The great masses therefore which excite envy, and tempt rapacity, must be put out of the possibility of danger. Then they form a natural rampart about the lesser properties in all their gradations ... The plunder of the few would indeed give but a share inconceivably small in the distribution to the many. But the many are not capable of making this calculation; and those who lead them to rapine never intend this distribution.[95]

The conservatives were anxious to demonstrate that the unequal distribution of wealth actually benefited the poor because the desires of the rich provided employment for the labouring masses. Thomas Malthus claimed that attempts to redistribute property equally among the whole population were doomed to failure. Even if the rich gave away their excess wealth their benevolence would only encourage the idleness of the poor, decrease the need for labour to provide the luxuries formerly desired by the rich and probably reduce production in general. Moreover, the excess wealth given away would never be enough to meet the demands of all those in want. Attempts to redistribute property would initially make all men poor, but would soon result in some men making determined efforts to restore inequalities of wealth. Malthus did not oppose all change or claim that all attempts to ameliorate the plight of the poor would be doomed to failure, but he was convinced that no government could greatly improve the conditions of the poor without reducing others to the same distressing circumstances. Human institutions could not prevent an unequal distribution of property or remove the evil consequences of poverty. The only solution was to hold down the size of the population while increasing the supply of food, but, unfortunately, any growth in the supply of food would stimulate the birth rate and result in the return of mass misery. In Malthus's view: 'It is, undoubtedly, a most disheartening reflection that the great obstacle in the way to any extraordinary improvement in society is of a nature that we can never hope to overcome. The perpetual tendency in the race of man to increase beyond the means of subsistence is one of the general laws of animated nature which we can have no reason to expect will change.'[96]

Other conservative theorists argued that, even if the redistribution of wealth could be shown to be beneficial, any government which attempted it would be exceeding its functions and betraying its purpose. No government had the right to decide that it would take away the private possessions of one man in order to give them to another simply because it calculated that the former had too much wealth and the latter too little. Subjects therefore had no right to demand that their government should institute social and economic changes which would deliberately interfere with the legal rights and private possessions of individuals. Social and economic reforms were not justified when they destroyed the liberty of the individual to enjoy what was lawfully his. Even those innovations which were designed to benefit the many at the expense of the few could not be regarded as a legitimate exercise of power. The chief end of government was limited to the preservation of law and order. This could only be achieved by protecting the possessions of individuals and by restraining men's passions. Governments could prevent much evil, but they could do little positive good. The permanent eradication of poverty was beyond the power of any government and the expropriation of private property was beyond its legitimate competence.[97]

3 The Justification of Established Authority

While the radicals condemned the existing political order and urged the need for extensive reforms in order to improve the constitution, the conservatives were most anxious to preserve the *status quo*. The radicals were convinced of the necessity of change, but the conservatives regarded innovation as a threat; and the greater the innovation the more they feared it. In their view the existing constitution was one of the best ever devised by man and, since absolute perfection could never be attained, it was the height of irresponsibility to attempt to make major changes. Even the best intentions and the most intelligent advice could lead to the most dreadful and fatal consequences when men tried to alter a political and social order which already produced considerable benefits. Reform once begun

312

could so easily lead to excessive change and finally end in violent revolution. In opposing even moderate reform Lord North once warned Parliament: 'every innovation ought to be watched with a jealous eye, because when once the spirit of innovation was abroad, it was impossible to say where it would stop.'[98] On a later occasion Mr Powys told the Commons that 'innovation was to be dreaded, and avoided as much as possible in all establishments.'[99] George Berkeley, in a sermon on the text of 'meddle not with them that are given to change', advised his congregation: 'I shall point out the danger and sin of making violent innovations in any constitution of government whatever, that has been long established, and to which the people have been accustomed quietly to submit.'[100]

In pointing out the virtues of the existing constitution, even to the extent of defending its apparent abuses, and in examining the principles which underlay all governments, the conservatives were seeking to defend the existing order and the prevailing distribution of authority. The radicals had to justify change, while the conservatives were content to approve of things as they were. The radicals claimed that the concept of universal and inalienable natural rights justified their attempts to create a democratic constitution and sanctioned their efforts to make a reality of their notion of an ideal society. The conservatives insisted that an effective even an ideal constitution was already in existence and they claimed that their examination of the natural state of man, of the origins of government and of the aims and purpose of civil government sanctioned the right of the propertied few to rule the many. To their immense satisfaction they discovered that the structure and distribution of authority which their philosophical inquiries recognized as legitimate was very like that which already existed in Britain in the late eighteenth century. The authority which the conservatives claimed ought to exist corresponded very closely in their opinion with the authority which did in fact exist.

In order to justify their proposals for a redistribution of authority the radicals appealed to the natural rights of man which they were confident they could discover with the aid of pure reason. In contrast, the conservatives tried to justify the existing political and social order by appealing to the will of God and to the test of experience. Like the theorists of order in the late seventeenth century the conservatives still believed that government was ordained by God and that the workings of civil society were at the mercy of divine providence. A

313

close scrutiny of their attempts to prove that the existing political order was entirely consistent with the best political order shows however that they also came to rely increasingly on the test of experience. While never abandoning their appeal to God as the source of all authority, the conservative theorists and propagandists began to develop a more pragmatic justification for accepting the prevailing political and social order in Britain.

The conservative defenders of the established order never developed a purely secular ideology and they never abandoned the conviction that ultimately it was God alone who sanctioned and supported all authority. While the radicals claimed that all men were created equal and had the inalienable right to political liberty, the conservatives insisted that God had ordained government in order to subdue the passions of men. In order to preserve society and to enable men to pursue their duty to God there had to be a firmly established authority. This was only possible where power was deliberately limited to the few and obedience was willingly rendered by the many. The right to govern and the duty to obey were both sanctioned by the will of God:

No man can lawfully govern himself according to his own will, much less can one person be governed by the will of another. We are all born in subjection, all born equally, high as well as low, governors and governed, in subjection to one great, immutable, pre-existent law, prior to all our devices, and prior to all our contrivances, paramount to all our ideas and all our sensations, antecedent to our very existence, by which we are knit and connected in the eternal frame of the universe, out of which we cannot stir. This great law does not arise from our conventions or compacts; on the contrary, it gives to our conventions and compacts all the force and sanction they can have; – it does not arise from our vain institutions. Every good gift is of God; all power is of God; – and He, who has given the power, and from whom alone it originates, will never suffer the exercise of it to be practised upon any less solid foundation than the power itself. If then all dominion of man over man is the effect of the Divine disposition, it is bound by the eternal laws of Him that gave it, with which no human authority can dispense; neither he that exercises it, nor even those who are subject to it.[101]

The conservative defenders of established authority insisted that neither power nor liberty could be regulated by an exercise of will, by the free and deliberate choice of men. Both originated in the will of God and must remain forever subordinate to his eternal law. By laying claim to universal and inalienable rights the radicals were as much a threat to morality and order as the most arbitrary tyrant. Their pride and ambition led them to elevate their will above that of God and their political rights above their moral duties. In order therefore to combat atheistical republicans who rebelled against God and nature it was essential to provide civil government with the support and sanction of religion. Public morality and political duties could never be separated from the Christian religion. An established church provided one of the strongest bonds of society and was an indispensable ally of the State. Religion encouraged all men to look beyond narrow self-interest to the pursuit of justice and it persuaded men to place power in the hands of those best fitted to exercise it. Those men who undermined organized religion or who sought to weaken the influence of the Established Church were enemies to all order and morality.[102]

The conservative theorists were confident that the existing political and social order in Britain corresponded as closely as humanly possible to the laws of nature and the commands of God. By securing a delicate balance between authority and liberty the British constitution reminded those in authority that they held their power as a trust and it allowed subjects to enjoy the freedom to protect their legitimate rights but not the power to destroy all order in the State. In order to convince the nation that the constitution could not be radically improved, however, the conservatives had to rely on more than just their interpretation of the laws of nature and the will of God. The radicals after all insisted that God created all men equal and that He granted all men the possession of inalienable natural rights. In order therefore to prove that what is, should be, the defenders of the established order increasingly appealed to the lessons of history and the test of experience. In doing so, pragmatism and prescription came to rival divine providence as the chief justification for the established order. In defending the political system conservatives continually claimed that, whatever its apparent abuses and irregularities, it worked in fact far better than any other and it produced the end-results which the British public most desired. When they explained the origins, development and aims of civil government the conservative theorists relied heavily upon the doctrine of prescription. Society and its political institutions, they insisted, had evolved over centuries. They were living organisms whose complexity was

315

beyond the grasp of any generation of men. They adjusted themselves slowly to the needs and desires of succeeding generations. Attempts to reform them on the basis of rational speculation would be futile at best and dangerous at worst.

The conservatives endeavoured to combine the two strands in their political ideology: their conviction that there was a higher moral law than any made by man and their pragmatic defence of existing institutions. They strove to prove that the authority which ought to exist in civil society did in fact exist in Britain. This can be seen most clearly in their efforts to prove that the ruling classes in Britain were fully justified in exercising power because they were the natural rulers of society. The conservative theorists insisted that only a minority of men in any society could be expected to possess the superior qualities needed to exercise political power. They were not however in favour of a meritocracy which would ensure that only men of proven abilities could govern. Their primary concern was to justify the existing system in which a small élite based on birth and fortune dominated British politics. This forced them to argue that those who actually exercised power were in fact those with the best right to govern. They insisted that the qualities needed to govern were possessed by the propertied classes, but not by the labouring masses. Edmund Burke at least was too wise and too honest to insist that the natural aristocracy which ought to govern was the same as the actual aristocracy of late-eighteenth-century Britain. He admitted that aristocratic arrogance needed to be checked and that an oligarchy could abuse its power. He also urged that the road to social eminence and political advancement should be open to men of genuine ability. Nonetheless, while Burke recognized that the ruling classes must always be ready to absorb into their ranks those men of ability who distinguished themselves in public service, he was convinced that it was more important to have men of property rather than men of talent in power: 'as ability is a vigorous and active principle, and as property is sluggish, inert, and timid, it never can be safe from the invasions of ability, unless it be, out of all proportion, predominant in the representation.'[103] Burke had no doubts that those who had long possessed substantial estates were best fitted to preserve both liberty and order because they were in the position to hold the middle ground between a brutal tyranny and a furious mob. Large proprietors were the essential ballast in the Vessel of State and it was not unnatural, unjust or impolitic to give them a pre-eminent position in the social and political order. While property is power it would require an act of unnatural tyranny to prevent the great proprietors exercising considerable influence over the affairs of government. Liberty itself could not survive if the natural influence of property could not operate. Thus Burke's concept of a natural aristocracy, his opinion of those who ought to govern, was equated in practice with the propertied classes who actually exercised authority in Britain in the late eighteenth century. When Burke detailed the qualities needed in governors and discussed how these were acquired, he made it absolutely clear that the propertied classes would inevitably provide the overwhelming majority of the ruling classes. Even those few men of distinguished abilities who, lacking birth and fortune, were allowed to enter the ruling classes must adopt the life style and attitudes of those born to rule. In doing so they would give evidence that liberty could only be preserved while property was respected and protected.[104]

Most conservatives in the late eighteenth century, even those who were ready to accept the designation of 'Tory', accepted the Revolution settlement and regarded themselves as the true upholders of the old Whig constitution. In developing their ideological offensive against the radicals however they attacked Locke's views on the natural state of man, on the origins of civil government, and on the sanctions which upheld and justified authority. They did this because they were convinced that the radical appeal to Lockean ideas was threatening to destroy the constitution and bring about social revolution. Yet an examination of their views on the aims and objectives of civil government shows that they still had much in common with Locke and the moderate Whigs of the late seventeenth century. They believed that the authority of the State over the individual should be limited and that no government should interfere unnecessarily in the life, liberty and property of its subjects. Most of all they were convinced that the chief purpose of civil government was to protect the rights of private property and they believed that this aim could best be achieved if active political power was restricted to those who owned property. They erected a moderately liberal State on deeply conservative foundations. Liberty rested on the rule of law and a stable social order and these could only be guaranteed by men of property. In their view liberty existed in order to defend property and property was the chief support and buttress of civil liberty. At

317

the same time very few of their radical opponents were social revolutionaries. The radicals of the late eighteenth century extended Locke's concept of natural rights until it embraced a demand for a democratic political order, but they did not abandon Locke's concern with the defence of private property. Their campaign for political liberty did not lead to an assault on the economic foundations of the prevailing social order. Not surprisingly this meant that the radicals were unable to defeat their conservative opponents in either a battle for power or a war of ideas. And yet it is important to recognize that the radicals did have a considerable influence on political opinion in the late eighteenth century. Their social conservatism ensured that the preservation of private property would remain a fundamental concern of the whole political nation. On the other hand their political radicalism and their preoccupation with the rights of man prevented the conservative reaction of the 1790s from utterly destroying the liberty of the subject.

The preservation of liberty and the protection of private property were political aims which were often and perhaps inherently in conflict with each other. Liberty and property were protected in the late eighteenth century, as they had been preserved ever since the late seventeenth century, because the forces of order and the friends of liberty were so strong that neither could eliminate the other. Although contemporaries and many foreign observers of the period praised the British constitution because it protected the liberty of the subject it is important to remember that the defenders of law and order generally held the upper hand. The concept of order however was never entirely divorced from the notion of liberty. The preservation of liberty and the protection of property were ideals which co-existed in a fruitful and surprisingly stable relationship. This relationship was not seriously threatened until the Industrial Revolution transformed the social and economic order in Britain and forced the nation to make the necessary political adjustments.

References

Unless otherwise stated the place of publication is London.

Introduction

1. My approach to this topic was undoubtedly influenced by Bernard Bailyn's *Ideological Origins of the American Revolution* (Cambridge, Mass., 1967) and by the criticisms levelled against Bailyn's approach by Gordon S. Wood in his article 'Rhetoric and Reality in the American Revolution', *William and Mary Quarterly*, 3rd ser., xxiii (1966), 3–32.

2. Herbert Butterfield, *George III and the Historians* (1957), p. 219.

3. See, e.g., Caroline Robbins, *The Eighteenth Century Commonwealthman* (Cambridge, Mass., 1959); Geoffrey Holmes, *British Politics in the Age of Anne* (1967); J. H. Plumb, *The Growth of Political Stability 1675–1725* (1967); Isaac Kramnick, *Bolingbroke and His Circle* (Cambridge, Mass., 1968); W. A. Speck, *Tory and Whig: The Struggle in the Constituencies 1701–1715* (1970); H. T. Dickinson, *Bolingbroke* (1970); and *idem* (ed.), *Politics and Literature in the Eighteenth Century* (1974).

4. This challenge to the Namierite interpretation of political action has been put best by Quentin Skinner in 'Some Problems in the Analysis of Political Thought and Action', *Political Theory*, ii (1974), 277–303; and 'The Principles and Practice of Opposition: The Case of Bolingbroke versus Walpole', in *Historical Perspectives*, ed. Neil McKendrick (1974), pp. 93–128. The approach has also been adopted by J. G. A. Pocock, 'Machiavelli, Harrington and English Political Ideology in the Eighteenth Century', *William and Mary Quarterly*, 3rd ser., xxii (1965), 549–83; and John Brewer, *Party Ideology and Popular Politics at the Accession of George III* (Cambridge, 1976), pp. 31, 96–111.

5. H. T. Dickinson, 'The Eighteenth-Century Debate on the Sovereignty of Parliament', *Transactions of the Royal Historical Society*, 5th ser., xxvi (1976), 189–210; and H. T. Dickinson, 'The Rights of Man: From John Locke to Tom Paine', in *Scotland, Europe and the American Revolution*, ed. O. D. Edwards and G. A. Shepperson (Edinburgh, 1976), pp. 38–48. Cf. *idem*, 'The Eighteenth-Century Debate on the "Glorious Revolution" ', *History*, lxi (1976), 28–45.

6. See, e.g., John Brewer, *Party Ideology and Popular Politics at the*

319

Accession of George III, pp. 139–60; G. A. Cranfield, *The Development of the Provincial Press, 1700–1760* (Oxford, 1962); R. M. Wiles, *Freshest Advices* (Ohio, 1965); and Ian R. Christie, *Myth and Reality in Late Eighteenth-Century British Politics* (1970), pp. 311–58.

Chapter 1

1. *Patriarcha and other Political Works of Sir Robert Filmer,* ed. Peter Laslett (Oxford, 1949), pp. 62, 93, 126. See also William Hickes, *Jovian* (1683), pp. 199–212 and Samuel Parker, *Religion and Loyalty* (1684), pp. 100–101.
2. *Patriarcha,* ed. Laslett, pp. 66–72, 81–4, 86–94.
3. Roger North, *A Discourse on the English Constitution,* probably written in the 1680s but first published in *The Scholar Armed* (2 vols., 2nd ed., 1800), i, 264.
4. Sir Philip Warwick, *A Discourse of Government* (written 1678, published 1694), pp. 123–5.
5. 13 Car. II, c. 30; 13 Car. II, c. 1; 14 Car. II, c. 4; 14 Car. II, c. 3.
6. Robert South, *Sermons* (6 vols., 3rd ed., 1704), i, 221.
7. Gilbert Burnet, *Vindication of the authority ... of the Church and State of Scotland* (1673), p. 14; Edward Stillingfleet, *A Vindication of the Answer to some late Papers* (1687), p. 389.
8. Printed in [Abednigo Seller,] *History of Passive Obedience* (1689), p. 108.
9. *The Judgment and Decree of the University of Oxford, passed in their Convocation, July 31, 1683, ...* (Oxford, 1683), p. 8.
10. Quoted by G. V. Bennett, *The Tory Crisis in Church and State 1688–1730* (Oxford, 1975), p. 103.
11. *The Poor Man's Help* (1689), p. 40. For patriarchalism in seventeenth-century England see Gordon J. Schochet, *Patriarchalism in Political Thought* (Oxford, 1975).
12. Filmer, *Patriarcha,* ed. Laslett, p. 57.
13. *Ibid.,* pp. 57–62, 74–5.
14. Robert Brady, *Complete History of England* (1685), i, xxxix–xl. See also Brady, *Introduction to the Old English History* (1684); J. G. A. Pocock, 'Robert Brady, 1627–1700', *Cambridge Historical Journal,* x (1951), 186–204; and Pocock, *The Ancient Constitution and the Feudal Law* (Cambridge, 1957), pp. 149–59, 182–228.
15. For Filmer's attempt to equate absolute monarchy with paternal authority see J. N. Figgis, *The Divine Right of Kings* (2nd ed., Cambridge, 1914), pp. 146–60.
16. W. H. Greenleaf, *Order, Empiricism and Politics* (Hull, 1964), chap. 2; and Arthur O. Lovejoy, *The Great Chain of Being* (Cambridge,

Mass., 1936), pp. 183–207.

17. Filmer, *Patriarcha*, ed. Laslett, pp. 92–5.

18. L. M. Hawkins, *Allegiance in Church and State: The Problem of the Nonjurors in the English Revolution* (1928); Charles Leslie, *The Rehearsal* (1704–9); *idem*, *The Best Answer ever was Made* (1709); *idem*, *The Constitution, Laws, and Government of England Vindicated* (1709); *idem*, *The Finishing Stroke* (1711); *idem*, *The Old English Constitution* (1714); Luke Milbourne, *The Measures of Resistance to the Higher Powers* (1710); *idem*, *The People not the Original of Civil Power* (1707); Henry Gandy, *Remarks upon Mr Higden's Utopian Constitution* (1709); George Harbin, *The English Constitution Fully Stated* (1710); *idem*, *The Hereditary Right of the Crown of England Asserted* (1713); George Hickes, *The Pretences of the Prince of Wales examin'd* (1701); *A seasonable and modest Apology in behalf of the Rev. Dr G. Hickes and other non-jurors* (1710); *The Debates in Deposing Kings; and of the Royal Succession of Great Britain* (1688); *An Essay upon Government. Wherein the Republican Schemes reviv'd by Mr Lock, Dr Blackal, &c are fairly consider'd and refut'd* (1705); *An Enquiry into the Nature of the Liberty of the Subject, and of Subjection to the Supreme Powers* (1706).

19. William Cobbett, *Parliamentary History of England*, v, 45–8. Hereafter cited as *Parl. Hist.*

20. *Memoirs of Sir John Reresby*, ed. A. Browning (Glasgow, 1936), p. 521.

21. Quoted by Keith Feiling, *History of the Tory Party 1640–1714* (Oxford, 1924), pp. 262–3.

22. For a modern account of the parliamentary debates of early 1689, see J. R. Western, *Monarchy and Revolution* (1972), pp. 284–325.

23. *Memoires of Thomas Bruce, Earl of Ailesbury*, ed. W. E. Buckley (2 vols., 1890), i, 237.

24. *The Autobiography of Sir John Bramston*, ed. P. Braybrooke (*Camden Society*, old series, xxxii, 1845), p. 355.

25. For a more detailed treatment of these appeals, see Gerald M. Straka, *Anglican Reaction to the Revolution of 1688* (Madison, 1962) and James C. Corson, 'The English Revolution and the Doctrines of Resistance and Non-Resistance, 1688–1714: A Study in Sovereignty' (unpublished Ph.D. thesis, Edinburgh University, 1934), pp. 204–71.

26. Thomas Comber, *A Letter to a Bishop concerning the present settlement and the new oaths* (1689), pp. 18–31. See also Edmund Bohun, *The History of the Desertion* (1689); *idem*, *The doctrine of non-resistance or passive obedience no way concerned in the controversies now depending between the Williamites and the Jacobites* (1689); and

321

William Lloyd, *A Discourse of God's way of disposing of Kingdoms* (1691).

27. *Parl. Hist.*, v, 756.

28. Filmer, *Patriarcha*, ed. Laslett, p. 62.

29. Gilbert Burnet, *A Sermon preached ... on 31 Jan. 1688/89* (1689), pp. 3, 13. See also *idem, A Sermon preached ... before his Highness the Prince of Orange, 23 December 1688* (1689); Edward Stillingfleet, *A Discourse concerning the Unreasonableness of a New Separation, on Account of the Oaths* (1689), p. 106; William Lloyd, *A Discourse of God's way of disposing of Kingdoms* (1691); Symon Patrick, sermon of 1689, in *The Works of Symon Patrick*, ed. A. Taylor (9 vols., Oxford, 1858), viii, 347–71; Robert Fleming, *The Divine Right of the Revolution Evinc'd and Apply'd* (1706); and Thomas Bradbury, *The Divine Right of the Revolution* (1709).

30. Francis Atterbury, *Sermons and Discourses on Several Subjects and Occasions* (2 vols., 1723), i, 258.

31. Filmer, *Patriarcha*, ed. Laslett, p. 106.

32. *Bishop Overall's Convocation Book, MDCVI* (1690), pp. 55–9.

33. William Sherlock, *The Case of the Allegiance due to Soveraign Powers, stated and resolved* (1691), p. 9.

34. *Ibid.*, pp. 15, 41, 50. See also *idem, A Vindication of the Case of Allegiance due to Soveraign Powers* (1691) and *idem, Their Present Majesties Government prov'd to be thoroughly settled* (1692).

35. See, e.g., Thomas Browne, *An Answer to Dr Sherlock's Case of Allegiance to Sovereign Powers* (1691); Jeremy Collier, *Dr Sherlock's Case of Allegiance considered* (1691); John Kettlewell, *The Duty of Allegiance settled upon its true grounds* (1691); George Hickes, *A Vindication of Some among Ourselves against the False Principles of Dr Sherlock* (1692); and Thomas Wagstaffe, *An Answer to Dr Sherlock's Vindication of the Case of Allegiance due to Sovereign Powers* (1692).

36. Anchitell Grey, *Debates of the House of Commons* (10 vols., 1763), x, 86. Hereafter cited as Grey's *Debates*. John Hampden, 'Some short considerations concerning the State of the Nation' (1692) in *A Collection of State Tracts* (3 vols., 1705), ii, 325.

37. *Letters of Humphrey Prideaux to John Ellis*, ed. E. Maunde Thompson (*Camden Society*, new series, xv, 1875), pp. 157–9.

38. Andrew Browning, *Thomas Osborne, Earl of Danby and Duke of Leeds* (3 vols., Glasgow, 1944–51), i, 432.

39. Hist. MSS. Comm., Bath MSS, i, 199.

40. A. Tindal Hart, *The Life and Times of John Sharp, Archbishop of York* (1949), pp. 332–3; and Leicester Records Office. Finch MSS. Box vi, bundle 22. Sharp to Nottingham, 31 March 1701/2.

41. Quoted by Geoffrey Holmes, *Religion and Party in Late Stuart*

England (1975), p. 23.

42. Geoffrey Holmes, *British Politics in the Age of Anne* (1967), pp. 279–80.

43. Henry Dodwell, *The Case in View* (1705), p. 4. See also *idem, A Further Prospect of the Case in View* (1707) and *The Case in View now in Fact* (1710).

44. *The Divine Institution of Magistracy* (1709), p. 4.

45. William Higden, *A View of the English Constitution* (1709), p. 13.

46. *The Works of George Berkeley*, eds. A. A. Luce and T. E. Jessup (Edinburgh, 1949–57), viii, 22–3.

47. *Parl. Hist.*, v, 756–68.

48. *A Collection of the Addresses which have been presented to the Queen, since the Impeachment of the Reverend Dr Henry Sacheverell* (2 vols., 1710), i, 1.

49. Huntington Library, California. Stowe MSS. 58, v, f. 126. Coke to James Brydges, 15 February 1709/10.

50. *The Examiner*, no. 35 (5 April 1711).

51. [Francis Atterbury,] *The Voice of the People, no Voice of God* (1710), p. 6.

52. Offspring Blackall, *The Lord Bishop of Exeter's Answer to Mr. Hoadly's Letter* (1709), p. 18.

53. [William Robertson,] *The Liberty, Property, and Religion of the Whigs* (1713), p. 10.

54. See, e.g., George Berkeley, *Passive Obedience, or the Christian Doctrine of not resisting the Supreme Power, proved and vindicated upon the principles of the Law of Nature* (1709); *The Revolution no Rebellion* (1709); *The Doctrine of Passive Obedience and Non-Resistance, as established by the Church of England* (1710); and [Michael Maittaire,] *The Doctrine of Passive Obedience, and Non-Resistance stated* (1710).

55. John Sharp, *A Sermon preached before the House of Lords, on 30 January 1700* (1700), pp. 20–21.

56. Leicester Records Office. Finch MSS. Box vi, bundle 22. Sharp to Nottingham, 31 March 1701/2.

57. Quoted by G. V. Bennett, *The Tory Crisis in Church and State, 1688–1730*, p. 105.

58. Blackall also referred to the sovereign legislature in *The Lord Bishop of Exeter's Reply to Mr Hoadly's Letter* (1709), pp. 22–3. In *The Divine Institution of Magistracy* (1709) Blackall was more equivocal. He did not support absolute monarchy, but he did stress the royal prerogative and accepted that the authority of kings might be ordained by God.

59. Jonathan Swift, *The Sentiments of a Church-of-England Man*,

with respect to Religion and Government (1708), in *The Prose Works of Jonathan Swift*, ed. Herbert Davis, ii (Oxford, 1939), p. 16; Swift, *The Examiner*, no. 33 (22 March 1711) and no. 39 (3 May 1711); George Berkeley, *Passive Obedience, or the Christian Doctrine of not resisting the Supreme Power* (1709); Wililam Higden, *A View of the English Constitution* (1709), pp. 22–48; and Higden, *A Defence of the View of the English Constitution* (1710), pp. 59–85.

60. *The Tryal of Dr Henry Sacheverell* (1710), p. 203. Sir Simon Harcourt, the principal manager of Sacheverell's defence and a leading Tory Member of Parliament, was the first to introduce this argument. *Ibid.*, p. 179.

61. *Parl. Hist.*, vi, 932.

62. 'The Letters of Henry St John to the Earl of Orrery, 1709–1711', ed. H. T. Dickinson, *Camden Miscellany XXVI* (4th series, 1975), p. 146.

63. *Bishop Burnet's History of His Own Time* (6 vols., Oxford, 1833), vi, 40.

64. Lincoln Records Office. Massingberd MSS. 20/93. William Massingberd to Burrell Massingberd, 1 April 1711.

65. Hist. MSS. Comm., House of Lords MSS, vi, p. xvii. For a more detailed treatment of the Tory views on the landed and moneyed interests, see Geoffrey Holmes, *British Politics in the Age of Anne*, pp. 148–82 and W. A. Speck, 'Conflict in Society' in *Britain after the Glorious Revolution 1689–1714*, ed. Geoffrey Holmes (1969), pp. 135–52.

66. Samuel Clarke, 'A Discourse concerning the Unalterable Obligation of Natural Religion' (1706) in *A Collection of Theological Tracts*, ed. Richard Watson (1785), iv, 189.

67. Henry Sacheverell, *The Perils of False Brethren both in Church and State* (1709), pp. 18–19. Cf. Sir John Pakington's attempt to lump Whigs and Dissenters together as 'a party of men that are against the church and government'. *Parl. Hist.*, vi, 153.

68. Gloucester Records Office. Sharp MSS. Bundle 3R. A country divine to Archbishop Sharp, 3 February 1705/6.

69. See, e.g., British Library. Add. MS. 27440, f. 84. Charles Allestree to Dr John Younger, c. 1702; and *Letters and Diplomatic Instructions of Queen Anne*, ed. B. Curtis Brown (1935), p. 99. Queen Anne to Lady Marlborough, 21 November 1702–4.

70. 'An Anonymous Parliamentary Diary, 1705–6', ed. W. A. Speck, *Camden Miscellany XXIII* (4th series, 1969), p. 83. For a more detailed treatment of the Tory defence of the Church of England, see G. V. Bennett, 'Conflict in the Church', in *Britain after the Glorious Revolution*, ed. Geoffrey Holmes, pp. 155–75; *idem, The Tory Crisis in Church and State, 1688–1730*; Geoffrey Holmes, *The Trial of Doctor Sacheverell*

(1973), pp. 21–47; and *idem, Religion and Party in Late Stuart England* (1975).

Chapter 2

1. John Locke, *Two Treatises of Government* (1689), I, para 81.
2. *Ibid.*, II, para 6.
3. For the early stages of this campaign, see B. Behrens, 'The Whig Theory of the Constitution in the Reign of Charles II', *Cambridge Historical Journal*, vii (1941), 42–71.
4. Locke, *Two Treatises*, I, paras 6, 11, 52–3, 55, 60–66 and II, paras 52, 53, 55. See also Algernon Sidney, *Discourses concerning Government* (published posthumously, 1698; 3rd ed., 1751), pp. 27–45; James Tyrrell, *Patriarcha Non Monarcha* (1681); Henry Neville, *Plato Redivivus* (*c.* 1681), in *Two English Republican Tracts*, ed. Caroline Robbins (Cambridge, 1969), p. 86; and Gordon J. Schochet, *Patriarchalism in Political Thought* (Oxford, 1975), chaps. ix and xiii.
5. E.G. *Some Remarks upon Government* (1689), pp. 12–13 and Peter Paxton, *Civil Polity* (1703), pp. 298, 503, 597–8.
6. J. G. A. Pocock, *The Ancient Constitution and the Feudal Law* (Cambridge, 1957), pp. 30–55.
7. *The Stuart Constitution*, ed. J. P. Kenyon (Cambridge, 1966), p. 21.
8. William Petyt, *Jus Parliamentarium: Or, the Ancient Power, Jurisdiction, Rights and Liberties of the most High Court of Parliament, revived and asserted* (written in the 1680s; first published 1739), p. 12.
9. Algernon Sidney, *Discourses* (3rd ed.), pp. 377, 412.
10. *Ibid.*, pp. 24–7, 74–5, 78–87, 243–9, 266–73, 413–17.
11. Locke, *Two Treatises*, II, paras 4, 6, 8, 57, 61, 63. See also *John Locke, Essays on the Law of Nature*, ed. W. von Leyden (Oxford, 1954), editor's introduction; and J. W. Gough, *John Locke's Political Philosophy* (Oxford, 1950), chap. I.
12. *Two Treatises*, II, paras 4–12, 172.
13. *Ibid.*, II, para 13.
14. *Ibid.*, II, paras 87–9, 95–131.
15. *Ibid.*, II, paras 134–42, 211–43.
16. C. B. Macpherson, *The Political Theory of Possessive Individualism* (Oxford, 1962), pp. 194–262. For Locke's emphasis on property, see C. E. Vaughan, *Studies in the History of Political Philosophy* (2 vols., Manchester, 1925), ii, 167–8, 180–81; J. W. Gough, *John Locke's Political Philosophy* (Oxford, 1950), pp. 64–92; and John Dunn, *The Political Thought of John Locke* (Cambridge, 1969), pp. 120–47.
17. Locke, *Two Treatises*, II, paras 25–51, 124, 134, 138–40, 193, 222.
18. *Ibid.*, II, paras 63, 119, 122, 138.

19. See, in particular, C. B. Macpherson, *The Political Theory of Possessive Individualism*, pp. 194–262 and *idem*, 'The Social Bearing of Locke's Political Theory', *Western Political Theory*, vii (1954), 1–22.

20. Peter Laslett, 'Market Society and Political Theory', *Historical Journal*, vii (1964), 150–54; Alan Ryan, 'Locke and the Dictatorship of the Bourgeoisie', *Political Studies*, xiii (1965), 219–30; John Dunn, 'Consent in the Political Theory of John Locke', *Historical Journal*, x (1967), 165–6; and M. Seliger, *The Liberal Politics of John Locke* (1968), chaps. ix and x.

21. Sidney, *Discourses* (3rd ed.), p. 75.

22. Tyrrell, *Patriarcha Non Monarcha* (1681), pp. 83–4.

23. Sidney, *Discourses*, pp. 149, 423.

24. Locke, *Two Treatises*, II, paras 131–4, 143, 150, 157–8, 243.

25. *Ibid.*, II, paras 208, 225, 230.

26. On this section, see J. P. Kenyon, 'The Revolution of 1688: Resistance and Contract', in *Historical Perspectives*, ed. Neil McKendrick (1974), pp. 43–69.

27. Sidney, *Discourses*, pp. 375–98.

28. Daniel Whitby, *An Historical Account of some things relating to the nature of the English Government, and the Conceptions which our Forefathers had of it* (1690), pp. 43–4.

29. See e.g. Gilbert Burnet, *An Enquiry into the Measure of Submission to the Supram Authority* (1688); R. Ferguson, *A Brief Justification of the Prince of Orange's Descent into England* (1689); *Pro Populo Adversus Tyrannos: Or the Sovereign Right and Power of the People over Tyrants, clearly stated, and plainly proved* (1689), pp. 7–13; *A Resolution of Certain Queries concerning Submission to the Present Government* (1689), pp. 1–23; *A Brief Vindication of the Parliamentary Proceedings against the Late King James IId* (1689), pp. 5–12; W. Atwood, *The Fundamental Constitution of the English Government* (1690); Matthew Tindal, *An Essay concerning Obedience to the Supreme Powers, and the Duty of Subjects in all Revolutions* (1694); and James Tyrrell, *A Brief Enquiry into the Ancient Constitution and Government of England* (1695).

30. *Vox Populi, Vox Dei: Being True Maxims of Government* (1709), p. 11. This important pamphlet has been attributed both to Daniel Defoe and Lord Somers, but on insubstantial evidence. It went through eight editions in 1709. It was reprinted in 1710 under the less provocative title, *The Judgment of Whole Kingdoms and Nations concerning the Rights, Power and Prerogative of Kings, and the Rights, Privileges and Properties of the People*, and went through a further six editions. Other pamphlets dealing with the contract theory include John Wildman, *A Letter to a Friend Advising in this Extraordinary Juncture How*

to Free the Nation from Slavery Forever (1689); *Political Aphorisms: Or, the True Maxims of Government Displayed* (1690); *The Claims of the People of England, Essayed* (1701); and Daniel Defoe's *The Original Power of the Collective Body of the People of England, Examined and Asserted* (1702).

31. Grey's *Debates*, ix, 20, 12.

32. *Ibid.*, ix, 12–15, 21–2. Bishop Burnet also feared that any claim that the government was dissolved might get out of hand 'for that might have been carried so far, as to infer from it, that all men's properties, honours, rights, and franchises were dissolved.' *History of His Own Time*, iii, 362.

33. Grey's *Debates*, ix, 25.

34. Hist. MSS. Comm., House of Lords MSS (1689–90), pp. 14–16.

35. Grey's *Debates*, x, 75.

36. *The Tryal of Dr Sacheverell* (1710), pp. 34, 74, 384–8.

37. Richard Claridge, *A Defence of the Present Government under King William and Queen Mary* (1689), p. 7. See also [Thomas Comber,] *A Letter to a Bishop concerning the Present Settlement and the New Oaths* (1689), pp. 4–11; [Thomas Long,] *The Historian Unmask'd* (1689), p. 8; [James Welwood,] *Vindication of the present Great Revolution in England* (1689), p. 20; *The New Oath of Allegiance Justified, from the Original Constitution of the English Monarchy* (1689), pp. 6–15; Daniel Whitby, *Obedience due to the present king notwithstanding our oaths to the former* (1689) in *Somers Tracts*, ed. Sir Walter Scott (1815), x, 297–8; *A Vindication of the late proceedings of the Parliament of England* (1689) in *Somers Tracts*, x, 263; and [Peter Allix,] *Some considerations touching succession and allegiance* (1689) in *A Collection of State Tracts*, i, 337.

38. Samuel Masters, *The Case of Allegiance in our present circumstances consider'd* (1689), p. 9.

39. James Tyrrell, *Bibliotheca Politica*, p. 808. See also, *ibid.*, pp. 177, 779–81; *An Essay upon the Original and Design of Magistracie* (1689), pp. 6–7; *The New Oath of Allegiance Justified* (1689), p. 21; *The Revolution Justified* (1697), pp. 15–16; *A Letter to Dr Lancaster, wherein the Resistance of the People and the placing King William on the throne, are vindicated from the odious imputations of Usurpation and Rebellion* (1697), pp. 7–12; Benjamin Hoadly, *The Measures of Submission to the Civil Magistrate considered* (1706), pp. 171–4; and *idem, The Original and Institution of Civil Government Discuss'd* (1710), pp. 125–7, 150–56.

40. *The Tryal of Dr Sacheverell*, p. 92.

41. Robert J. Frankle, 'The formulation of the Declaration of Rights', *Historical Journal*, xvii (1974), 265–79.

42. William Petyt, *The Ancient Right of the Commons of England Asserted* (1680) and *Jus Parliamentarium: Or, the Ancient Power, Jurisdiction, Rights and Liberties of the most High Court of Parliament, revived and asserted* (published posthumously, 1739).

43. Robert Atkyns, *The Power, Jurisdiction and Priviledge of Parliament; and the Antiquity of the House of Commons asserted* (1689), pp. 49–50.

44. Gilbert Burnet, *History of His Own Time*, ii, 205.

45. See, e.g., *Parl. Hist.*, v, 1070–1134; and Daniel Defoe's *Review*, iii, no. 151; iv, no. 49, no. 51, no. 69, no. 72; v, no. 106; vi, no. 20, no.53, no. 128; ix, no. 19, no. 20. For a general discussion of this question, see J. W. Gough, *Fundamental Law in English Constitutional History* (Oxford, 1955), esp. chap. x.

46. For the important debates on the Septennial Act, see *Parl. Hist.*, vii, 304–57.

47. John Locke, *Letters Concerning Toleration* (1689–92); *idem, The Reasonableness of Christianity* (1695); and G. R. Cragg, *From Puritanism to the Age of Reason* (Cambridge, 1966), pp. 114–25, 215–18.

48. Peter Paxton, *Civil Polity. A Treatise concerning the Nature of Government* (1703), pp. 54–5, 226; Edward A. Bloom and Lillian D. Bloom, *Joseph Addison's Sociable Animal* (Providence, 1971), chaps. 1–4 and J. G. A. Pocock, *The Machiavellian Moment* (Princeton, 1975), pp. 423–61.

49. Charles Davenant, *An Essay upon Ways and Means of Supplying the War* (1695) in *Works*, ed. Sir Charles Whitworth (5 vols., 1771), i, 16; Daniel Defoe, *An Essay upon Public Credit* (1710); and *idem, Review*, iv, no. 109; vi, nos. 30–32; vii, nos. 55, 62, 103, 117, 118, 130.

50. Geoffrey Holmes, *British Politics in the Age of Anne*, pp. 172–6.

51. Daniel Defoe, *Review*, ii, no. 3 (6 March 1705).

52. W. Pittis, *History of the First Session of the Present Parliament* (1711), p. 99.

53. Defoe, *The Original Power of the Collective Body of the People of England, Examined and Asserted* (1702), p. 18.

54. Paschal Larkin, *Property in the Eighteenth Century* (Cork, 1930), pp. 58–91.

55. Samuel Clarke, *A Discourse concerning the Unalterable Obligation of Natural Religion* (1706) in *A Collection of Theological Tracts*, ed. Richard Watson (1785), iv, 111–12.

56. James Tyrrell, *Bibliotheca Politica* (1694), advertisement. See also *idem, A Brief Enquiry into the Ancient Constitution and Government of England* (1695), p. 4.

57. *The Claims of the People of England, Essayed* (1701), p. 106. See also *A Discourse concerning the nature, power and proper effects of the*

present Conventions in both kingdoms, call'd by the Prince of Orange (1689) in *A Collection of State Tracts*, i, 219.

58. [Defoe,] *The Original Power of the Collective Body of the People of England, Examined and Asserted*, p. 18.

59. John Toland, *The Militia Reform'd* (1698), pp. 18–19. See also *Some Remarks upon Government* (1689), pp. 24–6; *Some Observations concerning the regulating of elections for Parliament* (1689), pp. 9–12; and the more detailed treatment of the Commonwealthmen in the next chapter.

60. John Locke, *Two Treatises*, II, para. 22.

61. Richard Claridge, *A Defence of the Present Government under King William and Queen Mary* (1689), p. 4. See also, Gilbert Burnet, *An Enquiry into the Measures of Submission to the Supram Authority* (1688), p. 3; *The Doctrine of Passive Obedience and Jure Divino disprov'd* (1689), p. 1; Daniel Defoe, *Jure Divino* (1706), p. vi; Benjamin Hoadly, *The Happiness of the Present Establishment and the Unhappiness of Absolute Monarchy* (1708), pp. 8–9; and *idem, St Paul's Behaviour towards the Civil Magistrate* (1708), pp. 11–12, 16.

Chapter 3

1. On the Whig side see, e.g., Gilbert Burnet, *An Enquiry into the Measures of Submission to the Supream Authority* (1688), p. 3; Robert Atkyns, *The Power, Jurisdiction and Priviledge of Parliament* (1689), p. 14; and Samuel Masters, *The Case of Allegiance in our present circumstances consider'd* (1689), p. 9. On the Tory side see the arguments of Sherlock, Dodwell, Higden, Sharp, Blackall and Swift cited in chapter one. The common ground between Whigs and Tories was clearly perceived by the anonymous author of *A Letter to a Friend: Occasion'd by the Contest between the Bishop of Exeter and Mr Hoadly* (1709).

2. *Parl. Hist.*, v, 758.

3. *Ibid.*, v, 765.

4. *Ibid.*, v, 832.

5. [Daniel Defoe,] *Some Reflections on a Pamphlet lately publish'd, entituled, An Argument shewing that a Standing Army is inconsistent with a Free Government* (1697); [*idem,*] *An Argument shewing that a Standing Army, with Consent of Parliament, be not inconsistent with a Free Government* (1698); [Lord Somers,] *A Letter, Ballancing the Necessity of Keeping a Land-Force in Times of Peace: with the Dangers that may follow it* (1697); Lois G. Schwoerer, *'No Standing Armies!'* (Baltimore, 1974), pp. 184–7; and J. R. Western, *The English Militia in the Eighteenth Century* (1965), pp. 94–103.

6. Dennis Rubini, *Court and Country, 1688–1702* (1967), pp. 100–101.

7. *Parl. Hist.*, v, 793, 838, and *The True Englishman's Choice of Parliament-Men* (1698).

8. *Parl. Hist.*, vi, 474; and British Library. Add. MS. 17677 DDD, f. 683.

9. *Political Thoughts and Reflections* (*c.* 1690) in *The Works of Halifax*, ed. J. P. Kenyon (1969), pp. 209–12. See also Charles Davenant, *Essays upon Peace at Home, and War Abroad* (1704) in *Works*, iv, 303–14. Though sometimes a critic of the Court, Davenant had just accepted a Court appointment when he wrote this.

10. *The Spectator*, no. 125 (24 July 1711).

11. Swift, *The Sentiments of a Church-of-England Man* (1708) in *Prose Works*, ed. Herbert Davis, ii (Oxford, 1939), pp. 13–14.

12. *Faults on Both Sides* (Part One, 1710), p. 55. See also *An Essay Towards the History of the Last Ministry and Parliament* (1710), pp. 8–10, 39–40.

13. *An Account of some late designs to create a Misunderstanding betwixt the King and his People* (1702), p. 13. See, in particular, Charles Davenant, *Essays upon Peace at Home, and War Abroad* (1704), in *Works*, iv, 287–302.

14. J. G. A. Pocock, 'Machiavelli, Harrington, and English Political Ideology in the Eighteenth Century', *William and Mary Quarterly*, 3rd series, xxii (1965), 549–83; *idem, The Machiavellian Moment* (Princeton, 1975), pp. 404–19.

15. Charles Davenant, *An Essay upon the Balance of Power* (1701), in *Works*, iii, 319.

16. John Trenchard, *An Argument, Shewing that a Standing Army is Inconsistent with a Free Government, and Absolutely Destructive to the Constitution of the English Monarchy* (1697); *idem, A Short History of Standing Armies in England* (1698); *idem, A Letter from the Author of the Argument against a Standing Army* (1697); Andrew Fletcher, *A Discourse concerning Militias and Standing Armies* (1697); John Toland, *The Militia Reform'd* (1697); and Lois Schwoerer, '*No Standing Armies!' The Anti Army Ideology in Seventeenth-Century England*, pp. 155–87.

17. Davenant, *Works*, iii, 320–25; iv, 146–7; Jonathan Swift, *The Conduct of the Allies*, in *Prose Works*, ed. Herbert Davis, vi, 41; *The People of England's Grievances* (n.d., but *c.* 1693); and *Parl. Hist.*, vi, 889.

18. Charles Davenant, *Works*, iii, 299–300; J. G. A. Pocock, *The Machiavellian Moment*, pp. 437–45; P. G. M. Dickson, *The Financial Revolution in England* (1967), chap. 2; and W. A. Speck, 'Conflict in Society', in *Britain after the Glorious Revolution*, ed. Geoffrey Holmes, pp. 135–52.

19. [Thomas Wagstaffe,] *A Letter to a Gentleman elected a Knight of*

the Shire to Serve in the Present Parliament (1694), pp. 6–8.

20. Quoted by E. A. Reitan, 'From Revenue to Civil List, 1689–1702: The Revolution Settlement and the "Mixed and Balanced" Constitution', *Historical Journal*, xiii (1970), 579.

21. *Parl. Hist.*, v, 671.

22. J. A. Downie, 'The Commission of Public Accounts and the formation of the Country Party', *English Historical Review*, xci (1976), 33–51; Dennis Rubini, *Court and Country*, pp. 68–92; and Geoffrey Holmes, *British Politics in the Age of Anne*, pp. 137–41.

23. Charles Davenant, *Works*, iii, 301–302.

24. Public Records Office. Shaftesbury papers, 30/24/46/no. 90. 'Essay on Public Virtue' (*c.* 1696), fol. 14. I am indebted to a former postgraduate student, Peter Robinson, for bringing this manuscript essay to my attention.

25. Henry Neville, *Plato Redivivus*, in *Two English Republican Tracts*, ed. Caroline Robbins, pp. 185–8.

26. *Some Remarks upon Government* (1689), pp. 26–7.

27. Walter Moyle, *An Essay upon the Constitution of the Roman Republic*, in *Two English Republican Tracts*, ed. Caroline Robbins, pp. 239–40.

28. *Parl. Hist.*, v, 744–52.

29. *Ibid.*, v, 829–32.

30. John Toland, *The Danger of Mercenary Parliaments* (1698), pp. 6–7. See also *Some Cautions offered to the Consideration of Those who are to Chuse Members to Serve in the Ensuing Parliament* (1695) and *A Letter to a Country Gentleman, setting forth the cause of the Decay and Ruin of Trade. To which is annexed a list of the Names of some Gentlemen who were Members of the last Parliament, and now are (or lately were) in Public Employments* (1698).

31. G. S. Holmes, 'The Attack on "the Influence of the Crown" 1702–1716', *Bulletin of the Institute of Historical Research*, xxxix (1966), 47–68.

32. John Toland, *The Art of Governing by Partys* (1701), pp. 70–73; and *Some Reasons for Annual Parliaments* (1693).

33. *A Letter to a Gentleman Elected a Knight of the Shire* (1695), p. 14.

34. 7 and 8 William III, c. 4.

35. 7 and 8 William III, c. 25.

36. Geoffrey Holmes, *British Politics in the Age of Anne*, pp. 143–4.

37. *Some Remarks upon Government* (1689), pp. 25–6; and Walter Moyle, *An Essay upon the Constitution of the Roman Republic*, in *Two English Republican Tracts*, ed. Caroline Robbins, pp. 237, 240–41.

38. Geoffrey Holmes, *British Politics in the Age of Anne*, pp. 145–6.

39. [Daniel Defoe,] *Considerations upon Corrupt Elections of Members to serve in Parliament* (1701); [*idem,*] *The Villainy of Stock-Jobbers Detected* (1701); John Toland, *The Art of Governing by Partys* (1701), pp. 100, 165–6; and *A Short View of the Apparent Dangers and Mischiefs from the Bank of England* (1707).

40. [Defoe,] *The Freeholder's Plea against Stock-jobbing elections of Parliament Men* (1701), p. 23.

41. Charles Davenant, *Works*, v, 52.

42. Robert Molesworth, *The Principles of a Real Whig* (1711), in *The Memoirs of John Ker of Kersland* (3 vols., 1726), iii, 205.

43. [Daniel Defoe,] *The Original Power of the Collective Body of the People of England, Examined and Asserted* (1702), pp. 14, 22–3. See also *idem, Legion's Memorial to the Commons* (1701), pp. 1–4; and *idem, Two Great Questions consider'd* (1707), pp. 10–11.

44. [Defoe,] *The Original Power of the Collective Body of the People* ..., p. 23; *The Electors Right Asserted* (1701), p. 1; *Some Reasons for Annual Parliaments* (1693), pp. 4, 8; and *Questions of Common Right* ... (*c.* 1695), p. 3.

45. *Some Remarks upon Government* (1689), pp. 24–6; *Some Observations concerning the regulating of elections for Parliament* (1689), pp. 9–12.

46. *Letters to Parliament-Men, in reference to some proceedings in the House of Commons* (1701), pp. 9–10.

47. *The Representative of London and Westminster in Parliament, Examined and Consider'd* (1702).

48. John Toland, *The Art of Governing by Partys* (1701), pp. 75–7.

49. [Defoe,] *The Freeholder's Plea against Stock-jobbing Elections of Parliament Men* (1701), pp. 16–17.

50. *Ibid.*, pp. 18–19.

Chapter 4

1. Changes in the structure of politics have been examined by J. H. Plumb, *The Growth of Political Stability in England 1675–1725* (1967), pp. 159–89; Geoffrey Holmes, 'Harley, St John and the Death of the Tory Party', in *Britain after the Glorious Revolution*, ed. Geoffrey Holmes, pp. 216–37; John B. Owen, *The Eighteenth Century 1714–1815* (1974), pp. 3–23, 94–122; A. S. Foord, *His Majesty's Opposition 1714–1830* (Oxford, 1964), pp. 13–109; and H. T. Dickinson, *Walpole and the Whig Supremacy* (1973), pp. 40–55.

2. Richard Cumberland, *A Treatise of the Laws of Nature* (1727), pp. 64–6, 314, 322–5; Henry Kames, *Essays upon several subjects in Law* (Edinburgh, 1732), pp. 100–101; David Hume, *A Treatise of Human*

Nature (1740), Book III, part 2, section ii; Francis Hutcheson, *A System of Moral Philosophy* (2 vols., 1755), i, 323; and Adam Smith, *Lectures on Justice, Police, Revenue and Arms*, ed. Edwin Cannan (Oxford, 1896), p. 15.

3. William Blackstone, *Commentaries upon the Laws of England* (7th ed., 4 vols., Oxford, 1775), i, 139. For Blackstone's preoccupation with the defence of property see Daniel Boorstin, *The Mysterious Science of the Law* (Cambridge, Mass., 1941), chap. ix. See also the *London Journal*, 6 March 1731 and 9 September 1732.

4. Adam Ferguson, *An Essay on the History of Civil Society* (1767), ed. Duncan Forbes (Edinburgh, 1966), p. 187. See also Bishop Samuel Squires, *An Historical Essay upon the Ballance of Civil Power in England* (1748), p. 49.

5. *Parl. Hist.*, xii, 463–4. A speech by Henry Fox. See also Blackstone, *Commentaries*, i, 171–2.

6. *Parl. Hist.*, xv, 744.

7. Some Whigs did of course endorse Locke's views. See, e.g., John Jackson, *The Grounds of Civil and Ecclesiastical Government Briefly Consider'd* (1718), pp. 6–8; and Thomas Bowles, *The Design and End of Civil Government* (Northampton, 1741), pp. 4–6.

8. See, e.g., Thomas Burnet, *An Essay upon Government* (Dublin, 1716), pp. 20–25, 75–6; and Roger Acherley, *The Britannic Constitution: Or, the Fundamental Form of Government in Britain* (1727), p. 27.

9. Thomas Burnet, *An Essay upon Government*, pp. 43–5; *idem, The Divine Authority of Government* (1726), pp. 19–25; William Hay, *An Essay on Civil Government* (1728), pp. 8–10, 12–14; *London Journal*, 8 April 1732, 9 September 1732, 1 September 1733; Edmund Keene, *A Sermon preached before ... the Lords Spiritual and Temporal, ... January 30, 1753* (1753), pp. 12–22; William Ashburnham, *A Sermon preached before the House of Lords ... on January 30, 1755* (1755), pp. 6–7.

10. *London Journal*, 2 June 1733.

11. Thomas Burnet, *An Essay upon Government*, p. 13. See also Blackstone, *Commentaries*, i, 34; *A Treatise on Government: Being a review of the doctrine of the original contract* (1750), pp. 13, 15–16, 43, 46–8; and William Hay, *An Essay on Civil Government* (1728), p. 11.

12. James Beauclerk, *A Sermon preached before the ... Lords ... January 30, 1752* (1752), p. 10.

13. Blackstone, *Commentaries*, i, 161–2.

14. *Ibid.*, i, 212.

15. Lord Hervey, *Ancient and Modern Liberty stated and compared* (1734), p. 47. See also Thomas Wise, *Religion and Loyalty* (1715), pp. 6–7; Thomas Burnet, *An Essay upon Government*, pp. 14, 43, 47–55, 69;

Edward Chandler, *A Sermon preached before the Lords ... on 30 January 1718* (1718), pp. 27–8; Samuel Croxall, *A Sermon preached before the House of Commons ... 30 January 1729* (1729), p. 13; Roger Acherley, *The Britannic Constitution* (1727), p. 95; *London Journal*, 11 November 1734; and George Fothergill, *The Danger of Excesses in the Pursuit of Liberty* (Oxford, 1737), p. 13.

16. Thomas Burnet, *An Essay upon Government*, pp. 53, 70; David Hume, 'Of the Original Contract', in *Essays Moral, Political and Literary* (Oxford, 1963), p. 459; and *King George's Title asserted* (1745), pp. 62–3.

17. The best interpretation of Hume's political views is in Duncan Forbes, *Hume's Philosophical Politics* (Cambridge, 1975). See also J. B. Stewart, *The Moral and Political Philosophy of David Hume* (1963) and *Hume's Theory of Politics*, ed. F. Watkins (1951). I have also profited from discussions about Hume with a former student, Roger A. Mason.

18. 'Of the Original Contract', in Hume, *Essays Moral, Political and Literary*, p. 456.

19. Hume, *A Treatise of Human Nature* (1740), Book III, part 2, section ii.

20. *Ibid.*, Book III, part 2, sections ii, v, and vii.

21. *Ibid.*, Book III, part 2, section viii; and 'Of the Origin of Government', in *Essays*, pp. 35–8.

22. *Treatise*, Book III, part 2, section x.

23. *Ibid.*, Book III, part 2, section ix.

24. *Ibid.*, Book III, part 2, section x; and 'Of Passive Obedience', in *Essays*, pp. 474–7.

25. 'Of the Liberty of the Press', 'Of the Origin of Government', and 'Of the Idea of a Perfect Commonwealth', all in *Essays*, pp. 8–12, 38–9, 499–515.

26. 'Whether the British Government inclines more to Absolute Monarchy or to a Republic', in *Essays*, pp. 48–53.

27. 'Of the Original Contract', in *Essays*, pp. 463–4. See also 'Of the Idea of a Perfect Commonwealth', *ibid.*, pp. 499–500.

28. 'Of Parties in General', 'Of the Parties of Great Britain', 'Of the Coalition of Parties', and 'Of the Protestant Succession', in *Essays*, pp. 54–62, 63–74, 478–86 and 487–8; Hume, *The History of Great Britain*, ed. Duncan Forbes (Pelican Classics, 1970), pp. 30–38; and Duncan Forbes, *Hume's Philosophical Politics*, pp. 261–90.

29. Adam Smith, *Lectures on Justice, Police, Revenue and Arms*, ed. Edwin Cannan (Oxford, 1896), pp. 9–13, 44–5, 58, 68–72. This work was based on a student's notes written in 1763.

30. Adam Ferguson, *An Essay on the History of Civil Society* (1767),

ed. Duncan Forbes (Edinburgh, 1966), p. 123. See also pp. 1–10, 16, 182.

31. *Ibid.*, p. 163.

32. *London Journal*, 1 September 1733 and 16 March 1734. See also Isaac Kramnick, *Bolingbroke and His Circle* (Cambridge, Mass., 1966), pp. 127–36.

33. *Daily Gazetteer*, 6, 12 and 26 July 1735.

34. *London Journal*, 16 November 1734; and Lord Hervey, *Ancient and Modern Liberty stated and compared* (1734), p. 24.

35. *Ibid.*, p. 40.

36. Blackstone, *Commentaries*, iv, 412–43. For Burke, see J. G. A. Pocock, 'Edmund Burke and the Ancient Constitution: a Problem in the History of Ideas', *Historical Journal*, ii (1960), 125–43.

37. David Hume, 'Of the Coalition of Parties', *Essays*, pp. 482–3.

38. Robert Wallace, *Characteristics of the Present Political State of Great Britain* (1758), p. 65.

39. *Parl. Hist.*, ix, 410.

40. *Ibid.*, xvi, 171.

41. *An Essay on Liberty and Independency* (1747), pp. 7–8.

42. *Parl. Hist.*, ix, 473.

43. Blackstone, *Commentaries*, i, 154–5. See also *Parl. Hist.*, xvi, 796; and Bernard Bailyn, *The Origin of American Politics* (New York, 1968), pp. 17–19.

44. *The Old Whig*, no. 1 (19 March 1719).

45. Richard Steele, *The Plebian*, nos. 1 and 2 (14, 23 March 1719).

46. *Parl. Hist.*, vii, 621. See also E. R. Turner, 'The Peerage Bill of 1719', *English Historical Review*, xxviii (1913), 243–59.

47. *Parl. Hist.*, viii, 847; and *London Journal*, 4 July and 19 September 1730.

48. *Parl. Hist.*, vii, 299–300. See also *Some Considerations on a Law for Triennial Parliaments* (1716).

49. *London Journal*, 25 August 1733.

50. Blackstone, *Commentaries*, i, 159–60.

51. *Parl. Hist.*, xvi, 612. See also *ibid.*, xvi, 170, and 'Parliamentary Diaries of Nathaniel Ryder 1764–7', ed. P. D. G. Thomas, *Camden Miscellany XXIII* (4th series, 1969), pp. 264–7.

52. Benjamin Hoadly, *A Preservative against the Principles and Practices of the Non-Jurors both in Church and State* (3rd ed., 1716), p. 65. The same conclusion was reached by the Rev. John Jackson, *The Grounds of Civil and Ecclesiastical Government Briefly Consider'd* (1718), pp. 18–28. The acceptance of the subordinate position of the Church is clearly seen in William Warburton, *The Alliance of Church and State* (1736). This did not prevent Warburton's becoming a bishop.

53. Hume, 'Of Parties in General', in *Essays*, p. 58.

54. Burke, *Thoughts on the Cause of the Present Discontents* (1770) in *Works* (Bohn ed., 6 vols., 1854–56), i, 367.

55. Hume, 'Of Luxury', in *Political Discourses* (Edinburgh, 1752), pp. 35–6. See also Adam Ferguson, *An Essay on the History of Civil Society*, ed. Duncan Forbes, pp. 245–62; Adam Smith, *Lectures on Justice, Police, Revenue and Arms*, ed. Edwin Cannan, pp. 195–6; and J. G. A. Pocock, *The Machiavellian Moment*, pp. 493–504.

56. *Some Considerations on Public Credit and the Nature of its Circulating in the Funds* (1733), quoted by Isaac Kramnick, *Bolingbroke and His Circle*, p. 52. See also *London Journal*, 11 July 1730, 1 April 1732; *Daily Gazetteer*, 20 September 1735, 7 April 1737; and Robert Wallace, *Characteristics of the Present Political State of Great Britain* (1758), pp. 64–5.

57. *Letters from a Moor at London to His Friend in Tunis* (1736), p. 27.

58. William Arnall, *Opposition No Proof of Patriotism* (1735), p. 18. See also *Parl. Hist.*, ix. 471–2; *ibid.*, x, 400–401; *London Journal*, 29 September 1733, 18 May 1734; *Free Briton*, 4 January 1733; *An Essay on Faction* (1733), pp. 7–14; *A Full and True Account of the Strange and Miraculous Conversion of the Tories in Great Britain by the Preaching of Caleb d'Anvers, Prophet and Apostle to these Nations* (1734); and Isaac Kramnick, *Bolingbroke and His Circle*, pp. 119–27.

59. *The Case of the Opposition Stated between the Craftsman and the People* (1731), pp. 13–16; William Arnall, *Opposition No Proof of Patriotism* (1735), pp. 3–6; *London Journal*, 23 June 1733; *Free Briton*, 11 May 1732, 18 January 1733, 28 June 1733; *Daily Courant*, 3 March 1733; Earl of Egmont, *Faction Detected by the Evidence of the Facts* (1743); and Henry Fielding, *A Dialogue between a Gentleman ... and an Honest Alderman ...* (1747) in *Henry Fielding: The Jacobite's Journal and Related Writings*, ed. W. B. Coley (Oxford, 1974), p. 32.

60. David Hume, 'Of the Independency of Parliament', *Essays*, p. 44; and Samuel Squire, *An Historical Essay upon the Ballance of Civil Power in England* (1748), pp. v–vii.

61. For the vigorous defence of a standing army by Court Whigs, see *Parl. Hist.*, viii, 1185; x, 395–401, 419–20.

62. *London Journal*, 5 October 1734. See also, *ibid.*, 17 May 1735.

63. Abraham Tucker, *The Country Gentleman's Advice to his Son* (1755), pp. 37–9.

64. *London Journal*, 19 October 1734. See also, *ibid.*, 12 October 1734; and *Parl. Hist.*, xi, 335, 346; xii, 879.

65. *Ibid.*, ix, 370; and Henry Fielding, *A Dialogue between a Gentleman ... and an Honest Alderman ...* (1747) in *Henry Fielding: The*

Jacobite's Journal and Related Writings, ed. W. B. Coley, p. 5.

66. *Parl. Hist.*, xi, 362–6. See also *ibid.*, ix, 378.

67. *London Journal*, 26 May 1733.

68. *Parl. Hist.*, xiii, 1078.

69. e.g. *ibid.*, xii, 474; *London Journal*, 5 May 1733, 26 May 1733, 2 June 1733, 1 September 1733, 5 January 1734; *Daily Gazetteer*, 23 November 1742; *The Rise and Fall of the Late Projected Excise, Impartially consider'd* (1733), p. 28; *A Letter to the Freeholders ... concerning their Duty before and after the Election of their Representatives* (1733), pp. 5–6; David Hume, 'Of the First Principles of Government', *Essays*, pp. 32–3; *A Letter to a Member of Parliament, concerning the present State of Affairs at Home and Abroad* (1740), pp. 2–6; *A Hint upon Instructions from the Electors to their Representatives in Parliament* (1742), pp. 5–7; *Seasonable Expostulations with the Worthy Citizens of London, Upon their late Instructions to their Representatives* (1742); and Lord Egmont, *Faction Detected by the Evidence of the Facts* (1743), pp. 100, 134.

70. *Parl. Hist.*, x, 557.

71. *London Journal*, 22 June 1734.

72. Thomas Burnet, *The Divine Authority of Government, with the measure of subjection stated, and the lawfulness of the Revolution demonstrated* (1726), pp. 19–20; George Fothergill, *The Danger of Excesses in the Pursuit of Liberty* (Oxford, 1737), p. 13; Edward Chandler, *A Sermon preach'd before the Lords Spiritual and Temporal ... on 30 January 1717–18* (1718), pp. 11, 27; Joseph Butler, *A Sermon preached before the House of Lords ... Jan. 30, 1740–41* (1741), pp. 14–16; and [Daniel Defoe,] *An Humble Address to our Soveraign Lord the People* (1715), p. 31. (Defoe at this stage in his career was seeking to make peace with the Court Whigs.)

73. *The Freeholder's Alarm to his Brethren: Or, the Fate of Britain determin'd by the ensuing Election* (1734), p. 22.

74. Douglas Hay, 'Property, Authority and the Criminal Law', in *Albion's Fatal Tree*, ed. D. Hay et al. (1975), pp. 17–63.

75. Daniel Defoe, *A Hymn to the Mob* (1715), pp. i–v; *idem, An Humble Address to our Soveraign Lord the People* (1715); *idem, The Great Law of Subordination consider'd* (1724); *Hyp Doctor*, 2 May 1736; *Daily Gazetteer*, 18 August 1736; and *The Freeholder's Alarm to his Brethren* (1734), pp. 5–7, 13.

76. Hay, *op. cit.*, in *Albion's Fatal Tree*, pp. 17–63.

Chapter 5

1. Isaac Kramnick, *Bolingbroke and His Circle*, pp. 177–81.

2. Thomas Gordon, *The Works of Sallust* (1744), p. 83.

3. *The Works of Lord Bolingbroke* (4 vols., 1844), ii, 114–20. See also *Parl. Hist.*, x, 384–6 for the speech by Lord Noel Somerset, a Tory, on this theme.

4. H. T. Dickinson, *Bolingbroke* (1970), p. 208.

5. Trenchard and Gordon, *Cato's Letters* (4 vols., 5th ed., 1748), iii, 151 (no. 84, 7 July 1722).

6. *Ibid.*, ii, 17 (no. 35, 1 July 1721).

7. *Ibid.*, iii, 160 (no. 85, 14 July 1722).

8. *Ibid.*, iv, 244–5 (no. 133, 15 June 1723).

9. *Gentleman's Magazine*, vi (1736), 367.

10. See T. W. Perry, *Public Opinion, Propaganda and Politics in Eighteenth-Century England* (Cambridge, Mass., 1962), which, despite its title, is a study of the Jewish Naturalization Act of 1753.

11. See, in particular, *The Character of an Independent Whig* (1719) and the fifty-three issues of *The Independent Whig* (1720).

12. Trenchard and Gordon, *Cato's Letters*, i, 179–80; ii, 85–7, 216, 228, 245.

13. *Ibid.*, i, 86–7 (no. 13, 21 January 1720).

14. *Ibid.*, i, 191–2, 257–61; iii, 84.

15. *Ibid.*, i, 11; ii, 16; and *An Essay on Civil Government* (1743), pp. 133–4.

16. Bolingbroke, *Works*, ii, 163–4.

17. *Free Briton*, 4 May 1732.

18. *Cato's Letters*, i, 11 (no. 3, 19 November 1720); i, 32 (no. 7, 17 December 1722); i, 43 (no. 9, 3 December 1720); iii, 119–206 (no. 90, 18 August 1722); iii, 206–10 (no. 91, 25 August 1722). Cf. *The Craftsman*, no. 114 (7 September 1728); no. 130 (28 December 1728); and no. 134 (25 January 1729).

19. *Common Sense*, 1 March 1740.

20. *Cato's Letters*, iii, 210 (no. 91, 25 August 1722). See also Historical Manuscripts Commission, Portland MSS, vii, 449. Wm. Stratford to the Earl of Oxford, 15 July 1727; and *The Craftsman*, no. 111 (17 August 1728); no. 114 (7 September 1728); and no. 123 (9 November 1728).

21. *Epistle to Bathurst* (1733), ll. 69–78.

22. There has been a great deal of work on how the literary world treated the theme of corruption. See, in particular, Isaac Kramnick, *Bolingbroke and His Circle*; Maynard Mack, *The Garden and the City* (1969); Peter Dixon, *The World of Pope's Satires* (1968), pp. 133–41; H. T. Dickinson, *Walpole and the Whig Supremacy* (1973), pp. 140–59; and *idem*, ed., *Politics and Literature in the Eighteenth Century* (1974), pp. 53–104.

23. Bolingbroke, *Works*, ii, 9–10, 160–68, 187–8, 281, 439–61; *The Craftsman*, no. 377 (22 September 1733); *Common Sense*, 2 April 1737,

12 July 1740; Hugh Hume, Earl of Marchmont, *A Serious Exhortation to the Electors of Great Britain* (1740), pp. 22, 25–6; James Ralph, *Of the Use and Abuse of Parliament* (2 vols., 1744); and James Shebbeare, *A Third Letter to the People of England, on Liberty, Taxes, and the Application of Public Money* (1756), pp. 30–31.

24. Bolingbroke, *Works*, i, 427.

25. See, e.g., *The Craftsman*, no. 182 (27 December 1729); and Hugh Hume, Earl of Marchmont, *A Serious Exhortation to the Electors of Great Britain* (1740), pp. 58–60.

26. Isaac Kramnick, *Bolingbroke and His Circle*, pp. 119–21.

27. *Cato's Letters*, i, 104–108 (no. 16, 11 February 1720); iii, 3–12 (no. 69, 10 March 1722); iii, 18–24 (no. 80, 9 June 1722); iii, 258–64 (no. 96, 29 September 1722).

28. *Works*, ii, 67.

29. H. T. Dickinson, *Bolingbroke*, pp. 194–7, 254–7.

30. *Cato's Leters*, i, 86 (no. 13, 21 January 1720); i, 96–7 (no. 15, 4 February 1721); i, 214–25 (no. 59, 30 December 1721); Hugh Hume, Earl of Marchmont, *A Serious Exhortation ...*, pp. 20–21; Henry Fielding, *The Champion* (Collected ed., 1741), p. 94 (10 April 1740); [John Campbell,] *The Case of the Opposition impartially stated* (1742), pp. 51–2; *An Essay on Government* (1743), pp. 138–9, 353–8; and John Shebbeare, *A Seventh Letter to the People of England* (1758), pp. 21–4.

31. *The Sentiments of a Tory* (1741), quoted in Donald J. Greene, *The Politics of Samuel Johnson* (New Haven, 1960), pp. 275–6.

32. Bolingbroke, *Works*, ii, 87–9, 401–402, 410. See also J. H. Burns, 'Bolingbroke and the Concept of Constitutional Government', *Political Studies* (1962), x, 264–76.

33. Edward Spelman, *A Fragment out of the Sixth Book of Polybius* (1743), preface, pp. v–ix; David Hume, 'Of Parties in General' and 'Of the Parties of Great Britain', *Essays*, pp. 55–61, 63–74; and Bernard Mandeville, *The Fable of the Bees*, ed. F. B. Kaye (2 vols., Oxford, 1924), i, 94–5, ii, 334; and *idem, Free Thoughts on Religion, the Church and National Happiness* (1723 ed.), pp. 341–2, 355–6.

34. Caroline Robbins, ' "Discordant Parties": A Study of the Acceptance of Party by Englishmen', *Political Science Quarterly*, 73 (1958), 505–29; and J. A. W. Gunn, ed., *Factions No More* (1972), pp. 80–94, 137–50.

35. See, e.g., *The Craftsman*, nos. 65, 71, 91, 93, 105 and 114; *Parl. Hist.*, viii, 1063–7, 1077–1166; and *Cato's Letters*, nos. 3, 7, 9.

36. *Parl. Hist.*, viii, 1325. See also Paul Langford, *The Excise Crisis* (Oxford, 1975).

37. *The Craftsman*, no. 114 (7 September 1728).

38. *Parl. Hist.*, viii, 953.

39. *Ibid.*, ix, 373. See also *ibid.*, xiv, 595, 1095.

40. *Ibid.*, vii, 508; viii, 61, 642–4; ix, 262; x, 387–93, 913–14; *Cato's Letters*, ii, 234–57 (nos. 94 and 95; 15, 22 September 1722); *The Craftsman*, nos. 185, 186 (17, 24 January 1730); John Shebbeare, *A Second Letter to the People of England. On the Foreign Subsidies, Subsidiary Armies, and their Consequences to this Nation* (1757), pp. 12–25; and Bolingbroke, *Works*, i, 304, 315, 339, 341, 371, 427; ii, 92, 129, 132.

41. *Parl. Hist.*, xiv, 158–9.

42. *Ibid.*, viii, 1249–50; x, 1387; Adam Ferguson, *Reflections Previous to the Establishment of a Militia* (1756), pp. 1–12; Edward Wortley Montagu, *Reflections on the Rise and Fall of Antient Republicks* (2nd ed., 1760), pp. 374–88; and J. R. Western, *The English Militia in the Eighteenth Century*, pp. 104–26.

43. *Parl. Hist.*, vii, 317. See also *ibid.*, vii, 299–357.

44. *Ibid.*, vii, 612; x, 456; xiv, 29–43; and xv, 160–61. See also *Common Sense*, no. 140 (6 October 1739); James Ralph, *Of the Use and Abuse of Parliament* (1744), pp. 717–18; and John Shebbeare, *A Second Letter to the People of England* ... (2nd ed., 1755), pp. 5–8.

45. *Parl. Hist.*, ix, 396–474; xii, 590; xiii, 1056–1107; Bolingbroke, *The Freeholder's Political Catechism* (1734); and *The Craftsman Extraordinary; in which the Right of the People to Frequent Elections of their Representatives is fully consider'd* (1734).

46. Paul Langford, *The Excise Crisis*, pp. 47–57, 172; *Parl. Hist.*, xii, 416–27.

47. Lucy S. Sutherland, 'Edmund Burke and the Relations between Members of Parliament and their Constituents', *Studies in Burke and his Time*, x (1968), 1005–1008.

48. *A Letter to a Member of this New Parliament, from a true lover of the Liberties of the People* (1742), p. 6.

49. *The Craftsman*, 30 December 1732.

50. Bolingbroke, *Works*, ii, 150–51; and Marchmont, *A Serious Exhortation to the Electors of Great Britain* (1740), pp. 16–17.

51. *Common Sense*, no. 142 (20 October 1739).

52. Thomas Carte, *A Full Answer to the Letter from a By-Stander* (1742), p. 206.

53. Quoted in *The Gentleman's Magazine*, iv (1734), 381; and xi (1741), 378. Cf. Marie Peters, 'The "Monitor" on the Constitution, 1755–65: new light on the ideological origins of English radicalism', *English Historical Review*, lxxxvi (1971), 706–25.

54. *Common Sense*, 15 April 1738, 6 October 1739, and 10 January 1741. See also Malachy Postlethwayt, *The Universal Dictionary of Trade and Commerce* (2 vols., 1751, 1755), ii, 415.

55. Quoted in *The Gentleman's Magazine*, xvii (1747), 329 *et seq.*

56. *Fog's Journal*, no. 285 (20 April 1734); and *Liberty and Right: Or an Essay Historical and Political on the Constitution and Administration of Great Britain* (1747), pp. 43–51.
57. G. A. Cranfield, *The Development of the Provincial Press 1700–1760* (Oxford, 1962), chap. 6.

Chapter 6

1. From a letter signed 'Considerator' in the *London Evening Post*, 7–9 September 1773. See also Catharine Macaulay, *Observations on a pamphlet, entitled, Thoughts on the Cause of the Present Discontents* (3rd ed., 1770), pp. 14–16; *A Letter to the People of Great Britain, on the present alarming Crisis* (1771), pp. 1–32; *Letters concerning the Present State of England* (1772), pp. 11–12; John Cartwright, *Take Your Choice!* (1776), pp. ix–xv; Richard Watson, *The Principles of the Revolution vindicated* (Cambridge, 1776), pp. 7–8; *The True State of the Question* (1784), pp. 9–12; and Joseph Priestley, *Lectures on History and General Policy* (Birmingham, 1788), p. 263.
2. *An Essay towards a Catalogue of Patriots, real and pretended* (1769), pp. xviii–xix; Joseph Towers, *Observation on Public Liberty, Patriotism, Ministerial Despotism, and National Grievances* (1769), pp. 15–17; a letter signed 'A Watchman', *The London Chronicle*, 18–20 April 1769; *Considerations on the Times* (1769), pp. 31–7; *Letters concerning the Present State of England* (1772), pp. 200–205; and Capel Lofft, *An Argument on the Nature of Party and Faction* (1780), pp. 8–11.
3. See, e.g., Richard Price, *Observations on the Nature of Civil Liberty* (7th ed., 1776), pp. 1–7; John Cartwright, *Take Your Choice!* (1776), pp. 2–4; and *Declarations of those Rights of the Commonalty of Great Britain, Without Which they Cannot be Free* (c. 1782).
4. Joseph Priestley, *An Essay on the First Principles of Government* (1768), pp. 24–5.
5. On this paragraph see, *ibid.*, pp. 10–17, 41–5; Francis Hutcheson, *A Short Introduction to Moral Philosophy* (2 vols., Glasgow, 1764), ii, 302–12, 326–9; 'Essay on Natural Liberty', in *London Magazine* (1769), pp. 260–61; *The Whisperer*, no. 3 (3 March 1770); letters signed 'Brutus' in *London Evening Post*, 8–10 September and 24–6 December 1772; Letter signed 'Cato' in *ibid.*, 17–19 November 1772; *Resistance No Rebellion* (1775), pp. 12–13; Richard Price, *Observations on the Nature of Civil Liberty* (7th ed., 1776), pp. 6–7; Richard Watson, *The Principles of the Revolution vindicated* (Cambridge, 1776), pp. 3–11; Letter signed 'Liberalis', in *London Evening Post*, 6 November 1777; and *A Letter to the Rev. Dr Cooper, on the Origin of Civil Government*

(1777), pp. 7–20, 37–8. The transmission of seventeenth-century radical political ideas into the eighteenth century is treated at length in Caroline Robbins, *The Eighteenth-Century Commonwealthman*.

6. Richard Price, *Observations on Reversionary Payments* (1771), p. 275; and Thomas Paine, *Common Sense* (1776), ed. Isaac Kramnick (1976), p. 65. See also Richard Price, *A Review of the Principal Questions and Difficulties in Morals* (1758; 2nd ed., 1769), p. 345; and Mary Wollstonecraft, *A Vindication of the Rights of Men* (1790), pp. 11–12, 40–41, 60–61.

7. Joseph Priestley, *Lectures on History and General Policy* (Birmingham, 1788), p. 323. See also, *idem*, *Miscellaneous Observations Relating to Education* (Bath, 1778), pp. 2–4.

8. Priestley, *First Principles*, p. 8. See also *ibid.*, pp. 3–8, 127–91. For a general view of the theory of progress in Britain, see J. B. Bury, *The Idea of Progress* (1920), pp. 217–37.

9. Richard Price, *A Review of the Principal Questions and Difficulties in Morals* (1758; 2nd ed., 1769), pp. 95, 119, 125; and *idem*, *The Evidence for a Future Period of Improvement in the State of Mankind* (1787).

10. William Enfield, *A Sermon on the Centennial Commemoration of the Revolution* (1788), p. 17.

11. Dissenters who campaigned for both religious toleration and political reform include Richard Price, Joseph Priestley, Thomas Paine, John Cartwright, William Godwin, James Burgh, John Disney, Mary Wollstonecraft, Capel Lofft, David Williams, Andrew Kippis, Thomas Brand Hollis, Joseph Towers, Thomas Walker, George Dyer and William Enfield. Liberal Anglicans who advocated political reform include John Wilkes, Christopher Wyvill, John Jebb, John Horne Tooke, and Granville Sharp.

12. Andrew Kippis, *A Vindication of the Protestant Dissenting Ministers* (1772), pp. 25–6.

13. David Williams, *A Letter to the Body of the Protestant Dissenting Ministers of all Denominations* (1777), pp. 23–4.

14. Joseph Priestley, *An Essay on the First Principles of Government* (1768), pp. 54–5.

15. Richard Price, *Observations on the Nature of Civil Liberty* (1776), pp. 21–2. See also Joseph Fownes, *Enquiry into the Principles of Toleration* (1772; 3rd ed., 1790), p. 17; Joshua Toulmin, *Two Letters on the Late Application to Parliament by the Protestant Dissenting Ministers* (1774), pp. 8–10; *Half an Hour's Conversation ... on the Test Laws* (1789), p. 2; *An Address to the Opposers of the Repeal* (1790), p. 16; and George Dyer, *An Inquiry into the Nature of Subscription to the Thirty-Nine Articles* (1789; 3rd ed., 1792), pp. 60–61. There

are useful accounts of the contribution of Dissent to political radicalism in Caroline Robbins, *The Eighteenth-Century Commonwealthman*, pp. 221–70; Anthony Lincoln, *Some Political and Social Ideas of English Dissent 1763–1800* (Cambridge, 1958); Richard B. Barlow, *Citizenship and Conscience* (Philadelphia, 1962); and Russel E. Richey, 'The Origins of British Radicalism: The Changing Rationale for Dissent', *Eighteenth Century Studies*, vii (1973–4), 179–92.

16. [Gilbert Stuart,] *An Historical Dissertation concerning the Antiquity of the English Constitution* (1768), pp. 39, 41, 221, 287; and [Obadiah Hulme,] *An Historical Essay on the English Constitution* (1771), pp. 4–7.

17. Catharine Macaulay, *Observations on a pamphlet, entitled, Thoughts on the Cause of the Present Discontents* (3rd ed., 1770), pp. 12–14.

18. *History of England* (1763; 5 vols., 1822 ed.), i, 2–3, 7n.

19. A letter signed 'Brutus', *London Evening Post*, 5–7 August 1773. For other radical criticisms of the Revolution settlement see John Cartwright, *Take Your Choice!*, p. xxiv; David Williams, *Letters on Political Liberty* (1782), pp. 18–22; *A Dialogue on the Revolution; between a Gentleman and a Farmer* (Manchester, 1788), pp. 13–14; and William Enfield, *A Sermon on the Centennial Commemoration of the Revolution* (1788), pp. 16–17.

20. On radical activity see, in particular, G. S. Veitch, *The Genesis of Parliamentary Reform* (1913); Simon Maccoby, *English Radicalism*, vol. i (1954); George Rudé, *Wilkes and Liberty* (Oxford, 1962); Ian Christie, *Wilkes, Wyvill and Reform* (1962); E. C. Black, *The Association: British Extra-Parliamentary Political Organization 1769–1793* (Cambridge, Mass., 1963); John Cannon, *Parliamentary Reform 1640–1832* (Cambridge, 1973); and John Brewer, *Party Ideology and Popular Politics at the Accession of George III* (Cambridge, 1976), pp. 139–200.

21. Published in *Aris's Birmingham Gazette*, 3 October 1774. Quoted by John Money, 'Taverns, Coffee Houses and Clubs: Local Politics and Popular Articulacy in the Birmingham Area, in the Age of the American Revolution', *Historical Journal*, xiv (1971), 15–47.

22. See Frank O'Gorman, *The Rise of Party in England: The Rockingham Whigs 1760–82* (1975).

23. Edmund Burke, 'Thoughts on the Cause of the Present Discontents' (1770), *Works* (6 vols., Bohn ed., 1854–6), i, 313.

24. *Parl. Hist.*, xx, 1297.

25. A. S. Foord, 'The Waning of the Influence of the Crown', *English Historical Review*, lxii (1947), 484–507.

26. *Sir Henry Cavendish's Debates of the House of Commons*, ed. J. Wright (2 vols., 1841), i, 15.

M

27. Edmund Burke, 'Thoughts on the Cause of the Present Discontents', *Works*, i, 375.

28. *Ibid.*, i, 379–80. On the interpretation of Burke's ideas on party I have relied upon John Brewer, *Party Ideology and Popular Politics at the Accession of George III*, pp. 55–76; *idem*, 'Party and the Double Cabinet: Two Facets of Burke's *Thoughts*', *Historical Journal*, xiv (1971), 479–501; and *idem*, 'Rockingham, Burke and Whig Political Argument', *ibid.*, xviii (1975), 188–201.

29. *The Correspondence of Edmund Burke*, ed. T. W. Copeland *et al* (9 vols., Cambridge, 1958–70), vii, 52–3. To Wm. Weddell, 31 January 1792.

30. John Wilkes, *Fragments and Anecdotes proper to be read at the present crisis by every honest Englishman* (1764), p. 41.

31. *Public Advertiser*, 8 February 1769.

32. The best study of Wilkes as a propagandist is in chapter 9 of John Brewer, *Party Ideology and Popular Politics at the Accession of George III*.

33. *A Collection of all Mr Wilkes's Addresses* (1769), p. 3.

34. *Middlesex Journal*, 10–12 July 1770; *London Magazine* (1769), pp. 132–3, 136, 193; and the *Town and Country Magazine*, i (February 1769), 109–110.

35. *Public Advertiser*, 13 June 1771.

36. *Parl. Hist.*, xviii, 1287–97.

37. See John Brewer, *Party Ideology and Popular Politics*, chap. 10.

38. Edmund Burke, 'Letter to the Sheriffs of Bristol' (1777), *Works*, ii, 27. See also *Parl. Hist.* xvii, 276; xviii, 478–540; xix, 358–9.

39. *Parl. Hist.*, xviii, 154 note. For similar views see *ibid.*, xvi, 99–100, 104–105, 872; xviii, 198–203; xix, 373–4.

40. *Ibid.*, xvi, 168.

41. *Ibid.*, xvi, 178. See also xviii, 164, 440–41.

42. *Ibid.*, xviii, 342–4, 597–8, 748–51, 1007, 1013; xix, 380; xx, 14–15; *Resistance No Rebellion* (1775), pp. 30, 46; and the petition from the City of London, 1775, in *Town and Country Magazine*, viii (1775), 221–2.

43. Willoughby Bertie, Earl of Abingdon, *Thoughts on the Letter of Edmund Burke, Esq. to the Sheriffs of Bristol* (Oxford, 1777), *passim*.

44. *Parl. Hist.*, xix, 570.

45. John Brewer, *Party Ideology and Popular Politics*, chap. 10. My own independent research confirms Dr Brewer's thesis.

46. *Parl. Hist.*, xvi, 177–80.

47. *Ibid.*, xvi, 747–55.

48. 'The Petition of the County of York', *The Annual Register* (1780), p. 338.

49. Christopher Wyvill, *Political Papers* (6 vols., York, 1794–1804), i, 232–3.

50. *Ibid.*, i, 228–43.

51. *Parl. Hist.*, xxi, 671–88; and *An Authentic Copy of the Duke of Richmond's Bill, for a Parliamentary Reform* (1783).

52. William Jones, *The Constitutional Criterion* (1768), pp. 12–14; *A Vindication of the Right of Election against the Disabling Power of the House of Commons* (1769), p. 14; *London Magazine* (1769), pp. 260–61; *London Evening Post,* 17–19 November 1772, 6 November 1777; *Parl. Hist.*, xix, 569–70, xx, 14–15; Granville Sharp, *A Declaration of the People's Natural Right to a Share in the Legislature* (1774), pp. 11, 16–17, 26–7, 238; and Willoughby Bertie, Earl of Abingdon, *Thoughts on the Letter of Edmund Burke, Esq., to the Sheriffs of Bristol* (Oxford, 1777), pp. 15–17, 22–8, 43.

53. Obadiah Hulme, *An Historical Essay on the English Constitution* (1771), pp. 141–7.

54. Richard Price, *Observations on the Nature of Civil Liberty* (7th ed., 1776), pp. 15–16.

55. See, e.g., *London Magazine* (1769), pp. 132–3, 136, 193; *Freeholder's Magazine*, ii (1770), 250; *Town and Country Magazine,* i (1769), 109–110; *London Evening Post*, 26–9 June and 29–31 July 1773; and 'An Address to the Freeholders of Middlesex ... on 30 Dec. 1779', in *The Works of John Jebb,* ed. John Disney (3 vols., 1787), ii, 460–63 and note.

56. John Cartwright, 'American Independence the Interest and Glory of Great Britain' (1774), in *English Defenders of American Freedoms 1774–1778*, ed. Paul H. Smith (Washington D.C., 1972), p. 156.

57. Jeremy Bentham, *A Fragment on Government and an Introduction to Principles of Morals and Legislation*, ed. Wilfred Harrison (Oxford, 1948), pp. 96–102.

58. James Burgh, *Political Disquisitions* (3 vols., 1774), iii, 428–34. See, in general, T. M. Parssinen, 'Association, convention and anti-parliament in British radical politics, 1771–1848', *English Historical Review* lxxxviii (1973), 504–10.

59. *The Works of John Jebb*, ed. John Disney, ii, 469–84.

60. Christopher Wyvill, *Political Papers*, iii, 66. Letter dated 15 August 1783. See also *ibid.*, v, 262.

61. *Reflexions on Representation in Parliament* (1766), p. 6 note. See also the essay by 'Regulus', in the *Political Register*, ii (1768), 218–42; and 'The Necessity of an equal Representation in Parliament', in the *London Magazine* (1770), pp. 449–50.

62. Obadiah Hulme, *An Historical Essay on the English Constitution* (1771), pp. 76, 153–4.

63. James Burgh, *Political Disquisitions*, i, 37. See also *ibid.*, i, 26–8, 36–8, 51–4, 87–94, 106–27.

64. *A Collection of the Letters which have been Addressed to the Volunteers of Ireland on the Subject of Parliamentary Reform* (1783), pp. 83–4. Richard Price to Sharman, 7 August 1783.

65. John Cartwright, *Take Your Choice!* (1776), p. 19.

66. *Ibid.*, pp. 62–3, 69; *idem, The People's Barrier against Undue Influence and Corruption* (1780), pp. 21–8, 56, 109; and *idem, Give us our Rights* (1782), pp. 4–6.

67. David Williams, *Letters on Political Liberty* (1782), pp. 79–80. See also Joseph Williams, *Parliamentary Reformation Examined* (1782), pp. 7–9; and Jeremiah Batley, *Address to the People of Great Britain of All Denominations, but particularly those who Subsist by Honest Industry* (1782).

68. One or two voices were raised against the inequality of the sexes, but even these campaigners did not demand the vote for women. See the *Middlesex Journal*, 18–20 October 1774; and the *Town and Country Magazine*, viii (1776), 507–8.

69. *Some Thoughts on a Parliamentary Reform* (1784), p. 16.

70. Joseph Priestley, *An Essay on the First Principles of Government* (1768), pp. 20–22.

71. Joseph Priestley, *Lectures on History and General Policy* (Birmingham, 1788), p. 304; and William Jones, *A Letter to a Patriot Senator* (1783), p. 30.

72. James Burgh, *Political Disquisitions*, i, 9, 11, 18; National Library of Wales. Price to Wm. Smith, 1 March 1790; John Cartwright, *The Commonwealth in Danger* (1795), pp. xxxv, ci–cii.

73. See, e.g., *London Magazine* (1770), pp. 556–9.

74. Joseph Priestley, *Lectures on History and General Policy*, pp. 279–80.

75. *Idem, An Essay on the First Principles of Government*, pp. 60–83.

76. Christopher Wyvill, *Political Papers*, iii, 60–61.

77. Catharine Macaulay, *Loose Remarks on Certain Positions to be found in Mr Hobbes ... with a Short Sketch of a Democratical Form of Government* (2nd ed., 1769), pp. 25–7.

78. William Ogilvie, *An Essay on the Right of Property in Land* (1781), pp. 11–12, 74, 87.

Chapter 7

1. *Parl. Hist.*, xxvii, 1332–8; and xxviii, 294–7.

2. *An Abstract of the History and Proceedings of the Revolution Society* (1790), pp. 14–15.

3. Andrew Kippis, *A Sermon preached at the Old Jewry, on the Fourth of November, 1788, before the Society for Commemorating the Glorious Revolution* (1788).

4. Richard Price, *A Discourse on the Love of Our Country* (1790), pp. 26–35, 40–42.

5. William Enfield, *A Sermon on the Centennial Commemoration of the Revolution. Preached at Norwich, November 5, 1788* (1788), pp. 8–9. See also *A Dialogue on the Revolution; between a Gentleman and a Farmer* (Manchester, 1788), pp. 13–14.

6. Laelius, *A Short Sketch of the Revolution; with observations on that event* (2nd ed., 1793), pp. 8–16; and William Winterbotham, *The Commemoration of National Deliverances* (1794), pp. 16, 25–30.

7. Thomas Paine, *Rights of Man* (1791–2), ed. Henry Collins (Pelican ed., 1969), p. 147. See in general C. C. Bonwick, 'Contemporary Implications of the American Revolution for English Radicalism', *The Maryland Historian* (1976), pp. 33–58.

8. *Memoirs of the life of Sir Samuel Romilly* (2nd ed., 2 vols., 1840), i, 356.

9. *The Life and Correspondence of Major Cartwright*, ed. F. D. Cartwright, p. 182.

10. Richard Price, *A Discourse on the Love of Our Country*, pp. 40–41.

11. *Parl. Hist.*, xxviii, 452–79.

12. Christopher Wyvill, *Political Papers*, iii, appendix, p. 144.

13. *Parl. Hist.*, xxix, 1301.

14. T. H. B. Oldfield, *An Entire and Complete History, Political and Personal, of the Boroughs of Great Britain* (3 vols., 1792), i, 59–66, 103–105, 123–5.

15. *The State of the Representation of England and Wales* (1793). This is reprinted in Christopher Wyvill, *Political Papers*, iii, 189–251.

16. E.G. *The Birthright of Britons* (1792), pp. 136–7; William Belsham, *Remarks on the Nature and Necessity of a Parliamentary Reform* (1793), pp. 27–38; *Letter on Parliamentary Reform* (1793), p. 34; and John Longley, *An Essay toward forming a more complete Representation of the Commons of Great Britain* (1795), pp. 9–11.

17. *Parl. Hist.*, xxx, 787–925; xxxiii, 644–735.

18. Christopher Wyvill, *Political Papers*, v, 262. See also Christopher Wyvill, *A State of the Representation of the People of England on the Principles of Mr Pitt in 1785* (York, 1793), pp. 33–46.

19. John Cartwright, *The Commonwealth in Danger* (1795), pp. xxxv, ci–cii, 93; *idem, An Appeal, Civil and Military, on the Subject of the English Constitution* (1799), p. 62.

20. Christopher Wyvill, *Political Papers*, v, 23. See also v, 51–2.

21. James Mackintosh, *Vindiciae Gallicae* (1791), p. 306.

22. *Ibid.*, pp. 294, 313–22, 330–32, 346–7.

23. Thomas Paine, *Rights of Man* (1791–2), ed. Henry Collins, pp. 63–4. See also pp. 65–7, 94, 113, 215.

24. *The Cabinet* (3 vols., Norwich, 1795), i, 27–35.

25. Thomas Paine, *Rights of Man*, p. 140.

26. *The Cabinet*, i, 178.

27. Mary Wollstonecraft, *A Vindication of the Rights of Men* (1790), pp. 67, 72; idem, *An Historical and Moral View of the Origin and Progress of the French Revolution* (1794), pp. 20–21, 72, 219.

28. James Mackintosh, *Vindiciae Gallicae* (Dublin, 1791), pp. 48–9.

29. Thomas Paine, *Rights of Man*, pp. 87–95.

30. William Godwin, *Enquiry Concerning Political Justice* (1793; 2 vols., 3rd ed., 1798), i, 158–69.

31. *The Works of Jeremy Bentham*, ed. John Bowring (10 vols., Edinburgh, 1843), ii, 501. Cf. *ibid.*, ii, 496–534; and Elie Halévy, *The Growth of Philosophic Radicalism* (1928; new ed., 1972), pp. 138, 143–9, 164–77.

32. Mary P. Mack, *Jeremy Bentham: An Odyssey of Ideas 1748–1792* (1962), pp. 409–66.

33. Thomas Cooper, *A Reply to Mr Burke's Invective* (1792), p. 65.

34. *Ibid.*, pp. 15–23, 60.

35. James Oswald, *Review of the Constitution of Great Britain* (3rd ed., 1793), p. 12.

36. Thomas Paine, *Rights of Man*, pp. 102–106, 144–5, 148, 152–3, 162–6.

37. *Ibid.*, pp. 186–7, 200, 206, 209, 220–24.

38. Thomas Paine, 'Dissertation on First Principles of Government' (1795), in *The Complete Writings of Thomas Paine*, ed. Philip S. Foner (2 vols., New York, 1945), ii, 577–81.

39. Thomas Paine, 'Letter Addressed to the Addressers on the Late Proclamation' (1792), *ibid.*, ii, 503–505.

40. William Godwin, *Enquiry Concerning Political Justice*, i, 124, 130, 214–16, 225–39.

41. *Ibid.*, i, 144–7, 167–70, 186, 214–16, 256–7; ii, 86–96.

42. *Ibid.*, i, 165–6.

43. *Ibid.*, ii, 119–20.

44. *Ibid.*, ii, 114–23.

45. James Mackintosh, *Vindiciae Gallicae* (Dublin, 1791), pp. 103–104.

46. John Thelwall, *The Natural and Constitutional Rights of Britons to Annual Parliaments, Universal Suffrage and the Freedom of Popular Association* (1795), pp. 46–8.

47. Public Records Office. TS. 11957/3502(1). Thelwall's 'Lecture Notes'.

48. Thomas Paine, 'A Serious Address to the People of Pennsylvania . . .' (1778), in *Complete Works*, ed. Foner, ii, 287.

49. Mary Wollstonecraft, *A Vindication of the Rights of Woman* (1792).

50. *Ibid.* (Everyman ed., 1929), p. 164.

51. *Parl. Hist.*, xxxiii, 726–7. 26 May 1797.

52. John Cartwright, *An Appeal, Civil and Military, on the Subject of the English Constitution* (1799), p. 17.

53. John Longley, *An Essay toward forming a more complete Representation of the Commons of Great Britain* (1795), pp. 4, 6.

54. 'On the Rights of Woman', *The Cabinet* (1795), ii, 42–8.

55. 'On the Rights of Woman', *ibid.*, i, 178, 184–5.

56. Mary P. Mack, *Jeremy Bentham* (1962), p. 464.

57. *To the Parliament and People of Great Britain* (1795).

58. Thomas Walker, *A Review of Some of the Political Events which have occurred in Manchester during the Last Five Years* (1794), pp. 46n–47n.

59. *Parl. Hist.*, xxxi, 738.

60. Thomas Paine, 'Dissertation on First Principles of Government' (1795), and 'Agrarian Justice' (1796), in *Complete Works*, ed. Foner, ii, 580; i, 611–12.

61. Thomas Paine, *Rights of Man*, pp. 249–62.

62. Thomas Paine, 'Agrarian Justice', in *Complete Works*, ed. Foner, i, 619–20.

63. George Dyer, *The Complaints of the Poor People of England* (2nd ed., 1793), pp. 2–3, 7, 13–14, 16.

64. 'A Letter to the Bishop of Landaff' (1793), in *The Prose Works of William Wordsworth*, ed. Alexander B. Grosart (1876), i, 16.

65. Daniel Eaton, 'The Village Association', in *Hog's Wash or Politics for the People*, 9 November 1793. For similar views see also [Thomas Bentley,] *The Poor Man's Answer to the Rich Associators* (*c.* 1793) and *Rights of Swine: An Address to the Poor* (5 January 1794), in *State Trials*, ed. W. Cobbett, T. B. Howell, *et al.* (34 vols., 1809–28), xxiv, 745–8.

66. John Thelwall, *The Rights of Nature against the Usurpations of Establishments* (1796). For his concern for the poor see Charles Cestre, *John Thelwall* (1906), pp. 150–66, 181–8.

67. John Thelwall, *The Natural and Constitutional Rights of Britons to Annual Parliaments, Universal Suffrage, and the Freedom of Popular Association* (1795), p. 43.

68. *Ibid.* See also *idem, The Rights of Nature*, pp. 18–19.

69. William Godwin, *Enquiry Concerning Political Justice*, i, 15–16; ii, 453–64.

70. *Ibid.*, i, 16.

71. S. T. Coleridge, 'A Moral and Political Lecture', in *The Collected Works of Coleridge*, ed. L. Patton and P. Mann (1971), i (*Lectures 1795 on Politics and Religion*), 12.

72. S. T. Coleridge, 'Conciones ad Populum', in *ibid.*, i, 48.

73. James Oswald, *Review of the Constitution of Great Britain* (3rd ed., 1793), p. 16.

74. Thomas Spence, *The Real Rights of Man* (1793). Originally given as a lecture in 1775 this work was reissued in 1796 as *The Meridian Sun of Liberty*.

75. Public Records Office. Home Office Papers 42/20. Resolution of the Delegates of the United Constitutional Societies.

76. *Thomas Paine: Representative Selections*, ed. Harry Hayden Clark (New York, 1944), Introduction, section vi.

77. Thomas Cooper, *A Reply to Mr Burke's Invective* (1792), pp. 31–2, 64–7.

78. George Dyer, *The Complaints of the Poor People of England* (2nd ed., 1793), p. 18. For other demands for public education for the poor, see [Thomas Bentley,] *The Poor Man's Answer to the Rich Associators*, p. 2; and Daniel Eaton, *Hog's Wash or Politics for the People*, 9 November 1793.

79. William Godwin, *Enquiry Concerning Political Justice*, i, 86. See also *ibid.*, i, 69, 92–3, 109–119; ii, 78–9.

80. *Ibid.*, ii, 240–53, 296–304.

81. *Parl. Hist.*, xxxi, 738.

82. See, e.g., *Address to the Inhabitants of Great Britain on the Subject of Parliamentary Reform* (6 August 1792) in *State Trials*, xxv, 590–92; *An Address to the Nation from the London Corresponding Society on the Subject of a Thorough Parliamentary Reform* (July 1793); and *Parl. Hist.*, xxxi, 706.

83. Thomas Paine, 'Letter Addressed to the Addressers on the Late Proclamation' (1792), in *Complete Works*, ed. Foner, ii, 499–505; and Joseph Gerrald, *A Convention the Only Means of Saving Us from Ruin* (1793).

84. T. M. Parssinen, 'Association, convention, and anti-parliament in British radical politics, 1771–1848', *English Historical Review*, lxxxviii (1973), 514–15; and G. S. Veitch, *The Genesis of Parliamentary Reform*, pp. 275–340.

85. *Ibid.*, pp. 299–320.

86. John Thelwall, *Sober Reflections on the Seditious and Inflammatory Letter of Edmund Burke to a Noble Lord* (1796), p. 56; and *idem*, *The Tribune* (3 vols., 1796), ii, 126.

87. William Godwin, *Enquiry Concerning Political Justice*, i, 257.

Cf. i, 268–84.

88. Thomas Paine, *Rights of Man*, p. 279; Thomas Spence, *The End of Oppression* (1795) in *The Trial of Thomas Spence*, ed. Arthur W. Waters (Leamington Spa, 1917), pp. 112–16; and James Mackintosh, *Vindiciae Gallicae* (1791), p. 344.

89. James Oswald, *Review of the Constitution of Great Britain*, pp. 52–3.

90. E. P. Thompson, *The Making of the English Working Class* (1963), pp. 176–95.

91. G. S. Veitch, *The Genesis of Parliamentary Reform*, pp. 318–19; and John Cannon, *Parliamentary Reform 1640–1832*, pp. 135–7.

92. William Godwin, *Enquiry Concerning Political Justice*, ii, 420–80.

93. Thomas Paine, *Rights of Man*, pp. 262–81.

94. Thomas Paine, 'Agrarian Justice', in *Complete Works*, ed. Foner, i, 611–17.

95. *The Speech of J. Thelwall at the General Meeting of the Friends of Parliamentary Reform* (1795), p. 14; and John Thelwall, *The Rights of Nature, against the Usurpations of Establishments* (1796).

96. James Oswald, *Review of the Constitution of Great Britain*, p. 59; *The Cabinet*, ii, 215–19 and iii, 281–95; and Mary Wollstonecraft, *A Vindication of the Rights of Men*, p. 140.

97. Thomas Spence, *The Real Rights of Man* (1793); and *idem*, *The Rights of Infants* (1797).

98. *The Cabinet*, i, 190.

99. John Thelwall, *The Natural and Constitutional Rights of Britons . . .*, p. 42.

100. Thomas Paine, *Rights of Man*, p. 279.

101. John Thelwall, *The Rights of Nature*, p. 19.

102. Norman McCord and David Brewster, 'Some Labour Troubles of the 1790s in North East England', *International Review of Social History*, xiii (1968), 366–83; E. P. Thompson, *The Making of the English Working Class*, pp. 112–14; and *The Early English Trade Unions*, ed. A. Aspinall (1949), pp. 1–35.

Chapter 8

1. William Blackstone, *Commentaries on the Laws of England* (7th ed., Oxford, 1775), i, 126–7.

2. *Parl. Hist.*, xxx, 900.

3. Thomas Walker, *A Review of Some of the Political Events which have occurred in Manchester during the Last Five Years* (1794), p. 17.

4. 'Of Political Evils', in *The Universal Magazine*, xxix (1761), 20.

5. *Parl. Hist.*, xvi, 796.

6. Josiah Tucker, *Four Letters on Important National Subjects* (1783), p. 98. See also *The Briton*, 11 September 1762; *The Universal Magazine*, xxix (1761), 19–20; and *A Letter on Parliamentary Representation* (2nd ed., 1783), pp. 34–5.

7. Francis Basset, *Thoughts on Equal Representation* (1783), p. 19.

8. *An Essay on the Polity of England* (1785), pp. 130–39.

9. Soame Jenyns, *Thoughts on a Parliamentary Reform* (1784), pp. 21–2.

10. William Paley, 'The Principles of Moral and Political Philosophy' (1785), in *The Works of William Paley*, ed. Edmund Paley (7 vols., 1825), iv. 396. See also *ibid.*, pp. 394–400; *An Inquiry into the Origin and Consequences of the Influence of the Crown over Parliament* (1780), p. 26; and *An Essay on Constitutional Liberty* (1780), pp. 27–33.

11. Soame Jenyns, *Thoughts on a Parliamentary Reform*, pp. 22–4.

12. 'Of Political Evils', *The Universal Magazine*, xxix (1761), 21–2. See also Robert Nares, *Principles of Government, deduced from Reason, supported by English Experience, and opposed to French Errors* (1792), pp. 96–97n.

13. Josiah Tucker, *Four Letters on Important National Subjects* (1783), pp. 28–9. See also *ibid.*, pp. 23–31.

14. George Pitt, Lord Rivers, *Letters to a Young Nobleman, upon Various Subjects, particularly on Government and Civil Liberty* (1784), pp. xxxi–xxxii; and *An Essay on Constitutional Liberty* (1786), pp. 83–7.

15. Robert Nares, *Principles of Government deduced from Reason ...* (1792), pp. 51–2. See also Soame Jenyns, *Disquisitions on Several Subjects* (1782), p. 130; *A Defence of the Constitution of England* (1791), p. 31; and Robert Fellowes, *An Address to the People, on the present relative situations of England and France* (1799), pp. 30–39.

16. William Blackstone, *Commentaries*, i, 171. See also *The Scots Magazine*, xxxvii (1775), 59.

17. Edmund Burke, 'Letters on a Regicide Peace' (1796), *Works*, v, 189–90.

18. George Pitt, Lord Rivers, *Letters to a Young Nobleman* (1784), pp. 118–19.

19. *Three Letters to Dr Price* (1776), p. 84. See also Thomas Gisborne, *An Enquiry into the Duties of Men in the Higher and Middle Classes of Society in Great Britain* (2 vols., 4th ed., 1797), i, 29–30.

20. Soame Jenyns, *Thoughts on a Parliamentary Reform*, pp. 9–13; and *Free Parliaments: Or, A Vindication of the Parliamentary Constitution of England* (1783), pp. 41–3.

21. Soame Jenyns, *Thoughts on a Parliamentary Reform*, p. 7.

22. *Parl. Hist.*, xvi, 705.

23. *Ibid.*, xvi, 696.

24. *Ibid.*, xxiii, 837.

25. *Ibid.*, xxiv, 988.

26. John Young, *Essays* (2nd ed., Glasgow, 1794), p. 78. See also *Parl. Hist.*, xvi, 99; *ibid.*, xxiii, 831; *ibid.*, xxiv, 989; Blackstone, *Commentaries*, i, 159; Samuel Johnson, *Taxation No Tyranny* (1775), in *The Political Writings of Dr Johnson*, ed. J. P. Hardy (1968), p. 118; Soame Jenyns, *The Objections to the Taxation of our Colonies by the Legislature of Great Britain, briefly considered* (1765), p. 6; 'Pacificus', in *The Gazetteer*, 10 December 1765; *Remarks on the Nature and Extent of Liberty* (Edinburgh, 1776), p. 13; *Three Letters to Dr Price* (1776), p. 121; George Pitt, Lord Rivers, *Letters to a Young Nobleman* (1784), pp. 282–3; and *Considerations on the Intended Reform in the Parliamentary Representation of the People* (1785), p. 7.

27. Lucy S. Sutherland, 'Edmund Burke and the Relations between Members of Parliament and their Constituents', *Studies in Burke and His Time*, x (1968), 1005–21.

28. Edmund Burke, 'Thoughts on the Cause of the Present Discontents' (1770), in *Works*, i, 367.

29. James Mackintosh, *A Disclosure on the Study of the Laws of Nature and Nations* (1797), p. 47.

30. William Paley, 'Principles of Moral and Political Philosophy' (1785), in *Works*, iv, 379–94. See also Josiah Tucker, *Four Letters on Important National Subjects*, pp. 68–71; Francis Bassett, *Thoughts on Equal Representation* (1783), p. 15; *A Letter on Parliamentary Representation* (2nd ed., 1783), p. 26; *Free Parliaments: Or, a Vindication of the Parliamentary Constitution of England* (1783), pp. 66–7; and *Considerations on the Intended Reform in the Parliamentary Representation of the People* (1785), pp. 8–9.

31. *Parl. Hist.*, xxx, 808–20.

32. Thomas Bray, *A Sermon preached before the House of Commons, January 31, 1763* (1763), pp. 6, 14.

33. Soame Jenyns, *Disquisitions on Several Subjects* (1782), p. 150.

34. *Correspondence of Edmund Burke*, vi, 42.

35. *Parl. Hist.*, xxiv, 988.

36. Edmund Burke, 'To the Sheriffs of Bristol' (1777), *Works*, ii, 30.

37. *Correspondence of Edmund Burke*, vi, 42.

38. *Parl. Hist.*, xvi, 170, 612; Samuel Johnson, *Taxation No Tyranny*, in *Political Writings of Dr Johnson*, ed. J. P. Hardy, pp. 108–109; and George Chalmers, *Second Thoughts: Or, Observations upon Lord Abingdon's Thoughts* (2nd ed., 1777), pp. 48–58.

39. *Parl. Hist.*, xvii, 276; xix, 358–9; xxx, 590; xxxii, 348; Burke, *Works*, ii, 27, 35, 423; *Corr. of Burke*, iii, 181–2.

40. *Parl. Hist.*, xxvi, 819–21, 826; xxviii, 16–22, 405–11; Soame Jenyns,

Disquisitions on Several Subjects, pp. 152–9; William Paley, 'Principles of Moral and Political Philosophy', *Works*, iv, 472–6; and William Belsham, *Essays Philosophical and Moral* (2 vols., 1799), ii, 129–30.

41. *Parl. Hist.*, xxxii, 357–8; Edmund Burke, 'Reflections on the Revolution in France', *Works*, ii, 285–306; *idem*, 'An Appeal from the New to the Old Whigs', *Works*, iii, 44–5.

42. Josiah Tucker, *The Respective Pleas and Arguments of the Mother Country, and of the Colonies, distinctly set forth* (2nd ed., 1776), pp. 22–3.

43. *Parl. Hist.*, xvi, 788–90; xxi, 175, 606; xxiii, 853; *Sir Henry Cavendish's Debates of the House of Commons*, ed. J. Wright, i, 280, 285, 287–8; Sir Robert Herries, *A Letter from a Member of the House of Commons ... on the Great Constitutional Questions lately agitated in Parliament* (1784), pp. 19–20; Robert Nares, *Principles of Government, deduced from Reason ...*, pp. 59–60; and Thomas Gisborne, *An Enquiry into the Duties of Men in the Higher and Middle Classes in Great Britain*, i, 203–10.

44. *Parl. Hist.*, xvi, 704–705.

45. *Ibid.*, xxxi, 495.

46. *Ibid.*, xxi, 603–15; xxiii, 853; xxv, 461; Josiah Tucker, *Four Letters on Important National Subjects*, pp. 59–60; *idem*, *A Treatise concerning Civil Government* (1781), pp. 257–73; *An Inquiry into the Origins and Consequences of the Influence of the Crown over Parliament* (1780), p. 12; Edmund Burke, 'A Letter on the Duration of Parliaments' (1780), *Works*, vi, 1–3; George Pitt, Lord Rivers, *Letters to a Young Nobleman*, pp. 333–7; *An Essay on the Polity of England* (1785), pp. 257–68; and *Considerations on the Intended Reform in the Parliamentary Representation of the People* (1785), pp. 11–12.

47. *Parl. Hist.*, xxx, 554–5. Burke's was of course the most influential voice warning the political nation to heed the warning of the French Revolution. See, in particular, his *Reflections on the Revolution in France* (1790) and *Letters on a Regicide Peace* (1796).

48. Arthur Young, *The Example of France, A Warning to Britain* (1793), pp. 41, 44n. See also *Parl. Hist.*, xxx, 612, 873–8, 892–3; *Thoughts on the New and Old Principles of Political Obedience* (1793), p. 32; *The Englishman's Political Catechism*, in *Liberty and Property preserved against Republicans and Levellers* (1793), no. x; John Young, *Essays*, p. 116; John Reeves, *Thoughts on the English Government* (1795), pp. 15–16; Sir Wm. Maxwell to the Duke of Buccleuch, 19 November 1792, quoted by G. S. Veitch, *The Genesis of Parliamentary Reform*, p. 250; and *The Debate on the French Revolution*, ed. Alfred Cobban (1950), pp. 347–80, 443–92.

49. Arthur Young, *An Enquiry into the State of the Public Mind*

amongst the Lower Classes (1798), p. 6.

50. Soame Jenyns, *Disquisitions on Several Subjects*, pp. 121–2.

51. George Pitt, Lord Rivers, *Letters to a Young Nobleman*, pp. 226–7.

52. Adam Ferguson, *Principles of Moral and Political Science* (2 vols., Edinburgh, 1792), ii, 463; and *An Address to the People of England* (1796), p. 11.

53. Richard Watson, 'The Wisdom and Goodness of God in having made both Rich and Poor' (1793), in *Miscellaneous Tracts* (2 vols., 1815), i, 449–93.

54. See Jacob Viner, *The Role of Providence in the Social Order* (Philadelphia, 1972), pp. 103–105.

55. George Horne, 'A Discourse on the Origin of Civil Government', in *The Scholar Armed* (2 vols., 2nd ed., 1800), i, 277; 'Of the Necessity of Distinction of Ranks in Society', in *The Scots Magazine*, lvi (1794), 241; and *A Letter to the Farmers and Manufacturers of Great Britain and Ireland* (1792), pp. 20–21.

56. Edmund Burke, *Works*, ii, 327; iii, 493–4; and *Parl. Hist.*, xxxviii, 434–5.

57. H. V. S. Ogden, 'The State of Nature and the Decline of Lockian Political Theory in England, 1760–1800', *American Historical Review*, xlvi (1940), 21–44.

58. Burke, *Works*, iii, 86.

59. *Ibid.*, ii, 368–9. See also Charles Parkin, *The Moral Basis of Burke's Political Thought* (Cambridge, 1956), pp. 6–29.

60. See, e.g., William Blackstone, *Commentaries*, i, 34; Allan Ramsay, *Thoughts on the Origin and Nature of Government* (1769), pp. 8–10; Jeremy Bentham, *A Fragment on Government* (1776), ed. Wilfrid Harrison (Oxford, 1948), pp. 34–5, 40–4, 49; Soame Jenyns, *Disquisitions on Several Subjects*, pp. 133–4, 268–70; William Paley, 'The Principles of Moral and Political Philosophy', *Works*, iv, 332–7; and George Horne, 'A discourse on the Origin of Civil Government' and 'Some Considerations on Mr Locke's Scheme of deriving Government from an Original Compact', both in *The Scholar Armed*, ii, 268–77, 289–96.

61. Josiah Tucker, *A Treatise Concerning Civil Government* (1781), p. 42.

62. Soame Jenyns, *Disquisitions on Several Subjects*, pp. 137–40; Samuel Horsley, *A Sermon preached before the Lords Spiritual and Temporal ... on January 30, 1793* (1793), p. 8; George Horne, in *The Scholar Armed*, i, 270–71.

63. Burke, *Works*, iii, 79. See also *ibid.*, ii, 363–4, 370.

64. Adam Ferguson, *Principles of Moral and Political Science* (2 vols., Edinburgh, 1792), i, 196–9, 262–3; ii, 206, 218–22, 237–44, 469–70; and Josiah Tucker, *A Treatise concerning Civil Government*, pp. 124–59.

65. Burke, *Works*, vi, 148. See also William Paley, 'The Principles of Moral and Political Philosophy', *Works*, iv, 373–4.

66. Edmund Burke, 'An Appeal from the New to the Old Whigs', *Works*, iii, 1–115; *ibid.*, ii, 289–306; William Blackstone, *Commentaries*, i, 211–13; Josiah Tucker, *A Treatise concerning Civil Government*, pp. 89–96; Robert Nares, *Principles of Government deduced from Reason* ..., pp. 139–40; John Young, *Essays*, p. 35; John Reeves, *Thoughts on the English Government* (1795), pp. 38–43; George Chalmers, *A Vindication of the Privilege of the People, in respect to the Constitutional Right of Free Discussion* (1796), pp. 65–7; *Parl. Hist.*, xxxii, 357–8; xxxv, 112; and T. B. Howell, ed., *State Trials*, xxvi (1819), 559–60.

67. Burke, *Works*, vi, 146–7. See also *ibid.*, ii, 442; *Parl. Hist.*, xxx, 900; and *Looker-On*, xxiii (26 May 1792), 179. For Burke's doctrine of prescription see in particular Russell Kirk, 'Burke and the Philosophy of Prescription', *Journal of the History of Ideas*, xiv (1953), 365–80; J. G. A. Pocock, 'Burke and the Ancient Constitution – A problem in the History of Ideas', *Historical Journal*, iii (1960), 125–43; and Paul Lucas, 'On Edmund Burke's Doctrine of Prescription; Or, An Appeal from the New to the Old Lawyers', *ibid.*, xi (1968), 35–63.

68. Burke, *Works*, viii, 59.

69. *Ibid.*, ii, 435.

70. *Ibid.*, iii, 340.

71. *Ibid.*, vi, 146.

72. *Ibid.*, ii, 422.

73. *Corr. of Burke*, vi, 95; *Sir Henry Cavendish's Debates of the House of Commons*, ed. J. Wright, ii, 318; Paul Lucas, 'Edmund Burke's Doctrine of Prescription ...', *Historical Journal*, xi (1968), 35–9.

74. William Paley, *Principles of Moral and Political Philosophy* (1785), pp. 407–408.

75. Burke, *Works*, ii, 365.

76. Soame Jenyns, *Disquisitions on Several Subjects*, p. 130. See also *A Defence of the Constitution of England* (1791), p. 53; Robert Nares, *Principles of Government deduced from Reason*, pp. 42, 44, 54–5; *Thoughts on the New and Old Principles of Political Obedience* (1793), pp. 14–18; and John Young, *Essays*, p. 13.

77. Burke, *Works*, iii, 326.

78. For Burke's views on prudence, see John Maccunn, *The Political Philosophy of Burke* (1913), pp. 38–49; Charles Parkin, *The Moral Basis of Burke's Political Thought*, pp. 109–30; Francis P. Canavan, *The Political Reason of Edmund Burke* (Durham, N. Carolina, 1960), pp. 3–26; and Gerald W. Chapman, *Edmund Burke: The Practical Imagination* (Cambridge, Mass., 1967), *passim*.

79. *Corr. of Burke*, vi, 48.

80. Burke, *Works*, vi, 114.

81. *Ibid.*, ii, 514–15.

82. *Ibid.*, 514. See also *ibid.*, iii, 79.

83. *Parl. Hist.*, xxviii, 434–5.

84. Josiah Tucker, *Four Letters on Important National Subjects*, pp. 110–12.

85. *Parl. Hist.*, xxxii, 467. See also *An Inquiry into the Origin and Consequence of the Influence of the Crown over Parliament* (1780), pp. 43–4; Josiah Tucker, *A Treatise concerning Civil Government*, pp. 421–2; George Pitt, Lord Rivers, *Letters to a Young Nobleman*, pp. lix–lx; 225–7; and William Paley, 'Principles of Moral and Political Philosophy', *Works*, iv, 340–41.

86. *Parl. Hist.*, xxvi, 819–21; *ibid.*, xxviii, 405–11; Soame Jenyns, *Disquisitions on Several Subjects*, pp. 152–9; and William Paley, 'Principles of Moral and Political Philosophy', *Works*, iv, 472–6.

87. Burke, *Works*, ii, 332. See also B. T. Wilkins, *The Problem of Burke's Political Philosophy* (Oxford, 1967), pp. 155–80.

88. Joseph Wimpey, *Letters occasioned by Three Dialogues concerning Liberty* (1777), p. 50. See also *Civil Liberty asserted, and the Rights of the Subject defended, against the Anarchical Principles of the Reverend Dr Price* (1776), p. 8.

89. For Burke's concept of natural rights see John Maccunn, *The Political Philosophy of Burke*, pp. 190–217; Russell Kirk, 'Burke and Natural Rights', *Review of Politics*, xiii (1951), 441–56; Charles Parkin, *The Moral Basis of Burke's Political Thought*, pp. 6–29; Francis P. Canavan, *The Political Reason of Edmund Burke*, pp. 103–44; R. R. Fennessy, *Burke, Paine and the Rights of Man* (The Hague, 1963), pp. 108–59; and B. T. Wilkins, *The Problem of Burke's Political Philosophy*, pp. 152–246. For similar contemporary views see William Blackstone, *Commentaries*, i, 124–43; and Adam Ferguson, *Principles of Moral and Political Science*, ii, 191–210.

90. Burke, *Works*, ii, 332.

91. *Ibid.*, ii, 332–3; and Adam Ferguson, *Principles of Moral and Political Science*, ii, 471–3.

92. *Parl. Hist.*, xxxi, 380.

93. Adam Smith, *The Wealth of Nations* (1776), Book V, chap. 1 (Everyman ed., 2 vols., 1910), ii, 199, 203. See also Adam Ferguson, *Principles of Moral and Political Science*, ii, 222, 238; Robert Fellowes, *An Address to the People, on the present relative situation of England and France* (1799), p. 38; and *Parl. Hist.*, xxxi, 380.

94. Burke, *Works*, ii, 423; and Blackstone, *Commentaries*, i, 139.

95. Burke, *Works*, ii, 324.

96. Thomas Malthus, *An Essay on the Principle of Population* (1798, Pelican ed., 1970), pp. 198–9. See also pp. 72, 95–102, 116–17, 133–41, 172, and 177–8.

97. Burke, *Works*, v, 83–109; *Corr. of Burke*, vi, 95; *Liberty and Property preserved against Republicans and Levellers* (1793), no. ix; William Paley, 'Reasons for Contentment, addressed to the Labouring Poor of the British Public', *Works*, iii, 320; J. M. A. Gee, 'Adam Smith's Social Welfare Function', *Scottish Journal of Political Economy*, xv (1968), 283–99; and Andrew Skinner, *Adam Smith and the Role of the State* (Glasgow, 1974).

98. *Parl. Hist.*, xxi, 601.

99. *Ibid.*, xxv, 455.

100. George Berkeley, *The Danger of Violent Innovations in the State exemplified from the Reigns of the Two First Stuarts* (Canterbury, 1785), p. 2.

101. Burke, *Works*, vii, 99–100.

102. *Ibid.*, ii, 362–6; John Maccunn, *The Political Philosophy of Burke*, pp. 122–43; and Charles Parkin, *The Moral Basis of Burke's Political Thought*, chaps. 6–7.

103. Burke, *Works*, ii, 324.

104. *Ibid.*, i, 322–3, 337; ii, 365–6; iii, 85–6; and vi, 170–71.

Index

359

commissioners of the salt duty, 113

common law, 62–3, 74, 82

common people, fear of, 16–17, 45, 69–70, 78, 87–90, 93, 101, 103, 116–17, 127–8, 136, 142, 146–7, 151–2, 154, 157–60, 162, 165–6, 168, 191, 237–9, 251, 270, 275, 279–81, 285, 287–90, 299, 303, 310–12, 317; support for, 212–13, 218, 227–31, 247, 248–9, 253–61, 265–9

Common Sense, 190, 191, 192

Commons, House of, 16, 18, 24, 27, 28, 30, 31, 41, 43, 49, 63–5, 74, 79–82, 89, 91, 93, 97–103, 108, 111–15, 123, 143–7, 152–7, 174–6, 179, 181–91, 195–6, 207, 211, 214, 215, 217, 219, 220, 223, 225–6, 229, 232, 237–9, 246, 274–89, 313

Commonwealthmen, 89, 103–6, 111–12, 115–17, 164–5, 204

Comprehension bill, 54

conquest theory, 34–5

constitution, *see* ancient constitution, balanced constitution *and* written constitution

Constitutional Society, 206, 260, 262

contract theory, supporters of, 57, 61, 65–79, 90, 197, 222, 234–5, 243–4; critics of, 16, 125, 128–9, 132–5, 138–40, 142, 291, 294–8, 299, 306–7

Convocation, 37, 148

Cooper, Thomas, 247, 261

Corinth, 111

Cornewall, Velters, 185

Cornwall, 117, 191, 226

Corporation Act (1661), 19, 54, 84, 148, 167, 202, 233, 308

corruption, fear of, 92, 102–18, 124, 150–1, 169–88, 191, 196, 200, 204, 207–8, 221, 256

Country party, 82, 91–5, 102–18, 121–4, 140, 148–50, 163–92, 195–7, 208

Court and Treasury party, 155, 174, 175, 182

Court of Common Pleas, 211

Court party, 91–102, 121–62, 169, 207–8, 277–8

Craftsman, The, 189, 191, 192

Crewe, John, 208

Cromwell, Oliver, 105, 184

Crosby, Brass, 219

crown, *see* influence of crown *and* prerogatives of crown

Danby, Thomas Osborne, Earl of, 32, 36

David, King, 60

Declaration of Independence (1776), 235

Declaration of Rights (1689), 75, 80

Declaratory Act (1766), 147, 215

Defoe, Daniel, 9, 87, 88, 116, 117

democracy, criticisms of, 16–17, 57, 58, 61, 64, 68, 69, 101, 127–8, 143–4, 149, 154, 157–8, 165–6, 187, 207, 225, 229, 274–6, 302; support for, 213–14, 220–1, 228, 229, 238, 243–50, 258

Derby, 262

Devon, 226

Digby, William, Lord, 75

Discourses upon Government, 73

Dissenters, 54–6, 79, 83–4, 91, 100, 150, 167, 178, 202–3, 220, 225, 232–3, 235, 240, 308

Dissenting academies, 56

Divine Institution of Magistracy, The, 44

divine providence, 35–7, 293, 295–6, 305–6, 313–15

divine right, doctrine of, 13, 15, 17, 19, 22–9, 33, 35–40, 42,